Frontiers in Economic History

Economic historians have contributed to the development of economics in a variety of ways, combining theory with quantitative methods, constructing new databases, promoting interdisciplinary approaches to historical topics, and using history as a lens to examine the long-term development of the economy. Frontiers in Economic History publishes manuscripts that push the frontiers of research in economic history in order to better explain past economic experiences and to understand how, why and when economic change occurs. Books in this series will highlight the value of economic history in shedding light on the ways in which economic factors influence growth as well as social and political developments. This series aims to establish a new standard of quality in the field while offering a global discussion forum toward a unified approach in the social sciences.

More information about this series at http://www.springer.com/series/16567

Emmanouil M. L. Economou

The Achaean Federation in Ancient Greece

History, Political and Economic Organisation, Warfare and Strategy

Springer

Emmanouil M. L. Economou
Department of Economics
University of Thessaly
Volos, Greece

ISSN 2662-9771 ISSN 2662-978X (electronic)
Frontiers in Economic History
ISBN 978-3-030-52696-2 ISBN 978-3-030-52697-9 (eBook)
https://doi.org/10.1007/978-3-030-52697-9

This Springer imprint is published by the registered company Springer Nature Switzerland AG.
The registered company address is: Gewerbestrasse 11, 6330 Cham, Switzerland

To my mother, Agoritsa, to my brother,
Dimitris,
to Vasso and Andreas for the unwavering
support
they provided me throughout this demanding
research
journey, to the memory of my father and the
many
scholars who focused their research on
ancient
Greek federalism

Foreword

This book skillfully analyses the ancient Greek federal state of Achaea—the Achaean Sympolity—which flourished in the late Classical and Hellenistic periods (ca. 323–146 BCE). It offers a detailed account, not only of the history of the Sympolity but of its economic, political, and institutional structures. It concludes with thoughtful and telling comparisons of the ancient Achaean Sympolity with modern federal states and the European Union. The book follows an interdisciplinary approach, combining political history with methodologies derived from economic theory—economic history, historical political economy, and institutional economics—as well as modern theoretical and methodological concepts from behavioural economics, constitutional theory, game theory, and international relations theory. This combination makes the work truly innovative: it will be of great value to historians and social scientists alike.

The book explores the beginnings of the formation of the Achaean Sympolity in a highly competitive geopolitical environment where shifting relations between friends, strong competitors and rivals—the kingdoms of Macedon, Sparta, and Epirus, the Hellenistic kingdoms of the East (the Seleucid, Ptolemaic, and Pergamene), other federal states (the Aetolian and Boeotian), as well as other important states such as Athens and Rome—were a constant challenge. The book persuasively argues that, despite a series of military setbacks and its final conquest by Rome, the Achaean Sympolity was a success as a historical paradigm and a federal experiment in the region of Achaea and the wider Peloponnesus. The main reasons for its success can be attributed to a series of innovative political and economic institutions, developed and gradually implemented on the basis of commonly accepted values and principles—notably freedom, equity, and autonomy. Crucial to this success were the choices and actions of its leaders, Aratus and Philopoemen. And yet equally crucially, those leaders never devolved into tyrannical despots.

Among these pivotal institutions was *isopoliteia* (the civil rights of every citizen of any member city-state guaranteed throughout a federal state); *asylia* (immunity) and *proxeny* (the granting of beneficial status to a citizen of another state in exchange for honorary titles with the purpose of promoting interstate trade); *enktesis* (the right to hold property in any member city-state within the territory of a federal state); the protection of property rights and the free movement of goods, people, and capital anywhere within the borders of the federation; interstate trade under free market economy principles; magistrates to supervise marketplaces throughout the Sympolity to prevent profiteering; and a mixture of direct and participatory democracy practices.

These and other institutions were part of a wider framework, grounded in explicitly *federal* values and principles. These key institutions, values, and principles allowed for monetary union; state provision of public goods—first and foremost, defence and security; arbitration between the member city-states when disputes between them arose; a justice system available to all Achaean citizens at the federal level; and the establishment of efficient road networks between city-states. The author develops his arguments by a careful reading of ancient writers and archaeological evidence, and with masterful reference to a large bibliography of contemporary scholarship, ranging across multiple literatures and languages.

Among the book's central arguments is that the Achaeans developed a sophisticated 'mixed' system of direct democratic-participatory and indirect procedures in decision-making on federal matters. This political system was complemented by economic practices. The result was the achievement of a bond of trust between the Achaean people across dozens of city-states and a sense of legitimacy at both local and federal levels. It was that trust and legitimacy that ensured the Achaean Sympolity's success and its enduring importance as a historical paradigm of practical federalism.

The author sheds new light on the current political situation by identifying problems and malfunctions within modern democracies. He draws on the history of the Sympolity to propose innovative solutions, thus making the book a useful source of policy ideas. He suggests ways that the Achaean federal paradigm might deal with a series of current global issues: European Union integration; the asymmetry of power and the increasing imbalance in the diffusion of economic prosperity among EU member states; democratic deficits in decision-making at the EU level; Brexit; and immigration. The book concludes with an impressive bibliography, a detailed and very helpful glossary, and a useful index.

In Chap. 1, the author analyses the key questions raised regarding the study of ancient Greek federalism with special reference to the Achaean federal state. This chapter introduces the variety of terms that developed in Ancient Greece to describe what social scientists now understand federal organisation to be, as well as the conceptual gaps between ancient and modern terms. It also explains the modern debate concerning the correct typological description of ancient Greek federalism (federation, confederacy, league, commonwealth) among historians and social scientists. The chapter demonstrates that the terms *Sympolity* and *Koinon* most accurately describe Ancient Greek federal states. Finally, this chapter explains the development of federalism in Ancient Greece (mainly in the Hellenistic Period 323–146), referring to a number of examples beyond the Achaean federal state.

Chapter 2 examines the formation and gradual development of a pan-Achaean political identity among the people of the Peloponnesus. It examines the reasons that lay behind the decision of the Achaean people to move from a strong-autonomy city-state model to a federal system in which city-states were integrated into a larger organisation. It shows how, after its re-establishment in 280, the Achaean Sympolity federal organisation survived and flourished until the second century. Finally, it explains the mistakes and the inconsistencies of the Achaean policymakers that finally led to the Sympolity's dissolution and its conversion into a Roman province.

Chapter 3 explains, through a *Defence Economics* perspective, why the Achaean Sympolity finally failed to offer adequate resistance to Rome and thereby forestall the latter's eventual triumph. The author compares the Achaean Sympolity to Rome by measuring their relative strength through state power equations. The chapter concludes with a game-theoretical analysis to evaluate the pros and cons of a key decision faced by Achaean policymakers: whether or not to resist Rome.

Chapter 4 provides an analysis of Aratus, one of the most influential and important leaders of the Achaean federal state. It describes his life and explains how his actions led to the rise of the Achaean Sympolity as a prominent state in southern Greece. It provides evidence of a series of strategic choices by Aratus regarding geopolitics, the revival of the federal trend throughout the Peloponnesus, his efforts to confront a formidable and dangerous enemy, Sparta under King Cleomenes III, and his key contribution towards shaping an alliance with the Kingdom of Macedon as a way of containing Sparta. The chapter further examines the evidence for a lost opportunity: the unification of the whole of the Peloponnesus through the incorporation of Sparta into the Achaean federal state.

Chapter 5 analyses the character and the actions of Philopoemen who, together with Aratus, is considered the most influential and important figure of the Achaean federal state. Philopoemen's choices in the political and military sphere guided Achaean federal policies throughout the period 245–213. During that time, the principal strategic goal of Achaea's visionary policymakers was finally achieved—the unification of the entire Peloponnesus under the Achaean federal state. It was not an easy task. The chapter analyses the implications, opportunities, difficulties, and problems that the proponents of the Achaean federal experiment faced before finally achieving their goal. The author argues that Philopoemen's leadership and character was the driver that made possible the final unification of the Peloponnesus.

Chapter 6 analyses the primary political institutions and organisation of the Achaean federal state. These included the pan-Achaean *Ecclesia*, a federal Assembly of citizens, where each citizen from every member city-state could participate under direct democracy procedures in decision-making, and the federal *Boule*, a Council, which functioned as a preparatory body proposing the issues to be discussed in the Assembly. The federal government centred on a *strategos* and the ten-man committee he headed, known as the *damiourgoi*. The *strategos* was both head of state and commander of the federal armed forces. The chapter also analyses the crucial institutions of *isopoliteia*, the concession and the sale of political rights, *asylia* (immunity), and *proxeny*. It further examines the procedures followed by Achaean policymakers in regard to resolving conflicts between city-states over territorial and civil matters. Finally, the chapter reviews the administrative organisation at the state and regional levels, the military organisation of the Achaean armed forces, and the 'Common Foreign and Security Policy' of the Achaean federal state.

Chapter 7 analyses the economic institutions of the Achaean federal state. The author provides evidence that the Achaean Sympolity was based on principles of economic freedom, market-type institutions, and monetary union among the member city-states, with a common currency. Property rights were protected by law through local and federal courts. This was highly beneficial for the development of commercial activity among the member city-states. The chapter then turns to a series of state economic policy issues: how public revenues and expenses were settled, and issues of the state budget, taxation, and public debt management. Furthermore, it analyses the provision of public goods under the discretionary supervision of the Achaean federal authorities. In the first instance, these were defence and the operational cost of the Achaean federal armed forces. Other public goods include the federal courts and a road network. Throughout, the author emphasises the positive economic externalities of public goods. The chapter also considers other social groups: women, orphans, *metics* (foreigners), and slaves. It concludes with a convincing demonstration that the value added of the political and economic institutions of the Achaean federal state was a critical reason for the success of the Achaean federal experiment.

Chapter 8 addresses further aspects of the functioning of the institutions of the Achaean federal state. It first provides a spatial decision model analysis between *Strategos* Aratus and King Antigonus III Doson, in order to show that Aratus' and Antigonus' decision to radically reform their foreign policy by forming an alliance between their two states was the result of a prudent evaluation of the trade-off policy, based on a cost–benefit logic. Then, having in mind the previous analysis as a whole, the author is able to answer the question of whether the Achaean state was a federation or a confederacy, coming down definitively in favour of the former. He then turns to the issue of the influence of the Achaean federal state on the American Founding Fathers in the course of debates leading to the US Constitution of 1787. Finally, he provides a comparison between the Achaean federal state and the European Union under a specific set of institutional intertemporal criteria. He argues that the institutions and the policies that were practised by the ancient Achaeans on a variety of issues (economic and social policy, foreign affairs, diplomacy, and defence) could serve as a source of inspiration for the future political and economic integration of the European Union.

In sum, this well-written book offers an innovative and a synthetic-interdisciplinary interpretation of the emergence of federal organisation in ancient Greece, focusing on one of the most best documented cases of ancient federalism. Economists, historians, political scientists, policymakers, and researchers alike will benefit from Dr. Economou's original, erudite, and thoughtful answers to an enduring question: how can many states act as one?

Josiah Ober

Tsakopoulos-Kounalakis Professor
in Honor of Constantine Mitsotakis,
Professor of Political Science and
Classics, Stanford University (USA),
Stanford, CA, USA
May 30, 2020

Preface

This work is a study of the historical evolution as well as the organisation and structure of the principal political and economic institutions of the Achaean federal state (*Sympolity*). The history of the Ancient Greek federal states is less well known than that of many of the individual city-states and kingdoms of the Ancient Greek world. It is true that examinations of that era, both in the Greek and international academic bibliography, have focused mainly on the cases of ancient Athens, Sparta, Macedonia, Thebes, Rhodes, and others. Fewer attempts have been recorded at examining the organisation, function, as well as the significant historical added value that might be afforded by the study of the Ancient Greek federal states. After all, the evolution of political systems and democracy in ancient times was not restricted to the level of the city-state alone but included that of the federal democracies as well.

There are four primary reasons we have focused our study on the Achaean federal state. First, from ancient primary historical sources as well as the modern Greek and international bibliography, it is apparent that the Achaean federal state was one of the most powerful and significant states during the Hellenistic Period (322–146[1]). Accordingly, it is worthwhile examining how the actions and deeds of the Achaeans influenced and contributed to the world of both the Classical (480–323) and Hellenistic Periods. After all, the Achaean federal state was not an isolated historical experiment that emerged as a result of new trends in the development of political systems at the crossroads of the Classical and Hellenistic Periods but also was a politico-historical entity whose actions influenced and contributed to the historical evolution of the Greek world of that time. One need only mention that the Achaean

[1]All triple-digit dates are before the Christian era.

state was the last bastion of Hellenism before the conquest of mainland Greece by the Romans, completed in 146.[2]

Secondly, one of the greatest historians who focused on the issue of Ancient Greek federalism, J.A.O. Larsen (1968, p. 215), argued that the Achaean federal state was the most important of all Greek federal states and the subject of the bulk of the literature about them. The available sources regarding the historical background, the organisation, and the foundations of the Ancient Greek federal states, attributed either to ancient authors such as Polybius, Plutarch, Livy, and Pausanias, or to inscriptions found, or to modern bibliography, provide a mosaic of scattered information garnered from a wide variety of sources. Accordingly, a very meticulous effort is required to assemble this information into a unified, comprehensive whole. On the other hand, if treated cautiously, those ancient sources, as well as surviving inscriptions at archaeological sites and the modern Greek and international bibliography, provide significant information to allow for a satisfactory description of the main political and economic institutions of the Achaean federal state in a manner that can provide a reasonably credible and representative picture of the historical reality of that time in terms of how the Achaean state functioned. This is one of the main aims of our research.

The third reason for choosing the Achaean federal state is that we believe that its political and economic structures provide a series of significant policy proposals that could be considered useful in confronting some of the impasses of today's societies. Said differently, we believe that the function of certain basic institutions of the politico-economic organisation of the Achaean federal state might provide ideas and suggestions for the improvement of the political systems, as well as (why not?) the economic performance of today's societies, such as the European Union.

The confirmed historical existence of the Ancient Greek federal states of the second half of the Classical Period (400–323) and throughout the Hellenistic Period (322–146) underscores that the state institutions developed in the Greek world were never static but evolved to a level that surpassed that of the city-state and included entire geographical regions. During the last quarter of the fourth century, as well as throughout the century that followed, the state reorganisation of the Greek world was extended to greater geographical entities, to large kingdoms such as that of Alexander the Great's successors, or federal states, both democratic and not. Larsen (1968, pp. 303–304) argues that during the third and the first half of the second century, the Greek world consisted largely of federal states.

As Ager (1997, p. 23) observes, the federal states functioned as a balancing mechanism in the face of the powerful monarchies that had arisen, a phenomenon all the more apparent during the Hellenistic Period. Ober (2015, p. 308) writes that the Achaean and Aetolian states were the most powerful federal states during the Hellenistic era. Although they never displaced the Macedonian Kingdom as the

[2]The Macedonian Kingdom of the Antigonids on mainland Greece had already been overcome by 168 by Rome. To the East, after 146, the Ptolemaic Kingdom in Egypt, the Kingdom of Pergamon in Asia Minor, and the Seleucid Kingdom in the Middle East continued to exist.

single most dominant player on the Greek mainland, they did, however, serve to limit the Macedonian king's ability to dominate the states of central and southern Greece.

Walbank (1993) interprets the phenomenon of federalism as the capacity of the Greeks to adapt to new political challenges by adopting novel solutions. He believes that federalism offered the means of offsetting the limitation of size and the relative weakness of the city-states. Concurring, Kralli (2017, p. 147) maintains that the development of federal structures was the result of the city-states' need to overcome their limitation of size, protect themselves against pressure from much larger external powers, and maintain a peaceful co-existence. Mackil (2013, p. 1), based on *An Inventory of Archaic and Classical Poleis,* developed by Hansen and Nielsen (2004), claims that by the end of the fourth century, over 40% of mainland Greece's city-states were members of a federal state. Specifically, she reports that 183 of the 456 Greek city-states recorded at that time in mainland Greece and the Peloponnesus were members. The percentage may even be higher, 46–50%, about half of all city-states, as it does not include city-states that were likely members of the peripheral regions of a federal state. However, this participation has not been verified by Hansen and Neilsen (Mackil 2013, pp. 305–306).

From the above, it is apparent that the governmental structure of the federal state was a phenomenon of vast significance to the evolution of political systems in the ancient world as well as in subsequent periods. Today, many of the states that have played and still play a significant and pivotal role on the international stage, such as the USA, Canada, Germany, Switzerland, Russia, India, Brazil, etc., are federations.[3] It is safe to say that federalism was a natural consequence of a series of historical developments that led to the objective necessity of adopting novel governmental formats from the fourth century and beyond.

Beck and Funke (2015b, p. 25) identify several causes that contributed towards this gradual development, maintaining that beyond common legislation, representative government, and the rules that governed interpersonal relations of their citizens, the Greek federal states prevailed as a governmental schema because of some additional crucial parameters such as common origin and the expression and projection of a common identity as a tribe through its morals and customs. Accordingly, one cannot underestimate the contribution of shared behavioural norms to the development of common collective action and behaviour. One must add, too, the fact that Alexander the Great's conquests as far as India led to the crucial rise in power of Macedon, overwhelming the city-states of Greece and beyond. The geopolitical amplification of Macedon, as well as that of the Kingdom of Epirus

[3]Many claim that even the European Union, in terms of its political integration (if it is ever realised), will move (probably) towards federalism, as envisioned originally by its creators, Konrad Adenauer, Alcide de Gasperi, Walter Hallstein, Jean Monnet, Robert Schuman, Paul-Henri Spaak, and Altiero Spinelli. See such a view in the *Memoirs* of J. Monnet (1951) as well as https://europa.eu/european-union/about-eu/history_en. For instance, Burgess (2000) sees the EU as an 'economic confederation'.

under Pyrrhus, etc., created the need (or the pressure) for broader cooperation within the Greek world between the city-states of central and southern Greece.

This cooperation was not accompanied necessarily by participation in any federal structure since not all city-states were interested in joining. For instance, in 242, the head of the Achaean federal state, the *strategos* Aratus,[4] attempted to persuade the Athenians to join, but without success. The Athenians were not eager to involve themselves in new military adventures nor direct confrontation with Macedon; also, the idea of being subjugated as part of a federation was not particularly attractive to them. In any event, it is more than likely that, after the geopolitical might of the Macedonians soared for many reasons, such as their victory at the Battle of Chaeronea in 338, followed by their liberation of Asia Minor, the neutralisation of the Persian threat, and the advance of the Greeks into Syria, Egypt, Persia, and the Indian continent, integration between the existing federations in metropolitan Greece accelerated since the member city-states realised that integration was essential to any attempt to confront Macedonian power.

Alexander's successors fought bitterly among each other for the hegemony of metropolitan Greece.[5] Meanwhile, during the same period, the fourth century, the Achaean federal state was gradually growing into a powerful politico-military force, which sought to resist Macedonian, Spartan, Aetolian, and Theban influence, as well as that of the Hellenistic kingdoms and later, in the second century, that of Rome. The city-states of mainland Greece (not all of them) enjoyed economic prosperity during this time due to cash inflows in terms of booty, precious metals, etc., and the rise of trade with the markets of the East. Of course, there were adverse side effects as the influx of gold into Greece from the Persian treasury caused its value to fall. Since gold, to a large extent, took the form of coinage, this resulted in the devaluation of its buying power. Furthermore, the wider use of slave labour led to a reduction in wages (Walbank 1993; Ober 2015).

The ability to bring in large numbers of slaves from Asia into metropolitan Greece shifted the labour supply curve to the right, in the language of contemporary economic theory, resulting in downward pressure on wages: lower-cost slave labour replaced free, wage-earning citizens in the Greek city-states. This became even more of a problem in the third century when Greece became the scene of extensive armed conflict. On the other hand, the prospects of easy wealth and the hope for a better future led to a significant migration flow of Greeks towards Egypt and Asia. Consequently, these migrations to and from the Greek metropolis affected the socio-economic structure of the Greek world. Significant development occurred in the Hellenistic kingdoms of Egypt and Asia, and the centre of economic activity gradually shifted from the Aegean to the East. Walbank (1993) believes that the

---

[4]The *strategos* was not only the general of the armed forces but was also the head of the state, as it will be further explained in detail.

[5]Often leading to open warfare such as between Antigonus I Monophthalmus (founder of the Antigonid Dynasty) and the *strategoi* Perdicas and Eumenes (323–321), or the Battle of Ipsus in 301 in Phrygia, Asia Minor.

competition between the two was one-sided, given the limited natural resources and small populations of the city-states of Greece in the face of the rapidly growing and heavily populated Hellenistic megalopolises of the East. The traditional great commercial centres like Athens and Piraeus were gradually superseded by new ones, such as Alexandria and Antioch, which now dominated the Mediterranean.[6]

This re-ordering of economic power affected the military balance as well, since the small armies that individual city-states could muster paled against the great professional/mercenary armies of the Hellenistic monarchs, backed by ample funds, supplies, and armaments. As will be demonstrated in the case of the Achaean federal state analysed here, as well as the other Greek federal states such as the Aetolian,[7] one of the basic reasons they were formed was for cooperation in defence. They had realised that allied they could achieve much more than each one on its own, not only in terms of defence but also in other aspects of social life, such as economic cooperation.

Having described in general the historical background out of which the Achaean federal state rose, we close this introduction by presenting the structure of the analysis that follows. In the first chapter, we examine certain key crucial issues concerning the analysis of the Greek federal states which we believe are necessary to consider so that, given from the outset a series of assumptions, the analysis in the subsequent chapters has a more cohesive structure. In the second chapter, we analyse the political history of the Achaean federal state in its two phases—before and after 280, and until 146, when it was conquered by the Romans, marking the completion of Rome's conquest of Greece.

The third chapter provides an analysis of the final defeat of the Achaean federal state by Rome through an interpretation of modern *Defence Economics* theory. Chapters 4 and 5, in continuity with Chap. 2, briefly examine the political and military actions of the two great generals of the Achaean state, Aratus and Philopoemen, both of whom were so instrumental in its rise to power, while Chaps. 6 and 7 refer to the political and economic institutions of the Achaean state, presenting in the bibliography for the first time, to the best of our knowledge, what we believe to be a number of innovative interpretations and approaches.

Chapter 8 analyses four critical issues regarding the previous analysis. It provides (i) a spatial decision model analysis regarding the strategic choices between the *strategos* Aratus, the head of the Achaean state, and King Antigonus III Doson, the ruler of Macedon, regarding their alliance, (ii) an analysis regarding a crucial issue: whether the Achaean state was a federation or a confederacy, through a *Constitutional/Institutional Economics* approach, (iii) the influence of the Achaean federal state on the formation of the American Constitution of 1787, and (iv) proposals that

---

[6]For the development and the evolution of the economy of Ptolemaic Egypt, see Manning (2003, 2004, 2007), von Reden (2010), and our own work, Economou and Kyriazis (2019a).

[7]With regard to the Aetolian federal state, a powerful entity both politically and militarily, with a democratic government and bordering the Achaean Sympolity, see, among others, Mackil (2013), Economou, Kyriazis, and Metaxas (2015), and Kralli (2017).

the Achaean federal state may provide for the further integration of today's European Union.

This innovative effort in analysing and interpreting the organisational structure of the Achaean federal state that follows forms the basis for a broader interdisciplinary research philosophy that draws from several fields of study: *Political History, Economic History, Institutional Economics, Defence Economics, Behavioural Economics, Economic and Political Sociology, Political Science, Strategic Studies, International Relations Theory*, etc. This allows for a more integrated approach to the issue rather than a 'dry' interpretation of the facts seen only through the prism of an isolated analysis methodology.

The quotations of ancient authors that we cite in the main body of this book are based on translations provided by the Perseus Digital Library of Tufts University.[8] There is a citation list of these ancient sources in our bibliography. We also provide a Glossary explaining the ancient terms we use in the book as well as an Appendix. Adopting Thucydides' view that history is philosophy through example, we feel that the analysis in these chapters has a dual role: not only to provide information regarding how the Achaean federal state was organised and operated in practice but also to provide ideas and policy proposals which might improve the procedures of decision-making in modern democratic societies regarding economic policy issues.

Finally, I must express my gratitude to the following members of the academic community for their comments and suggestions on specific issues that arose during accumulating and managing the scientific material of this project. First and foremost, I must thank my colleague Prof. Dr Nicholas C. Kyriazis (University of Thessaly), with whom, so far, I have co-written a series of books and articles in academic journals and collective volumes as well as a book in Greek on Ancient Greek federalism.

Moreover, I am also indebted to Josiah Ober (Stanford University) for the time he devoted for the preparation of the *Foreword* and his overall view of this book and to George C. Bitros (Athens University of Economics and Business) and Ioannis L. Konstantopoulos (University of Piraeus) for our extensive and fruitful discussions on a variety of academic issues. Beyond that, I extend my thanks to my colleagues in the Department of Economics of the University of Thessaly, Messrs. Michel Zouboulakis, Christos Kollias, Theodore Metaxas, and Paschalis Arvanitidis who were members of my doctoral thesis related to federalism issues, as well as to George Halkos, Stephanos Papadamou, Lucas Zachilas, Andreas Stergiou, and my friend and colleague Dr Nikolaos A. Kyriazis, with whom I have cooperated on various projects, including co-authorship of numerous academic papers.

Moreover, I am also indebted to George Tridimas (Ulster University), Manfred Holler (Hamburg University), Geoffrey Hodgson (Loughborough University), Carl Hampus Lyttkens (University of Lund), also being a member of my doctoral thesis, Dimitris Kyrtatas (University of Thessaly), Bas van Bavel (Utrecht University), Dr

[8]See http://www.perseus.tufts.edu/hopper/

Ioannis-Dionysios Salavrakos (National and Kapodistrian University of Athens), and Dr Annita Prassa (PhD National and Kapodistrian University of Athens) for their comments and suggestions regarding various issues that are related to this book.

I also thank Dimitri Politis for undertaking the tedious task of translating the work into English, Andreas Gkouvas for his continuous and tireless support and cooperation on a series of technical issues during the preparation of this book, archaeologist George Stamatis, the journalists Rossana Popota, Sotiris Polyzos, Vasso Kyriazis, Glykeria Hydraiou, Dimitris Rallis, and Photis Spanos, as well as Sotiris Karagounis. Finally, I would like to thank the editors of this new series, Professors Claude Diebolt (University of Strasbourg) and Michael Haupert (University of Wisconsin–La Crosse) for the continuous encouragement and fruiful cooperation we had, as well as the Springer staff and especially Niko Chtouris, Associate Editor of Economics and Political Science for all the wonderful collaboration we had during the preparation of this book.

Volos, Greece
May 2020

Emmanouil M. L. Economou

Contents

About the Author

Emmanouil M. L. Economou is an Adjutant Lecturer at the Department of Economics, University of Thessaly. In 2014, he received his Doctorate from the same university in the analysis of "Economy, institutions and warfare", with a degree, "Excellent". His research focuses on economic history, institutional economics, international political economy, public economics, and defence economics.

He has contributed to the international academic bibliography with seven academic books in English and Greek (one to be published in 2021), with 29 papers in internationally recognised reference journals (such as *Journal of Institutional Economics* (2), *European Journal of Law and Economics*, *Defence and Peace Economics*, *Homo Oeconomicus, Economics of Governance*, *Evolutionary and Institutional Economics Review*, *Peace Economics, Peace Science and Public Policy*, and *Journal of Central Banking Theory and Practice* (2)), with 20 papers in academic book chapters (collective volumes), and he has participated in 36 international and Greek audience Conferences.

He is a reviewer/external reviewer of four scientific journals, three of which are the internationally acclaimed *Journal of International Financial Markets, Institutions & Money, Journal of Institutional Economics*, and *Research in Economics* and is a member of the Laboratory of Economic Policy and Strategic Planning (ERGO. POLIS) of the Department of Economics, University of

Thessaly. Many articles by him (of economic, political/institutional, and historical interest) have been published in journals for the general public (*Foreign Affairs, The Hellenic Edition, Economic Review, Illustrated History,* and *The Reader*). He also writes in the Greek press on economic, political, and historical issues.

List of Abbreviations (Ancient Authors' Works)

Aristophanes 'Acharnians'	'Arist. Ach.'
Aristophanes 'Peace'	'Arist. P.'
Aristotle 'Athenian Constitution'	'Arist. Ath. Const.'
Aristotle 'Oeconomica'	'Arist. Oec.'
Aristotle 'Politics'	'Arist. Pol.'
Demosthenes 'Against Midias'	'Dem. Mid.'.
Diodorus Siculus 'Historical Library'	'Diod. Hist.'
Herodotus 'The Histories'	'Herod. Hist.'
Homer 'The Iliad'	'Hom. Il.'
Homer 'The Odyssey'	'Hom. Od.'
Isocrates 'Panathenaicus'	'Isoc. Pan.'
Livy 'History of Rome'	'Liv. Hist R.'
Pausanias 'Description of Greece'	'Paus. Des.'
Plato 'Laws'	'Plat. L.'
Plut. 'Agis'	'Plut. Ag.'
Plut. 'Aratus'	'Plut. Arat.'
Plut. 'Cleomenes'	'Plut. Cleo.'
Plut. 'Demetrius'	'Plut. Dem.'
Plut. 'Philopoemen'	'Plut. Philop.'
Plut. 'Solon'	'Plut. Sol.'
Polybius 'Histories'	'Polyb. Hist.'
Strabo 'Geography'	'Strb. Geo'
Thucydides 'History of the Peloponnesian War'	'Thuc. Hist.'
Xenophon 'Constitution of the Athenians'	'Xen. Ath. Con.'
Xenophon 'Hellenika'	'Xen. Hell.'
Xenophon, 'Memorabilia'	'Xen. Mem.'

List of Figures

List of Tables

Chapter 1
Introduction: The Methodology of Analysing the Institutions of the Achaean Federal State (*Sympolity*)

1.1 The Key Questions Raised by the Study of Ancient Greek Federalism and the Achaean Federal State

Before proceeding further in an analysis of the Achaean federal state, one must consider the issue of the precise meaning of the modern terms league, federation, confederacy, and the ancient terms *sympolity*, common *polity*, *koine sympoliteia*, or *Koinon* (*Koina*, in the plural) used to identify Greek federal states. This must be clarified at the outset because the international academic bibliography is inconsistent in this respect, perplexed not only by the lack of specific data from surviving ancient sources but by the fact that those basic sources (Polybius' *Histories*, Plutarch's *Parallel Lives*, Titus Livy's *History of Rome*, Xenophon's *Hellenica*, Diodorus Siculus' *Historical Library*, Pausanias' *Description of Greece*, Strabo's *Geographica*, Thucydides' *History*, etc.) do not use a consistent and coherent typology in their terminology. This has resulted in many divergent views that have been expressed in a variety of interpretations by contemporary researchers.

In general, the tendency in the international academic bibliography has been to use the term *league* to identify the phenomenon of federalism in Greek antiquity (e.g. Achaean League, Aetolian League) or, to a lesser extent, the terms, *confederacy* or *federation*. In our opinion, the term *league* is not very definitive, as it does not contain sufficient explanatory power regarding what we describe here. There is a problem, too, with the modern Greek terms *omonspondia* (federation) and *synomonspondia* (confederacy); although they are not interchangeable, they are both used alternatively indiscriminately. The term 'federation' regarding the Greek federal states has been adopted by, among others, Freeman ([1893] 2013), Champion (2013, pp. 120–21), Gabrielsen (2013, p. 342) as well as by myself and my colleagues in Economou et al. (2015), Economou and Kyriazis (2015a, b, 2016a, c), while the other term, 'confederacy', by Flensted-Jensen (1996), Finer (1997, p. 231, Vol. I), Kralli (2017), Richard (2009) and Gagarin (2010, p. 13). Still others, such as Larsen (1968), use both interchangeably.

E. M. L. Economou, *The Achaean Federation in Ancient Greece*, Frontiers in Economic History, https://doi.org/10.1007/978-3-030-52697-9_1

What will emerge from this research, in the case of the Achaean federal state, is that the terms *federation* or *confederacy* are clearly more appropriate in describing its political form than *league*. The latter was adopted in earlier decades by Caspari (1917), Larsen (1925, 1952, 1973), Badian (1952), Roebuck (1955), de Laix (1973), Briscoe (1981) and, to a large extent, has prevailed—unfortunately, given that it is generally not sufficiently supportive of the more appropriate description we advocate herein. Jacob Larsen, who devoted much of his academic life to the study of the Ancient Greek federal systems and, in 1968, published an integrated and organised examination on the subject entitled *Greek Federal States*, in which he uses the terms *federation* and *confederacy* interchangeably.[1] For instances where descriptions in primary sources were insufficient, he turned to the term *looser organisations*.

McInerey (2013) uses the ancient term *koinon,* noting (p. 466) that the source of the word comes from the Greek word for society, *koinonia*. Mackil (2013), throughout her extensive and superb treatise, *Creating a Common Polity,* adopts the term *koinon* and describes as federal only those governmental and economic institutions whose determination is clearly characterised as such. The term *koinon* denotes the federal state (in the plural, *koina*). It literally means 'something in common', in our case, a common identity and polity. More specifically, Larsen (1968, p. xiv) writes that *koinon* means the commonwealth, or the federal state or government, often in opposition to the local community or government.

The measured approach of Larsen, McIenery and Mackil can be characterised as 'diplomatic'. They shy from adopting terms which might prove problematic in their interpretive dynamics. Another expression that is mentioned by Polybius in various passages (such as in 11.41.11., 11.44.4), by Thucydides (Hist. 6.4.1) and Xenophon (Hell. 5.2.12) is *Sympolity* (or *Sympoliteia*), or *Koinopoliteia*, or *Koine Sympoliteia*, all meaning 'joint polity' (Walbank 1985, pp. 24–26; Beck and Funke 2015b, p. 14). Larsen (1944, 1968, p. xv) characterises *sympolities* (plural form) as 'true federal states' and as 'an organisation embracing a number of cities' or as 'sharing of citizenship' or as 'merging of two cities into one with a single citizenship'.

He provides a further definition regarding *sympolity* (ibid., pp. 7–8):

> With the development of the federal state something new and something different had been born. The Greeks finally indicated this by adopting a new name to describe the form of the federal state from one point of view. This word is *sympolity*, which can best be interpreted as a union of city-states or the common citizenship of citizens of several city-states.

R. Davis (1978, p. 14), having given an admittedly efficacious translation of the term *Sympolity* as 'fellow citizenship' or as 'sharing of citizenship', supports that meaning with the following additional interpretations: 'sharing of citizenship or a common political life', or a 'union of several states in which there is an exchange of

[1] An earlier book by him with the title *Representative Government in Greek and Roman History* was published in 1955.

civic rights'.[2] As we will analyse below, the Greek federal states boasted *isopoliteia*, the granting of political rights to all the citizens of a *sympolity*. We will show that aside from the institutions of *enktesis, asylia, epigamia* and *isopoliteia*, the citizens of member city-states possessed unlimited personal civil and political rights (including that of the vote) throughout the *Koinon*.[3] Davis (1978, p. 22, ftn. 17) adopts the term of the older, important historian Georg Busolt from his essay *Griechische Staatkunde* (1920) who, regarding the Greek federal states, argued that:

> Their member states were called *poleis* in the official language and in the literature. As the state organization of a *polis* is represented in the *politeia*, in the same way, the constitution of several *poleis* united into a single federal community is represented as *Koinopoliteia* or *Sympoliteia*. The federations called *Koina*. The concept of *Koinon* comprises every political or nonpolitical association and community. Similarly, a *polis* was a *Koinon*. In a narrow sense, a *polis* as a unified subject must be distinguished from a *Koinon* as an association of a number of *poleis*. In this way, *Koinon* took on the meaning of a federal community.

Davis (1978, p. 20) points out the basic elements of value-added provided by participation by a city-state in a federation, according to the Greek experience:

> ...First, the gradual movement, by will or force,[4] towards 'association', 'fraternization' or indeed, 'integration', rather than anything we call 'fusion', 'merger', or 'unification'. And the reasons for this relate to the age, the culture, and the circumstances—always the urge of mutual protection, conquest, retaliation, peace, sometimes the attraction of common cults; and everywhere the move to association is tempered by one of the most significant features of the Hellenic culture, pride of the polis. Second, if the Hellenic experience begins with relatively simple forms of tribal and city-state associations... it is clear that these associations broadened and matured into more extensive, more complex, more 'institutionalized' political systems, though boundaries between them, as Ehrenberg[5] tells us, were not always very clear: *amphictyonies*, into *symmachia* and *symmachia* into *sympoliteia*[6]...Third, there is, at all stages, from their first appearance and throughout their growth and ultimate demise, a rich variety in their size, form, complexity, cohesion, symbols of commonality, interaction, the individual strength of each polis, their relative power towards the central 'authority' the power if the most important single figure in the league, the *strategos* or 'general', and the extent to which military and civil functions were mingled in his office.

On this point, Davis ascertains and verifies the view of Riker (1964) who, in studying the constitution and institutions of the USA, etc., argued that, for a federation to be viable, distribution in terms of power between the member states should be sufficiently balanced as to achieve an equilibrium between the members.

---

[2]For the issue of typology on how these political entities, which are the next step after the city-state organisation, R. Davis (1978) in Chap. 2 provides an extensive analysis. See as well, Beck and Funke (2015a).

[3]Xen. Hell. 5.2.19; Polyb. Hist. 3.2.7, Mackil (2013, pp. 102, 237–238, 255–262, 495–499, 2015).

[4]However, during the analysis, it will become evident that at least the majority of city-states chose to become members of the Achaean state voluntarily and not by force, although, as Polybius reports (2.38.7), there were instances of force, while after 191, the large geographical unities such as Sparta, Messenia and Elis, for geopolitical reasons, were—probably—drawn into a Sympolity by force.

[5]See Ehrenberg (1964).

[6]For *amphictyonies* and *symmachiai*, see below.

They must all participate in the benefits of common action. If one member is tending to become much more powerful than the rest, then that member will tend to manipulate them, putting the federation at risk of becoming a hegemony under a strong state. The powerful member will tend to turn the others into satellites. Riker's view can be supplemented by the fact that the tendency to create an imbalance between members of a federation might have an even more decisive result than that of leading to one member acting as a hegemon over the others, as Oates (1972) writes in his seminal work, *Fiscal Federalism.* A case in point is that of the Boeotian *Koinon* (federal state) and its most powerful member, Thebes. It can lead to the 'absorption' of the other members by the powerful into a form of union (but not federated). In effect, any imbalance of power between members, in the end, may even lead to the dissolution of a federal state. Plutarch (Philop 8.1–2) provides his own, admittedly colourful but on-point 'constitutional' definition of what the Achaean *Sympolity*[7] was:

> The commonwealth of the Achaeans was first raised to dignity and power by Aratus, who consolidated it when it was feeble and disrupted, and inaugurated a Hellenic and humane form of government. Then, just as in running waters, after a few small particles have begun to take a fixed position, others presently are swept against the first, adhere and cling to them, and thus form a fixed and solid mass by mutual support, so the Achaeans, at a time when Greece was weak and easily dissolved and drifting along by individual cities, first united themselves together, and then, by receiving into their number some of the cities round about which they had aided and assisted in shaking off their tyrants, and by uniting others with themselves in a harmonious civil polity, they purposed to form the Sympolities into a single political body and one power.

Based on this passage of Plutarch, in Chaps. 6 and 7 we will mainly extensively analyse why the success of the Achaean Sympolity should be largely attributed to its supranational economic and political institutions and to the successful intraregional economic/commercial cooperation that had developed among them (see among others, Mackil 2013, 2015; Economou et al. 2015; Economou and Kyriazis 2016a, c). As Ober (2015, p. 224) argues, in Achaea and Aetolia, as in other regions of Hellas, informal cooperative intraregional relations deepened to become the institutional foundations of federal states.

In concluding with that definition, it is worth adding Walbank's view (1993) that the meaning of *sympolity* relates to a group of cities in a broadly based organisation in which some, not all, individual rights are granted in exchange for becoming stronger as a whole. This was a manifest development in a world where a monarchy with its vast territories was undermining the importance of individual cities. The disadvantages of the old city-states' autonomy had already begun to become apparent. Walbank argues that the two major and most powerful *sympolities* were the Achaean and Aetolian. One can, of course, mention the Boeotian *Koinon* which, though it had an administration of political institutions based on a democratic

---

[7]Having already given a clear definition of what *Sympolity* means, from this point on and throughout the rest of the book we will mainly use this term to describe the Achaean federal state. Sometimes we may also use the term *Koinon* (common polity) which is almost identical.

philosophy, it differed (in 'constitutional' terms) from the *sympolities* mentioned above.

As will be discussed further down, there were instances when cities which, after they had joined a federal state, attempted to withdraw, such as in the case of Pellene, a member of the Achaean Sympolity. According to Polybius (Hist. 2.45.1–2.46.3), in 235, several city-states (Tegea, Mantinea, Orchomenos and Caphyae) which had joined the Achaean federal state in 235, 2 years later, changed their minds and chose to join the Aetolian federal state, but eventually returned to the Achaean. Moreover, as will be discussed in detail in 4.3, according to Plutarch (Arat. 38.8), the King of Sparta, Cleomenes III, was open to joining the Achaean Sympolity, but with the intention of playing a leading role in it. Because of the rivalry between Aratus and Cleomenes III, this never materialised. Of course, as will be discussed below, initially in 192, Sparta, obliged by the circumstances to join the Achaean Sympolity, after a short time, seceded. However, in 189, against her will, she was forced to rejoin the Sympolity (Livy Hist. 38.34.3).

Accordingly, as mentioned above, the issue of the accuracy of a single identifying term describing the Greek phenomenon of federalism is neither easy nor does it form the basic core of the analysis carried out herein. More significant is to assess what kind of added value these political cases yielded in the past, and if and to what extent they are useful for today to serve as inspiration for contemporary (but also intertemporal) political and economic problems in need of solutions. In any event, in this book's analysis, we have chosen to adopt the term *sympolity*. This term is quite similar to that of *Koinon*, which Mackil (2013) prefers, but we adopt *sympolity* because a large part of the international bibliography accepts this term to denote a federal structure,[8] and because, as Walbank (1985, p. 24) argues, the word was frequently used denoting federal states in Hellenistic times. Finally, Kralli (2017, p. 149) notes that the term *sympolity* is used by Polybius[9] 16 times as a technical term (16 in all), while the word *Koinon* is used only three times (Polyb. Hist. 2.70.5; 4.60.9; 28.19.3).

At appropriate instances, as per our judgement, we use the modern terms 'federal state' and 'federation' when it is clear that we are describing a federal practice, policy or institution, refraining from using the term 'confederacy' since we believe its meaning offers less than the term 'federation' towards understanding the political integration of the Ancient Greek city-states into supranational structures. In Sect. 6.5, we explain why we believe that the Achaean state, from a typological point of view, was a 'composition', a 'synthesis' of federation and confederation, but the federal elements are much more recognisable than the 'confederate' ones.

We should also stress that the true number and significance of Greek federal states cannot be determined accurately due to the paucity of vital historical sources. Also,

[8]For example, see among others, some of the experts in the field: Walbank (1985, p. 24–26), Nielsen (1996), Mackil (2013), the collective volume of Beck and Funke (2015a) and Kralli (2017).

[9]Who, along with Plutarch and Titus Livy, is the main source regarding the history of the Achaean federal state.

those states did not present the same governmental and institutional set-up; likely, there were significant differences in a number of aspects, i.e. military organisation, currency policy, etc. (Mackil 2013, p. 336). Some federal states with a democratic regime include, among others, Arcadia, the Aegean islands, that of the Acarnanians, of the Chalcideans, and the Magnetes; the Lycian state in Asia Minor, that of the Hetaians, of the Locrians, of the Free Laconians, etc. aside from the Boeotian *Koinon*, and the Aetolian and Achaean Sympolities, which, according to the sources and the analysis that follows, lay claim to having been institutionally and politico-economically the most 'integrated' and accordingly, present the greater academic interest.

There were, as well, non-democratic federal states, such as the Thessalian and that of Cyrenaica. If one adds to that a number of other sympolities referred to in the ancient texts or that have been examined by modern researchers, such as the Bottiaeans of Macedonia, the Phocis, that of the White Mountains in Crete, the loose federalism of Elis, of the Locrians, the Euboians, then it becomes apparent that the phenomenon of federalism in Greece was widespread in its application, and varied widely in structure and institutional organisation. It cannot be ignored, given that simply adding up those mentioned above, their number exceeds 25.[10] In our view, what constitutes sympolities or *Koina* are political forms of voluntary and free union of independent states in a unified, supranational entity to undertake common action in several areas including defence, foreign policy, a common currency, etc., often accompanied by a common constitutional treaty.

Finally, a particularly interesting attempt to clarify the above cases were those of Larsen (1944) and Davis (1978, p. 13) who have studied the attempts by the Greeks at forming federalist governments beginning in the Archaic Period (750–510), concluding with four basic formats:

- *Amphictyonies*
- *Symmachiai*, meaning alliances of city-states ostensibly free and autonomous, or *semi-federal alliance*s
- *Sympolities,* or 'truly' federal states
- *Alliances* or agreements for common peace between city-states

One should refer, as well, to the methodology in the analysis of Mosse (1967), who proposes three formats:

- *Alliances* of a military character formed by the rival cities Athens and Sparta
- The *Koinon* of the Greeks founded by King Philip in 338

[10]For the historical background regarding most of these federal states, see Larsen (1968), Mackil (2013) and the papers in the recent collective volume edited by H. Beck and P. Funke *Federalism in Greek Antiquity* in detail. In Epirus, during the period 231–168, the Council of the Epirotes, also a form of federated state, appears to have functioned on a democratic basis (Cross 2015, pp. 109–112). For the Free Laconians *Koinon* in the Peloponnesus, see Cartledge and Spawforth (2002). For the Lycian *Koinon*, see also Larsen (1956, 1957). For the *Koinon* of Hetaians, see Thuc. (Hist. 3.42, 4.78) and Strabo (Geo. 9.43).

- Specific *federations* of city-states, e.g., the Boeotian

The terms *amphictyonies* and *symmachies* demand a brief elaboration: as for the *amphictyonies*, it has been determined that these existed as early as the eighth century, functioning throughout the wider Greek world. According to Brock and Hodkinson (2000, pp. 25–26), the earliest began to appear during the Archaic Period and were autonomous communities with common ethno-racial characteristics, concentrated around a cult centre containing a temple. The intent was more effective political and military cooperation. The centre was located at a neutral geographical location so no single city-state could claim primacy. The best-known are the Delphic *amphictyony* (founded in the seventh century), that of Calabria[11] and the Greek *amphictyonies* of Asia Minor, the Ionian Dodekapolis (12 city-states), the Dorian Hexapolis (6 city-states) and the Aeolian Dodekapolis (12 city-states).[12]

As for the *symmachies* (alliances), Ehrenberg (1964) writes that the *symmachia* (in singular) began as a comradeship-in-arms or a military alliance concluded for a longer period, that is to say, as a normal inter-state relation. From the middle of the sixth century, a new form arose, although the old still survived. This new form was an alliance of a leading state with a number of others, not limited in time or by any specific aim, implying a leading position of the one state in war, and soon also in politics, loosely organised at first, but clearly an attempt at a unit transcending the single state. We shall describe *symmachies* as an 'alliance under a Hegemon' and shall assign to it the Lacedaemonian or Peloponnesian League, the First and Second Athenian Leagues and the League of Corinth under the leadership of the Kingdom of Macedon.

He further explains that we are clear in our own minds that these 'leagues' were not federal units. Larsen (1944) refers to the major instances of ancient alliances, the Peloponnesian Alliance (or League) that was formed sometime during the sixth century and lasted until 371, the Athenian Alliance, the Delian *Symmachia* (its first phase lasting from 478 to 470 and the second from 378 to 355) and the Greek Alliances of Phillip and Alexander from 338 to 322 (Alliance of Corinth), that of Dimitrius Poliorcetes (303–302) and the successors of the Macedonians that followed (229–221). Although they are of interest, as much for their institutional structure and their function, as for their wider historical impact through their action, they were unable, however, to evolve into organised and viable federal political entities and, for several reasons,[13] remained military alliances focussed on geopolitics and defence.

---

[11]Its centre was the island of Poros, located in the Saronic Gulf, off Attica in central Greece.

[12]For a detailed examination of the *amphictyonies*, both Greek and non-Greek, among others, Larsen (1944), Roebuck (1955), Rathjen (1965) and Forrest (2000) offer valuable information.

[13]In view of our specific purpose herein, we will not examine the *amphictyonies* any further other than to note that, in a general sense, they served as the 'ancestors' of the *sympolities*; nor will we examine further the *symmachies*. An examination of both the *amphictyonies* and the *symmachies* is provided by Tausend (1992).

Returning to the *sympolities*, a number of historians claim,[14] the initial spur to their creation was defence against a superior rival, which, in the case of the Achaean Sympolity, referred mainly to the powerful state of Macedon to the north on the Greek mainland and Sparta to the south, and to a lesser extent, the neighbouring *sympolities* of central Greece (Aetolian, Boeotian[15]). Then why did the city-states of the broader region of Achaea not simply settle for a military alliance along the successful lines of the Athenian and Peloponnesian, but went further, organising into a federal structure?

As we will show in Chap. 7, federalism in Achaea (and in most of the other federal states) was based on a series of vital elements such as the common Achaean racial identity, the geographical proximity between neighbouring cities, their common customs and traditions as well as the critical issue of common defence and security. An additional crucial reason, as much for the Achaeans as it was for a substantial number of other Greek cities[16] for not settling only for a military alliance but proceeded towards federalism was the substantial value-added of mutual economic cooperation. We should mention at this point that cooperation between cities along broad lines was not a new phenomenon. Unions of villages or *komai* (meaning small cities), also known as *koina*, already existed in prior centuries and, in one sense, the federal *Koina* were a continuation of those older ones with an advanced, more sophisticated form of organisation. As has already been referred to and will be emphasised below, a significant institutional characteristic of the sympolities was *isopoliteia,* the right of citizens to exercise their political rights in any member city-state.

What differentiated the *sympolities* from the alliances (Athenian, Peloponnesian etc.) was that the philosophy behind their creation foresaw the cooperation in drawing up a common policy between the members, without allowing for any one member to strive for hegemony. The governmental form of a sympolity, in its ideal shape and when not distorted by hegemonistic tendencies of the more powerful cities, functioned as a unity, but without restricting the freedom of its members; instead, it constituted a strong, unified political entity, capable of guaranteeing their security and independence. It was the answer of the Greeks that aspired to defend their autonomy and political rights in the face of the rising power of the Hellenistic kingdoms that rendered the role and the future of isolated, small city-states tenuous, since, as federations, they disposed of sufficient economic substance to finance powerful, professional armies. As Walbank (1993) notes, in the face of the economic assets of the monarchs, the individual city-states seemed like dwarfs.

---

[14]Champion (2013, p. 121), Economou et al. (2015), Economou and Kyriazis (2016a).

[15]The Boeotian *Koinon* was reconstituted in 379 but had already been organised in a group of 11 administrative regions well before, in 431. They consisted of 31 cities whose population were not necessarily of a homogeneous makeup. For the Boeotian *Koinon*, see, among others, Mosse (1967), Larsen (1968), Buckler (1980), Mackil (2013) and Beck and Ganter (2015).

[16]Which by the end of the fourth century amounted to some 46–50% of all recorded city-states.

A response to the power gap created by the existence of strong kingdoms had to be given, and that response came in the form of a federal state, either in a democratic or an oligarchic configuration. As it turned out, the strongest federations turned out to be the democratic ones, with one of the three major ones being the Achaean, the subject of our study.

Chapter 2
The Achaean Sympolity (389–146): The Political History

2.1 The Period 389–280: Political and Military Developments

As we know from *The Iliad* (2. 574–575), Homer employed the term *Achaeans* to refer to all the Greeks of the era of the Trojan War, at around 1250.[1] However, in the centuries that followed, the term eventually came to refer only to the inhabitants of the northwestern Peloponnesus. During the Early Iron Age (ca. 1100), according to descriptions by Herodotus (Hist. 7.94) and Strabo (Geo. 8.7.1), the region of Achaea had suffered extensive destruction due, to the Dorians' incursion into the area. Gradually, the region began to recover and Homer, in his catalogue of ships (and peoples) in *The Iliad* (2. 574–575), refers to those who lived in the eastern part of Achaea as *Aigaleians, Kaukones* and *Epeians*. The reconstitution of a new 'pan-Achaean' identity began to assert itself as of the ninth century, as Mele (2002, p. 76) claims. Rizakis (2015, pp. 118–119), however, disputes this, believing this occurred in stages after the Homeric epics were written,[2] a process not completed until the sixth century.

Rizakis (2015, p. 119), with Pausanias (7.1.4) in mind, claims that the initial process of forging a unified Achaean identity occurred during the intense rivalry between the Ionian-descendant Aigaleians and the Aeolian-descendant Achaeans inhabiting the region. This rivalry of the two tribal groups revolved around the acceptance, at a pan-Achaean level, of the deity each side supported; the former supported the Heliconian Poseidon, protector of their capital Helice, while the latter,

[1]Contrary to research studies such as that of Kirk (1965) that claim that the Trojan War occurred around 1100, other authors believe that it occurred at an earlier time. For example, Forrest (1966) offers a possible chronology of around 1215, while D'Amato and Salimbetti (2011) estimate that, in fact, Troy was destroyed after a brutal siege around the end of the thirteenth and the beginning of the twelveth century.

[2]Around 750, at the beginning of the Archaic Period.

E. M. L. Economou, *The Achaean Federation in Ancient Greece*, Frontiers in Economic History, https://doi.org/10.1007/978-3-030-52697-9_2

the Achaeans, supported Zeus, protector of their most important city, Aegion (Ehrenberg 1964). Finally, it was the cult of Zeus Omorios (or Omarios) that prevailed as associative of a common Achaean identity. Perhaps the adoption of that version of Zeus was not accidental given that Zeus Omorios was considered the protector of love and friendship among neighbours.

There followed further cementing of that common identity among the cities of northwestern Peloponnesus. One possible significant impetus for this was the threat the Achaeans faced from Sicyon to the east and from Sparta to the south.[3] The trend for political integration of the region into a unified entity (Finer 1997, p. 375), became apparent during the Persian Wars (490 and 480–479) where, according to Herodotus (Hist. 1.145.1), the Achaeans were a unified nation, boasting a form of military and broad political cooperation between 12 city-states. These were Pellene, Aegeira, Aeges, Boura, Helice, Aegion, Rypai, Patrai, Pherae, Olenos, Dyme and Tritaia (Caspari 1914; Rahtjen 1965; Walbank 1993). Strabo (Geo. 8.7.5) and Pausanias (Des. 7.1.6–8), as had Herodotus, describe the political cooperation between the 12 city-states of this part of the Peloponnesus on which the common Achaean identity was forged: each of the 12 regions that Strabo called *merides* consisted of seven or eight municipalities. The most important city in the wider region throughout history from the Mycenean up to the Classical Period had been Aegion which became the capital of the Achaean federal state. In all probability, the capital of the federation was initially Helice, with Aegion becoming the capital after an earthquake destroyed the first (Larsen 1968, p. 87).

According to Rizakis (2015, p. 120), cooperation between these 12 *merides* was still under development during the time of the Persian Wars, so it was not yet fully coherent and functional. In today's terminology, a *merida* can be considered a district or regional unit. There seem to be divergent views on this issue. Some researchers claim that the greater political cooperation between the Achaean city-states did not occur until the first half of the fifth century (ibid. p. 121), while others claim that it can be found in a much earlier period, between 570 and 550 (Larsen 1968, p. 83; Tausend 1992; Mele 2002). This second group relies mainly on a comment by Polybius (Hist. 2.39.1–6) which claims that the Achaeans had established colonies in Magna Graecia on the Italian peninsula and that some of these cities, such as Croton, Sybaris and Caulonia, had adopted their customs and laws from the Achaean prototype. Morgan and Hall (1996) cast doubt on this, while Walbank (2000) defends it.

Mackil (2013, pp. 49–52) elaborating on Morgan and Hall's reasoning (1996), rests on the important element concerning the limited role of the Achaeans as a single political entity during the Peloponnesian War (431–404), something which could reinforce the view that a strong and politically integrated federal state had not yet come into being. Thucydides (Hist. 5.82.1) writes that:

[3]As of the sixth century, the Spartans were intent on expanding their hegemony and power throughout the Sympolities (Rizakis 2015, p. 120).

> The next summer the people of Dium, in Athos, revolted from the Athenians to the Chalcidians, and the Lacedaemonians settled affairs in Achaea in a way more agreeable to the interests of their country.

Larsen (1968, pp. 87–89) places this incident as having occurred in 417 and, based on what Thucydides wrote, argues that during that period, Achaea had become democratic, meaning that democracy had already spread throughout the entire region of Achaea. However, he also believes (ibid. p. 82) that it can almost be taken for granted that aristocratic and oligarchic regimes functioned in Achaea before 417. Gradually, over time, references to the 'nation of the Achaeans' appeared more and more frequently in the ancient sources (Xen. Hell. 4.6.1; Strabo Geo. 8.7.3; Paus. Des. 10.18.1–3). Rizakis (2015, p. 121) argues that the political union of the Achaeans occurred sometime after 417 when, with the help of Sparta, they expanded their influence beyond the borders of Achaea, up to the shores of Aetolia. However, Mackil (2013, pp. 49–52) notes that the fact that no reference exists in the ancient sources that refer clearly to the Achaeans as a political entity that fought as such in the Peloponnesian War renders problematic any claim that the Achaean Sympolity existed at that time. In any event, Xenophon (Hell. 4.6.1) tells us that shortly before 389, the Achaeans as a unified state entity granted the men of Calydon the right of citizenship in the Sympolity. Accordingly, by 389 at the latest, the Achaean Sympolity had been formed and was functioning.

One additional conclusion is that one could be a citizen of the Sympolity and still retain citizenship in his home city-state (Rizakis 2015, p. 123). This provides proof enjoyed the privilege of dual citizenship—in other words, *isopoliteia*, as we mentioned in our introduction and will analyse further in due course. The privilege of freedom of action in commercial activity, etc., anywhere within the Sympolity was enjoyed by any citizen of a member city-state, under the regime of *isopoliteia, asylia, proxeny,* etc., as we will elaborate in detail in Sect. 5.2. According to Polybius (2.41.), at the time the Calydonians acquired citizenship, the Sympolity already included a significant number of members, including Olenos, Helice, Patras, Tritaia, Leontion, Aegion, Aigeira, Pellene, Boura and Ceryneia, and functioned without problems up until the rise of Macedon under her kings, Philip II and Alexander III. In 389, the Sympolity maintained an alliance with Sparta, dating from the time of the Peloponnesian War. Thus, one can state that the existence of the Achaean federal state can be verified for the period 389 to 146, whereas, in all probability, it was already in existence as early as 417.

It is known that after the significant victory of the Boeotian *Koinon* (or rather, more specifically, the Thebans, under the leadership of Epaminondas and Pelopidas) at Leuctra (371), Thebes became the dominant military power in mainland Greece. The Boeotians considered it a wise strategic move to forge ties with the cities of the northern Peloponnesus. Around 370, Pellene, one of the city-states of the Achaean Sympolity, taking advantage of its good relations with Sparta, followed an autonomous path in relation to the other members of the federation. Pellene may have even withdrawn from the Sympolity for a year, or an even longer period. Further to the apostasy of Pellene, Xenophon (Hell. 7.1.15–18) claims that, although the

Sympolity retained its structure and function, the wider region of Achaea was in a state of 'stasis' (revolt). Unfortunately, ancient authors do not indicate what they mean by that.

Perhaps a general state of sociopolitical upheaval was taking place, but there is no indication as to why. Aside from Pellene, there may have been other city-states that, to a greater or lesser extent, may have wanted to be free of the Sympolity, but this cannot be verified with any certainty. With the Boeotian *Koinon* being the strongest military power in Greece at the time, the case of Pellene gave Epaminondas an opening to intervene in Achaea, invading it with a powerful force. Robinson (2011, pp. 26–27) claims that from 417 to 366, there was a powerful oligarchic trend in Achaea. He writes that for the Classical period, evidence remains scarce. Polybius' passage about Achaean democratisation goes on to claim that, despite various troubles, Achaea attempted to keep its *koinon politeuma* (the commonly established polity) democratic through to the time of Alexander and Philip (2.41.6). According to Robinson, this might suggest that democracy was the norm for most of the fifth and fourth centuries; however, it is known that Achaea was oligarchic by 366. In that year, Epaminondas led the Thebans in an invasion of Achaea with the goal of making the city-states their allies. Initial successes led to negotiations with aristocratic leaders known as *beltistoi* (the 'best of the people') from the Achaean cities.

When Epaminondas invaded the Sympolity with the ultimate aim of making the Achaean city-states allies of the Boeotian *Koinon*, he was approached by the *beltistoi*, who wielded significant influence in the exercise of political power. Epaminondas assured them, despite the tense situation, that none of them would be exiled, nor would there be any change in the government, meaning that the oligarchs would retain their privileges and influence (Xen. Hell. 7.142). However, potent pressure from radical (i.e. democratic) circles in Achaea, reinforced by corresponding efforts by the democratic leadership of its neighbour to the south, the newly formed Arcadian Sympolity, contributed to altering the options and plans of the Boeotian *Koinon's* federal Assembly. Consequently, Epaminondas diverged from his initial inclination to deal with the Achaean oligarchs, abandoning them in favour of the local grassroots radical pressure groups, who in the end prevailed, introducing a democratic polity throughout the region. Boeotian participation in establishing democratic government was pivotal: the oligarchs were exiled, and in each city-state of the Achaean Sympolity, a temporary governor was installed—the *harmostes*—charged with smoothing the transition to a new government composed of radical democrats. However, in practice, this new regime did not last very long and gradually, the oligarchs returned to power in many Achaean cities (Xen. Hell. 7.1.43, 7.2.11, 7.3.4). Robinson (2011, p. 26) argues that the aristocratic exiles banded together and launched a successful military campaign, one by one, capturing the cities and bringing about the elites' restoration, after which Achaea pursued a strongly pro-Spartan foreign policy. The oligarchy thus attested for 366 may have had its start in 417, for according to Thucydides (5.82.1) in that year the Spartans—had just affected an oligarchic coup to topple the democracy in Argos and 'settled Achaean affairs, which previously had not been favourable'.

Up to this point, the facts one can draw from the above are as follows: the Achaean Sympolity was created around 417, but certainly not much later than that. At first, it functioned on a democratic basis. There may have been a few cases of city-states being under oligarchic control, probably for a short term. The issue of providing a precise definition regarding the political status of each of the Achaean city-states during the 417–338 period is quite difficult since, according to Kralli (2017, p. xxxi), most Peloponnesian city-states in the Classical Period were either oligarchic or constitutionally unstable or, in any case, had not enjoyed the experience of a robust democracy. This does not necessarily contradict the view of Larsen (1968), who argued that around 417, democracy had already spread throughout the entire region of Achaea if we take into account that, according to Aristotle, the term 'oligarchy' covers a variety of regimes.[4]

In practice, these views mean that during the first period of the Achaean Sympolity, from 417 or 389 to ca. 281, there was quite a confusing situation regarding the precise status of political institutions and regimes in each city-state (either democratic or oligarchic) due to the harsh antagonism between the democratic and the oligarchic groups for gaining (or regaining) political power in each city-state. It is safe to argue that there were cases of city-states where the status of the political regime changed (either from democracy to oligarchy, or vice versa). However, what is crucial is that the political ideology of the Achaean Sympolity was certainly democratic, and the member-city-states had to conform to it in one way or another. As will be shown in Sect. 6.1, it is certain that during its second period (280–146), the Sympolity, for its time, gradually developed a very high level of democratic federal organisation, a characteristic of which was the necessary correlation of the democratic governmental structures at the city-state level with those at the federal. For instance, as will be analysed in greater detail below, while the federal Council was a representational body, it is important to note that its members were elected locally, through democratic procedures. Accordingly, during the period 417–338, although there were instances of city-states being under oligarchic administration, these were gradually replaced by democratic regimes as the Sympolity, over time, developed and honed its operational structures and institutions.

Within this framework, it is almost certain that Epaminondas and the Boeotian federal government were heavily involved in the political developments prevailing in the Achaean Sympolity during the 370s to reduce or restrain the dynamics of its development as it manifested itself in the years that followed. There followed the period of Macedon's imposition of its supremacy in southern Greece, marked by the Battle of Chaeronea in 338 and the defeat of the Boeotian–Athenian military alliance that resulted in the destruction of Thebes. Then, under Macedon's leadership, came the campaign against the Persians, which led to the conquest of their empire. In

[4]Aristotle (Pol. 1279b 17–19) connects oligarchy with constitutional authority in the hands of those in possession of property, especially landed property. Aristotle (Pol. 1293a 12–34) classifies four varieties of oligarchy, depending on the size of the estates (from small to large) and the political power of those holding it (Ostwald 2000, pp. 391–393).

metropolitan Greece, Macedon's supremacy was unchallenged, even if the reins of power were not held by Alexander the Great himself but his surrogate, the general Antipater.

It seems that throughout Achaea, the Macedonian influence was so pervasive that it gradually led to the imposition of tyrannical regimes in its cities, with administrations controlled by the Macedonians. This influence became even stronger when, in 331/330, the King of Sparta, Agis III, attempted to draw all the other states in the Peloponnesus (including the Achaean) into an anti-Macedonian military campaign, which ultimately failed. From what is known, it seems that Macedonian influence over Achaea became even more asphyxiating, in reprisal for the latter having joined the Spartan effort. On this issue, Larsen (1968, pp. 215–216) notes that the Achaean state was in existence in 302 when the Achaeans were listed among the members of the Hellenic League at the time of its revival by the Macedonian King Demetrios I Poliorcetes. The Kingdom of Macedon had established many garrisons in Southern Greece, for example, in Athens as of 294 and, later, in Achaean city-states such as Cerynea, Boura and Aegion. Larsen believes that there was never any formal dissolution of the Sympolity before its reorganisation in 281/280; what happened was merely that Macedon controlled so many of its members that the Achaean federal government had practically ceased to function.

To summarise, the reasons responsible for the malfunction of the Achaean Sympolity before its reorganisation in 280 were: first, the upheaval in the Sympolity caused by intense internal confrontation between democratic and oligarchic circles during the period 417 to 366 that certainly acted as a deterrent to further consolidation in the dynamics of politico-economic integration and strengthening of the Sympolity. Second, the interference of the Boeotians in the internal affairs of the Achaean city-states may not have been only 'arbitrational'. They may have been trying to prevent the further strengthening of the Sympolity by their military presence in the region and by any other means, both legitimate and not. One such method may have been to offer various incentives to certain corrupt individuals who might serve Boeotian interests within Achaean city-states, while purportedly acting in those cities' interests. Such individuals could, for example, promote repudiating the federal form of governance in favour of restoring the city-state's full sovereignty, appealing to nationalist sentiment. Alternatively, they might support the political integration of the Sympolity, as long as this policy remained in favour of Boeotian strategic aims. Such forms of corruption were not at all impossible to have occurred; they were characteristic during the Peloponnesian War as the two pro-Athenian and pro-Spartan camps applied pressure on the smaller and weaker Greek city-states.[5]

Third, the pervasiveness of Macedonian influence, coupled with active interference by the Macedonian leadership in all matters and affairs of the Achaean Sympolity as the Boeotians had done previously, obviously reinforced anti-federalist tendencies. After all, the Macedonians had successfully installed anti-federalist,

[5]This phenomenon was not exclusive to the Ancient Greek world but has been endemic everywhere and forever, common to all societies worldwide.

pro-Macedonian tyrannies in many cities in place of the federalist administrations of the first Sympolity. Fourth, there is always a possibility that some flawed actions by federalist governments had occurred in matters of administration, in foreign policy and security, or economic policy, gradually creating a climate of general dissatisfaction amongst the political leadership as well as among the citizens of the individual city-states. For example, if an unpopular policy of high taxation had been adopted to meet a specific federal fiscal target,[6] this may have sparked an outcry and a rejection of the federal structure in its entirety by a group of citizens because of its threat to their wealth and well-being, on a personal and collective level.

Lastly, and this is something that reinforces the view that the Achaean Sympolity, after 338, had lost a large measure of its cohesion, functionality and autonomy as a unified and independent political entity against the other powerful states of that time is the fact that when the Lamian War took place in 323/2, as far as we know, the cities of the Achaean Sympolity did not participate in the anti-Macedonian coalition (Diod. Sic. 18.15.8–9; Plut. Dem. 11.4).[7]

2.2 The Reconstitution and Evolution of the Achaean Federal State (280–146)

Around 280, the Sympolity of the Achaeans was reconstituted as local pro-democratic groups of politicians succeeded in overthrowing oligarchs controlled by Macedon from several important city-states (Polyb. 2.41.10). This was strongly related to the fact that the Macedonian king at that time, Antigonus II Gonatas, was distracted, engaged in a fierce struggle with Ptolemy Keraunos over the throne of Macedonia, and had suffered a naval defeat by him in late 281–early 280. Thus, the Achaean city-states had a great opportunity to take the initiative and get rid of Macedonian garrisons while Macedon was plagued by internal conflicts (Kralli 2017, p. 116).

Larsen (1968, p. 84) argues that the new Achaean Sympolity was regarded as the continuation of the old. Its reconstitution was relatively rapid. As Polybius relates (2.41.10), it began with two members, Dyme and Patra, expanding quickly to four

---

[6]On this critical issue of the sustainability of federal structure in terms of its economic aspect and parameter, we offer an extensive analysis in Sects. 7.2 and 7.3.

[7]With Alexander the Great's death in 323, almost immediately, an extended coalition of military forces was formed to overthrow the Macedonian influence in southern Greece, serving under the command of the Athenian general, Leosthenes. Despite initial successes, in the end, in September of 322, a Macedonian force 40,000 strong defeated the allied army of 25,000 *hoplites* (infantrymen) from all parts of southern Greece at the Battle of Crannon, near the Pineos River. Coupled with defeats of the Athenian fleet at Echinades in 323 and Amorgos the following year, the war ended with Macedonian power consolidated over all of Greece. For further reading on this war, known as the Lamian War, see Habicht (1999).

with the addition of Tritaia and Pherae. Soon after, this number expanded to 7 and within 6 years, the Sympolity had at least ten member cities. Aside from those already named, these were Aegion, Boura, Ceryneia, Leontion, Aegeira, Pellene and, probably, Olenos (Rahtjen 1965; Walbank 1993). In effect, the revived Sympolity built on the same key cities that had formed its earlier composition. In 275, Aegion expelled the local Macedonian garrison and joined the resurrected Sympolity. In the city of Boura, the pro-Macedonian tyrant was assassinated, while in neighbouring Ceryneia, the local tyrant resigned (Polyb. 2.41.13–15). Plutarch (Arat. 29.5) informs us that one of the basic strategies employed by the 'governor' of the new Sympolity, the *strategos* Aratus, from the start of his tenure was to remove all the tyrants that ruled the city-states in the region. Most of those who did not surrender voluntarily met an ugly fate, such as that of Aristippus, tyrant of Argos, who was pursued by Aratus' forces to Mycenae where he was put to death.[8]

Figure 2.1 depicts the segmentation of the Peloponnese peninsula. In the north (within the circle) is the region of Achaea which formed the nucleus of city-states that constituted the reborn Achaean Sympolity during the first years of its formation (280–252). In 251, Aratus added Sicyon to the Sympolity and, in 243, wrested strategic Corinth and Acrocorinth from Macedonian rule. In 235, he added Megalopolis and 6 years later, Argos. Acrocorinth had immense strategic value because it overlooked the entrance into the Peloponnesus from mainland Greece. It was a formidable fortified city and anyone who controlled it could hold back the passage of any military force, whether by land or by sea.

Kralli (2017, p. 156) writes that under Aratus' leadership, from 251 on, the Achaean Sympolity started expanding into the wider area of the Peloponnese peninsula, regions that were not Achaean in geographical terms. This means that this expansion was no longer related solely to reunifying the Achaean nation but served an ambition to unify the Peloponnesus as a whole, under a federal umbrella. Larsen (1968, p. 218) writes that this period of the liberation of city-states from tyrants or the voluntary relinquishing of power by tyrants whose city-states then joined the Achaean Sympolity, culminated with the inclusion of Argos in 229. Thus, between 243 and 228, thanks to the success of this expansionary policy put in place by Aratus, most cities of the Corinthian Isthmus, Arcadia and Argos had become members of the reborn Sympolity (Walbank 1993).

According to Plutarch (Cleo. 3.4), from the beginning, Aratus hoped to unite the Peloponnesians into a federal structure believing this was the only way for them to defend themselves from outside aggressors. Kralli (2017, pp. 158–159) comments on Polybius' (2.43.3) view that Sicyon joined the Achaean Sympolity because of Aratus' faith in the Achaean polity, arguing that this view reflects more of an idealistic conception of Aratus than the political reality in the Peloponnesus. According to Plutarch (Arat. 9.5–6), the incorporation of Sicyon was due to the

[8]One more example of the fate usually accorded to any tyrant who no longer enjoyed the people's favour, is that of Ipparchus, Ippias' brother, who was murdered by Armodius and Aristogeiton in 514 in Athens. The Thirty Tyrants met a similar fate in 404.

Fig. 2.1 The ancient regions of the Peloponnesus. The Achaean region is depicted in circle. Source: http://www.greeceathensaegeaninfo.com/a-greece-travel/a-maps/map-ancient-pelopon nese-lg.jpg (last accessed on 30 May 2020)

need of shielding it both from internal upheaval and from King Antigonus II Gonatas' aggression by making it a part of a larger, politically stable entity. As the first non-Achaean city-state to become a member after the rebirth of the Sympolity in 280, the incorporation of Sicyon was an important achievement since Sicyon was a much bigger city-state than the average Achaean, famed for its artists at the time (Plut. Arat. 13.1–2). Thus, the incorporation of Sicyon increased the Sympolity's prestige, appealing to potential would be pro-Achaean non-member city-states from the Peloponnesus. The Achaean city-states in western Peloponnesus were not only threatened by Macedon but also by the neighbouring Aetolian Sympolity. Kralli (2017, p. 159) correctly points out that at the same time, the growing Aetolian power might have appeared threatening enough to make Aratus, the Sicyonians, and the Achaeans think that they had to expand in order to protect themselves.

It is also important to note that the reconstitution of the Achaean Sympolity was essentially a voluntary choice by its members (Mackil 2013, p. 99), clearly indicating, for the most part, that participation was considered mutually advantageous, although later, there were cases of forced participation (2.38.7). Polybius (2.38.19–20) writes that some city-states became members through compulsion at first, but over the years they found their participation in the Sympolity to be beneficial. This was the case until 191 when the city-states of southern and western Peloponnesus such as those in the regions of Sparta (Laconia), Messenia and Elis, joined more for geopolitical reasons and less by free will.

While Ehrenberg (1964) estimates the total number that became members during the entire 280–146 period to have been approximately 60, below we will argue that this number is much higher and, at the peak of its expansion in 191 and beyond, the Sympolity included at least 103 city-states (See Table 6.2 in 6.5). The Sympolity's rapid revival and its acquisition of new members are significantly connected with the boost in politico-military dynamics that occurred under the leadership of its able (and historically most important) *strategoi*, Aratus and Philopoemen. Both were democratically elected as heads of state and led the Sympolity to the apogee of its power from 245 to 213 and 209 to 182, respectively.[9] As will be discussed in Sect. 6.1, the *strategos* were elected for a 1-year term and concurrently served as the political leader of the Sympolity as well.

However, in 279, the year after the Sympolity was revived, its military power was still relatively weak. It was at this time that Gallic armies invaded Greece, even attacking the sanctuary at Delphi. Only a military expedition from Achaean Patras attempted to defend the oracle from pillage and destruction. None of the other members of the Sympolity participated in this effort to save the sanctuary, probably because of their lack of military capacity. Throughout the period from 280 to 227, the Achaean Sympolity was focussed on repelling Macedonian and Spartan dominance. In 272, it tried to cultivate an advantageous relationship with the Kingdom of Epirus, inviting its able King Pyrrhus to bring an army to Achaea to join it in a campaign to displace Macedonian influence in the Peloponnesus since he had been so successful against the Macedonians in mainland Greece. Achaea also took part in the Chremonidean War of 267–261. However, Achaea was unable to draw into its sphere of influence strategically important Corinth which remained in the hands of the Antigonids of Macedon.

As mentioned above, the period 245–213 was marked by the commanding presence of the *strategos* Aratus of Sicyon who intensified the Sympolity's anti-Macedonian policy. In 245, the Achaeans, together with the Boeotian *Koinon*, declared war on the Aetolian Sympolity, attacking Aetolia on several fronts, including the city-state of Ozolian Locris. The Aetolians, confirming that at that time they were at the peak of their power, counterattacked and crushed the Boeotian forces at Cheroneia (Plut. Arat. 16.1; Polyb. Hist. 20.4.5; Scholten 2000, pp. 85–86).

[9]Chapters 4 and 5 analyse in greater detail the major political and military actions of both Aratus and Philopoemen.

Although the Boeotian *Koinon* suffered a resounding defeat, the Achaeans managed to reap a benefit: Aratus was able to bring Corinth into the Achaean fold in 243 (Plut. Arat. 18.2–22.9, 23.4; Polyb. 2.43.4). The Aetolians counterattacked, invading the territory of the Achaean Sympolity from the north. The Achaeans, however, conceding the enemy forces' superiority, chose not to confront them in battle and instead concentrated on defending Pellene, probably considering it to be vital strategically. This strategy, in the end, proved to be decisive since the Achaeans were not defeated, and in the spring of 240, drew Cynaetha into the fold of the Sympolity. Cynaetha was a small city in northern Arcadia, near the latter's border with Achaea.

Eventually, the Sympolity was able to achieve peace with the Aetolians (Plut. Arat. 33.1–2; Polyb. 2.44.1; Larsen 1975). Moreover, in a striking 180° turn, the two sympolities forged a mutual defence alliance in the face of the recent geopolitical shift after the two powerful kingdoms to the north, Macedonia and Epirus, had reached a mutual understanding. Certainly, this alliance between the two powerful democratic sympolities of Central and South Greece occurred right after Antigonus Gonatas' death in 239 (Polyb. Hist. 2.44.1). Larsen (1975, p. 171) characterises this as 'the most hopeful alignment of Hellenistic times'. He is right in the sense that if the two sympolities had managed to retain that alliance longer than they did, perhaps jointly they might have faced first Macedon, and later Rome, more effectively.

During the next decade, 240–230, the Achaeans pursued their policy of gradual expansion to reconstitute the original Sympolity and expand it further. Their efforts included several political moves such as in Acarnania, the ousting of the tyrant ruler of Argos to add that important city to the Sympolity, the inclusion of the city-state of the Cleonae as well as powerful Megalopolis after its ruler, Lydiades, agreed to relinquish his rule in 235. Lydiades not only renounced tyranny and surrendered his city-state to the Sympolity, but he was also later elected *strategos* and proved himself very capable (Plut. Arat. 30.2–8). The Sympolity then expanded further into Arcadia, absorbing the cities of Heraia, Cleitor and Thelpousa (Polyb. 2.44; Plut Arat. 30.3). The incorporation of Megalopolis, however, brought the Sympolity and Sparta into conflict as that city was at the core of resistance against Sparta's expansionary policy. This led to confrontation when Cleomenes III became King of Sparta (Freeman [1893], 2013; Mackil 2013, p. 107). The Theban *strategos* Epaminondas had selected the particular location to found the city of Megalopolis for it to serve as a fortified 'barrier' against the Spartans. Its walls were considered impregnable. Megalopolis, beyond its strategic value, also happened to be where some of the most famous weapons-manufacturing workshops in the Greek world were located. Cleomenes was very much aware of this and was eager to bring the region under his control.

The Achaean-Aetolian alliance, although it proved advantageous for the expansion and strengthening of both democratic sympolities, was not without its ups and downs, such as the significant defeat inflicted on Aratus at Phylakia when the Macedonian king, Demetrius II, invaded the Peloponnesian peninsula during the so-called Demetrian War which took place sometime between 239 and 227 (Plut. Arat. 34.2–3; Grainger 1999; Mackil 2013, p. 107). In any event, the absorption of new territory and members continued with the inclusion of the city-states of Aegina,

Ermione and the greater part of Arcadia and later, the important city-states of Argos and Phleious (Plut Arat. 34.7, 35.1–5; Polyb. 2.44). In 229, the Spartans under Cleomenes III attempted to enhance their presence in central Peloponnesus, raiding the city-states of eastern Arcadia such as Tegea, Mantineia, Orchomenos and Caphyae which had been incorporated into the Achaean Sympolity in 235. According to Polybius (Polyb. 2.46.8–9), in 233, these cities changed their minds, choosing to defect and join the Aetolian Sympolity. This was in the Aetolians' interest as it served to restrict the Achaeans' dynamic. Fine (1940), however, disputes Polybius' account. Admittedly, it is difficult to reconcile the timeline convincingly. It is odd that initially, in 235, these city-states decided to join the Achaean Sympolity and then, just 2 years later, suddenly opted to switch allegiance and joined the Aetolian.

The question arises as to whether the Achaean–Aetolian alliance would not have been adversely affected by the Aetolians accepting city-states of the Achaeans without prior consultation with the latter. It is highly unlikely that the Achaeans would have agreed to such an arrangement given that it contradicted the very essence of Achaean strategy under Aratus which, according to Plutarch (Cleo. 3.4), was the incorporation of all the Peloponnesus into the Sympolity. Cooperation between the two sympolities did not last very long. It was yet another sign of the fragility of the Greek world's geopolitical environment, with alliances signed, then, a brief time later, renounced, either formally or not; false friendships; little credibility in the development of any stable foreign policy, anticipatory attacks against opponents—literally, an endless Greek *Machtpolitik*.[10]

It appears that even the Hellenistic 'international' security system was characterised by a state of *anarchy*, in terms of modern *International Relations Theory*. According to that theory, the absence of a dominant military power with the capacity—as an overriding regulatory authority in terms of transnational relations—to enforce terms and rules of behaviour within a specific security system,[11] forces states to seek to ensure survival at any price.[12] In conclusion, the fierce competition between the Hellenistic states confirms the view of Hans Morgenthau (1948), one of the leading thinkers of the *Realist School* of *International Relations Theory*, who held that (pp. 4–15) the basic characteristic of international politics is the struggle to acquire power. As a driving force, this is something universal, independent of space and time—an ageless, 'Thucydidean' view of international relations.

In 228, Cleomenes attacked Megalopolis, and the Achaean Sympolity declared war on Sparta. Most of the fighting took place on Achaean soil and, although the

---

[10]*Power politics* (in German: *Machpolitik*), as it is called in *International Relations* theory. It is a state of relentless antagonism in defending a nation's interests through threats or militaristic and economic policies designed to intimidate others to one's advantage. For further reading, see Morgenthau (1946, 1948) and Wight ([1946], 1995).

[11]As was the British Commonwealth during the nineteenth century or the USA for a period after 1991 with its victory in the Cold war, creating a so-called unipolar world.

[12]For the determination of *anarchy* in *International Relations* Theory, see the seminal work of Kenneth Waltz, *Theory of International Politics* (1979), as well as Milner (1991).

Sympolity suffered a significant defeat in 227 at Mt. Lycaeum, near Megalopolis, it nevertheless managed to defend its integrity successfully. Thanks to its able *strategos* Aratus, it even succeeded in regaining control of Mantinea. The Sympolity suffered yet another big defeat that same summer, at Ladoceia, near Megalopolis (Plut. Arat. 36.1–5; Tarn 1928). By 226, Cleomenes, by reorganising his forces and instituting his social reforms, was able to make Sparta a force to be reckoned with, with ambitions of becoming once again the Peloponnesus' dominant power.[13] In 226, Cleomenes himself led a 20,000-strong army of Spartan and allied *hoplites* against the city-state of Dyme. To defend their member, the Achaeans, led by their *strategos,* Hyperbatos, deployed at Ekatonbaion, where they once again were defeated.

By 224, most Peloponnesian cities had passed to the Spartan camp, assenting to adopting Cleomenes' proposed social reforms as they were applied in Sparta. Intending to put an end to endless conflict, he offered to incorporate Sparta as a leading member of the Achaean Sympolity on condition he was appointed the Sympolity's head. It was unsuccessful, through no fault of his own, because he fell ill and was unable to put his case to the Achaean Assembly in person. Meanwhile, of course, Aratus was doing his utmost to forestall Cleomenes' plans (Plut. Arat. 38.). According to Plutarch (Cleo. 16.1–3.), Cleomenes' illness altered the course of Greece's history because it gave Aratus enough time to change the Achaeans' minds and resume negotiations with the Macedonian king, Antigonus III Doson (Michalopoulos 2016).

Cleomenes' appeal to the Achaeans never took place (Cleo. 17.2–4) and thus, a Peloponnesus unified under a single political administration, better able to confront Macedon and later, the new rising great power, Rome, never came to pass.[14] Seeing the Sympolity in a desperate situation, Aratus felt obliged to turn to his mortal enemy, the king of Macedon, Antigonus III Doson, offering him Acrocorinth as an

[13]It is worthwhile to refer, even briefly, to Cleomenes III's reform programme. He began by continuing the significant reforms instituted by one of his predecessors, King Agis IV (Plut. Ag.). A man of profound self-awareness and resolve, he donated all his property to the state and urged his relatives and friends to do the same. In 227, he discarded the institution of *ephors*, exiled the wealthiest citizens and recognised as Spartans many of the *perioikoi, hypomeiones, apeleutheroi*, foreigners and *helots* in order to expand the ranks of his army (which he armed with long spears, like those of the Macedonians) to 4000 warriors. Realising Agis' ambitious reforms, encouraged and supported ideologically by his wife Agiatis, to whom he was devoted, and by the stoic philosopher Sphairos Boristhenetes, Cleomenes forgave debts and mortgages, appropriated the land and redistributed it in 4000 shares, restored the *agoge*, the educational system instituted by the Spartan lawmaker Lycurgus, and resumed the common meals (known as *syssitia*), the black broth and red garments of the *homoioi hoplites*. In short order, he consolidated his position as well as that of the city, acquiring a great deal of power. Only in name did he retain the Spartan institution of dual kingship. Regarding the social strata of Sparta of *periokoi, hypomeiones* and *apeleutheroi,* see Cartledge (1979, 1987), while with regard to the *hoplites*, the citizen-soldiers of the Ancient Greek city-states, who were armed primarily with shields and spears, see, among others, Cartledge (1987), Hanson (1998) and Kagan and Viggiano (2013).

[14]The final failure of Sparta to achieve a broader geopolitical and economic status quo on the Peloponnesian peninsula through its incorporation into the Achaean Sympolity appears to us to

incentive. However, Aratus' manoeuvring in leading the Sympolity into a 180° geopolitical turn to a collaboration with Macedon in 227 abrogated its strategic anti-Macedonian alliance with the Aetolian Sympolity (Briscoe 1981). It met with success as the Macedonian forces defeated the Spartans in a decisive battle at Sellasia in 222 (Polyb. 2.65; Plut. Cleo. 27.4–28.8; Philop. 6.1; Mackil 2013, p. 113). As a result, the risk of the Sympolity's dissolution because of the war with Sparta was averted.

During the time of the so-called Social War of 221–217, the alliance between the Aetolian and Achaean Sympolities collapsed in 220 when the Aetolians crossed the Gulf of Corinth and attacked western Achaea and, along with their ally, Elis, raided and pillaged the cities of Patras, Pherae and Tritaia and then proceeded toward Messene. According to Thucydides (1.5.3) and Polybius (4.3.1–5), the march of the Aetolians across Achaea was accompanied by raids for plunder into adjacent regions. That view may have been an exaggeration, coloured by Plutarch's prejudice against the Aetolians which often appears in his work.

When representatives of Patras and Pherae cities protested at the pan-Achaean Assembly, a measure mandating military action was passed. However, the Achaean armed forces were crushed by the Aetolians near Caphyae (Polyb. 4.11–12). The war continued over the following years, with the Achaeans, in addition to the Aetolians, also having to face the Spartans from the south who were now closely allied with the Aetolians (Polyb. 4.16.12–31). In 219, the Spartans invaded the region southeast of Argos and laid siege to Megalopolis. At the same time, the Aetolians invaded western Achaea and laid waste to areas around Dyme, Tritaia and Pherae, defeating a force mobilised to push them back and forging on to destroy several fortified sites protecting the cities of Dyme and Thelpousa.

Those city-states, in particular, were prone to a first-strike attack by the Aetolians. The challenge for a country to adopt first-strike capability is to strip the enemy of his offensive means, making him incapable of taking aggressive action afterwards. Elis was a perpetual ally of the Aetolians, never having sought to join the Achaean Sympolity, very likely afraid of harming its prestige as the home of the Olympic Games. It thus facilitated the Aetolians in transferring troops through Elis to attack Achaea along a second front. It was to the Aetolians' advantage to stage that attack from the southwest, through Elis, aware that in the event of failure or the need to regroup, it could be done by withdrawing to safety on friendly territory (see Fig. 2.1).

---

exhibit similarities with today's relationship between the European Union and the UK, especially after the Brexit vote of June 2016. Is the UK part of the European family or the Anglo-Saxon world in a 'coalition' of the USA–UK–Canada? Is it in the UK's interest to parallel Sparta's 'isolation on the island', and seek its independence, retaining its national currency, in memory of a *Pax Britannica* (which today translates into a handful of strategic possessions scattered throughout the planet, such as its base on southern Cyprus, the Falkland Islands in the South Atlantic or the Straits of Gibraltar) instead of sacrificing a measure of its independence in exchange for a strong place in a supra national EU? The English, as the strongest factor in the UK, in the referendum of the 24 June 2016, chose to turn its back on the EU. Only the future will tell how wise that decision was.

Facing both the Aetolian and Spartan forces at the same time put the Achaeans in a difficult position. The city-states of the western part of Achaea suffered greatly while Messenia remained under the control of Sparta who continued to pursue her ambition to extend her influence throughout the region. It seems that the Spartans, despite their significant defeat at Sellasia in 222, a pivotal event in the evolution of that city-state's history, continued to wield considerable power in the region. Due to the lack of sufficient sources, one can only make assumptions as to its military capacity after 222. It must be noted that Antigonus III Doson's successor on the Macedonian throne, Philip V, in 219, decided to intervene in the confrontation between the two sympolities on the side of his ally, the Achaeans. That alliance had remained intact from the time of Aratus' dramatic switch in foreign policy in 227. The Macedonians conducted military campaigns in Epirus and Acarnania, freeing many city-states from Aetolian control, and then proceeding to invade Aetolia itself, sacking the cities of Stratos and Calydon and bringing the city-state of Eniades under its influence. In 218, they continued their successful military incursions throughout the Peloponnesus.

It is important to note that the Achaean Sympolity's failure to defend its members successfully led many of them to refuse to pay the *eisphora* tax to the federal treasury. Furthermore, the Sympolity's troops, as professional *hoplites*, were no longer as eager to offer their services due to delays in payment. Faced with these dire circumstances, it was necessary to reactivate the aged but experienced *strategos*, Aratus, who was once again re-elected in 217/6. His first act was to ask the federal Assembly to pass a *dogma* (bill) to establish and fund a federal mercenary force of 8500 *hoplites* and 500 horsemen, and a conscripted force of 3000 *hoplites* and 300 horsemen, as well as six fully operational *triremes* (warships), three based in ports of Argolis (the Sympolity's eastern flank) and the other three off the coast of Patras and Dyme in the west.

It seems that the realisation of Aratus' proposal bore fruit as the Achaean Sympolity consequently scored a series of victories over the Aetolians (Polyb. 4.59–60; Mackil 2013, p. 119). The Sympolity gained further significant victories in 207 when, under the leadership of the *strategos* Philopoemen, who thoroughly reorganised the Sympolity's forces, it managed to inflict significant defeats on the Spartans and their allies in Messene. The leader from Megalopolis reorganised the Achaean military forces and introduced new weaponry, such as the *sarissa* spear of the Macedonians, a development that contributed significantly to improving the Achaeans' fighting ability (Fig. 2.2). He also supplied his men with larger, more durable shields. Furthermore, he even inspired a change in the behaviour of the young, especially those old enough for military service, who had become too accustomed to leading an idle life of pleasure and luxury (Plut. Philop. 9; Paus. Des. 8.50.1–2; Anderson 1967). As a result, the alliance between the Achaean Sympolity and the Kingdom of Macedon weakened significantly. It had been formed to confront Cleomenes's then-powerful Sparta. But after Philopoemen's victories, Achaean power throughout the region had been restored, and Philopoemen was able to rid the Sympolity of Macedonian influence.

Fig. 2.2 A unit of an Achaean *phalanx* of *hoplites* (based on the Macedonian formation), as reorganised by Philopoemen. Source: *History of the Hellenic Nation*, Vol. 3/1. With the permission of Ekdotike Athinon Publications, Athens

2.3 The Achaean Sympolity During the Second Century. Achieving Political Integration Before the Fall

The issue of the Achaeans' deliverance from Macedonian influence came to the fore again in 200, when the new rising decisive factor in the Hellenistic geopolitical equation, Rome, once again interfered in the internal affairs of mainland Greece.[15] Upon an appeal by the Athenians, the Rhodians and King Attalos I Soter, the ruler of Hellenistic Kingdom of Pergamon, Rome sent *legati*[16] to both the Aetolian as well as the Achaean Sympolities, seeking to impact political developments in the region, enlisting the federations as allies to put an end to Macedon's dominance (Errington 1969, pp. 70–75, 81–84).

This was achieved in 199 when the Roman general, Titus Quinctius Flamininus, upon instruction by the Roman Senate, declared war on Macedon. Significant regions of Thessaly, Phocis, Locris and the greater part of Euboea fell to the Romans while their opportunistic allies, the Aetolians, raided areas still controlled by the Macedonians. In the fall of 198, as Flamininus was besieging Phocian Elateia, the Achaeans received a delegation from the Romans and their Greek allies seeking to persuade them to abandon Macedon and join them. In his fateful speech to the Achaean Assembly, the *strategos* Aristaenus pointed out the Sympolity's

[15]Rome had first intervened in the internal affairs of Greece during the First Macedonian War (215–206). At that time, it sought a cooperation with the Aetolian Sympolity against Rome's powerful enemy, Hannibal of Carthage, in return for assisting Aetolia in her conflict with Philip V of Macedon.

[16]The *legati* were high-ranking officials of the Roman army, although the title was also given to Rome's diplomatic emissaries sent by the Senate on missions to foreign countries. Emissaries of foreign countries to Rome were also referred to as *legati*.

vulnerability to an attack by the Roman fleet on the northern shores of the Peloponnesus, as well as to an attack by the Spartans under the tyrant Nabis from the south. The Achaeans decided to end their alliance with Philip and ally themselves with Rome, Attalus of Pergamon and the island of Rhodes (Livy 32.19–23), fearing Philip V was no longer able to protect them from either the Romans or Nabis (Livy 32.19.6–10, 21.15–20, 26, 29–31).

Probably, the Achaeans must have grasped that Roman power would prevail as the decisive factor in Greek affairs in mainland Greece. One can say that, in the short run, it was the right choice: the Sympolity dodged confrontation with Rome, allowing it to maintain its political status. However, putting an end to its cooperation with Macedon and allying with Rome against its former allies, a policy to which Philopoemen adhered, was a very truly fateful decision because it led to a variety of consequences which we analyse below. Eckstein (2018, p. 244) writes on this issue that many Greek state officials knew they were walking a tightrope', complying with Roman wishes when necessary but retaining as much freedom of action as possible.[17] Polybius addresses this delicate political problem in his depiction of a debate ca. 184 between the Achaean statesmen Philopoemen and Aristaenus on how to retain Achaean honour and independence when dealing with the Romans (24.11–13). Aristaenus urged giving in immediately whenever the Achaeans were faced by a Roman request or demand since resistance to Rome would ultimately not work, and it would only anger the Romans—and to no purpose, since the Achaeans would ultimately have to give in. Philopoemen instead was for fighting for one's legal rights under the Sympolity's formal treaty of alliance with Rome, and only bending to Roman demands at the last moment, if the Romans were particularly insistent.

In any case, the Achaean Sympolity, lacking sufficient military capacity to determine its own future, was obliged to choose sides, either the Macedonians or the Romans and their allies. The Achaeans benefitted from Macedon's defeat at the Battle of Cynoscephalae in 197, being allowed by the Romans to incorporate Corinth as a 'reward', although forced to accept a 'temporary' Roman garrison. Identifying with Roman geopolitical aspirations served to boost the Sympolity's power dramatically. By 191, excepting Elis, Laconia, Messene and Argos, all the other city-states of the Peloponnesus had become members of the Sympolity.

In fact, Corinth had been liberated by the Achaeans themselves, without Rome's help, since allegedly, on the same day that the Romans defeated the Macedonians at Cynoscephalae, the Achaean army, comprised of 5000 men under the command of the *strategos* Nikostratus, defeated a Macedonian army of 6000 men and 700 Corinthian youths under the command of Androsthenes (Livy 33.14–15). The Achaean army's success was largely due to the reforms Philopoemen had instituted back in 209 (Larsen 1968, p. 396). The confrontation between Nabis and Rome in the

[17]For the geopolitical background and the balance of power between city-states, federal states and kingdoms in mainland Greece during the early second century BCE two Fine (1940) and Eckstein (2007, 2018) provide important evidence.

Peloponnesus that ended in Sparta's defeat and further loss of power led to several Laconian coastal cities being incorporated into the Achaean Sympolity. Flamininus decided to pull out the Roman garrisons from Demetrias (Thessaly), Chalcis and the fortress of Acrocorinth and leave Greece. Then, Nabis' sudden death allowed Philopoemen to take advantage of the power vacuum to incorporate Sparta and the rest of Laconia into the Sympolity.[18] Almost at the same time, western Peloponnesus and its city-states of Elis and Messene were also incorporated.

It appears that Rome's involvement in Greece led to a substantial geopolitical upscaling of the Achaean Sympolity which now included important cities such as Argos, Corinth (including Acrocorinth) and Sparta. Possibly, the Romans appreciated the fact that the Achaeans disavowed their alliance with Macedon and allied with Rome. Not having any other reliable ally in Greece, only enemies (Macedonia, the Aetolian Sympolity, Sparta[19]), perhaps Rome felt that having an ally in southern Greece, with geopolitical footholds in mainland Greece as well, willing to go along with its overall policy for the region, was worth in return allowing the Achaeans to consolidate their hold over their own turf, the Peloponnesus.[20]

Despite Sparta having become a member of the Sympolity in 192, it had not been a voluntary choice. The Spartans appealed to Rome to return the hostages the Romans had taken during the Sparta-Rome conflict in the Peloponnesus in 195. They also demanded the return of coastal areas that the Romans had handed over to the Sympolity. In the end, only the first demand was granted (Livy 36.35.7). With Sparta unwilling to swallow her new circumstances as a member of the Sympolity, the Achaeans turned to attempting to incorporate the region's remaining free regions of the Peloponnesus, Elis and Messenia. The first appeared willing to consider this, but Messene baulked, appealing to Flamininus to intercede. Flamininus proposed a very diplomatic solution: requesting (or ordering) the Achaeans to abandon Messenian territory that had seized in exchange for the city-state's rejoining the Sympolity as it had a few years earlier before reneging (Liv. Hist. 36.31.1–9; Polyb. 22.10; Paus. Des. 4.29.11).

The descriptions in the ancient sources portray how fluid the situation in the Peloponnesus was, and probably in the rest of mainland Greece, as well. It is uncertain whether Flamininus simply recommended or outright demanded compliance from both the Achaean Sympolity and the Messenian city-states with his wishes. Moreover, Flamininus' insistence that, although the region of Messenia was to be incorporated into the Achaean Sympolity, Achaean troops could not be stationed there seems contradictory; if Messene were to be a federal unit, it stood to reason that it would not object to having federal troops stationed on its soil. From all

[18](Livy Hist. 34.22.5–24.7, 34.25.1–41.10, 35.37.1–3; Plut. Philop. 15.4–5; Paus. Des. 8.51.1)

[19]At that particular time Sparta was considered as an enemy by Rome (Forrest 1968).

[20]Something similar has occurred many times in history. For instance, the contemporary multifaceted support of Israel by the USA, from 1948 to date, rests on the argument that Israel is traditionally its reliable ally in the Middle East through which the USA can project a part of the broader design of its global overriding grand strategy.

the descriptions, it appears that the Romans saw their relationship with the Achaeans as one between a powerful state, Rome, and its satellite, the Sympolity.

It is obvious that it suited Rome to have an independent but weakened Sparta in the region, just strong enough to keep the Achaean Sympolity from gaining further strength through a politico-military unification of the entire peninsula. Any dynamism on the part of either the Achaeans or the Spartans would be curbed by their perpetual mutual animosity—arbitrated by Rome. This allowed the Romans to portray themselves not as conquerors of Greek territory but as benevolent arbitrators and peacemakers, interested only in 'maintaining stability' in the region. An attempt by Sparta to challenge the Sympolity's authority over the whole of the Peloponnesus occurred again in 189/8 when the Spartans rebelled, demanding independence, putting the future of the city to the arbitration of the Roman general, Fulvius Nobilior. He, in turn, directed both the Spartans and the Achaeans to appeal directly to Rome for a solution. The fact that the Achaean Sympolity agreed to this was an indirect recognition of Rome's right of de facto intervention in her affairs. Rome's reply was ambiguous, along the lines of 'as far as the Lacedaemons are concerned, nothing must change' (Livy 38.32.9). The Achaeans interpreted this to mean they were entitled to handle the issue as an internal matter and thus had the right to further their campaign to integrate cities into the Sympolity (Mackil 2013, p. 132).

Philopoemen took the initiative to move against Sparta to pull it back into the Sympolity, with the backing of some pro-Achaean Spartans. Clashes occurred, resulting in the death of some 74 rebel Spartans. Philopoemen ordered the destruction of the city's walls, the abolition of Lycurgus' laws and the acceptance of the Achaean federal legislation's supremacy (Livy 38.33–34). Again, the 'anti-federalist' Spartans appealed to Rome, and again, Rome intervened. The Achaeans were obliged to heed the Roman insistence on restraint. It was obvious that Rome was openly intervening in the internal affairs of the Achaean state. Mackil (2013, p. 133), based on Polybius (23.4–16), characteristically argues that:

> The full cost of Philopoemen's decision to align the Achaeans with Rome in order to secure their independence from Macedon was now being revealed. The Romans expected that their resolutions would be followed, but doing so sometimes required the Achaeans to violate their own laws and reverse their own ratified decisions. They had indeed achieved independence from Macedon but were quickly becoming subordinated to the Romans.

Mackil (p. 133) notes very aptly that while the Achaeans managed to create a state unifying all of the Peloponnesus (even though it was a complicated mosaic of city-states), in the end, they were not able to suppress the discontent of members like Sparta, on integration during the final phase of the Sympolity's existence. The reasons for this are numerous, but here we focus on the most substantial. Mackil is right in characterising the Achaean Sympolity as a mosaic: although homogeneous in many fundamental respects such as a common Achaean/Hellenic ancestry, language and culture, each city-state presented its peculiarities (some more, some less significant), in terms of how it was organised as a state, or how it designed its foreign policy, etc. Accordingly, the homogenisation required by a federal structure was no easy matter and required a substantial period of adjustment for federal institutions to be accepted into the consciousness and practical behaviour of the Achaean citizens as a whole. The crucial element in the survival of the Achaean Sympolity was familiarisation of its citizens with the practices and functions of its institutions; obviously, to achieve that, what was required was time.

In the case of Sparta/Laconia as well as the city-states of Messene and Elis, that did not happen since their integration, with the view of uniting all of the Peloponnesus under a single administration, was not distinguished by any eagerness on their part to participate. For Sparta and the greater region of Laconia, it was accomplished only by enforcement through the Sympolity's military power and the diplomatic machinations of Philopoemen to convince leading citizens to make Sparta a member, partly by compulsion, partly by persuasion (Plut. Phil. 15.4; Kralli 2017, p. 343). For the Messenian city-states and the whole of Elis, on the other hand, it was geopolitical necessity that forced their hand. Kralli (2017, p. 181), based on Plutarch (Cleo. 3.5), believes that Aratus' plan for a unified Peloponnesus (with the exception of Sparta) were not seen positively by the Eleans nor by some, or even many, Arcadian city-states which were more favourably disposed toward the Spartans. It appears, however, that the real reason behind the reluctance of those Arcadian city-states to join the Achaean Sympolity was not their aversion to federalism (after all, during the 370–235 period, they were members of the erstwhile Arcadian Sympolity); instead, it was for reasons of defence.

Scholten (2000, pp. 159–161) and Kralli (2017, p. 181) mention that the Achaean defeat at Phylakia (located between Tegea and Sparta) in ca. 233/2 by Bithys, the Macedonian general, and the ensuing turmoil in the area, could very well have alarmed the eastern Arcadians as to the Achaeans' ability to defend them effectively; it made them turn to the Aetolians for assistance. Walbank (1984, p. 451) suggests that the fact that the Arcadian city-states decided to remain in the Achaean Sympolity was more fear of the possible consequences they might face if they seceded. A decisive factor that led to the incorporation of the Arcadian poleis into the Achaean Sympolity was the decision of Megalopolis to become a member. Soon after, Mantineia and the other eastern Arcadian poleis joined as well, if only as a means of self-protection (Kralli 2017, p. 182).

Regarding the Messenians, Pausanias (4.29.6) argues that after 272, the Messenians were unwilling to join the Achaean Sympolity for fear of reviving their ancestral hostility with Sparta. At least some of them may have wanted to join the Sympolity but chose not to do so for security reasons (fear of Spartan reprisal). This strategy continued unchanged until 210 when, along with King Attalos of Pergamon and the Illyrians, the Eleans, the Spartans and the Messenians joined the Roman–Aetolian alliance, in response to that of the Achaeans and Macedonians. This situation, however, changed radically when, in April 191, the Romans defeated the alliance of the Aetolian Sympolity and King Antiochus III of the Seleucid Empire at Thermopylae.[21] Then, according to Errington (1969, pp. 131–132), the loss of Aetolian protection, combined with fear both of the Romans and the Achaeans, who had very recently violently incorporated Sparta, led the Eleans, encouraged by Rome, to agree to become members of the Sympolity. The Messenian city-states were also invited to join, but did not give any reply to the Achaean envoys and instead prepared for war. Rome intervened at this point, however, ordering the Messenians to join the Sympolity anyway, which they did in 191 (Kralli 2017, pp. 324–326).

The above views stress how volatile the situation in the Peloponnesus was at that time, and it underscores the fact that the Arcadian city-states, Messenians and the Elians especially, become members of the Achaean Sympolity basically for geopolitical reasons. According to Kralli (2017, p. 329), the facts mentioned above are proof that the unification of the entire Peloponnesus under the Achaean Sympolity was but an illusory situation. However, in Chap. 7, we provide evidence that participation in the Sympolity led to considerable economic benefits due to interstate commerce among its more than 100 member city-states (including those recalcitrant regions of Messenia, Laconia and Elis). That means that even if a large number of Arcadian, Spartan/Laconian, Elian and Messenian city-states were at first disgruntled by their having been 'encouraged' to join the Achaean Sympolity, their negativism might have gradually eased as they reaped the rewards of better economic conditions through the commercial activity because of their participation in the federal structure.[22]

In the spring of 191, the Spartans decided to leave the Sympolity. Less than a year had passed since they had joined. The Achaean *strategos* at the time, Diophanes, having recently established a cooperation with Roman forces, thought to make an example of them. Despite the advice and recommendation by Philopoemen for restraint, Diophanes and the Roman *legate*, Titus Flamininus, entered Laconia and prepared to launch an attack against Sparta (Plut. Phil. 16.1–2). Thanks to Philopoemen's intervention, however, Sparta rejoined the Sympolity without conflict (16.3–4). A short while later, however, in autumn of the same year, followers of the tyrant Nabis succeeded in overthrowing and exiling Sparta's pro-Achaean faction. The Spartans went further, renouncing their membership in the Sympolity. In the winter of 191/0, they sent a delegation to Rome demanding the return of a number of small neighbouring cities to their political jurisdiction as well as five hostages Flamininus had extracted from Nabis. This time, Philopoemen intervened aggressively, bringing Sparta back into the fold in 188 by force of arms. Again, the Spartans responded by sending a delegation to Rome, this time asking for her to intervene to allow the repatriation of Spartan citizens that had been exiled for anti-federalist activity (Polyb. 23.18.1–2). In the middle of 184, two former Spartan

[21]On the invitation of the Aetolians, Antiochus had arrived in late October 192 to liberate Greece from Roman suzerainty but failed and turned back (Livy 35.32.1–33.11, 36.16–19; 36.35.11; Polyb. 20.8).

[22]We return to this issue in Sects. 7.3 and 7.4.

exiles, Areus and Alcibiades, confronted the representative of the Sympolity, Apollonidas, on the floor of the Roman Senate concerning the events that followed Philopoemen's entry into Sparta a few years earlier. The Achaean federal authorities deemed this high treason and both men were sentenced in absentia to death. The Achaean *strategos* at the time, Lycortas, was obliged to state the Sympolity's case for this before Rome's representatives, a clear indication that it was now in a position of finding it necessary to explain its actions to a higher authority, Rome.

The following year, the city-state of Messene,[23] controlled by an oligarchic movement led by an adventurer, Denocrates, declared its secession from the Achaean Sympolity. The Achaeans put down the rebellion by force, bringing Messene back into the fold. It was only then that Rome decided to back the Sympolity, imposing a financial embargo on the Messenians (Polyb. 23.17.3). This episode had lasting effects, setting off a chain of events as the entire western part of the Peloponnesus peninsula, including the rest of the Messenian city-states (southwestern Peloponnesus) and Elis (northwestern Peloponnesus), those that had not initially joined, were quickly integrated into the Sympolity.

This was undoubtedly a huge accomplishment as the Sympolity had finally achieved the ultimate goal of its overriding strategy: the political integration of the whole of the peninsula under the aegis of the Achaeans. In fact, Philopoemen's victory over Sparta in 191 meant all of the southeastern Peloponnesus had been absorbed into the Sympolity, albeit by force. The Achaeans' defeat of Messene in 183 then saw the integration of the city-state into the Sympolity as well. It was the culmination of the Sympolity's expansionary policy, the political vision of Aratus and his fellow dreamers, realised by the great *strategos* Philopoemen. For assurance that their action to suppress Messene's apostasy would not add to complications for the Sympolity, the Achaeans appealed to the Romans. The latter not only chose not to support them but warned them they would not do so even if larger city-states, such as Corinth or Argos, attempted to secede. This inconsistent stance of Rome proves that her ultimate aim was to become the regulator of Greece's internal affairs. As Larsen (1935, p. 209) characteristically observes, the only freedom Greece had was to arrange her internal affairs in line with Rome's wishes.

Polybius describes the crucial events that followed: his own father, Lycortas, the *strategos* in 182, was responsible for bringing Sparta back into the Sympolity[24] and advocated for the return of all exiles not related to anti-Achaean activity. Mackil (2013, p. 134) acknowledges that, in Polybius' account, Lycortas' stance was not unique and that there were other, even more, submissive proposals considered in favour of further satisfying Rome's demands. This is supported by the fact that almost right after Lycortas' proposal, the Roman Senate became even less accommodating, demanding the return of all exiles who were against the federalisation of the Peloponnesus under the Achaean Sympolity. Polybius (24.13–18) mentions that Callicrates and Hyperbatus, two of Lycortas' political opponents, on their own

[23]Messene was one of the major city-states in the region of Messenia in southwestern Peloponnesus.

[24]Having, in 184 or 183, obviously again renounced its membership.

initiative (it appears), travelled to Rome and, testifying before the Senate, appealed for it to publicly censure those Achaean politicians that were not willing to satisfy so easily Roman demands. Upon hearing their testimony, the Senate decided to accept the appeal, perhaps in a show of Roman supremacy over the Sympolity, or possibly to test the Achaeans' reaction to Rome's manipulations—or both.

But from Polybius' account, there was something more, indicative of Roman diversionary policy and hypocrisy: the Senate accepted to hear and act on testimony from unauthorised political personae of the Sympolity. This management of bilateral relations not only through official channels but through unofficial as well, was certainly not ethical. Clearly, in her relations with the Greek world, Rome's grand strategy was based on a tactical policy of divide and conquer. It was a particularly successful policy, playing one against the other, in line with whatever geopolitical or geo-economical goal benefitted Rome at any given time, serving to weaken the Greek states which gradually were transformed either into its satellites or its tributaries. Polybius notes that this subversion was already occurring in the internal politics of the Sympolity. The Romans had infiltrated 'their people' to promote their interests. Polybius ascribes selfish motives to Callicrates and Hyperbatus, considering them disastrous for all Greeks, especially for the Achaeans. In Mackil's (2013, p. 134) view, although granting that Polybius' account, to a degree, may have been biased, it nevertheless indicated that the situation, at least from that decade on, both in terms of the Sympolity's internal affairs as well as its relations with the Romans, was leading to disaster. Upon his return from Rome, in 180/179, Callicrates proposed to the Achaeans that they accede to the Romans' demands and allow the return of all anti-federalist exiles, both Spartan and Achaean (Polybius. 24.10.14–15). All this provides much food for thought.

To begin with, concerning the motives of Callicrates and Hyperbatus, it is obvious that they deserved Polybius' characterisation of them as great consular woes. Their motives were obviously personal and selfish: their continued presence in the political arena as state officials meant they were in a position to handle the economic affairs of the state. This was also indicative of a general decline in ethics in the Achaean political world, a malady not exclusively Achaean, but obviously panhellenic as well. It goes far in explaining why Rome eventually subjugated Greece. While Philopoemen, Lycortas, their advocates and other 'patriots of the pan-Achaean ideal' were trying to hold back the Roman incursion and forestall their satellisation of the Sympolity, another political faction was undermining them.

This scheming group portrayed themselves as extreme pro-Roman, as 'holier than the Pope', to use a modern expression. Callicrates managed to be elected *strategos* of the Sympolity for the year 180/79. First off, he sought and achieved the return of the Spartans who had fought against federalisation (which was in Rome's interest). Along with Hyperbatus, they convinced their fellow citizens to repatriate and reinstate all who had been exiled from the Sympolity for their transgression, under the laws of the state.[25] Subsequently, with a series of acts, Callicrates succeeded in undermining every vestige of freedom and independence that, over the ages, the Sympolity had fought so hard to achieve.

Additional food for thought is provided by the issue of the social/class dimension of the makeup of the part of the population that appeared to be resigned to the new status quo, i.e. to a relationship of reduced sovereignty of their homeland vis-à-vis Rome. That was an issue that was not limited to the Sympolity but to all of Greece, and highlighted by the Battle of Pydna, for example. An analysis of the class and socio-economic aspects of this battle, however, is not within our purview here. Suffice it to say, though, that this opportunistic attitude passes through a class prism. That Callicrates, although unpopular for most Achaeans, managed in 180 to be elected *strategos* was probably due less to support from a group of citizens at large at one of the federal assemblies, and more to his strong backing from pro-Roman oligarchic circles. However, the fact that the post of *strategos* was filled by open vote by the federation's citizens in a scheduled pan-Achaean federal Assembly could only mean two things: first, that, of those present at the Assembly, at least in that year, 180, oligarchic citizens voting for Callicrates outnumbered their opponents. This could reasonably be attributed to the Assembly being dominated by oligarchic circles because simple citizens of modest means from outlying regions often found it difficult to afford to abandon their work to participate in the Assembly, as well as pay for travel to and from it.[26]

An alternative scenario is that the oligarchic circles had somehow managed to influence enough of their compatriots of the lower strata in Callicrates' favour. This cannot be excluded. In any event, the fact that the Achaeans had reached a point where they gave the highest post in the Sympolity to an adventurer like Callicrates does not mean that his authority would not repulse the democratic masses. The consistent support given by Callicrates and the political faction that shared his views and backed him in favour of subservience to the Romans did not endear him to his compatriots, the majority of whom despised him. The pro-Roman faction of Callicrates, Andronidas and their cohorts repulsed most Achaean citizens. Polybius (30.29) refers to an occasion sometime after 180, during the annual Antigoneia festival in the city-state of Sicyon. The citizens going to the public baths demanded that the waters be changed if Romans or followers of Callicrates and Andronidas had bathed in them. Moreover, the latter were jeered whenever they appeared in public spaces, and even schoolchildren taunted them, calling them traitors. The extent of the revulsion their compatriots felt was so great that they were effectively shunned. It was one thing for the Sympolity to have followed a prudent, pragmatic and responsible foreign policy, one developed within the context that had developed and in

[25]Within this group of men that accepted Callicrates' view was no small number of 'useful idiots', to use the description attributed to Josef Stalin, men who were either naïve or incapable of rational judgment, blindly supporting pro-Roman policy in Achaea at the expense of their homeland's interests.

[26]On this issue, see Briscoe (1974) and our own work, Economou and Kyriazis (2016). Below, in Sect. 6.1, we analyse this in detail.

which it was called to ask—quite another to slavishly follow a policy of subservience to the Romans, as represented by Callicrates and his cohorts.

Returning to this issue of international relations, gradually, the relationship between the Achaean Sympolity and Rome deteriorated progressively because of the latter's frequent meddling in issues of the Peloponnesus city-states which the Sympolity considered to be internal matters, not subject to interference by third parties (Badian 1952). In effect, although with an ever-dwindling effect, the Sympolity did manage to retain its sovereignty until 146, when the Romans defeated it at the Battle of Leucopetra. Regarding all the above, there is an alternate view: both the political movers and shakers as well as the average Achaean citizen may have become very much aware of Rome's might. Her remarkable resilience when faced with profound challenges, turning around and defeating the Carthaginian general Hannibal at the Battle of Zama in 202, confirmed her status as the dominant power in the Mediterranean, and extended that power into the Hellenic world.

In 197, during the second Macedonian War, the Romans defeated Macedon, their most powerful rival in Greece, at the Battle of Cynoscephalae and, 29 years later, by 168, had virtually turned its erstwhile ally, the Aetolian Sympolity, into a Roman province. In 180, the only states in Greece who theoretically were in a position to challenge Roman expansion were the Kingdom of Macedon to the north, though significantly weakened after its defeat in 197, and the Achaean Sympolity in the south, which, on the surface, remained an ally of Rome. For their part, the Hellenistic kingdoms in the east lacked sufficient power to oppose Roman imperialism in the form of a *Drang nach Osten* toward the east. Excepting the Battle of Pydna in 168, the only serious challenge by the Greco-Macedonian kingdoms of Alexander's successors in mainland Greece during the second century was the campaign by the able King Antiochus III the Great of the Seleucid Kingdom, who attempted to contribute to the Aetolian Sympolity (which, at that time, had abandoned its alliance with Rome). However, as mentioned above, his forces were defeated by the Romans at Thermopylae in 191. The Romans then proceeded to carry the war into Asia Minor, attacking Antiochus' forces, again defeating his army at Magnesia in 190 (almost parallel to Hannibal's defeat off Sidon in North Africa). The result was that a significant part of western and central Asia Minor had fallen into Rome's hands.

The new and decisive defeat of Macedon under King Perseus at Pydna in 168, during the third Macedonian War (171–168),[27] made it clear that the margin of resistance to Rome's broader geopolitical objectives had narrowed significantly. The first encounter in that war between the two rivals had ended in a Macedonian victory at Callinico in Thessaly (171). However, despite that victory, the balance of power failed to tilt in Macedon's favour. Devastating Roman raids in central Greece followed, and Rome took Boeotia. The once-powerful *Koinon* of the Boeotians was officially abolished. In 170, the Romans sent ambassadors to Aegion, the

[27]The battle saw the further ascendancy of Rome in the Hellenistic world and the end of the Antigonid dynasty, whose power traced back to Alexander the Great.

Sympolity's capital, to inform the Achaeans that Rome considered even silent support for Perseus a hostile act. Accordingly, the Sympolity proposed sending troops under Polybius to fight alongside the Romans. The gesture was rejected, possibly because the Romans were unsure of the Sympolity's motives, since, up to that time, the latter had been Macedon's allies. It is not quite clear whether its gesture was purely voluntary or necessitated by the force of cold, geopolitical reality. Perhaps the Achaeans weighed the potential benefits from Macedon's defeat against the consequences of not identifying with the Romans—a timeless dilemma.

Moreover, the Romans appeared to be pursuing a corrosive policy of undermining the administrative jurisdiction of the Achaean Sympolity, sending *legati* to every Achaean city separately to determine each one's sentiments regarding Rome. In fact, Polybius (30.13.1–11), and Livy (45.31.9–11) report that in cities of Aetolia, Acarnania, Epirus and Boeotia where anti-Roman sentiments were perceived, the local authorities were asked to surrender the ringleaders to be tried in Rome. Their man in the Achaean Sympolity, Callicrates, pounced on that to rid himself of his political rivals, claiming they had been conspiring with Perseus, Rome's main rival in Greece. These men agreed to defend themselves before the Roman Senate. The Romans asked Callicrates for a list of over 1000 names of the main opponents of Roman policy in Greece. This list included Polybius who, along with the others, was exiled to Italy as a de facto hostage of the Romans (Mackil 2013, p. 138).[28] The stationing of Roman legions on Greek soil and the recent defeat of the Macedonians did not give the Achaean nobles of whom Callicrates was suspicious little room for manoeuvre so they chose to accept their fate.

It is almost certain that from the moment the Achaean Sympolity had agreed to the unacceptable (in terms of today's code of international justice) demand to exile to Italy all those Achaeans who opposed Roman ambitions, it had essentially turned into a satellite state of Rome. It is also certain that the loss of 1000 significant personalities of the Sympolity deprived the state in the future of able administrative executives both at the federal and the city-state level. It is possible that if the Sympolity had not been deprived of the service and abilities of those individuals, it might have better prevented its dissolution in 146, or at least delayed it. In other words, perhaps the intervention by at least some of those personalities, like Polybius, in the subsequent history of the region might have prevented the worst scenario from coming to pass (critical missteps in managing foreign policy, confrontation with Rome and consequent defeat). As for the more than 1000 Achaeans who travelled to Rome to mount their defence, the Romans chose to regard them as guilty a priori. In 167, they were exiled to cities all over Sicily and Italy. Back home in Greece, this served to enrage the popular will as most were now deeply affected by this tactic of

[28]By many researchers, Polybius is considered Thucydides' heir in terms of the objectivity and critical thinking in his work, and forefather of strict historical research in its modern scientific meaning. Some historians, however, have cast doubt on that objectivity at specific points in his work. Because of his origins (He was the son of the *strategos* Lycortas who was never cast in the role of Rome's man in Achaea but was a stout defender of political neutrality during the Romans' war against Perseus of Macedon), he obviously paid the price personally, living in exile in Italy.

division and gradual neutralisation of Greek power that Rome was pursuing. This exile lasted for 17 years. It was not until 150 that Polybius was finally permitted to return home. Meanwhile, the traitorous stance of the pro-Roman and mostly oligarchic politicians, like Callicrates, generated intense antipathy and loathing in the democratic masses, as illustrated by the incident at the baths of Sicyon mentioned above.

Regarding that period, from 168 to 150, information from surviving sources is sparse, but the Achaean Sympolity did continue to function, politically and economically, although always with a foreign policy that did not stray far from Roman interests (Mackil 2013, pp. 139–140). When the exiles returned in 150, few of the 1000 men were still alive, suggesting that their living conditions had been less than ideal. Of course, it is fair to say that, when they were exiled, being of some standing in their respective communities, many were already middle-aged.

During the winter of 170/169, the Roman generals Popilius and Octavius were transferred from Thessaly (where they commanded a part of what was essentially an occupying force in mainland Greece) to southern Greece. The purpose of this was to visit the city-states of the Peloponnesus to project an image of diversity in the Roman Senate and persuade the Greeks that it had legislated that Roman commanders were not authorised to take any action, military or other, without express authority from the Senate (Poly. 28.3.3–4). Of course, their sojourn there had another purpose as well: to recruit new willing associates—and to strike fear in those who resisted. To that end, in every city, they made it clear that they were very much aware of the local political situation, and were also aware of who they felt was suitable to take on administrative posts, those who were 'politically correct' in Roman eyes, in addition to those already promoting Roman interests. Moreover, Polybius (30, 31.1–15) indicates that polarisation had reached such a point that anyone who chose the 'wrong camp', i.e. anti-Roman, was liable either to be put to death by Rome's agents or forced into suicide.

In 151, a Spartan, Menalcidas, became *strategos*, the first—and last—Spartan to be elected to that post (Paus. 7.11.7). This fact should not be ignored and nor denied the value it deserves. As has already been stressed, the position of *strategos* was for 1 year and was the highest office in the Sympolity. The *strategos* had a host of responsibilities and his decisions determined the fate of the state. Elected by direct vote of the pan-Achaean Assembly, he was not necessarily beholden to any particular voting bloc (if such existed), but to the body of all citizens. It must have taken a great deal of courage to vote as *strategos* for someone who, until fairly recently, had been a leader of a state with which the Sympolity had been at war and was now the source of considerable problems, not least of which was the delay in implementing the process of federalisation, which, if it had been achieved earlier, might have given the Sympolity the foundations for a longer lifespan.

One might interpret the fact that Sparta and the Achaean Sympolity had not clashed for 37 consecutive years (188–151) and that the former was now a member of the latter to mean that the differences between the two states had been resolved and their historic differences bridged.[29] However, it seems that such a notion cannot be firmly supported, for two basic reasons: The first concerns the assumption made above that, after 188, Sparta had eschewed its politico-military might in order to exercise an independent foreign policy, at least in terms of the existing situation in the Peloponnesus. The city-state's loss in human assets, combined with the explosive collapse in the morale of the once all-powerful state of the period 750–371, was so severe after 189 that Sparta had been reduced to being just one more city of the Hellenistic period, however deeply the Spartans denied it. In effect, the peace that prevailed during that period owed less to the Sympolity having succeeded in convincing Sparta and the rest of Laconia's city-states that it was in their interest to join, and more to Sparta's military weakness which precluded her generating a new geopolitical status quo in the peninsula strong enough to challenge the Sympolity.

The second reason is that during the time of the conflict between Aratus and Cleomenes III, from 229 to 222, the Achaean Sympolity and the Kingdom of Sparta were involved in a confrontation the likes of which had never been seen before for the winner, it meant that he would be positioned to impose his will on his opponent, while the loser would be obliged to abandon any hope of maintaining a credible politico-military posture. In other words, this clash between the Achaean Sympolity and Sparta was not a routine confrontation generated by a geopolitical environment but hid something far more fundamental: he who prevailed would become the undisputed regulator of developments for the whole of the Peloponnesus peninsula. Yet, that confrontation between the two nations resulted in a critical loss of power for both participants, not just Sparta: both gradually were transformed into satellites of Rome and, eventually, into her provinces.[30]

As mentioned above, that the Achaeans elected a Spartan as their *strategos*, in the highest post in the state's hierarchy, represents a profound conviction in their ethos: seeing, beyond the trees and well into the forest, progress and prosperity for each city-state, for the good of the Sympolity and the whole of the Peloponnesus. It reveals an abiding faith in the transcendence of the concept of federalism. Achaean citizens and their political hierarchy (for the most part) had understood that, despite Sparta's previous corrosive role of antagonist in terms of the viability and evolution of the federal experiment, her integration into the Sympolity would be preferable to her exclusion. Although Sparta was no longer as mighty as she had been before Sellasia in 222, the prestige of her name and her inclusion as a geographical unit would be an asset to the Sympolity, increasing its power and prestige.

Before we proceed with our analysis, at this point, we should comment on the fact that with the election of the Spartan Menalcidas, the Sympolity acquired its first

[29]As happened, for example, in the case of France and Germany after 1945, thanks to the formation of the European Economic Community (EEC) in 1957.

[30]One can see a parallel in other cases. The clash between the Byzantine and Persian empires in 622–628 CE and that between Nazi Germany and the Soviet Union in 1941–1945 had a similar dimension: the full prevalence of one against the other, an utter defeat resulting in profound consequences for the loser.

leader who was not from a member city-state under democratic governance. Of course, while Sparta in 151 was no longer governed under its old 'historic' package of laws, a 'peculiar kind of oligarchy', in the words of Rhodes (2007, pp. 58–60), based on the *Great Rhetra*[31] of Lycurgus, its government was not democratic. As far as we know, there was no other non-democratic city-state within the Sympolity, at least at that time. What this probably means is that while Sparta became a full member of the Sympolity in 188, the latter's leaders demanded that Spartans had to accept the Achaean 'constitution' only at the federal level. In other words, there was no demand that the Spartans align their political system with democratic principles, as did the other member city-states. This is another point where historical and archaeological sources provide no information, as far as is known. That non-democratic city-states could be members of the Sympolity theoretically existed as a possibility but based on the political reality concerning its functions, at least during the period from 280 until 146 for which sources are more numerous and reliable, this does not seem to have been the case. Therefore, in the case of Sparta, for the reason mentioned above, the Achaeans were willing to make a one and probably the only exception to the rule.

When Menalcidas' 1-year term as *strategos* ended, he was accused by Callicrates of having secretly requested of Rome that Sparta is allowed to leave the Sympolity (Paus. Des. 7.11.7). When or even whether this actually happened is not clear (Mackil 2013, p. 141). Menalcidas rejected the accusation and was eventually acquitted, probably having bribed his successor, the last *strategos* of the Sympolity, Diaeus, earning the fury of the Achaean citizenry who demanded he is punished. Taking into account the shady past of Menalcidas' accuser, Callicrates, it is not unlikely that the former was the victim of any conspiracy and sycophancy. What is certain, though, is that unfortunately, this led to a sequence of events that hastened the final clash with Rome and contributed to the dissolution of the Achaean Sympolity and the loss to its political independence. Diaeus, attempting to evade the charge of bribery, tried to distract his fellow citizens' attention by accusing the Spartans of violating the treaty whereby Sparta had joined the Sympolity by appealing to Rome directly to be assigned territory whose ownership was in dispute. Direct appeals to third parties by members of the Sympolity were not allowed.

This incident leads to some speculation: to begin with, whatever Diaeus' motives, the new *strategos* of the Sympolity was right. The Spartans' request for Rome to intercede in resolving their issue essentially went against principle since a paramount legitimate state existed—the Achaean federal government, to whom they should have appealed directly. On the other hand, Sparta obviously did not want to be in the Sympolity, membership having been imposed on her. Although it had been a member for 37 consecutive years, nevertheless, her citizens' attitudes in favour of

[31]For the *Great Rhetra,* the oldest set of laws that has been saved in fragments and dates from the seventh century, which is the first written Ancient Greek 'constitution' of laws, upon which the sociopolitical and military organisation of the Spartan state was based, see, among others, Cartledge (1987, 2003, p. 29).

independence and against participation in a multilateral federal schema still had not changed. It seems the Spartans found it difficult to accept that, for the times, the prevailing trend in the architecture of the new 'international system', in terms of security and international and economic relations, demanded that a city-state be a member of a federation or part of a large kingdom. Sparta, bound by a set of principles and values from a bygone era, lived on its memories, trapped by them to some extent in a labyrinth of thoughts, ideas and proposals of outdated perception and, as a result, declined further, losing what little power that remained, becoming a minor state and, from the second century on, a tiny possession of the Roman state of little geopolitical or economic value.

Diaeus led a campaign into Laconia to persuade Sparta and the Achaean acquisitions in the area to accept federalism, enforce a policy along the lines of 'speak softly but carry a big stick', replacing diplomacy with raw military muscle, characterised by modern theory as *hard power* (Nye 1991, 2009, 2011). Diaeus encouraged the Spartans to hand over those who were trying to pull Sparta out of the Sympolity. Twenty-four individuals were singled out, and Diaeus demanded they be exiled. The Spartans, conscious of their weakness in the face of the Sympolity's strength, agreed. However, on the initiative of one member of their Senate, Agasisthenes, they allowed those men to escape. To appear cooperative, though, they sentenced them to death in absentia. The 24 men escaped to Rome.

Representatives of both the Spartans and the Achaeans separately converged on Rome. The Spartans included a complaint regarding her borders with Megalopolis to the north. Menalcidas represented Sparta, while the Sympolity sent Diaeus and Callicrates; however, only Diaeus finally showed up, Callicrates having died on the journey to Rome. In the Senate, the encounter of Menalcidas and Diaeus deteriorated into a shouting match of insults (Paus. 7.12.8). The Romans may have appeared as merely interested observers, but in private, they must have been quite pleased with the state of their guests' affairs and its divisive nature, right in line with Rome's aspirations!

According to Pausanias (7.12.7–9), the Romans promised to send an arbitrator to help resolve the situation, yet another indication of how, de facto, the Sympolity had forfeited a measure of its sovereignty by accepting the active intervention of a foreign power on what was essentially a domestic issue. Upon their return, the two representatives each brought his own version of events home concerning the Roman decision: Diaeus announced that thanks to him, the Achaeans had been granted the right to force the Spartans to kneel before Achaean hegemony, while Menalcidas claimed that he had managed to take Sparta out of the Sympolity. It was pathetic that on such a serious matter as the viability not only of the city-states of the Sympolity but of Sparta as well, their representatives acted so irresponsibly, choosing to lie to the citizens of their respective cities.

Perhaps they were unaware of how critical the situation was or, they were aware, but each chose to appear as the 'winner' of the negotiations to gain some personal political advantage. Irresponsible actions by irresponsible men that in the end, led to the whole of the Peloponnesus becoming a Roman province not long after. Given the usual Roman delaying tactics of divide and conquer, the likelihood of the consul issuing any clear decision was minimal. Probably, the consul stood back, 'gaining time', observing the two parties embroiled in an argument without end which could only lead to further introversion and reduction in the power and dynamics of the states they each represented.

In 148, with a decision on the matter not forthcoming from the Romans, the Spartans again renounced their membership in the Sympolity. As had the Corinthians, they may have been pushed behind the scenes by the Romans to carry out their act of secession. If the Romans had actually done that, it would have been just one more act in Rome's broader plan to reduce further the Sympolity's power. But before the arbitration team could set off from Rome, the Achaeans took the initiative and created a fait accompli: the *strategos* at that time, Damocritus, ignoring the advice (or commands) of the Roman general Quintus Caecilius Metellus,[32] led an army to Sparta in an attempt to bring her back into the Sympolity.

The Achaean forces were victorious as Spartan military capabilities were limited. According to Pausanias (7.13.3), the Spartans suffered some 1000 casualties from among the cream of the city-state's youth. Damocritus chose not to besiege the city, not to provoke the Romans further. Of course, the Achaeans were furious at this, deeming it traitorous, levying a fine of 50 *talents* on their *strategos* and forcing him into exile. This brings up two important points. The first concerns the fact that an elected head of the government and armed forces had been removed from his post. Dismayed by Damocritus' handling of the campaign, the Achaeans elected to get rid of him, probably by vote at an extraordinary federal Assembly, which actually could be summoned, according to the circumstances, and which was called *synkletos* as we will discuss further in 6.1. This was not unusual in Ancient Greece since, from the fifth century on, the recall of an officer of the state was not uncommon in the Athenian Democracy in the event of dereliction in the performance of one's duty. The case of Damocritus indicates that this extended to the democratic federations as well. The second point regards the size of the fine levied on Damocritus. It is unclear whether that was the standard sum by which an act of treason was punished, or whether he was tried by a special committee of the Sympolity or some federal tribunal that settled on such a very large fine. One *talent* was equivalent to 6000 *drachmae*; during the third century, the daily wage of a labourer was approximately 1.5 *drachmae* (Loomis 1998).

This generates two more issues: if the standard fine for treason was 50 *talents* and Damocritus did not have the means to pay such a sum, he may have been imprisoned, have had his property confiscated, or suffered some other alternate punishment; no relevant record exists. If, on the other hand, he did have the capacity to pay the fine, this may confirm our belief that, at least at the highest levels of government, the Sympolity was led by wealthy oligarchic elements. However, not enough data exists to support this with any certainty. Of course, if that had been the case, we propose that the accusation of treason was based not so much on

[32]The situation was so confusing and fluid that whether the Romans' advice was just that or, in fact, a demand is not easy to assess with any certainty.

Damocritus' refusal to tear down the walls of a rebellious city to avoid conflict with Rome (which might have had unforeseen and uncontrollable consequences, risking even the very essence of the Sympolity),[33] but rather on the fact that Damocritus—and probably other wealthy Achaeans—possessed such vast funds in the first place, funds that were never placed, directly or indirectly, at the disposal of the Sympolity to boost defence spending and recruit mercenary troops, etc., thus helping to ensure its survival.

One must not overlook the fact that the second century was a time when the average citizen of the Sympolity, as well as the rest of the population of mainland Greece, to a lesser or greater extent, had lost a part of his wealth, resulting in either social uprisings with financial demands[34] or emigration from mainland Greece toward the wealthy Hellenistic kingdoms to the east. All this must be considered in light of the critical stage reached at that time in terms of the Sympolity's future viability, given that its earlier campaign against Sparta, its participation in 'international' conflicts (the Macedonian Wars) and the interventions of Macedon and, later, of Rome (in its various iterations), all these seem to have exhausted the Sympolity. It appears that the real traitors to the Sympolity were those who had amassed great wealth at the expense of their fellow citizens instead of applying it in support of the struggle to strengthen and maintain the Sympolity's independence. It is certain that if it could be proven that Damocritus actually paid the fine, then the view that the leadership of the Sympolity was in the hands of a clique of oligarchs, often making decisions without the consent of the Achaean citizenry, could be more easily supported. That, however, is not clear from the sources. Moreover, there is no evidence from the sources that the annual federal assemblies consisted only of oligarchic elements. Accordingly, the view that the Sympolity's government functioned along class lines cannot be proven and should be considered suspect, at least to some extent.

Returning to Diaeus and his term as *strategos*, in 150, after he had replaced Damocritus, he reoccupied the territory around Sparta and then pursued throughout all of Achaea anyone who had expressed pro-Spartan sentiments during her confrontation with the Sympolity (Paus. Des. 7.13.1–5). Menalcidas took his own life; Pausanias (Paus. Des. 7.13.8) writes that 'he was the clumsiest of generals and had previously ruled the Achaeans as the most unjust of men'. This observation is significant because it clearly states that the Spartan *strategos* was among the worst, if not the worst, the Sympolity had ever suffered. We speculate that this was not so much a matter of ability but more because he did not possess a mentality forged by a federalist consciousness, much like the vast majority of Spartans, and all he did was to undermine the Sympolity's effectiveness and evolution.

[33] In this light, we suggest that the Achaeans judged their *strategos* too harshly, condemning him for an issue of lesser significance, unable to see the 'bigger picture'.

[34] As will be analysed to a greater extent in Sect. 4.3 (with reference to the social and reform programme of King Cleomenes III and its appeal to the member states of the Sympolity).

Taking this further, one must consider what the Achaeans did in this respect. Even though Menalcidas was head of state and, according to the Achaean federal laws, had broad powers, on the other hand, that 'constitution' was democratic, and he presided over a federal Council, i.e. a democratically elected executive power, as will be further expounded in 6.1. If Menalcidas, as Pausanias claimed, had ruled over the Achaeans so badly, why then did no member of the government protest? Why was there no programmed pan-Achaean federal Assembly that year, nor an extraordinary one called, at which citizen(s) might have called him to account? These are questions that the sources do not address, making it difficult to answer with any absolute, or even relative, certainty.

As a result of these events, the last phase of the drama began in the spring of 147: the Roman *legate* Aurelius Orestes who had promised in 149 to mediate the Achaean-Spartan confrontation, finally arrived in Corinth and called to Assembly all who held public office in all the cities of the Sympolity (Paus. Des. 7.14.1–2).[35] He announced the decision of the Senate that the Achaean Sympolity must relinquish the memberships of Sparta, Corinth, Argos, Heracleia Trachinia and the Arcadian Orchomenos, on the grounds that those city-states were not Achaean in nationality and had only recently been incorporated into the Sympolity. If the Roman demands were to be satisfied, it would have meant the loss of significant territory and the return to the Sympolity's borders to where they had been before the Cleomenean War of 229–222. The Achaean officials were shocked. The Romans' demand essentially meant the Achaean leadership's voluntary acceptance of the partial dismemberment of the Sympolity. It was certain that that was something that even the most ardent Romanophiles in Achaea would have difficulty swallowing. Perhaps the Romans were 'tugging at the rope', choosing to elevate tensions with the Sympolity, possibly considering that by not responding overtly to Damocritus' refusal to toe the line on attacking Sparta it would be sending the wrong message concerning Rome's ability to impose her will. They were clearly applying an overt *hard power* policy, applying coercion backed by her military power.

The Romans could argue they were free to act in this way—not at all appropriate for a mediator, of course—because the Achaeans had ignored their 'recommendation' and marched into Sparta without their approval. By their general behaviour, it was obvious the Romans felt they had a right to intervene in the affairs of the Sympolity, treating it as a protectorate. It may have been that certain influential circles in the Roman Senate aimed to settle the issue of the Sympolity once and for all and convert the territory it controlled into a province of Rome. The demands of the Romans may have purposefully unrealistic, meant to provoke an opportunity for them to intervene in force and put an end to Achaean independence.

How could the Achaeans have accepted such an outlandish demand, equivalent to the partial dissolution of their nation? Could the Romans themselves who made that

[35]It is possible that Pausanias mistakenly did not clarify that the call was actually for the highest-ranking officials of each city. Lower-echelon personnel were not party to decision-making at that level; thus, their participation would have made little sense.

demand actually have believed that the Achaeans would accept it? And even if there were politicians who might have been willing to sign on to such humiliation, as there always have existed in the course of history, surely, they would have been in the minority. What politician, no matter how craven, would put his signature to a treaty ceding territory, knowing that he might suffer on a personal level, be characterised as a traitor, putting his political future at risk? Therefore, the whole handling of the Achaean issue by Rome's leadership was intentionally objectionable, requiring the application of demands that no sovereign state, and no responsible political leadership, could reasonably even consider, let alone accept and satisfy.

For their part, the Achaeans reacted strongly. The leadership, grasping the general tone of Orestes' message, did not bother to hear it in its entirety, calling instead for a special Assembly. Upon learning of the Romans' demands, the populace was enraged, accusing the Spartans as being responsible because they had been the main reason for Rome's frequent intervention in the Sympolity's affairs. Pausanias (7.14.2) characteristically notes:

> When the Achaeans heard the decision of the Romans, they at once turned against the Spartans who happened to be then residing in Corinth, and arrested everyone, not only those whom they knew for certain to be Lacedaemonians, but also all those they suspected to be such from the cut of their hair, or because of their shoes, their clothes or even their names. Some of them, who succeeded in taking refuge in the lodging of Orestes, they actually attempted even from there to drag away by force.

The abuse of Spartans was accompanied by a general sense that this time the Achaeans were determined to resist Rome's demands. There was a great deal of commotion, protests directed at the Roman envoys, who were eventually ejected from the Assembly. Strabo (Geo. 8.6.23) believed that the very lives of the envoys were in danger, something that Polybius (38.9.1–3) rejected, considering the events had been overdramatised. In any case, the Romans' handling of the situation reveals an arrogance in the face of an (ostensibly) allied state. The Romans had not travelled to Corinth as arbitrators as they had promised but as bearers of decisions that had already been taken, simply demanding they be implemented. For their part, the Achaeans did not attempt to negotiate with the Romans. The *strategos*, Diaeus, along with Callicrates, was summoned to Rome; the journey was not a success, even though in the debates, the Sympolity was represented by her head of state. As we mentioned above, Callicrates died during the journey, leaving the Sympolity, as Pausanias (Des. 7.12.2) noted with biting irony, denied the services of a stout defender of its interests:

> …being the worst rascal of his time, one who could never resist a bribe of any kind…the most abominable wretch in all of Greece.

The situation became even direr for the Achaeans in the autumn of 147 when Diaeus was replaced as *strategos* by Critolaus of Megalopolis, known for his anti-Roman rhetoric. After having been rebuffed at Corinth, the Romans returned with a new embassy, insisting on the implementation of their demands, offering their services in arbitrating the end of the state of war between the Achaean Sympolity and Sparta. Critolaus was determined not to accept the Roman demands (Polyb.

38.9–10) and rejected any interference whatsoever, infuriating the Romans. During the winter of 147/6, Critolaus prepared for war, taking care to gather sufficient assets to fund his efforts. It appears that the Sympolity's citizens approved of this since, according to Polybius (38.11), they authorised the expansion of the powers of the *strategos*. What Polybius writes suggests that both the citizens of the Sympolity as well as her leadership were of a mind to accept a clash with Rome if it proved unavoidable. Only this explains the effort to prepare for war. Consequently, the Sympolity's government declared war on Sparta, and by extension, on Rome as well (Mackil 2013, p. 143). In their effort, the Achaeans were not alone, being reinforced by forces sent by other cities from all over the Peloponnesus, from Boeotia, Phocis, Locris and even some regions of the Ionian islands (Paus. Des. 7.14.6, 7.15.5).

In his effort to persuade the Achaeans, Critolaus appealed more to emotion than logic, to valour, and against compromise. Critolaus aimed to enhance his purpose with the character of a broader anti-Roman uprising. Before and after the Peloponnesian Wars, Greek city-states and political unions (kingdoms, federations) both had always been constantly at odds with each other, grappling to broaden their power.[36] In 146, the consequences of the internecine conflict of past centuries were at last fully perceived. Behind the Achaean Sympolity, there crystallised an effort to undertake joint action by city-states and federations throughout all of Greece, some of which had just become Roman possessions and regretted their short-sighted action. All were now sending what military forces they possessed to join those of the Sympolity as a 'last line of containment' against the Roman flood.

Another facet of the Achaeans' decision to confront Rome, if this were to become inevitable, is the social makeup of those for and against this choice. At the critical Assembly that took place in Corinth, Polybius reports, a great number of average citizens participated for the first time, tilting the decision decisively. As has already been made clear, each citizen had the right to one vote in the federal pan-Achaean Assembly. As we have stated earlier, those who wanted to avoid conflict with Rome were, generally, those same oligarchic circles who rushed to declare their acceptance of the Romans' demands (officially referred to as 'proposals' and 'suggestions'). But at that particular historical moment, there was a large number of ordinary citizens aware of the critical state of the situation. Perhaps even some oligarchs also expressed their opposition to Orestes' demands, attempting to associate themselves with the broader popular verdict. Most oligarchs, however, appeared to prioritise their own interests, hoping to reap the benefits and retain their privileges and wealth in the event of an Achaean defeat (which, to be fair, was the most likely outcome). They chose their 'security' and indirect allegiance to Rome instead of resistance, not eschewing, however, whatever opportunities resistance in favour of national

[36]Only during one brief period, the time of Philip II and Alexander the Great (337–323) was the Greek world united under a common administration (the Congress of Corinth known also as the Panhellenic Congress, during the winter of 338/7), even if, in some cases, that union was affected violently. After Alexander's death, these separatist tendencies reasserted themselves, evidenced by the Lamian War of 323–322, perhaps the last attempt by Athens to regain a leadership role in the political realities of Greece.

independence might create. Ordinary citizens, on the other hand, were more inclined to resist outright since, not possessing the nobility's wealth, all they risked was their lives.[37]

2.4 The Final Phase of the Drama: The Dissolution of the Achaean Sympolity and Its Conversion into a Roman Province

In 147, a significant part of the Roman military forces in Greece was based in Macedon. The year before, under the command of Quintus Caecilius Metellus, they had suppressed an uprising by the Macedonians under Andriskos, a claimant to the throne, at the second Battle of Pydna. As Metellus' term of service in Greece was ending and he was about to be replaced by Lucius Mummius, presumably fired by personal ambition, he decided to move against the south to force the Achaeans to give up Sparta and the other city-states that had been recently absorbed into the Sympolity, in accordance with the demands of the Roman Senate that Augustus Orestes had proclaimed in Corinth the year before.

Arriving at the city of Heraclea Trachinia in Phthiotis which was under siege by the Sympolity, Metellus sent an embassy to Critolaus demanding he put an end to the siege immediately. The Romans presented themselves as the defenders of Spartan independence as well as that of the Phoceans and Euboeans who were being pressured by the Thebans. These latter were now allied with the Achaeans who were besieging Trachinia obviously on their account. The demand was rejected. With a powerful force under his command, Metellus chose not to wait for Lucius Mummius and instead attack the Achaeans himself. As Metellus' troops approached Critolaus' army, the latter either chose not to defend the pass at Thermopylae or, according to another version, was caught by surprise. Metellus crossed the Sperheios River and met the Achaeans at Scarpheia in Locris. Of that confrontation, Pausanias (7.15.4), with an ironic disposition against Critolaus, writes:

> Critolaus and the Achaeans took to flight, but at a short distance from Scarpheia they were overtaken by the men of Metellus, who killed many and took about a thousand prisoners. Critolaus was neither seen alive after the battle nor found among the dead. If he dared to plunge into the marsh of the sea at the foot of Mount Oeta he must inevitably have sunk into the depths without leaving a trace to tell the tale.

Perhaps Critolaus' effort might have had better luck if, after abandoning Heracleia, he had successfully managed to barricade himself in Thermopylae and await reinforcements from Diaeus. Perhaps Critolaus had indeed been caught by surprise and was forced to fight at Scarpheia. In any event, Metellus descended toward Thebes and Athens and confirmed Rome's dominion of both (or incorporated

[37]We provide a further analysis of this issue in Chap. 3.

them into Roman territory as possessions). The Thebans abandoned their city, and the Achaeans, Megara. Pytheas, the Theban leader, or *Boeotarch*, who came to the aid of the Achaeans, was captured and executed. After Critolaus' crushing defeat and the loss of most of the Sympolity's army, Diaeus took over as *strategos* under dire circumstances. The Achaeans, despite their rout at Scarpheia, were in no mood to capitulate. In an attempt to rebuild his forces, Diaeus released 12,000 slaves from bondage and enlisted them into the army. He managed to scrape up a few more lightly armed fighters as well as 500 horsemen. A force of 14,000 infantry and 600 horsemen, Achaeans and Arcadians, gathered at Corinth, along with anyone else who could carry a weapon. The fighting capabilities of this force was dubious. In particular, as far as the slaves were concerned, nothing is known if any of them, before their enslavement, had had any military training or experience.

At that point, more Roman forces arrived, under the command of Mummius, Metellus' replacement. The two armies combined under Mummius and marched southward to the Peloponnesus peninsula. That force now comprised 23,000 legionnaires and 3500 horsemen (Paus. 7.16.1–8). The ratio in terms of infantry (1:1.64) was not insuperable, but that of cavalry was heavily in favour of the Romans (1:7). The Achaean forces and their Arcadian allies were arrayed so that their left flank lay along the walls of Corinth. On the right flank, facing Leucopetra, Diaeus had placed his cavalry. With his left flank along the walls, he could not be outflanked from that side. He placed his heavy infantry of *phalangites,* armed with their formidable *sarissa* spears, in the centre, and 500 horsemen on his right flank. Perhaps he hoped that if his cohesive centre could contain the Roman legionnaires, he might prevail and launch a counterattack. As we have mentioned above, after Philopoemen's reforms, the *hoplites* were now armed with the *sarissa* spear, an exceptionally effective and much-dreaded weapon. Mummius, for his part, placed his legionnaires at the centre and his cavalry on his left flank.

On the first day, neither side took any initiative. That night, however, Diaeus launched a raid that met with some success, causing some damage and escaping with 600 shields. The Romans, though taken by surprise, were quick to react and repelled the raid. The battle that was to determine the fate of the Achaean Sympolity began the very next day. The Romans sent their legions against the Greek *sarissa*-bearers who succeeded in holding them off. Several attempts by the legions to break the Achaean line met with failure, repelled by the heroism of the Greeks. As long as the Greeks' flanks remained intact, the Romans were unable to break through the *phalanx.* Finally, Mummius used his 'strong card' and committed his cavalry, which heavily outnumbered that of the Greeks. Unable to hold the Romans off, the Greek cavalry was crushed. The combined forces of infantry and cavalry then turned on the *phalangites,* who, despite a heroic stand, were finally defeated. The Romans' victory was complete.

Those who survived fled to Corinth but chose to throw down their arms. The rest returned to their homes. Diaeus escaped to Megalopolis, killed his wife and committed suicide. Mummius' forces swarmed into Corinth; the cruelty that he and his men exhibited there was unprecedented: every man they found was put to death, and all the women and children sold into slavery, as were Corinth's slaves, regardless if they were freemen or not. Finally, the city was burned to the ground and the ashes scattered. The fabulous artefacts of Corinthian art were stolen and sent to Rome. Part of the city's territory was handed over to Sicyon. Corinth had been one of the most important commercial cities of the Greek world and a formidable competitor of Athens—at least, during the Classical Period.

The painful events of Corinth had a sequel. The Achaean Sympolity capitulated, and all of Greece became a Roman province. The walls of fortified cities were torn down, and all spaces and structures where assemblies took place were demolished. Local democratic administrations were replaced with oligarchic and the institutions of the Achaean city-states were abolished, including the one that allowed a citizen of Achaea to own property in any other city-state of the Sympolity. (Paus. 7.16.9), which, as we will examine later in 7.1, constituted a key institutional element in the operational principles of the Greek federations, in general. Finally, sometime during the first century CE, by decree of the Roman emperor, the whole of Achaea was united as a single provincial unit. Achaea eventually became the name for all of Greece, as a unified administrative entity.

Chapter 3
Interpreting the Defeat of the Achaean Sympolity by Rome Through a *Defence Economics* Perspective

3.1 The Socio-Economic Aspects Regarding the Strategic Choice of War Over Peace

Polybius ascribed a great deal of responsibility for the defeat at Leucopetra to the leaders of the Sympolity, Diaeus and Critolaus, deeming them demagogues who swayed their citizens towards direct confrontation with mighty Rome, resulting in the dissolution of the Achaean Sympolity and Corinth's destruction (Polyb. Hist. 38.9–10; Champion 2013, p. 127; Mackil 2013, p. 142). Polybius' description is brutal: the Achaeans in effect fell victim:

> to the worst of men, hated by the gods, who turned their nation into a ruin.

This judgement is rather unfair, made in retrospect, with the outcome of the war a given. Mackil (2013, p. 142) notes in this respect that Polybius, an Achaean, was in an awkward position having to act as an apologist for Rome and her policy in the Peloponnesus and across the Sympolity. It is obvious that Polybius, although in principle an objective observer, does not want to offend his Roman readership, concentrating on the Achaeans' failings and sidestepping the Roman machinations that contributed so massively to the gradual debilitation of the Sympolity's power and its eventual destruction. Characterising Diaeus and Critolaus as those mainly responsible for the destruction of the Sympolity, Polybius, probably mistakenly, correlates their attempts at social reform with critical errors by Critolaus on military matters and in the Sympolity's relations with Rome.

Critolaus could have followed a more accommodating stand to avoid direct confrontation with Rome. But one can reasonably assume that he was simply expressing what the average Achaean citizen was feeling, resigned to war, fed up by the many years of the Roman Senate's constant interference and obvious ambition to exert its dominance over the Sympolity. In this light, Polybius perhaps focused on Critolaus the greater share of responsibility to avoid putting off his

E. M. L. Economou, *The Achaean Federation in Ancient Greece*, Frontiers in Economic History, https://doi.org/10.1007/978-3-030-52697-9_3

Achaean readership. In any event, responsibility for what transpired must be shared as much by Critolaus and Diaeus, as by the average citizens of Achaea.

The decision by the Achaean people to object to the dissolution of their federal state by defying Rome's demands may be expressed in modern terms as expressed in the bibliography on the theory of *conflict and settlement*. This essentially relates to the dilemma of war or peace, through an economic perspective, based on the research field of *Defence Economics*. According to this theory, Nation A will try to avoid conflict with Nation B when its citizens, as economically active units, determine that the damage incurred to them on a personal level by war outweighs the possible advantages of waging it.

According to, among others, Caruso (2006, p. 53), Massoud and Magge (2012), Cortes and Montolio (2014) and Economou and Kyriazis (2016), when a rationally thinking citizen in economic terms or the state itself decide to engage in or avoid or abstain from waging war, they take into consideration the *opportunity cost*[1] that results from the potential loss of wealth due to war. This means that between the strategic choice of peace or war lies the parameter of the economic evaluation of the *opportunity cost* each option entails.

In the case examined here, the Achaean socio-economic stratification consisted of a larger number of ordinary citizens of modest means and a small number of wealthy oligarchs. The latter, as Polybius writes, were not at all eager for war, considering that the likelihood of victory over Rome was, at best, minimal. In defeat, they risked losing their wealth. For them, the opportunity cost would be high. In economic terms, the opportunity cost to the far more numerous ordinary citizens would be much lower. It is no surprise that the choice to go to war was made by the lower social strata.[2] To round out the picture of what was surely the most critical decision ever taken regarding the Sympolity's fate, condensed in a single question—war with Rome or peace?—and decided by national referendum, one must note that after the rejection of negotiations over Rome's demands for the Sympolity to be dissolved, in a desperate attempt to address the peremptory needs that confrontation with powerful Rome would entail, the Sympolity passed measures benefitting the lower classes, unprecedented in its history.

Specifically, it decided to cancel all debts and free 12,000 slaves. The latter act was no doubt related to the need to quickly rebuild the army's capacity so that the Sympolity could respond to possible military engagement. These measures, social reforms equivalent, one could say, to those of King Cleomenes III in Sparta during 227–222,[3] were, however, not passed based on any strategic plan, but were based on the compelling need to save the nation. Of course, these measures, once passed,

---

[1]For the novice in Microeconomic Theory, the *opportunity cost* of Good A is determined in terms of sacrificing another Good that could have been produced for consumption with the same production factors used in the production of Good A.

[2]For a similar dilemma faced by the Athenians during 355–322 during the Eubulus and Lycurgus era as the Athenian *tamiai tis koines prosodou* (Ministers of Economics, in a sense), see Economou and Kyriazis (2016).

[3]On this, we refer further in Sect. 4.3.

would have been very difficult to recall later. Whether the Sympolity succeeded in avoiding a fateful confrontation with Rome, perhaps through some last-minute agreement to de-escalate, or achieved the improbable, a military success over Rome—either way, a 'new order of things' had come to pass in Achaea. Former slaves could now demand political rights, their position strengthened by having been elevated to the status of a *hoplite*. There was no turning back.

A similar radical change in the socio-economic structure of a regime, followed by a new package of values and institutions replacing the older institutional framework, known as *path dependence and change*,[4] occurred previously with the reforms of Cleisthenes and the establishment of democracy in early fifth century in Athens[5] and in Sparta with the socio-economic reforms of the kings, Agis IV and Cleomenes III, as will be further discussed in Sect. 5.3. If the Sympolity were to survive, 'it would never be the same' after that because, to save itself and its political regime as a whole, oligarchic groups were obliged to accept changes that they would never have even considered, not then nor at any other time in the future. This is a clear example of the parameter of war as a potential mechanism that de facto initiates a sequence of events that ultimately leads to socio-economic and sociopolitical change.

At this point in time, the Sympolity succeeded in galvanising the populace with a combination of nationalist and socialist fervour, daring to confront Rome and assuming the role of defender of Greek independence. This left Sparta in the demeaning role of the moral enabler of Rome's aggression.[6] Ironically, the traditionally conservative Achaean Sympolity's policymakers, which had first appealed to the Macedonians and later to the Romans to confront the socially revolutionary tendencies of the Spartans, Cleomenes III and Nabis, ended up resigned to adopting the social reforms that it had fought so hard to forestall. Sparta, which under Cleomenes III had been the leading actor in the struggle against the Macedonians, and the tip of the spear of reformist trends, in the end, found herself supporting the Roman conqueror (Shimron 1972, p. 134).

---

[4]On *path dependence,* see the significant work of David (1985) and Arthur (1989) and for the implementation of this theoretical concept in the case of Classical Athens, see Kyriazis (2006), Kyriazis and Metaxas (2010) and our own, Economou and Kyriazis (2019b).

[5]For Cleisthenes to effect his reforms in 508/7, he gave more rights to the lower income citizens. A short time later, Themistocles further improved the status of the *thetes*, giving them the right to serve as contracted oarsmen in the navy, simultaneously increasing public expenditure through the improvement in the public good of defence. Full electoral rights and the right to stand for election were granted to all Athenians, independent of income, with the reforms of Ephialtes in 462 (Economou and Kyriazis (2019b).

[6]In this respect, during this last period of the Greek world's independence, Sparta, sadly, followed a path that stained its legacy and the grandeur of its achievements of earlier centuries.

Table 3.1 The most significant ally of the Achaean Sympolity in each period

Period (BCE)	Basic allied state
First phase: (389–281 BCE)	
(389–372)	Sparta
(371–338)	*Koinon* of the Boeotians
(337–281)	Kingdom of Macedon
Second phase: (280–146 BCE)	
(280–272)	Aetolian Sympolity
(271–268)	Kingdom of Epirus (Pyrrhus)
(267–261) [Chremonidean War]	Athens, Sparta, Ptolemaic Kingdom of Egypt
(245–240)	*Koinon* of the Boeotians, Ptolemaic Kingdom of Egypt
(239–228)	Aetolian Sympolity
(227–169)	Kingdom of Macedon
(168–148)	Roman Republic
(147–146)	Reconstituted *Koinon* of the Boeotians (?)

3.2 Measuring the Strength of the Achaean Sympolity Against the Roman Republic Through State Power Equations

Based on the above analysis, the question arises whether the fate of the Peloponnesus could have been different if other policies had been followed and the Achaean Sympolity had avoided the series of critical strategic mistakes in crisis management it took against Rome, as well as relative to the other powerful political entities of the Hellenistic Period—Macedon, Sparta, the Boeotian *Koinon* and the Aetolian Sympolity.

It may have behoved it to have worked harder to maintain its alliance with the Aetolian Sympolity during 239–227, first as a powerful anti-Macedonian coalition and then as anti-Roman. Then again, perhaps there should have been a greater effort by Aratus, as the political leader of the Sympolity, and King Cleomenes III, the two most powerful men in the two states, to avoid conflict and work together to form a powerful pan-Peloponnese front against Macedon, which was already in geopolitical decline, and, even more importantly, against the rising power of Rome. This would have meant Sparta participating as a leading member of the Sympolity and which would have been a decisive factor before the Battle of Sellasia when Sparta was a capable force, recently reorganised by Cleomenes.[7] Based on all the above and the relevant sources, Table 3.1 presents the major allied nation(s) of the Achaean Sympolity in each period throughout its life, those that were most aligned with the promotion of her grand strategy. The table shows that in its 243 years of existence, it changed allies 11 times, each alliance lasting an average of 22 years.

[7]We examine this issue further in Sect. 4.3.

Historical experience, both ancient and modern, confirms that a short span of 22 years is not long enough to allow for building a productive, long-term relationship in terms of International Relations.[8] Table 3.1 indicates that during the fourth century, the first phase of its existence, the Sympolity's alliances lasted an average of 36 years. This results from dividing the 108 years of the first phase (389–281) by the three distinct alliances: with Sparta, the *Koinon* of the Boeotians and the Kingdom of Macedon. By the same reasoning, the Sympolity's alliances during the second phase (280–146) each lasted an average of only 16.75 years since it had formed eight alliances during the 134 years of that phase. These statistics reveal that during the second phase, the duration of the alliances had dropped to less than half of the first period, revealing how fluid the geopolitical situation had become during the second and third centuries, certainly more volatile than it had been during the fourth century.

This essentially supports our contention that, as we have already discussed, the Hellenistic world was in the throes of a *machtpolitik* which, over time, instead of waning, was increasing in intensity, its features becoming more apparent. The frequent alternations of alliances, the constant changes in allies with which the Sympolity maintained either diplomatic or particular relations, the conversion of former friends into enemies, and vice versa, all failed to surprise whenever they occurred. Two more observations based on Table 3.1 are the fact that the Sympolity identified with Macedonian interests during the period 337–280, something which was not really by choice, but happened because Macedon had interfered openly in her affairs, installing pro-Macedonian tyrants (or, more accurately, tyrant-puppets) in her cities, turning her to a large extent, into a satellite state.

It is not even certain that the Sympolity essentially functioned as an independent state during that period. In other words, during that time, it probably lacked true independence, any federal administration and an independent foreign policy. Additionally, one notes that the Sympolity allied itself militarily three times with the Boeotian *Koinon*, in 371–338, 245–240 and 147–146. It should be noted at this point that at that third time, 147–146, it is not even certain that the *Koinon* had been formally resuscitated in some way, in one of its earlier iterations, since the Romans had dissolved it after the Battle of Pydna. This illustrates the 'paradox of the Achaean Sympolity's power'. From its history, it is apparent that both during the first phase as well as the second, it steadily kept adding more and more city-states. This meant that theoretically, it should have been gaining power both economically and militarily as it was gaining in manpower as well as productive assets (land, infrastructure)—especially late in the second phase, from 190 on, when, as the ancient sources relate, the Messenian cities and those of the regions of Elis and Laconia were integrated into the Sympolity, and the whole of the Peloponnesus had come under its political/administrative control.

---

[8]One example of a successful military alliance in antiquity was the First Athenian Alliance, functioning between 478–404, i.e. for 64 years. Today, NATO, with the dominant participation of the USA, has functioned from 1949 until today (2020), i.e. for over 70 years. Its antagonist alliance, the Warsaw Pact, functioned only for 36 years (1955–1991).

Table 3.2 The major battles of the Achaean Sympolity during 243–146 BCE

Year	Event	Result
243	Battle of Corinth	Defeat of the Macedonians and the fall of Corinth to the Achaeans.
227	Battle of Mount Lycaion	Defeat of the Achaeans by the Spartans
226	Battle of Megalopolis	Defeat of the Achaeans by the Spartans
226	Battle of Dyme	Defeat of the Achaeans by the Spartans
222	Battle of Sellasia	Victory of the Macedonians (mainly) and the Achaeans over the Spartans
209	Battle of Larissos	Victory of the Achaeans over the Aetolians and the Elians
208	Battle of Mantinea	Victory of the Achaeans over the Spartans
201	Battle of Tegea	Victory of the Achaeans over the Spartans
195	Battle of Argos	Defeat of the Spartans by the Romans on behalf of the Achaeans
192	Battle of Gytheion	Indecisive battle between the Achaeans and the Spartans
192	Battle of the Barbosthenon	Victory of the Achaeans over the Spartans
188	Battle of Sparta	Defeat of the Spartans and the occupation of Sparta by the Achaeans
183	Battle of Messene	Victory of the Achaeans over the Messenians
147	Battle of Scarpheia	Defeat of the Achaeans by the Romans
146	Battle of Leucopetra	Defeat of the Achaeans by the Romans and the dissolution of the Sympolity

The question arises then, why was the Sympolity unable to put up a stronger resistance to Rome? This is not an easy question to address. All one can say for certain is that the outcome of the Battles of Scarpheia and Leucopetra demonstrated that the Sympolity was simply not ready for a full and decisive confrontation with Rome. Militarily, it appears that it did not have sufficient reserves in manpower during the period 147/6. A reserve is a highly significant factor in the arsenal of a nation at war, as, of course, is logistics (van Kreveld 1977). This is demonstrated by the fact that after Scarpheia, Diaeus, lacking reserves, tried to carry on resistance against Roman penetration into the Peloponnesus by liberating a significant number of slaves whose battle worthiness, for the most part, was doubtful and enlisting them into the army.[9]

Table 3.2 presents some significant battles of the Sympolity during the period 241–146. We believe that the inability of the Achaeans to mount a significant resistance to Rome is due to the significant erosion in power, not only of the Sympolity but of all the other political entities of the Hellenistic world because of the prolonged state of war that had long dominated their interrelationships. When in 147/6 Rome decided to move against the Sympolity, she probably found it 'exhausted', in internal disarray as a result of the fragmentation of society along democratic and oligarchic lines, into pro- and anti-Roman factions, and with most

[9]We revert to the issue of the Sympolity's military organisation in Sect. 6.4.

Table 3.3 The factors that determine the power of a state

P: *Power*
Econ: The economic strength, the level of development and long-term economic performance
Mil: Military strength
Tech: Level of technology
Geo: Geographical location, the extent of geographical territory and its makeup
Dem: Demographic factors, population size, age structure and fertility rate
Hc: Quality of human capital such as the average level of education
Nr: Natural resources and wealth-producing assets
Ps: Sociopolitical characteristics such as internal and external legitimacy, cohesion
Mor: State of morale, beliefs, will, commitment to goals
Lead: Quality of leadership and administrative structures
Al: Alliances
Int: Other internal factors such as intangible resources and cultural capital
Ext: External environment such as the power of other geopolitical entities and actors

Source: Knorr (1956), Cline (1977, 1980), Rummel (1983), Baldwin (1985), Bartholomees (2012), Heiggs (2012), Copeland (2014), Arvanitidis and Kollias (2016), and Kollias (2017)

city-states struggling to maintain the Sympolity's democratic foundations while others, fewer in number, were attempting to break away.

Amidst this environment of uncertainty and erosion that had developed, it appears, at least for the period 147/6, the Sympolity lacked capable leaders in her military arm. If personalities such as Aratus, Philopoemen, Lycortas or Polybius had been in charge of military strategic and tactical planning, perhaps the Sympolity might have avoided defeat or, at least, have maintained some measure of independence. Another contributing factor may have been the fact that capable members of the Sympolity's administrative personnel were absent at that critical juncture, probably because of the forced exile of over 1000 Achaean citizens who, as discussed above, had been accused of anti-Roman activities. Perhaps if these people, Polybius, for one, had been present, they may have tilted the decision-making process away from the series of wrong decisions that contributed to the Sympolity's dissolution.

At this point, and related to the above analysis, using modern methodological tools and, specifically, the equations of measuring state power, we aim to evaluate the Achaean Sympolity's strategy against Rome's during the last phase, the decisive period between 200 and 146 that ended with her ultimate defeat. Equations for measuring state power have been developed by scholars such as Christos Kollias, Ray Cline and R. J. Rummel. The equation of power, based on Kollias (2017, pp. 58–60), is expressed as follows, consisting of the following 13 variables:

$$\mathrm{P} = \mathrm{f}\ (Econ, Mil, Tech, Geo, Dem, Hc, Nr, Ps, Lead, Al, Int, Ext) \qquad (3.1)$$

These variables are identified in Table 3.3 Of course, Kollias (2017, pp. 57–60) recognises that other factors should also be considered, which would still far from exhaust the number of individual elements that determine the total power of a state.

Table 3.4 Evaluation of the strength of the Achaean Sympolity relative to the Roman Republic

P: *Power*	Achaean Sympolity	Roman Republic
Econ: Economic strength	2	5
Mil: Military strength	2	5
Tech: Technological level	4	5
Geo: Geographical location and extent	3	5
Dem: Demographics	1	5
Hc: Quality of human capital	2	5
Nr: Natural resources and wealth-producing assets	2	4
Ps: Sociopolitical characteristics	3	4
Mor: State of morale, beliefs, will, commitment to goals	4	5
Lead: Quality of leadership and administrative structures	2	5
Al: Alliances	1	1
Int: Other internal factors	2	5
Ext: External environment	5	5
Total	33	59

However, for this analysis, one can take the above variables to be representative of the total to a large and satisfactory extent. With the above in mind, we aim to offer a measurable—as far as feasible—valuation of the power of the Achaean Sympolity compared to that of Rome to ascertain if and to what extent it was feasible to adopt the strategy pursued by Diaeus and Critolaus, who had the support of the majority of Achaeans, against the policy of appeasement supported by Callicrates and the wealthy elite.

Before embarking on such an analysis, it must be noted from the outset that this is an ex-post critical assessment with all the disadvantages that presents in terms of the objectivity of an independent researcher. Furthermore, the methodology we follow is, to a degree, arbitrary as the 13 variables selected are scored on a scale of 1 to 5. It could be argued that the significance of each variable is not equal in determining power. For the analysis to be even more correct, each variable should be accompanied by a separate weighting factor to indicate the importance one should attribute to it. That, however, is very difficult to determine. For instance, what ratio should be attached to the variable *Econ.* relative to *Mil.*, or *Econ.* to *Lead*? Such issues cannot be easily determined so, for that reason, in Table 3.4 below, we offer an assessment that does evaluate each variable, but which, however, does not assign a weighting factor to each one.

Furthermore, unfortunately, statistical and cliometric data to support our arguments regarding the grading of each variable do not exist so we have arrived at our grades based on the general descriptions and whatever relevant evidence are available in the primary sources and modern bibliography. Therefore, the result is the aggregate effect of the balanced variables and assumes a priori that the final result for both states, aside from the element of subjectivity regarding the assigned grades, can only be approached as an abstraction/accepted through an abstract approach.

It is worthwhile to attempt to give a contemporary explanation regarding assigning a rank to each variable, as well as on the final accumulative result. Regarding the variable *economic might and economic development potential*, Rome was in the process of economic growth and geopolitical expansion. The Sympolity, for its part, as we have already mentioned, was plagued by social problems of an economic nature, so one cannot talk of growth. According to Bresson (2016), the prosperity of the Greek world had come to a halt with the conquest of Macedon by Rome in 168; this was followed by the conquest of the remnants of the free Hellenistic states in mainland Greece.[10] Having in mind all the above, the ranking given Rome is 5, while that to the Sympolity, 2.

As for *military strength*, here, the facts are indisputable: Rome without question possessed the most powerful military machine in the known world, while the Sympolity, worn down by endless conflict with Sparta, the Aetolian Sympolity, Macedon, as well as internal socio-economic tensions, lacked battle-worthy armed forces, evidenced by the slapdash conscription of manpower to fill her army's depleted ranks which led to the two defeats at Scarpheia in 147 and Leucopetra the following year. In any event, Rome was capable of fielding a force of 100,000 men. During the Second Carthaginian War at the Battle of Cannae in 216, the Roman forces are estimated to have amounted to 70,000 men. Rome, in other words, disposed of inexhaustible reserves.

As for the *level of technology* factor, from descriptions in the primary sources and available data, we can assume that the two protagonists were comparable in terms of means of production, but concerning the level of military technology, the Roman legion generally outranked the Greek phalanx to some extent. As we have mentioned above and will examine in greater detail in 5.3, the Achaean forces had been reorganised by the great *strategos* Philopoemen of Megalopolis along the lines of the Macedonian *phalanx* and had achieved a series of significant victories. However, the general feeling from examining the primary sources is that, more or less, they had been debased by the time of the conflict with Rome in 147/6. Accordingly, we rank Rome as a 5, and the Sympolity as a 4.

As for *geographical location*, both states possessed significant geostrategic positions. Rome, however, having conquered a great deal of territory and expanded its hegemony over a far larger geographical expanse than the Sympolity, outweighed her in that respect as well. In 146 Rome controlled the entire Italian peninsula, the Dalmatian Coast, northern and central Greece, Macedon, Epirus, Thessaly, the eastern and central sections of the Iberian Peninsula and Carthage (what is now Tunisia), what was once the Carthaginian Empire. The ranking here is Rome 5, the Sympolity 3.

---

[10]For the reasons that caused the decline in economic growth of the Greek world sometime during the Late Hellenistic period, see Ober (2015) and Tridimas (2018).

Regarding *demographic factors,* it is obvious that Rome had a vastly larger population base than the Sympolity. The latter indeed consisted of over 103 city-states in 191, but none had a large population, except for a few major centres such as Megalopolis, Argos, Corinth and Sicyon. On this subject, in the bibliography, there are a few demographic studies that offer estimates on the population of the various regions of the Mediterranean at that time. According to Frier (2000), the Italian Peninsula had a population of 7.6 million, Sicily, 0.6 million, Sardinia and Corsica another 0.5 million and the Iberian Peninsula, around 7.5 million. In total, the Roman Empire's population was 13.6 million. The population of the Greek Peninsula as a whole was no more than 3 million and, at that time, in fact, was generally in decline, suffering from a low birth rate and emigration to the Hellenistic kingdoms to the East as the cream of Greek youth left to seek a better fortune there. Population is a significant measure of the power of a nation since the larger it is, the more public income can be generated through taxation.

If one assumes that the standard of living and average income levels in Rome were more or less on a par with those of Achaea, then the sheer difference in numbers ensured that Rome had far greater prospects for expansion and growth, thus earning a ranking of 5. To Greece, with her population numbers significantly lower and in a general decline, as mentioned above, only a ranking of 1 can be assigned to the Sympolity. Further contributing to this low number is that, during this period of 186–146, the Sympolity was no longer exhibiting the level of social cohesion of earlier times because of the gulf that had evolved between the wealthy few and the lower social strata.

Concerning the next variable, *the quality of human capital,* here, the lack of data obliges us to assign an equal ranking to both of them. But, if in *human capital,* we also include those citizens serving in the armed forces, there is no doubt that the result would have been in favour of Rome. Therefore, we rate Rome with a 5 and the Sympolity with a 2. In terms of *natural resources and wealth-producing assets,* we assume an advantage to Rome if only because its greater territorial extent implies access to significantly more assets in terms of agriculture and mining. Given that, Rome is assigned a ranking of 4 (since, in 146, she had not yet reached the pinnacle of her territorial expanse), while the Sympolity receives a 2. As for *sociopolitical characteristics*, we have mentioned above the gulf that had opened in the Sympolity between the wealthy and the masses. Accordingly, we assume that during the period 183–146, she did not exhibit the cohesion of earlier times. We assign a 4 to Rome and a 3 to the Sympolity.[11]

With regard to the next variable, *morale,* Rome's constant victories leave no room to doubt that the Romans had generated a state of high morale within her legions' ranks. For their part, though not possessing the superb organisation and the record of success of the Romans, the Achaeans did possess a formidable will to resist

[11]Obviously, many parts of our argument regarding grading require further investigation and references, but that goes beyond the basic targeting of our research and the scope of presenting these tables here.

submission to Rome on the battlefield. Here, Rome earns a 5, while the Sympolity a respectable 4. As for the *quality of leadership,* as we have shown, the Roman generals in Greece were efficient, able and experienced. Opposing them, the *strategos* Critolaus proved himself grossly unequal to the task and was soundly defeated at Scarpheia in 147. Diaeus, on the other hand, performed far better at Leucopetra the following year, offering a respectable showing, his troops exploiting what few opportunities presented themselves as best as they could against a superior force. For this variable, the Romans are assigned a 5 and the Sympolity a 2.

In terms of the variable *alliances*, Rome did not appear to have been based on alliances. It appears that in 146, Romans had little need for them in any case. Conversely, the Sympolity's alliance with the Thebans proved unequal to the circumstances since it did little to contribute to the Sympolity's military strength. However, to be fair, one must measure the Sympolity's flexibility in respect of forging a truly effective alliance in terms of, e.g. financing or calling on assistance from Egypt or another Hellenistic kingdom, given that any nation that allied against Rome risked incurring her wrath—with its attendant consequences. For these reasons, we assign both states a ranking of 1.

As for *internal factors,* because of the grave internal social friction plaguing the Sympolity during that period, we assign a 2 to her, while Rome warrants a 5. For the last factor, the *external environment*, although the Romans had succeeded in imposing their will on most of mainland Greece, they had not yet achieved complete control of the Eastern Mediterranean. However, they had successfully incorporated Carthage into their territory. The Achaeans, on the other hand, had succeeded in uniting the greater part of the Peloponnesian peninsula. On the surface, it appears that both states had achieved their goals in terms of their external environment and international relations. Given that, we assign both a 5. The final tally of 33 for the Achaean Sympolity is significantly less than the 59 for Rome; it is certain that if the Achaean planners of foreign policy and military strategy had considered the circumstances in this manner, they would have made every effort to avoid war rather than seek it.

Another measure of power is the equation of R. Cline (1977, 1980). This one is expressed as follows:

$$P = (C + E + M) \times (S + W), \tag{3.2}$$

where

P: power
C: critical mass, i.e. area and population
E: economic capabilities
M: military capabilities
S: strategic purpose/targeting
W: will to follow the national strategy

The first three variables (C + E + M), were already covered above and values assigned to Rome and the Sympolity, respectively. Regarding the next two, (S + W),

Rome presented clear strategic targeting (S), expressed as her projection of power by the acquisition of new territory and, in the case of the Greeks, by taking advantage of their endless divisive squabbling and cleverly applying a strategy of divide and conquer. Rome's ambition was to acquire new territory or, alternatively, to establish satellite states and protectorates within her area of influence. Her will to follow her national strategy (W) appears to have been unified and unchanging since; despite differences occasionally expressed in the Senate, in terms of her foreign policy, the Roman Republic presented a fairly targeted strategy. Accordingly, we grade these two parameters with a 5.

Conversely, the Achaean Sympolity, especially in 147/6, could not present a *unified strategic purpose* (S). On the one hand, politicians such as Damocritus, Critolaus and Diaeus sought to expand the Sympolity's geographical territory as a means of increasing her power, while on the other, leaders such as Aristaenus, Menalcidas and Callicrates hoped to restrain her territorial ambitions and power with the aim, through compromise and appeasement in dealing with Rome, to ensure the Sympolity's viability. Here the Sympolity scores a 2 out of 5.

Also pertinent is the situation prevailing in terms of the *will to implement the high national strategy* (W). During the federal Assembly meetings, there did not appear to be any consensus, a general common understanding concerning the management of defence issues. Instead, the Assembly was a body split into two diametrically opposed camps: on the one side, those in favour of enlarging and strengthening the Sympolity and on the other, those open to satisfying all, or almost all of Rome's demands. The chasm between the two sides on this critical issue was too wide to allow for a foreign policy to be drawn up that reflected a common national strategy. Consequently, the strategy changed according to which of the two groups succeeded in electing as *strategos* (and government) one of its own adherents. For this reason, for this variable, the Sympolity—generously, we must add—is assigned a 2. In this light, the equations for each are as follows:

$$P_{\mathrm{ROME}} = (C + E + M) \times (S + W) = (5 + 5 + 5) \times (5 + 5) = 15 \times 10 = 150 \tag{3.3}$$

$$P_{\mathrm{ACH.SYMP.}} = (C + E + M) \times (S + W) = (1 + 4 + 2) \times (2 + 2) = 7 \times 4 = 28 \tag{3.4}$$

The result of Cline's equation emphasises the gulf between the two nations even more dramatically than Kollias's model of 13 variables. In any event, both agree that the difference in power between the two was obvious, and for that reason, the Sympolity should have avoided armed conflict. In this light, Polybius was vindicated in his observations, comments and criticisms. On the other hand, as mentioned above in 1.4, the crucial question of what degree of flexibility any Achaean *strategos* would have in undertaking a policy of appeasing Rome by partial dissolution of the Sympolity is not very realistic. Except for the few supporters of Callicrates and his cohorts and their pro-Roman sentiments, the vast majority of candidates for *strategos* were unlikely to countenance accepting what was essentially Rome's ultimatum vis-à-vis the secession of Sparta and the Sympolity's wider regions, Corinth, Argos, etc.

This was not necessarily because they were such great patriots but rather because none of them was willing to put his seal to a treaty which later could be cause for him to be either accused of treason or be assigned criminal responsibility or both. Cline's mathematical formulation (1977) for measuring power is similar to that of Rummel (1983). They both include the psychological factors that play a crucial role in determining power and the capacity to achieve goals.

$$P = C \times I \times W, \tag{3.5}$$

where

P: denotes power for achieving the aims of a state's grand strategy
C: denotes the material means for achieving those aims
I: denotes the level of focus in achieving said aims (this is almost the same as the variable S in Cline's equation)
W: denotes the will to achieve the aims (this is similar to Cline's variable W)

Although we acknowledge that the variable C may mean a combination of economic and military means, for reasons of simplicity, we limit the analysis to military strength, which is in line with the C in Cline's equation. Accordingly, in this case, we consider C to be defined as military means and strength. With these clarifications in mind, the following numerical outcomes result from the application of Rummel's equation with respect to Rome and the Achaean Sympolity.

$$P_{ROME} = C \times I \times W = 5 \times 5 \times 5 = 125 \tag{3.6}$$

$$P_{ACH.SYMP.} = C \times I \times W = 2 \times 3 \times 2 = 12 \tag{3.7}$$

Finally, we compare the two cases through Bartholomees' (2012) equation, which is:

$$R = M \times W, \tag{3.8}$$

where

R: denotes the total ability of the enemy in a real warfare situation scenario
M: the military means, such as the manpower ceiling (soldiers, officers, etc.)
W: the will of a state to resist. The logic of this equation is almost the same as Cline's and Rummel's equations. Having in mind these data, the outcome is:

$$R_{ROME} = M \times W = 5 \times 5 = 25 \tag{3.9}$$

$$R_{ACH.SYMP.} = M \times W = 2 \times 2 = 4 \tag{3.10}$$

As a general comment, all the equations of measuring state power and power potential denote that Rome would have been the indisputable winner if the disputes between the Roman Republic and the Achaean Sympolity came to war. Thus, war as a means of solving the problems of the Sympolity, was, it seems, the worst possible option and it should have been avoided; perhaps if more experienced, virtuous and capable politicians had handled the foreign and economic affairs, it might have been. But, unhappily, it seems that the Sympolity had run out of that kind of politicians, such as Aratos, Lycortas and Philopoemen. Instead, men such as Callicrates, Andronidas, Menalcidas, Critolaus and Diaeus prevailed, leading to the collapse of the Sympolity and the subjugation of its citizens to foreign masters.

3.3 The Game-Theoretical Approach Regarding Peace or War Strategy of the Achaean Sympolity Versus the Roman Republic

This approach, briefly described above, may also be presented through *Game Theory*. This theory was developed as a branch of economics and refers to the study of competitive interdependency with an emphasis on the process of decision-making by more than one player; in other words, a process whereby the way people or groups of people take decisions in an environment of mutual competition. Simply said, it is the study of taking strategic decisions in a situation of cooperation and conflict.[12]

In the instance under discussion, the game concerns the issue of providing defence as a public good. According to this game, the two basic strategies the Achaeans had to face against Rome can be condensed to two: (i) consent/appeasement (ii) resistance through the projection of force/military power. Table 3.5 presents a simple game which, based on the above two strategies, offers four pairs of outcomes: According to the pairing's first scenario, whereby both states choose peace as strategy, the Sympolity gets a 3, Rome, an 8. This is because, for the Sympolity to ensure peace, she must submit to the demands of Rome and divest members. This is how the Sympolity can avoid war, defeat and disaster. Because this means the partial loss of territory, she receives a low grade of 3, while Rome receives an 8. Rome, in turn, does not receive the top grade of 10 because if she had gone to war and won, she would have geopolitically erased a rival state and acquired all its infrastructure (productive capacity, capital and labour), thus increasing its power even further. Accordingly, for Rome, the strategy of peace, though beneficial, giving her a high return, is not the most advantageous.

[12]*Game Theory* was widely applied during the Cold War and is still used in studying the arms race, the nuclear threat and the balance of power between superpowers, among others.

Table 3.5 Game and numerical payoffs with reference to the Achaean Sympolity's war and peace strategy

Rome			
Achaean Sympolity		**Peace strategy**	**War strategy**
	Peace strategy	**(3, 8)**	**(1,10)**
	War strategy	**(10, 5)** (unrealistic)	**(7, 5)** Victory of the Sympolity **(1, 9)** Defeat of the Sympolity

The second scenario (1, 10) refers to the case where the Sympolity decides to avoid any escalation and clash with Rome, while the latter, regardless, decides to settle the situation in the Peloponnesus once and for all in her favour. In that case, the Sympolity's defeat would be a foregone conclusion as it will not have made any preparations for war against a seasoned and numerically superior force, led by experienced and capable commanders. The result: the defeat of the Sympolity and its dissolution (return 1), while Rome would have conquered new territory, further increasing her might (return 10).

The third scenario (10, 5) is where the Sympolity decides to do battle, led by a pervasive pro-war sentiment in its leadership (the *strategoi* Critolaus and Diaeus) and an aroused populace, while Rome seeks a peaceful solution through diplomatic channels regarding the extent of her influence in the region. This scenario assumes the Roman strategists as pacifist idealists, a utopian notion, 'too good to be true', whereby the weaker party is the aggressor seeking armed conflict while the far stronger party seeks to avoid it. Obviously, this is an unrealistic scenario in practice.

The last scenario that leads to a war strategy has two parts. If Rome were to be defeated (8, 5), her power in the region would be severely diminished. However, as she would remain the most powerful state in the eastern Mediterranean, such a defeat would not be catastrophic for her as she could easily regroup militarily and geopolitically and she could try again to achieve a critical victory over the Sympolity in the battlefield in the future. For the Sympolity, however, victory would be an accomplishment of titanic proportions that would enhance her might and influence, ensuring her survival. However, to remain the dominant power in the region's geopolitical equation would require maintaining a consistent and high degree of readiness, which implies the channelling of almost all the resources of the federal budget into defence spending. This would affect economic prosperity, putting a dent in the state's macroeconomic aggregates. The Sympolity thus would achieve Return 7 due to much greater defence spending, and perhaps even inflation, as extra coinage is struck to cover the increased spending. This situation could cause excessive public deficit that could lead to the deterioration of the economy in the long run.

In this scenario, if Rome were to win, the result would be total defeat and the dissolution of the Sympolity (Return 1), and while Rome would gain new territory and infrastructure, her victory would not have been without some measure of cost in terms of expenditure and loss of personnel to achieve her victory. The material cost to Rome, of course, would be offset by the spoils of war (Return 9). The end result of this game is that the Sympolity should have avoided armed conflict since the probability of her prevailing over Rome, the strongest power in the region, was nothing more than a fanciful hope. However, the cost of accepting peace was also adverse (Return 1), implying the progressive surrender of the Sympolity's power to Rome and its transformation into a satellite state, a protectorate. For any politician of the Sympolity to take such a decision would have doomed his political career, destroying his prestige and future reputation.

The fact of the matter is if one were to see this dispassionately and from the safety of hindsight, which is not always totally objective, the Sympolity should have sued for peace but chose instead to take the risk. It felt it could prevail over Roman ambition and secure its independence and leadership role in the Peloponnesus (Scenario 3). At the same time, the Sympolity was aware that it risked everything with its choice in the two battles that followed. Its final defeat did not gratify those who believed that it had any hope for victory.

There is one more scenario worth examining before wrapping up this chapter. This refers to the possibility of the Achaeans having one last chance if, after the defeat at Scarpheia, they had sought mediation to achieve peace. It may have resulted in the Romans imposing more onerous conditions but, on the other hand, it might have ensured the Achaean Sympolity's survival, although in a diminished state. It is not known whether this option was discussed by the members of the Achaean governing council under Diaeus or whether an extraordinary convocation of the federal Assembly was called on the issue. There may have been some discussion on it in one form or another, but there is no such relevant mention in the existing sources. And so, in a general sense, the Sympolity chose the path of glory instead of a slow but inglorious death as a satellite state of the Roman Empire under a regime of reduced sovereignty where its prospects for better days in the future as an independent entity in the path of history would have been minimal if not non-existent. Instead, the Sympolity, as part of the Hellenistic world, was unable to escape the general inherent vulnerabilities and pathologies that contributed to the subjugation of the Greek world to a rapidly ascendant Rome.

However, while having described the failings that led to the final defeat of the Achaean Sympolity, this chapter cannot close without noting its significant contribution to the city-states and citizens that comprised it. This issue is what will be addressed in the chapters that follow. In brief, what we hope to make clear with the evidence we will offer is that the Achaean Sympolity, at least during the period of its economic and geopolitical apex, under the leadership of Aratus and Philopoemen, achieved a complex of highly sophisticated economic institutions combined with a higher level of national security for its members which they may not have otherwise achieved had they remained on their own.

In this respect, Ager (2015, p. 472) confirms the historical significance of the Achaean and Aetolian Sympolities acting as protective 'umbrellas' for its member city-states in an *anarchic* world and, at the same time, protecting members from confrontation and warfare amongst themselves. If only for this, the historical contribution of these two *sympolities* in a Greek world fragmented into small cities and towns was crucial, at least during the time they were at the peak of their economic and politico-military strength, in guaranteeing its citizens the benefits of cooperation, security and prosperity.[13]

[13]For the Aetolian Sympolity, see among others, Larsen (1968), Grainger (1999), Scholten (2000), Mackil (2013), Beck and Funke (2015a), Economou et al. (2015) and Kralli (2017).

Chapter 4
Aratus of Sicyon: The Great Leader of the Achaean Sympolity During the Period 245 and 213

Before proceeding to an analysis of the political and economic institutions that constituted the Achaean Sympolity, we feel it is appropriate, in this chapter and the next, and in continuing our general critique of the Sympolity's history, to analyse the work of its two most prominent figures, the *strategoi* Aratus and Philopoemen. During the 243 years of the second phase of the Sympolity's existence, those two personalities stand apart for their leadership qualities, contributing definitively to the strengthening of the Achaean Sympolity to be, from the middle of the third until the middle of the second century, one of the most important states of the Hellenistic Period.

It is worth noting that these two towering figures did not come from the original 'core city-states' listed in Sect. 2.1, those that constituted the Sympolity's first phase, from ca. 389 to ca. 281. Aratus was from Sicyon, while Philopoemen was from Megalopolis. It was thanks to Aratus that Sicyon joined the Sympolity in 251 and Megalopolis in 235. This latter city had been founded in 370 to serve as the capital of the Arcadian *Koinon* (370–362). Its founding had been promoted by the Theban *strategos* Edaminondas to serve as the centre of the Arcadian people, as well as to act as a counterweight to the hegemonic tendencies of neighbouring Sparta. Despite its brief lifespan (370–362), the Arcadian *Koinon* was a particularly interesting example of a federation (see Economou and Kyriazis 2015). To populate Megalopolis, the inhabitants of some 40 villages throughout the region were transplanted there. The city was reinforced with emancipated ex-*helots* (ex-slaves) who, thanks to Epaminondas' military activities, had escaped from Sparta. This addition of ex-*helots*, no doubt was designed to ensure that the new city would never entertain any friendly tendencies towards Sparta (Paus. Des. 27; Diod. Hist. 15.94). In due course, Megalopolis grew into a powerful city, capable of fielding an army of 15,000 *hoplites* (Diod. Hist. 18.70–71). Of course, given the total strength of the Achaean Sympolity's forces, Diodorus Siculus' estimate is an obvious exaggeration.

The fact that neither of these two great leaders was from any of the core city-states of the Sympolity can probably be explained in at least two ways: in the first, it was their extraordinary qualities, their innate acumen and insight, that transcended

E. M. L. Economou, *The Achaean Federation in Ancient Greece*, Frontiers in Economic History, https://doi.org/10.1007/978-3-030-52697-9_4

geographical origins, as both were able to distinguish the significant benefits for the wider region of the Peloponnesus arising from the affiliation of all its city-states under the umbrella of the Sympolity, a sentiment that resonated throughout the peninsula. The second relates directly with the first: both leaders were aware of the importance of their city-states in the context of the Peloponnesus. They both surely felt that their participation in the Sympolity could only strengthen it and, by extension, through the function of the federal structures, create the conditions for their own city-states to grow stronger, gaining significant comparative advantages. These two men were zealous believers in the value of the federalisation of the Peloponnesus under a unified structure that would extend the Sympolity beyond its core, creating the conditions for a pan-Peloponnesian federal state. In this light, applying a contemporary perspective, Aratus and Philopoemen were the 'Fathers' of a 'United States of the Peloponnesus', mirrored centuries later by the Founding Fathers of the American Nation or the European Union. On this, Polybius (2.40.1–2) writes:

> When at length, however, the country did obtain leaders of sufficient ability, it quickly manifested its intrinsic excellence by the accomplishment of that most glorious achievement, the union of the Peloponnesus. The originator of this policy in the first instance was Aratus of Sicyon; its active promotion and consummation was due to Philopoemen of Megalopolis; while Lycortas and his party must be looked upon as the authors of the permanence which it enjoyed.

As we will demonstrate in this and the next chapter, these two powerful personalities, Aratus and Philopoemen, were responsible for significantly expanding the Sympolity and enhancing its prestige. There were other worthy *strategoi*[1] as well, such as Lycortas, Polybius' father, but unfortunately, the ancient sources and the modern bibliography are insufficient in providing evidence regarding their lives and deeds.

4.1 Aratus: A Young Exiled Sicyonian in Argos Becomes *Strategos* of the Achaean Sympolity

Aratus was born in 271 in Sicyon, the son of Cleinias, the leader of the city-state's democratic faction, who had put considerable effort into normalising Sicyon's political situation after it had endured the impact of a series of tyrants that had ruled it for several decades. His efforts finally bore fruit when he and a colleague, Timocleidas, were elected to the leadership of the city-state (Plutarch, Arat. 2.1). Democracy had finally been restored after 50 years of tyranny. This occurred at about the time of the start of the Chremonidean War that began in 267.

Walbank (1933, p. 30) believes that Cleinias established diplomatic relations with the Ptolemaic Kingdom of Egypt as well as with King Antigonus II Gonatas of

[1]In Sect. 6.4, we provide a detailed list of all the Achaean *strategoi* and their term of office.

Macedon with the intention they help the city, mainly economically. His foreign policy was otherwise neutral. However, in 264, Timocleidas died, and there was an uprising in the city led by Abantidas, the son of Paseas, resulting in the assassination of Cleinias as well as all his supporters and relatives. Abantidas was not satisfied with those crimes but even attempted to have young Aratus murdered. Young Aratus' survival was due to an ironic twist, as he was saved by Soso, the sister of his family's murderer (Plutarch's Arat. 2.3–4). Abantidas established tyranny once again in Sicyon.

Aratus childhood was a veritable 'trial by fire' as he not only had to suffer the psychological shock of his entire family's murder but his own exile as well, as Soso, to keep him safe, had him sent to Argos. Aratus grew up in the company of fellow exiles from Sicyon, many of them friends of his family, and nurtured an abiding hatred of tyranny. Plutarch records that as he was growing up, Aratus trained in wrestling, aiming to compete in pentathlon games and triumph, which he eventually succeeded in doing (Plut. Arat. 3.1–3.2). As Aratus grew, his popularity spread. His appearance was imposing, enhanced by his robust physique.

In 251, when Aratus was 20 years old, Nicocles became the new tyrant, in Sicyon, having assassinated Paseas, the previous tyrant's father, Abantidas, who had also been murdered. The political situation in the city-state was particularly unstable, uncertain and volatile. Plutarch (Arat. 3.4) informs us that in Nicocles' short reign of just 4 months, he committed numerous atrocities. Obviously, he resorted to such actions to consolidate his power. At the same time, Sicyon was in danger of losing its independence as the Aetolian Sympolity had the city-state in its sights.[2] Even though Aratus did not even live in Sicyon, by sheer contrast, Nicocles' behaviour served to enhance the former's persona, already characterised by the high moral standard he demonstrated in his daily life (Plut. Arat. 4.2–3).

It is worth noting that although Aratus lacked political experience and in 251, was just 20 years old, he had already taken the initiative and was active in efforts to remove Sicyon's tyrant ruler, appealing for backing from Macedon's King, Antigonus II Gonatas, as well as the Hellenistic kingdom of Egypt of Ptolemy III Euergetes. However, seeing that the prospect of these two kingdoms to participate in any effort to overthrow Sicyon's political regime was unlikely, Aratus, joined by his fellow exiles, decided to act independently and made plans to overthrow the tyrant quickly, without resorting to an extended conflict for which he lacked the necessary forces. It was very likely that Nicocles was receiving economic and military support from Macedon as it is well-known that Antigonus at that time was providing backing to pro-Macedonian city-states of the Peloponnesus.

The attempt of Aratus and his companions to overthrow the tyrant was successful. In a night raid, they managed to penetrate the walls of the city and shortly before dawn, disabled the sentries and proceeded to the tyrant's headquarters and overpowered him and his men, without bloodshed. The conspirators then sent out

---

[2]In the absence of a common border between Sicyon and the Aetolian Sympolity, the Aetolians' aim in absorbing the city-state was obviously part of a long-term strategy.

messengers to inform the city's inhabitants of what had occurred. A large number of citizens gathered and sped to the tyrant's house, setting it afire. Nicocles, however, managed to escape through the sewer system (9.1–4). That the people reacted in this manner, eager to punish the last tyrant of the city, clearly reveals that Nicocles had not succeeded in winning over much of the populace. Aratus reinstated some 80 exiles Nicocles had expelled, as well as another 500 citizens expelled by previous tyrannical administrations, restoring their property to them (9.4). Aratus then followed up this significant accomplishment with an equally important act: aware that after 50 years of tyranny, passions were still raw and the situation fluid, he proposed the integration of Sicyon into the neighbouring Achaean Sympolity (9.5). It appears he believed that as a member of the Sympolity, a democratic regime and political stability would be better secured, both in the immediate as well as the distant future. By uniting with the Sympolity, Sicyon, which was normally part of greater Corinth, effectively surrendered her identity as a Doric entity (9.6–7).[3]

Aratus consequently exhibited a particular concern for the Sympolity's further development and, as Plutarch (11.1) reports, made personal efforts in this respect, distinguishing himself as the commander of the federal cavalry. Plutarch adds that despite the personal glory Aratus had achieved, he always put himself at the disposal of the current Achaean *strategos,* whether the latter was from a city-state the size of Dyme or Tritaia or some other, smaller city. Later, Aratus received a gift from Ptolemy III of Egypt of 25 *talents*, a large sum for that period,[4] but he did not keep it, but instead, donated large sums to those citizens in need, and the rest for ransoming prisoners of war. Sometime later, Aratus travelled to Egypt to come to an understanding with Ptolemy who, at that time, was at odds with the Macedonians. The perilous journey put him at risk of capture by the Macedonian warden of Hydra. Ultimately, the journey was especially beneficial as he was able to win Ptolemy's favour and a gift of 150 *talents* for Sicyon, 40 of which he brought back to the Peloponnesus while the balance was sent in instalments (Plut. Arat. 12–13). Aratus invested these funds to great effect to the favour of the public welfare of his city, in contrast with previous leaders who, when receiving such gifts, tended to waste them.

Aratus chose integrity, transparency and the promotion of the interests of his city over the opportunistic accumulation of personal wealth, instead, distributing these transferred funds in the following way: a large part was granted to citizens with the view to put an end to the conflicts and inflamed passions that had persisted in the city for decades. Aratus aimed to establish a concord between the wealthy and the poor and to create a climate of security for all citizens. He figures as one of the great

[3]The political leadership of today's EU members that had joined from Eastern Europe during the great expansion of the Union in 2004, 2007 and 2013 obviously were similarly motivated. The former Soviet satellites realised that by joining the European Union, political stability, democratic governance and economic development would be better secured. Similarly, a few decades earlier, Greece joined in 1980–1981, and Spain and Portugal in 1986, all three having emerged from dictatorial regimes (Greece 1967–1974, Spain 1939–1975 and Portugal 1925–1975).

[4]As already mentioned, a *talent* was equal to 6000 *drachmae* at a time when the average daily wage of a worker was 1.5 *drachmae*. Twenty-five *talents*, therefore, was a particularly large sum.

political personalities of the ancient world, characterised by history as being exceptionally honest and fair in managing public monies, denying personal enrichment in favour of the welfare of society and the public interest.[5] He refused to use his position of power to coerce his fellow citizens but instead chose persuasion and conciliation. His fellow Sicyonians honoured him with a bronze statue inscribed at the base with the following (14.4):

> The counsels, valorous deeds, and prowess in behalf of Hellas, which this man has displayed, are known as far as the Pillars of Heracles;[6], but we who achieved our return through thee, Aratus, for thy virtue and justice, have erected to the Saviour Gods this statue of our saviour, because to thy native city thou hast brought a sacred and heavenly reign of law.

The ulterior aim of Aratus' strategy was to rid all the city-states of the wider region of their Macedonian garrisons. He understood that a realistic and enduring process of federalisation of the Peloponnesus rested on two preconditions: the weakening and eventual elimination of Macedonian influence in the region and the development of initiatives between the city-states aimed at this objective. This was a conscious decision of Aratus which, however, bore a cost: it irrevocably disturbed relations between the Achaean federal state and the Kingdom of Macedon. Moreover, in a diplomatic twist, the Macedonians joined forces with the Aetolian Sympolity initially to confront Achaean activity in their region and, at a later stage, to break up the Achaean Sympolity and divide her territory between them.[7] In response, Aratus tightened relations with Ptolemy III of Egypt in the name of the Sympolity.

Aratus then drew up an ingenious plan to relieve Acrocorinth from the Macedonian control (Plut. Arat. 16.2–5). He had come into contact with Erginos, a Greek from what is now Syria, whose one of three brothers, Diocles, a member of the Macedonian garrison in Acrocorinth, had discovered a section of the city walls whose height was only 15 feet tall accessible through an outcropping of boulders by a hidden path (18.7). Aratus promised the brothers a large reward of 60 *talents* if the incursion was successful and, in the event of failure, one talent plus a house in Sicyon for each. After a daring raid on the Macedonian garrison, Acrocorinth fell to Aratus, who followed up by taking the seaside city of Lechaeum as well. A fleet of 25 Macedonian ships was among the spoils taken, a substantial naval force much if not all of which were incorporated into the Achaean navy.

The inhabitants of Corinth opened the gates of their city to the Achaean troops that arrived to support the taking of Acrocorinth (Plut. Arat. 20–22). It was a

---

[5]He ranks among other such great personalities such as the Athenians Aristeides and Phocion, the Theban Epaminondas, Philopoemen of Megalopolis and the kings of Sparta, Agis IV and Cleomenes III.

[6]The Pillars of Heracles stood where Gibraltar, a British Overseas Territory, now stands.

[7]This reminds the Molotov–Ribbentrop Pact, a non-aggression agreement between the Soviet Union and the Third Reich which, in advance of their simultaneous invasion of Poland, essentially divided that hapless nation between them.

voluntary, conscious choice. The Macedonians had occupied Corinth from around 338–234. With the incorporation of Sicyon, Calydon, several cities of Ozolian Locris and, now, Corinth, the impressive territorial gains of the Sympolity under Aratus had created an inescapable reality in the northern Peloponnesus. According to Walbank (1933, p. 37) and Kralli (2017, p. 156), Corinth's inclusion signaled one more milestone: it had altered the character of the Sympolity since the term Achaean had now taken on a connotation more political rather than national. The Sympolity had extended its territory well beyond the limits of broader Achaea.

4.2 Aratus and the Achaean Sympolity's Expansion into the Leading Power in Southern Greece

After Corinth's liberation, Aratus continued the Sympolity's expansionary policy, adding the cities of Heraio and Lechaeum (Plut. Arat. 24.1). Megara followed, renouncing Antigonus' hegemony, and soon after, the cities of Troezen and Epidauros (24.3). Aratus then invaded Attica in 242 and tried to persuade the Athenians to join the Sympolity. To sweeten his offer, he freed the island of Salamis from the Macedonians, sending its inhabitants to Athens. However, his troops resorted to destruction and looting, of which Aratus certainly disapproved, aware that this could only cause problems to his ulterior plan: to push back the Macedonians, liberating city-states from their hegemony, introducing them to democracy and incorporating them into the Sympolity.

Aratus, emboldened by his success in expanding the membership of the Sympolity, did not abandon his efforts and, during the period 235–232, conducted military operations against the Macedonian garrisons in Athens and Piraeus, hoping to persuade the Athenians to join the Sympolity. For several reasons, these attacks had the opposite effect, earning him the Athenians' disapproval. The reluctance of the Athenians to entertain the possibility of joining the Sympolity was probably due to their unwillingness to become involved in new military adventures. Perhaps, too, the prospect of becoming a part of a federation did not strike them as particularly attractive. Although Athens in the middle of the third century no longer possessed land forces to be reckoned with, her citizens, no doubt, found it difficult to escape the memory of their city's past glory, unable to come to terms with the realities of the era in which they now lived. Possibly, her history as the leading city-state of the glorious First and Second Athenian Leagues prevented her on a psychological level from seriously considering the possibility of becoming a part of a federation of which she would not be the dominant leader, as in days of old.

Aside from Athens, another victim of this *path dependency* was Sparta. In this new, Hellenistic era, the two were no longer the major regulatory, geopolitical powers controlling political events, with the exception, perhaps, of a resurgent Sparta as a military power during the reign of Cleomenes III (235–222). One final comment regarding Aratus' strategy vis-à-vis the Sympolity and Athens: he persisted in trying to have Athens join because he believed that her participation would be significant and objectively beneficial to the federation's future. But why? Because of Athens' history and the prestige it would lend to the Sympolity? Because of her still-powerful fleet? Although the Achaean Sympolity's membership included many coastal city-states, the federation never developed a naval force of consequence; its military and geopolitical power rested on its land army. Perhaps at the time, Aratus was seeking Athens' accession to the Sympolity (242–232), the Athenian fleet was still a force to be reckoned with, or at least powerful enough for him to want to take advantage of the opportunity to reinforce his own naval forces. One cannot exclude this. Or perhaps Aratus wanted control of Attica because of Athens and Piraeus' strategic location in Greece between north and south. And it may be that all these hypotheses do not exclude each other.

Despite Aratus' lack of success, he was not deterred but continued to implement his political programme regarding expanding and strengthening the Sympolity. To this end, he persuaded his ally, Ptolemy III, to expand Egypt's alliance and support to the whole of the Sympolity. Because of Aratus' successes on behalf of the Sympolity, the Achaeans had come to believe he was the most qualified and re-elected him *strategos* although the position was for only a single-year term, as based on the Achaean federal 'constitution' the same person could not serve two consecutive terms. The way Plutarch (24.4) relates the issue, it is not clear as to whether Aratus was re-elected anyway or whether, since for the year he was not eligible, he continued to serve essentially as such behind a figurehead *strategos*, a man of his choosing.

By that time, 234, Aratus had already served as *strategos* for the years 245 and 243 and had continued to do so from 241 on. Since the Sympolity forbade consecutive service as a matter of principle (24.4), believing that it might lead to manipulation and corruption of its institutions,[8] the fact that Aratus was re-elected again and again could only have meant that he was an exception to this rule because of his immense popularity among the citizens of the Sympolity. That Aratus believed firmly in cooperation and support among the city-states to achieve progress and prosperity, as a precursor of the Fathers of the US Constitution and the visionaries who created today's European Union, is confirmed in Plutarch (24.5), where he reports:

> ...For [Aratus] considered that the Greek states which were weak would be preserved by mutual support when once they had been bound as it were by the common interest, and that just as the members of the body have a common life and breath because they cleave together in a common growth, but when they are drawn apart and become separate they wither away and decay, in like manner the several states are ruined by those who dissever their common bonds, but are augmented by mutual support, when they become parts of a great whole and enjoy a common foresight.

[8]This principle is basic to many modern democracies—regrettably, though, not to all. For instance, based on the *22nd Amendment to the Constitution*, passed on 24 March 1947, the US president cannot serve for more than two consecutive terms.

It would not be an exaggeration to argue that beyond the various relevant definitions which the modern academic bibliography attribute to the notion of federation and federalism in general (see, for example, Riker 1964; Davis 1978; Burgess 2000; de Figueiredo and Weingast 2005; McInerney 2013), which is interconnected with *fiscal federalism*[9] the definition attributed by Polybius to Aratus is, if analysed in depth, in our opinion, a practical definition which could even adorn some of the best academic arguments by eminent modern researchers regarding the correct typology of what a federation really is and how its success and viability are ensured for perpetuity.[10]

Aratus exhibited an iron will in his quest to overthrow all the pro-Macedonian tyrannies in the region. His next focus was the important city-state of Argos, and he devised a plan to assassinate the city's tyrant, Aristippos (25.1). The plan worked, but he was unable to capitalise on that success to take the city because the Macedonian forces stationed there intervened in support of Aristippos' brother, Aristomachus, to gain control and safeguard the city from Aratus' forces (26–29). It was clear by now that relations between Aratus and Antigonus had ruptured irrevocably. Aratus deepened the links between the Sympolity and the Ptolemaic Kingdom, to Antigonus' obvious alarm. Aratus' ambition to overthrow all the region's tyrannies had pitched the Achaean Sympolity into direct conflict with Macedon's interests.

Aratus, undeterred by his failure in Argos, turned his focus to Megalopolis, a powerful city-state under the control of a tyrant, Lydiades, very likely backed by the Macedonians. Lydiades, in contrast to previous instances of tyrannies, weighed his options and realised his political future would best be served by surrendering control of his city to the Sympolity and casting his lot with it. Megalopolis' entry into the Sympolity was a significant event because along with the city-state, it inherited her traditional animosity towards Sparta. That meant that future relations between the Sympolity and Sparta would be affected, with a greater likelihood of becoming chillier because Megalopolis' influence within the Sympolity grew rapidly. Confirming this was the fact that, after 235, most of the Sympolity's *strategoi* were from Megalopolis. After Megalopolis, yet another tyrant, Nearchos of the Arcadian Orchomenos, ceded to the Sympolity, following Lydiades' example. He was likely encouraged by the fact that the Achaeans, after all, had so appreciated Lydiades that they had even elected him as *strategos*, and elected him to that post alternately with Aratus over the next several years, from 234 to 229 (Plut. Arat. 30.1–5).

This phenomenon should be considered an act of particular political courage on the part of the Achaeans as they were trusting the highest office of the democratic, 'supranational' form of government to which they belonged to someone with a distinctly non-democratic past. Such a move could not have been devoid of some measure of political risk. Was it possible for Lydiades to govern in a political

[9]We analyse this issue in Sect. 7.4.

[10]On this issue, we will revert in detail in Chaps. 6 and 7.

environment markedly different from that to which he was accustomed? After all, his experience had been based on the format city-state/tyranny, with nationalistic, non-democratic characteristics, while the new constitutional schema he was asked to serve was based on the format federation/democracy, whose characteristics were 'internationalist' and 'supranationalist'.[11]

Plutarch (30.5–6) mentions that Lydiades exceeded the expectations of his new fellow citizens. It seems that not only did he manage to adapt quickly to the new state of affairs, but also he became consumed with an ambition to surpass Aratus' achievements, proposing new ideas, one of which was the campaign against the Spartans. Lydiades turned out to be an adept politician with a strong personality, evolving into a dangerous competitor to Aratus. The latter opposed Lydiades' plans; Plutarch notes that he seemed to envy Lydiades (30.6). The Achaeans once more honoured Lydiades in 231, electing him *strategos* again; once more, Aratus tried every means to prevent that, without success. Moreover, the Achaeans, deeming Lydiades had performed his duties well during that term, re-elected him again for the third time in 229. The two alternated the post over 5 years, Lydiades in 233, 231 and 229, Aratus in 232 and 230 (Russell and Cohn 2012, p. 36).

It is not known whether Aratus' antipathy towards Lydiades had to do with the former's vision of the Sympolity's future or his own personal ambitions (or vanity). Plutarch offers no illumination on that; as on so many other issues already mentioned, one can only make reasonable assumptions. One could consider that Aratus' antipathy was due to his political beliefs and innate hatred of tyrants, stemming from the trauma suffered during his childhood because of Sicyon's tyrant. Perhaps Aratus feared that Lydiades harboured a secret agenda, gaining the acceptance and trust of the Achaeans, only to manipulate events in his favour, reviving old practices from his time as Megalopolis' tyrant. Perhaps it all boils down to the possibility that Aratus, despite his many admirable qualities, had a flaw—that of jealousy. It is not impossible, after all, jealousy is a very human quality. If he were jealous, he had a legitimate reason to be: after so many sacrifices, dangers and hardships he had endured, risking health and wealth for the good of the Sympolity, it must have been painful to watch his fellow citizens acknowledging another leader in his place.

In any event, for his part, it appears that Lydiades, overestimating his capabilities, rashly attempted to remove Aratus entirely by having him excluded from public life. The Achaeans instead chose to support Aratus (Plut. Arat. 30.8). Lydiades had not realised that Aratus had become embedded in the Achaeans' consciousness as the 'Sympolity's faithful soldier'. That singular appeal, built up over the years by Aratus, step by step, had been overlooked by Lydiades. Ultimately, the factor that indisputably characterised the Sympolity's political stage best was Aratus himself, whose reputation was enhanced even further.

Another one of Aratus' accomplishments had to do with the Sympolity's relations with its neighbours to the north, the Aetolians. The two sympolities first came into conflict in 241 at the border city of Megara when the Aetolians decided to invade the

[11]Not in the racial sense since all the actors here were Greeks.

Peloponnesus. However, upon the death of Antigonus II Gonatas in 239 (Polyb. 2.44.1) and the accession of his son Demetrius II (later deemed 'Aetolicus'), followed by the election of Pantaleon as *strategos* of the Aetolian Sympolity, Aratus came to believe that the time had come for a radical change in the geopolitical status quo of southern Greece. Demonstrating that diplomacy often requires not only sagacity but audacity as well, Aratus, taking advantage of the new developments, took the initiative and contacted Pantaleon. The two drew up an alliance between the two democratic sympolities which until recently had been in a state of war. By doing so, the Aetolians, who until then had been maintaining good relations with Antigonus, renounced their alliance with the Macedonians.

As a result, although relations between the two sympolities generally had never been very good because of their differing interests in the broader region, their mutual anti-Macedonian stance constituted reason enough for the two to conclude an alliance (an ephemeral one, as it turned out, lasting from 235 to 227). To that end, the two *strategoi* put aside differences to confront the authoritarian-tyrannical regimes Antigonus had imposed on city-states in central and southern Greece and expand their influence, the Achaeans in the Peloponnesus and Attica, and the Aetolians in pushing back the Macedonians' ever-tightening noose. Aratus hoped a victory would put an end to Macedonian influence in Attica, allowing that region which included both Athens and Piraeus to join the Sympolity (Grainger 1999, p. 223). The so-called Demetrian War followed, a 12-year-long conflict lasting from 239 to 228/227—with a few interruptions—between the Macedonians and the two allies (Polyb. 20.5), the latter supported by Ptolemy III of Egypt. Hostilities between the two sides marked the period from 236 to 232 throughout Acarnania and the Peloponnesus.

In 237/236, Aratus made one last series of attempts to draw Athens into the Sympolity, all of which met with failure. In his final attempt, after failing to invest Piraeus, during the retreat to Thriasio, he broke a leg and was forced to undergo several surgeries, continuing to campaign from a litter (Plut. Arat. 33). One can safely surmise that Aratus, by carrying on bravely despite his wounds, must have inspired even greater loyalty in his troops (Plut. Arat. 33). However, as the war between the two sympolities and Macedon wore on, in 232, Macedonian forces under the command of the general Bithys crushed Aratus' army at Phylacia (probably somewhere near the source of the Alpheios River). This was probably the first so decisive a defeat suffered by Aratus. In the meantime, Demetrius invaded Boeotia and Aetolia. Taking advantage of the opportunity, the Acarnanians rose up and defected from the Aetolian Sympolity.

Despite the setbacks in Boeotia and failure at incorporating Athens into the Sympolity, the geopolitical stage was changing with the Achaean Sympolity gaining in strength while Macedon was weakening. The Achaeans now controlled an area that extended from the Gulf of Patras in the west to the Saronic Gulf in the east, including a large portion of Arcadia and all of Argolis (Fig. 1.1). Most of the remaining cities of Arcadia, as well as Aegina and Ermione, joined the Sympolity (Plut. Arat. 34.5–7). Obviously, for many less dynamic, weaker city-states on the Greek geopolitical stage, the balance of power had shifted, forcing them either to abandon their neutrality or their covert acceptance of Macedonian hegemony and openly join the Sympolity.

In 229, Demetrius II Aetolicus died and, as his son Philip was underage, the regency was assumed by Antigonus III Doson. At the time, Macedon was in an extremely difficult position not only because the Dardanians, a tribe to the north, had violated the border but also because the Aetolians had gained control of a large part of Thessaly and were putting a great deal of pressure on the pro-Macedonian regime in Boeotia. The Athenians, meanwhile, had bought their city's freedom from the head of the Macedonian garrison while the tyrants of Argos, Ermione and Phleious had relinquished power, allowing those city-states to join the Achaean Sympolity (Walbank 1993). Taking advantage of these developments, Aratus, along with the Aetolians, grasped the opportunity to resume hostilities against the Macedonians, intending to free all the remaining pro-Macedonian tyrannies in southern Greece. This final phase of the Demetrian War (228/7) saw Aratus turning his attention once more to Argos, the city where he had grown up and whose tyrant, he had failed to overthrow years before.

Aristomachus was now the ruler, having succeeded his brother Aristippus. Aratus demanded of Aristomachus that he relinquish power, as he had done of Lydiadas, the tyrant of Megalopolis, back in 235. Aristomachus agreed, aware that his hold on power did not rest on the popular acclaim of his subjects but rather on the force of arms. Given the rising tide of democracy in the Peloponnesus, his position was becoming increasingly less tenable. His choice proved correct as, in 228, the Achaeans, as they had done with Lydiades before, elected him *strategos* (Plat. Ar. 35.3). By that year, the Achaean Sympolity had expanded markedly. Aristomachus, as Lydiades before him, was eager to invade Laconia, perhaps to achieve a few victories and enhance his appeal to his new subjects. Aratus, realising that such an adventure could prove exceedingly dangerous, forbade him to do so. The new king of Sparta, Cleomenes III, was an imposing force and becoming more and more dangerously powerful. When Aritomachus, as *strategos*, demanded of Aratus that he submit to his order and participate in his campaign, the latter reluctantly agreed. However, when Cleomenes' army made its appearance, Aratus prevented Aristomachus from attacking, earning Lydiadas' censure. In the ensuing confrontation between the two, Aratus came out on top, being re-elected *strategos* for a twelfth term (Plut. Arat. 35.5–7).

4.3 Aratus and Cleomenes: Two Great Men and the Lost Opportunity for the Unification of the Peloponnesus Under the Achaean Sympolity

Cleomenes ascended to the throne of Sparta in 235. A descendant of the Agiades royal family, he succeeded his father Leonidas II. His first act of geopolitical significance was to forge a politico-military alliance with the Aetolians who, alarmed by the increasing power of their neighbour, the Achaean Sympolity, thought it wise to support the Spartans as an effective counterweight in the Peloponnesus. In 228, the city-state's *ephors* sent him to invest the border fortress Athenaion that both Megalopolis and Sparta were contesting. His success so alarmed the Achaeans that they called for an extraordinary federal Assembly and declared war on Sparta. They took Megalopolis' side in this affair because Cleomenes seized not only the fortress but the city itself as well, which happened to be a member of the Sympolity—an act of aggression that could not be ignored (Kralli 2017, p. 207). Obviously, from the perspective of the Achaean's grand strategy, the incident was a clear *casus belli*.[12]

On this point, Daubies (1973, p. 149) notes that, in fact, two imperialist entities, one from the north, another from the south, were vying for control of Arcadia. Aratus who, at that time, was not serving as *strategos* but must, at least, have been in command of a section of the Sympolity's army (not specified in the sources), staged a surprise nighttime raid on Tegea and Orchomenos which, at that time, were not members of the Sympolity. His supporters in the two cities failed to provide sufficient backing, forcing Aratus to withdraw before his effort came to Cleomenes' attention. It is not unlikely that among the many achievements of Aratus, he had acquired expertise in infiltrating cities, employing raids under cover of darkness, supported by fifth columnists in his targets. On this occasion, however, he met with failure.

Cleomenes advanced towards Arcadia but received orders from the *ephors* to turn back. That same year, Aratus took Caphyae, an act that the Spartans bound to see as one of aggression since the Aetolian Sympolity had conceded that city to Sparta. The *ephors* sent Cleomenes to take counteraction at the head of an army of 5000 men. On his way to Argos, Cleomenes bypassed Megalopolis and proceeded towards Arcadia, occupying the small city of Methydrion. He then marched into Argolis, raiding and looting along the way. Aristomachus, the erstwhile tyrant of Argos and now the Sympolity's *strategos* rallied a force of 20,000 infantry and 1000 horsemen to halt Cleomenes' advance.

Plutarch (Cleo. 4) tells us that Aratus cautioned Aristomachus to hold back and refrain from any engagement because he felt that, while the Achaeans outnumbered the enemy (4:1, plus 1000 horsemen), the latter outclassed them. Aristomachus was finally persuaded and did hold back. Ironically, Aratus was consequently accused of cowardice. In 227, Cleomenes attacked Megalopolis, while Aratus turned his attention to Elis, hoping to take Elida, a key city-state in Elis because it was the Aetolians' foothold in the Peloponnesus and a potential threat. As mentioned in 2.2, relations between the wider region of Elis in northwestern Sympolities and the Aetolians were very friendly, especially after 267. Obviously, for the city-states of Elis to maintain

[12]In almost an identical situation during the Cold War, the doctrine under which any attack of the Soviet Union on any NATO member would simultaneously mean an attack on all the other members states of the NATO alliance.

their independence and resist being drawn into the Achaean Sympolity, they needed a powerful ally who had no desire to see the Achaeans increase their power.

For their part, the Aetolians saw Elis as staging ground for intervention into the heartland of the Peloponnesus. Larsen (1975, p. 164) asserts the inhabitants of Elis were, in effect, subservient to the Aetolians, though we believe that assignment cannot be easily proven and should be considered suspect, at least if it was meant to apply to all the city-states within the region. Walbank (1933, p. 81) notes that by controlling Elis, Aratus intended to sever the ties between the two regions. Perhaps he intended to take a few more strategically significant city-states there as well. Cleomenes, moving up through Arcadia, attempted to block Aratus' effort and, while the latter tried to avoid a confrontation, because of the easy mobility of Cleomenes' troops, the Spartan army caught up with the Achaeans at Mt. Lycaeum. In the ensuing battle, the Achaeans suffered a crushing defeat (Plut. Cleo. 5; Polyb. 2.51.3).[13]

The ancient sources do not offer any explanation as to why the Sympolity's forces were so inferior. The responsibility for their defeat can only be ascribed to Aratus himself as he was serving as *strategos* at the time and accordingly was responsible for the readiness and quality of his troops. Although the Achaeans' defeat had been significant, Aratus nevertheless did succeed in incorporating the city-state of Mantinea into the Sympolity, thanks to help from his allies within the city walls, whose contribution proved decisive (Polyb. 2.58.1). Aratus installed a garrison and granted citizenship to all the city's *metics*[14] (Plut. Arat. 36.1–3). He realised that by 'upgrading' the Mantinean *metics*' status to full citizenship, he was providing them with an incentive to fight for and defend the city—if necessary, with particular zeal. This was a time when many city-states in Greece, because of a lack of a sufficient number of free citizen-*hoplites*, sought alternative methods of defence, such as hiring mercenaries, as did the Arcadians, or as Aratus did, offering *metics* and slaves citizenship in return for armed service.

Aratus saw that it was preferable to avoid or minimise loss of life on all sides when investing a city by relying on 'unorthodox', indirect strategies rather than conventional siege: in various city-states throughout the Peloponnesus, he established a network of supporters. The resulting successes dampened the Spartans' appetite for further military adventures, and they began to rebel against Cleomenes' military campaigning. Plutarch (Ar. 36.4) reports that when that same summer Sparta confronted Megalopolis, nevertheless, Aratus rushed to its defence, although he avoided any direct clashes with Cleomenes, despite the Megalopolitans' anxious appeals. However, after Aratus was once again replaced at the end of his term as *strategos* by Lydiades, the battle finally did take place. Lydiades was killed before the city gates, heroically defending his hometown, Megalopolis (Plut. Arat. 38.3–4). This was the second crushing defeat of the Sympolity's army in a year. Lydiades'

[13]For the clash between Aratus and Cleomenes III, see Michalopoulos (2016) in detail.

[14]As will be further explained in Sect. 7.5, *metics* were citizens of Greek cities who relocated to another city-state such as Athens, in search of work, either temporarily or indefinitely.

death had a considerable impact on the people and led to Aratus being accused of having forsaken Lydiades. The Achaeans, consequently, restricted further funding for Aratus—a part of which he would have intended to allocate to hiring mercenaries—to the bare minimum, and that, only in the event of imminent military action (37.5).

Was Aratus acting in self-interest, deliberately intending for Lydiades to die in battle, initially encouraging him to advance and then denying him sufficient support, hoping to be rid of what was, yes, a comrade-in-arms and compatriot, but also a dangerous and very able political rival in the Sympolity's power structure? Such an accusation is not indicated in any of the sources, nor has it been proposed by any modern researcher as far as we know. However, it is something that cannot be dismissed outright and should be considered a possibility, given Aratus' acknowledged temper and his undeniable skill at operating behind-the-scenes. On the other hand, who could have guaranteed that Aratus would survive the defeat and not meet the same fate as Lydiades? In any event, Aratus' defeat did cause him a considerable loss of face among his fellow citizens as a *strategos* capable of defending the realm, as we have mentioned above. The suggestion that Aratus countenanced the destruction of his army to rid himself of Lydiades as a rival is extreme and most likely is baseless. What seems to have been the case was that Cleomenes III's superiority as a military leader over Aratus and the other Achaean senior officers was undeniable. They were simply not up to the task of successfully confronting him militarily, hence their continuous defeats.

Cleomenes acted with humility and tolerance towards the citizens of Megalopolis and did not allow his troops to occupy the city, proposing an alliance instead. Of course, this was not feasible in the short- or even mid-term, given that most of the inhabitants were former *helots* from Sparta; it was not easy to erase centuries of hatred quickly. Megalopolis remained an anti-Spartan entity. At this point, Cleomenes, no longer considering the Achaeans as a foe of any particular consequence and having triumphed and enhanced his stature in Sparta, decided that the time was ripe to implement his reformist socio-economic programme as briefly discussed in Sect. 2.2. Aratus, in the meantime, disappointed and embittered by his loss of face, thought of resigning but then changed his mind. In the spring of 226, believing that circumstances in Sparta had turned fluid because of Cleomenes' efforts at reform, Aratus tried taking the initiative and called the Achaeans to arms. This time, he was victorious, even capturing Megistonus, Cleomenes' father-in-law; during the hostilities, 300 Spartans were killed (Plut. Arat. 38.1). Cleomenes responded promptly: he invaded and pillaged the region of Megalopolis. This occurred in May and June of 226.

Soon after, the inhabitants of Mantinea asked Cleomenes to intervene and throw out the Achaean garrison from their city. This obviously put Mantinea at odds with the Sympolity. Cleomenes agreed and, in a night raid, successfully attacked the city and forced the garrison's surrender, probably assisted by pro-Spartan elements within the city walls (Polyb. 2.58.4; Plut. *Cleo.* 14.1; Ar. 39.1). It seems that Cleomenes was an accomplished staff officer and studied and learned from his opponent. In effect, the conquest of Mantinea was achieved by adopting the tactics on which Aratus had based many of his previous successes. Cleomenes then advanced to Tegea and from there, into the heartland of the Sympolity, intending to force the Achaeans to confront him in a decisive battle. Heading a force of 20,000 Spartans and allies, he forged on towards the city-states of Dyne and Phares, taking both. Under the *strategos* Hyperbatos (who had succeeded Aratus), the Achaeans assembled a large force in an attempt to cut the Spartan advance short. At Hekatombaion, the armies met and the Achaeans, once again, were crushed (Plut. Cleo. 14.2; Ar. 29.1; Polyb. 2.51; Walbank 1933, p. 90).

From that point on, Cleomenes was free to move at will throughout the Achaean Sympolity; no city felt secure. All were vulnerable to attack by the Spartans at any moment and were without recourse to federal troops to help in their defence. Aside from the loss of any effective military capability on the part of the Sympolity since, with the latest crushing defeat, it no longer had credible military forces at its disposal, the Achaeans suffered yet another significant blow at this point: Ptolemy, obviously determining that the Sympolity was a lost cause and a waste of funds, decided to cut off economic support (Walbank 1984, p. 464). In the following year, 225, Hyperbatos' term came to an end and, although the Achaeans asked Aratus to take over once more, he refused. Timoxenos was thus elected to succeed Hyperbatos (Plut. Arat. 38.2). Aratus was denounced once more, this time accused of abandoning the state in its hour of need. Plutarch (36.6) notes that Aratus was also faulted for not consenting to Cleomenes' proposal to be appointed the Sympolity's leader since he felt himself unable to confront the Spartan king successfully. After all, Cleomenes' ostensible aim coincided with Aratus' desire to defeat Macedon.

It would be worthwhile at this point to provide some additional historical context to these events. After his string of military successes, Cleomenes, by nature a dynamic, restless spirit, continued to take the initiative. He took Corinth and other significant cities of the Sympolity. He was an extremely able military commander as evidenced by the speed with which his forces were able to move from one part of the Sympolity to another. Cleomenes never occupied the city-states he took, nor did he station garrisons in them. On the contrary, he affirmed their full freedom and independence. Instead, he arrested high-ranking Achaean officials with the hope of indoctrinating them with his vision of socio-economic reform for all of the Peloponnesus. Many of these officials, in fact, were persuaded and later fought on Cleomenes' behalf. Moreover, any city that had an oligarchic leadership was encouraged to abandon it and install a grassroots government in its place (Plut. Cleo. 17.3, Ar. 39.4). These facts may mean that, at the time, some city-states of the Sympolity were not democratic but were ruled by oligarchic regimes. Cleomenes also favoured cancelling the debts of city-states that were facing economic hardship.

This approach was very wise because he did not project himself as a heartless conqueror but instead as the Achaeans' reasonable 'partner', as an idealist who did not necessarily seek the dissolution of the Sympolity but sought a new era, with fresh ideas and socio-economic trends that would benefit everyone. Cleomenes proved to be the ablest and most brilliant of Aratus' opponents. Moreover, his vision seems to have gradually taken firm root because a revolutionary climate spread throughout almost the whole of the Sympolity. The lower classes saw Cleomenes as a hero and liberator. A significant number of cities had split from the Sympolity, including Pellene, Pheneos, Caphyae, Argos, Cleonae, Phleious, Epidaurus, Troezen, Ermione, Corinth (except for the fortified city of Acrocorinth), etc. Obviously, during that period, many cities, including Aratus' hometown of Sicyon, had become disillusioned with the internal politics of the renowned *strategos* and the Sympolitian leadership in general and were willing to break away and accept Cleomenes as a ruler with a licence to advance his socio-economic revolution even within the heart of the Sympolity. Aratus was troubled by this ominous trend since it threatened to disrupt the Sympolity's entire socio-economic structure, installing populist reforms such as the cancellation of the city-states' debts and the redistribution of land. Aratus, grounded on a considerably more conservative ideological socio-economic platform, was not in favour of accepting such radical reforms which, in addition to those that had been adopted in Sparta, extended to a new Solonian *seisachtheia* (or debt abolishment), as had occurred in Archaic Athens in 594.

Unlike the past, the third century was marked by great social upheavals, generally on economic grounds. Over 60 uprisings of this sort were recorded in mainland Greece during the Hellenistic Period, most in the Peloponnesus, against only 5 or 6 throughout the Classical Period. The basic demands in these uprisings were the redistribution of land and debt forgiveness. Where they were successful, they were accompanied by drastic socio-economic adjustments such as the redistribution of the wealth of the upper classes among the insurgents, expansion of the political body and the liberation of slaves (Rostovtzeff 1941, pp. 206–208, 210–214; Mendels 1982).[15] Fearing the worst, Aratus resorted to an act unprecedented for the Sympolity. Without authorisation from any member of the Achaean government, through two of his friends, Cercidas and Nicophanes, he came into contact with the Macedon's King Antigonus III Doson, asking for support in evicting the Spartans from the Sympolity's territory (Plut. Arat. 38.11). He even succeeded in enlisting the Megalopolitans to request Antigonus' support formally as well. This occurred in 226.

Aratus was essentially acting on his own, illegally, not holding any official position of authority in the Sympolity at that time. In effect, what he was proposing ran counter to the very basis of the Sympolity's overriding strategy vis-à-vis Macedon. Moreover, he had acted behind the scenes to persuade a member city-state, Megalopolis, to request Macedonian support, essentially inviting Macedon to interfere in the Sympolity's affairs. On this issue, Larsen (1968, p. xviii) argues that the Megalopolitans applied for help from Antigonus only after first securing permission from federal authorities. This is crucial as it proves that one of the strongest and most prestigious of the Achaean member city-states did not take initiatives regarding foreign policy without the knowledge of the Sympolity's authorities. This

[15] In another study by Economou and Kyriazis (2019), we refer to the social uprisings in medieval Europe, focussing on the High Middle Ages in England. Many of the demands of the insurgents, such as Wat Tyler and John Ball in 1381, were similar to those of the uprisings of the Hellenistic Period.

means that, in a broader context, the Megalopolitans accepted in practice one basic federal principle, which is that any issue of the foreign policy of a single member city-state must have the approval of federal supranational policymakers. Larsen makes it clear that foreign policy and diplomacy ultimately rested with the federal authorities.

At this stage, Aratus held back on informing the Achaean leadership, hoping that there might still be an opportunity to deal with Cleomenes by the Sympolity's forces, perhaps with support from the Aetolians or the Athenians (Plut. Arat. 41.3; Walbank 1984: 466). This shows that even at this late stage, Aratus was hoping to avoid drawing the Macedonians into the affairs of the Peloponnesus if he could enlist military support from elsewhere. The *strategos* at that time, Timoxenos, pressured by circumstance, opened negotiations with Cleomenes. This initiative may have been instigated by the Sympolity's leadership or as a result of an extraordinary federal Assembly, or even both, but that remains unknown.

The Spartan king, perhaps aware of Aratus' behind-the-scenes contacts with Antigonus, felt it better to come to an understanding with the Sympolity before Aratus' machinations bore fruit. In that light, he accepted Timoxenos' appeal, proposing the Achaeans agree to a truce and appoint him *hegemon* of the federation. Moreover, Aratus would be put in command of the Achaean armed forces. The term, *hegemon*, used by Plutarch (Ar. 41.6) is typologically problematic because it can be interpreted that Cleomenes intended to transform the Sympolity into a kingdom under his authority. On this issue, Plutarch is not at all clear what exactly the position Cleomenes demanded from Timoxenos entailed. Could the Achaeans accept a head who would concurrently retain the privileges of a king in his own state, even if that state became a member of the Sympolity, and yet also be the federation's *strategos*? All the sources make it quite clear that this was forbidden under the Achaean Sympolity's 'constitution'. Anyone who held the post of *strategos* was forbidden from concurrently holding any post in his home city-state. If the Achaeans were to agree to Cleomenes' precondition, under what authority would he govern the Sympolity?

In the previous instances of the tyrants Lydiades and Aristomachus, the transformation of their city-states into democracies was relatively easy. The two men simply resigned their offices and 'reconfigured' themselves as democrats by participating normally in the new structures of the Sympolity. Conversely, Sparta, despite Cleomenes' reforms, remained a kingdom and it is difficult to conceive of Cleomenes accepting to be a *strategos*, especially if restricted to a one-year term without the right to repeat until a year had passed as the Achaean 'constitution' stipulated, especially at that time, having soundly defeated the Sympolity on the field of battle again and again. Moreover, was it at all realistic to expect Cleomenes to be welcomed to lead the Sympolity's army?

As Walbank (1993) observes, accepting Cleomenes' precondition would have not only meant a loss of independence but would have been a radical change in the very social order of the Sympolity. The populists' view of Cleomenes as a saviour was inherently misplaced. A new Sympolity, with Sparta as its dominant member, would have appeared as an upgraded version of the old Peloponnesian Alliance in which

Sparta had always held the leading role in decision-making. Kralli (2017, p. 240) writes on this point that it is hardly likely that the Spartan king would stand as a candidate for election to the annual *strategia* (the post of *strategos*). On the contrary, he would assume the role of a permanent hegemon, and in a Sympolity led by him, Aratus would be reduced to a simple member of the Sicyonian elite. Kralli (p. 245) does note that we do not know whether federalism was unacceptable to Cleomenes since he was not the typical Spartan king: the Sparta of his time was much weaker than that of the fifth century. Thus, it would not have been unimaginable if Cleomenes, a king who had effectively abolished the dual kingship, did stand for election to the *strategia* as Lydiades or Aristomachos had. In that sense, the problem was transferred by Cleomenes to the leaders of the Sympolity: were they willing to accept the transformation of the Sympolity into a loose federation that would include land reallocation, wealth redistribution and a new-member state, with possible hegemonic aspirations such as Thebes of the Boeotian *Koinon*? The answer was probably no.

Larsen (1975) and Walbank (1993) believe that sincere dialogue with Sparta, on an equal footing, would have been a blessing and would have contributed greatly to the unification of the Peloponnesus. In any event, it would have meant an end to the destructive warfare and loss of human life and natural resources of the past. But such an outcome could have been possible if the leaders of the two sides had been anyone other than who they were: under Cleomenes and Aratus, a substantial, functional and lasting political union of the Peloponnesus was an impossibility. Cleomenes, who had beaten the Sympolity soundly on the battlefield on four occasions, as a king himself, would never settle for an elected office, and especially one that lasted just 1year and could not be repeated until another year had passed. And for personal reasons, Aratus could not countenance his life's work, the ascendance of the Achaean Sympolity's supremacy, to end up in the hands of the Spartan king.

Nor did he believe that the Sympolity could survive as an autonomous politico-economic entity under the authority of or the significant control of its institutions by Sparta. Furthermore, Aratus, most likely coming from and identifying with the wealthier strata of Achaean society, was not open to the idea of a radical shift in the socio-economic structure of the Sympolity along the lines of Cleomenes' reforms in Sparta. Even if Cleomenes had no intention of introducing his reforms beyond Sparta, Aratus had no way of knowing this a priori. Only later did it become apparent that the former did not have a plan to extend his reforms throughout the Peloponnesus. It may have been that if the confluence of politico-military circumstances that followed had evolved differently, he might have proceeded to do so, but as they did not, he restricted his reforms to Sparta alone.

Aratus managed to put an end to efforts at conciliation and cooperation of the Sympolity with the Kingdom of Sparta. He was aware that if Cleomenes took over the military affairs of the Sympolity, that would have meant the end of his service as *strategos* in the future. Beyond any patriotic motive, his ego could not easily accept that he might never have the opportunity again of being elected *strategos*, a post that offered fame, glory and, very likely, substantial monetary reward offered by the Sympolity to its 'first citizen'. Piper (1986, p. 58) provides a very substantive reasoning of why the inclusion of Sparta/Laconia in the Achaean Sympolity was not a realistic scenario: he argues that Cleomenes represented the old ideal of the *polis*, while Aratus the new federal state. Federalism was unacceptable to Sparta because she differed too much from the cities already absorbed by the League. Finally, she was greater than any city-state of the Achaean Sympolity, and her traditions were wholly inconsistent with mere membership in any federal structure.

After the negotiations had collapsed, Cleomenes despatched a herald to the Achaeans to inform them that he was resuming military action and, in a show of insolence, almost took his rival Aratus' birthplace, Sicyon, by resorting to treachery. However, he did attack Pellene, where the Achaean *strategos* was killed, and later, took the cities of Pheneos and Pantelion. Plutarch (Ar. 39.4) does not name that *strategos,* but it is unlikely that it was Timoxenos since he is mentioned as *strategos* in later events, in 224, for instance, during open hostilities between Macedon and the Sympolity (Plut. Cleo. 20.8). It may be that Plutarch was referring to another officer and not the *strategos*—perhaps a field commander.

The citizens of Argos immediately rejected the Sympolity and welcomed Cleomenes, while the Phleiasians even accepted a Spartan garrison. In general, the federal Achaean unification procedure seemed not to have been so secure in a large number of the member city-states of the Sympolity. Throughout the entire federation there now prevailed a climate of apostasy in favour of Cleomenes that had gained considerable impetus, propelled by interests in every city that sought radical policies and reforms and were willing to adopt Cleomenes' proposal (39.4–5). Aratus, seeing the Sympolity coming apart, took over as *strategos* in 225, once again elected by the Achaeans as the most capable of dealing with the dangerous circumstances rocking the Sympolity. Upon his election, he asked the federal Assembly that he be assigned a personal guard; despite having led the Achaeans for a total of 26 annual terms up to that point, nothing now seemed to guarantee his safety.[16] Then he appealed to the Aetolian Sympolity as well as Athens for help and was rejected by both (41.1–3). By the middle of 224, Cleomenes controlled Eastern and Central Peloponnesus (see Fig. 1.1), while the Sympolity had been cornered into the northwestern part of the peninsula, to the region from which it had been originally formed ca. 417 (or in 389).

Aside from assistance from Macedon, any alternative help seemed either less realistic or more damaging. As mentioned above, Aratus had sounded out the Aetolian Sympolity and Athens, and perhaps even Ptolemaic Egypt. Relations between the two great sympolities had soured over who controlled the four important Arcadian cities of Mantineia, Tegea, Caphyae and Arcadian Orchomenos, forever the subjects of contention between the two, and Aratus feared an alliance between the Aetolians and Spartans. In any event, any hope of military help from Ptolemy III was unrealistic as the latter was an ally of both the Sympolity and Sparta and was unlikely to insert himself in their dispute. Moreover, he had no desire to get embroiled in military action in Greece. Decades earlier, during the Chremonidean War (267–61), by sending a fleet of warships, the Ptolemaic Kingdom had supported

[16]In his original text, Plutarch mistakenly credited Aratus with 33 terms.

the anti-Macedonian alliance comprised of many city-states of southern Greece, principally Athens and Sparta. However, it had refrained from clashing with Macedonian land forces, leaving its allies at their mercy, unable to avoid eventual defeat.

For 3 months, Cleomenes hesitated, undecided as to how to handle the situation. In the meantime, Aratus was no doubt actively seeking support from the Macedonian king. He sent two envoys to Antigonus Doson to emphasise that if Cleomenes were not stopped, there was a possibility that he would ally with the Aetolians, subdue all of the Sympolity and the Peloponnesus, creating an anti-Macedonian alliance that would likely include the Boeotian *Koinon*. This notion that the Aetolians and Spartans were in secret negotiations for joint action in the Peloponnesus, as Polybius claims (2.49), does not seem to be reflected in following events, according to Urban (1979, p. 131) and Walbank (1984, p. 462). After all, the Aetolian Sympolity, at least seemingly and formally, continued to be an ally of the Achaeans. Of course, this did not really mean that much since, although the Aetolians did maintain an anti-Macedonian stance, they were never noted for the stability of their alliances. For his part, Antigonus, probably taking all the above considerations into account, agreed to join with the Achaean Sympolity militarily, deeming it in Macedon's best interests for the time being. He did not delay long in moving into the Peloponnesus (Plut. Arat. 43.1). For his part, Aratus was finally able to persuade his fellow citizens of the necessity of Macedonian intervention on behalf of all the Sympolity, although many may have been incensed that he had acted behind the scenes. Plutarch notes that the Achaeans even accepted the decision to hand over Acrocorinth to Antigonus in exchange for his military support (Plut. Arat. 42.2). It was apparent that the Sympolity had found itself in marginal straits.

It may have been that the state hierarchy of the Sympolity, especially those representing the interests of the wealthy oligarchs, accepted the alliance with Macedon as a 'necessary evil'. After all, aside from the demand to hand over strategic Acrocorinth, Antigonus had no intention of challenging the status quo in Achaea, nor the interests of the powerful, wealthy groups and oligarchs in a position to affect political developments. In that respect, Cleomenes III was a far greater threat to them than Antigonus. If Cleomenes were to prevail, it could not be excluded that he might proceed at some point to the redistribution of wealth and income to the lower strata, to the detriment of the interests of the Achaean oligarchs and other affluent circles. That was very likely the reason Aratus' behind-the-scenes machinations escaped punishment. There was no doubt that Aratus had remained the prime factor in the political developments of the Achaean Sympolity.

Cleomenes, although the master of the military situation after his string of victories, vacillated, losing considerable momentum. Had he acted more boldly, more in tune with his innate temperament, he might have defeated the remaining forces of the Sympolity, ultimately vanquishing it. It is difficult to believe that Cleomenes was not aware to some extent of Aratus' negotiations with the Macedonians and that Antigonus was heading towards the Peloponnesus. In retrospect, it could be argued that Cleomenes was not able to take sufficient advantage of his military successes to translate them into achieving his political programme which, in its more extreme form, would have been the dismemberment of the Sympolity, and in its milder form, its conversion into a 'loose' federation with Sparta as head, controlling developments in all critical issues concerning the Peloponnesus.

The alliance agreement between the Achaean Sympolity and the Kingdom of Macedon which had been approved by the Achaean federal Assembly in Argos was signed in the small town of Piges in Boeotia. Consequently, Macedonian forces returned to the Peloponnesus, this time as allies, to serve alongside the existing Achaean garrisons. Upon Antigonus' arrival in Argos in 224, Cleomenes thought it prudent to withdraw to Mantinea. He was fully aware of the Macedonian army's superiority (Walbank 1984, p. 467) and was unwilling to engage it in open battle, one that was likely to prove decisive. It seems that Cleomenes' determination and drive with which he had faced and prevailed over the Sympolity were cut short by his realisation that the military power of the Macedonians was superior to that of any other Greek city-state or federation.

Plutarch (Arat. 44.4–5) provides a very significant piece of information at this point. He reports that, one by one, all the city-states from which Cleomenes withdrew quickly rejoined the Achaean Sympolity. Obviously, in the climate of polarisation that prevailed in the region, plunged as it was in a state of chaos, switching camps, according to the direction in which the wind was blowing, was a prudent strategy. This phenomenon has been observed many times, even in recent history.[17] The Achaean city-states, although still harbouring sympathy for Cleomenes and his reforms, were indeed not about to risk more bloodshed at the hands of the surging Macedonian forces, especially given that he was abandoning them as he retreated southward. In any event, there was no resistance to rejoining the Sympolity since it had become apparent that Cleomenes was in no hurry—if he had intended at all—to implement his socio-economic reforms outside of Sparta. He had made no effort to encourage the enthusiasm of the inhabitants of the Achaean city-states for reform. Realising he was not willing to provide solutions for their problems and concerns, they abandoned him as easily as they had reached out to him. For instance, Plutarch (Cleo. 20.3) reports that once the citizens of Argos realised Cleomenes did not intend to relieve their debts as they had expected, turned on him, and were assisted by a military force under the command of the *strategos* Timoxenos (20.4) despatched from Sicyon.

Taking the above into account, one could argue that Cleomenes failed to build on his initial military successes by devising a workable strategy at a tactical and political level. This is something that Germany, too, in the two world wars of the twentieth century failed to do, to mention a modern historical example. Of course, there may have been overriding reasons for his failure to do so about which we can only speculate. When he initiated operations on the Sympolity's territory, he had hoped for quick and easy victories, which, admittedly, he did achieve in 228/227, just as the

[17]For example, Italy, an ally of the Axis during WWII, once her political hierarchy realised in 1943 CE that the Third Reich was losing the war, and after the Allies had landed in Sicily, rushed to overthrow the Fascist regime of Mussolini, joined the Western powers, declared war on Germany and restored democracy.

Germans had achieved in 1939–1941 CE with their *blitzkrieg*. Perhaps Cleomenes consequently became aware that he did not have enough military strength nor, equally significant, financial support to wage an extended campaign to break up the Sympolity before the Macedonians arrived on the scene.

Did he believe in a political solution that would serve Spartan interest? If so, he failed since during the years 225–223 when there were no large-scale military confrontations, Cleomenes was unreasonably inactive at the diplomatic level and failed to persuade the Achaean city-states that the programme he was proposing was feasible. Finally, which of the two conditions of war would prove more effective? Military power (with Cleomenes as warlord) or diplomacy (with Aratus as the seasoned diplomat)? In this case, diplomacy prevailed over military power as the decisive factor.

What followed is, for the most part, familiar, and we have already referred to the events at key points: Antigonus moved his troops into Sympolitan territory, clearing the city-states of their Spartan garrisons one by one. Cleomenes continued withdrawing to the south. Aratus once more drew disapproval, this time for not having done anything to prevent the murder of the Sympolity's sitting *strategos* Aristomachus, Argos' former tyrant, by an enraged mob (Plut. Arat. 44.6). In Plutarch's description, one can sense that the citizens of Argos had despaired over recent developments, taking out their frustrations on Aristomachus and his followers. According to Phylarchus, a chronicler of Cleomenes, Aristomachus was tortured before being put to death; Polybius (2.59) denies this.

That the Macedonian intervention in the region was accompanied, as one would have expected, by events that betrayed the fact that at that moment, the Sympolity was in a state of 'compromised national sovereignty' vis-à-vis Macedon is attested by the surrender of Corinth and the fortress of Acrocorinth to the Macedonians. Further evidence of that is provided by Macedon's stipulation that the wages of Macedonian troops were to be covered by the Sympolity, a ban on sending out missions to or drawing up treaties with third parties without the express permission of the Macedonian king, a demand that ceremonial sacrifices, processions and games be performed in honour of Antigonus, insistence that all statues of Argos' tyrants be restored and those of other revered past leaders of Argos be removed, as well as the arrest of certain anti-Macedonian elements of the city and their execution or delivery to the slave markets of Macedon and expropriation of their property (Plut. Arat. 45.5–7). The denial of the Sympolity's freedom to establish diplomatic ties with other states not approved by Macedon constituted a clear denial of a nation's right to have an independent government and not be reduced to the status of a protectorate. In effect, with its militarily weakened condition, the Sympolity was in no position to restrict Macedon's actions on its territory.

One by one, the city-states of the Sympolity renounced any pro-Spartan policy they may have had adopted. An exception was Arcadian Orchomenos, where Antigonus was forced to fight; resistance was crushed, and the city looted. In light of Orchomenos' fate, Mantinea quickly surrendered (Plut Ar. 45.6–9; Polyb. 2.56.1–9). Antigonus then cautiously proceeded throughout the Peloponnesus, clearing out pro-Spartan pockets of resistance, avoiding any hasty confrontations because Cleomenes continued to maintain strong support in many city-states. Antigonus' aim was first to clear the Peloponnesus of any Spartan remnants, then turn on his foe inside Laconia itself.

In the end, the new alliance's objective was achieved quickly as Antigonus' forces won their only encounter with Cleomenes' army, at Sellasia in 222 (Plut. Arat. 46.1), despite the Spartans' heroic resistance evoking memories of the grandeur of the old Sparta of the Archaic and Classical Periods. Antigonus fielded an army of 27,600 *hoplites*, 1200 horsemen, to Cleomenes' 20,000 infantry, in that final great battle between two Greek kingdoms, that of the north and that of the south. The Achaeans contributed a force of 4300 *hoplites* (Kralli 2017, p. 118). Cleomenes fled from Sparta, escaping to the court of the king of Hellenistic Egypt, Ptolemy IV Philopator, remaining there for 3 years, ostensibly as a guest, but in effect, a virtual prisoner. He attempted to stir up a rebellion by the Alexandrians against Ptolemy but failed and, soon after, in 219, committed suicide. Such was the inglorious fate of the last great ruler of Sparta.

Antigonus treated the Spartans with leniency, merely asking of them to restore the old governmental status quo, and insisting Sparta join the Sympolity (Plut. Cleo. 30.1). The laws of Lycurgus once again were set aside, and Sparta did join (Livy Hist. 38.34.3). As a member, she was obliged to adopt the Achaean 'constitution' and the gamut of legal and institutional provisions that entailed. As did the Romans later, Antigonus Doson's leniency towards the Spartans was not only based on magnanimity but cold calculation as well. If Sparta, the Sympolity's traditional and eternal rival, were to be weakened too much, it might have led to the Sympolity gaining too much power, something that ran counter to the Macedonians' overriding strategy for the Peloponnesus. The Sympolity's historic anti-Macedonian stance was not something Antigonus could ignore; for him, the Achaeans remained a precarious ally (Shimron 1972, p. 60). As a result, Antigonus did not resort to looting or other barbarities against Sparta, nor did he take any measures that would further weaken the kingdom.[18]

The Achaeans bestowed great honours on him for his actions. But, because of the rigours of the campaign in the Peloponnesus, Antigonus died and was replaced on the Macedonian throne by Philip V. At around the same time, the Aetolians began to launch raids on the Achaean territory, looting the cities of Dyme and Patras, and occupying the city of Messene. Because the Sympolity's *strategos* at that time was felt to be lazy and timid, his service was terminated 5 months before its end, and Aratus was once again elected in his place. However, his efforts to reverse recent developments failed. In the end, he was defeated by the Aetolians at Caphyae, not through any fault of his own, but because 'the Achaeans were untrained in body and

[18]This was the thinking, too, of the Allies after WWII in 1945. Germany, although responsible for the devastation of much of Europe for the second time in a single century, the Allies, taking into consideration the position of intellectuals such as J.M. Keynes, did not impose a new ultra-punitive treaty like that of Versailles after WWI (1919). With the Marshall Plan of 1948 and the Truman Doctrine, they provided considerable economic support to Western Germany so it could recover and join the ranks of the Western Alliance.

not concerned with war' (Plut. Arat. 47.1–5). Plutarch's comment reveals that at that time, the Achaean Sympolity did not have a viable armed force, mainly because its citizens did not seem to exhibit any will to fight on its behalf to save it. It was thus inevitable that the Achaeans would then appeal again for help from the Macedonians, handing them an opening to intervene directly in the politics and internal affairs of the Sympolity (Plut. Arat. 48). From 224 to 199, it remained a steadfast ally of the Macedonian Kingdom (Walbank 1993).

4.4 The Last Phase of the Life of Aratus: The Dream and the Reality

In contrast to their eminently capable fathers, the new Macedonian King, Philip V, and Aratus' neophyte politician son, Aratus the Younger, proved themselves very much unequal to the circumstances. Philip was never frank about his actual intentions vis-à-vis the Achaean Sympolity and actively interfered in its affairs. For example, in the case of the uprising in Messene, the manner in which he intervened ultimately led to an even wider chasm between the ruling class and the rest of people of the wider region of Messenia, instead of providing any real attempt at conciliation (Plut. Arat. 49.3–5). Philip applied the age-old strategy of divide and conquer to allow himself the excuse to intervene in the Sympolity's internal affairs and those of the Peloponnesus at large, aligning his actions with the interests of Macedon's overriding strategy regarding Southern Greece. A similar policy was followed later by the Romans, as we saw in detail in Chap. 2.

That Philip was not equal to the standard set by previous worthy kings of Macedon, neither in terms of leadership nor in terms of moral character, is attested to by Plutarch. In Arat. (50–52), he explains that Philip initially did follow Aratus' counsel because of the latter's undeniable stature, hoping to take advantage of the breadth of his experience in politics. However, once he felt firmly secure in his grip on power, he began to undercut Aratus because he felt him to be a hindrance to his own brazen behaviour, as well as to his efforts to interfere in the affairs of the Sympolity actively. As for his morals, Philip, for a spell, lived at the home of Aratus' son. During that time, he corrupted his host's wife and had an erotic liaison with her; he even seduced his host (49.2, 50.2–3)! That was how Philip honoured the home that was hosting him!

What is indisputable is that how Aratus met his death was a far cry from his value and contribution to his homeland. Plutarch (Ar. 51.4) mentions that as time passed, Philip became more and more tyrannical and morally corrupt. Deciding that the time had come for him to be rid of Aratus, Philip had the Macedonian *strategos* Taurion murder him discreetly, gradually poisoning him while Philip was far away in Macedon. Pretending to befriend Aratus, Taurion frequently shared meals with him, during which he secretly administered a slow-acting poison to his victim's food and drink. Aratus soon began to develop a fever that eventually rose; he developed a persistent cough and felt himself slowly weakening (52.3). He eventually realised what was transpiring but, too weak to resist, shortly before the end, in pain and coughing up blood, he confided to a friend, 'This is one's reward for befriending a king' (52.4).

He died in Aegion, the capital of the Sympolity, in 213. The Achaeans, acknowledging their great loss, wanted to honour Aratus' death in Aegion, but the citizens of his birthplace, Sicyon, insisted strongly he be buried there instead. Because burial within the city walls was considered sacrilege in Sicyon, the city appealed to the oracle at Delphi for a way around that. The oracle responded by advising that any place that hosted Aratus' body would be sacred; thus, there would be no sacrilege. Aratus' remains were interred at a central spot in Sicyon which was henceforth called the *Arateion*. For many years, he was attributed honours commemorating the day when he had returned to Sicyon from Argos, many years earlier, freeing the city from a tyranny that had lasted for decades.

Evaluating the aggregate work of Aratus, because that is the only fair way to judge a person, there is no doubt that he and Philopoemen, who we will examine in our next chapter, were the two greatest political figures of the Achaean Sympolity of the Hellenistic Period. Aratus was the benefactor of Sicyon, having delivered that city-state from tyranny, and the man most responsible for laying the groundwork for the political union of the Peloponnesus through the strengthening and political integration of the Sympolity. Aratus can be seen as one of the most prominent 'fathers of the Achaean political constitution'.

One final comment concerns to what extent the undeniably great work of Aratus actually took hold. Before he was murdered, Aratus had succeeded in ensuring the Sympolity would not be broken up as a result of the actions of Cleomenes III. But that had come at a great price: the Achaeans had been forced to appeal for support from the Kingdom of Macedon, which did provide that help but imposed onerous terms on the Sympolity. Aratus must have left life rather saddened since the future of the Sympolity remained uncertain. He may have felt that what he had created with such great effort and sacrifice had not borne the expected fruit. Had he not been murdered by Taurion, he may have been able to combine his name and actions with those of the other great political figure of the Achaean Sympolity, Philopoemen, who, at that time was on the 'ascendant', having already exhibited signs of his worth, and who Aratus in all probability had met. As will be explained in the next chapter, the commander of the Achaean armed forces who fought together with the Macedonians at Sellasia was Philopoemen. We consider it highly unlikely that he had not met the head of state at that time, Aratus.

The reemergence of the Achaean Sympolity that Aratus did not live to see would be ensured by Philopoemen in the years that followed.

Chapter 5
Philopoemen of Megalopolis: 'The Last Great Greek'

5.1 Preface to Sellacia: A New Great Leader Is Born

Philopoemen was born in Megalopolis, Arcadia in 253, the son of Crauges who Plutarch (Philop. 1.1) characterised as 'enlightened in every sense'. Crauges died when Philopoemen was a child and Cleandros, a friend of his father who was indebted to him, undertook the boy's upbringing. Even from an early age, Philopoemen showed signs of 'a brave and regal character' (1.2). As he grew, his education was undertaken by Ecdilus and Demophanes, followers of the philosopher Arcesilaus who, at the time, was the director of the Plato Academy in Athens.

One can surmise that the two prominent personalities of Megalopolis were both ardent democrats. According to Plutarch, it was they who liberated Megalopolis from tyrannical rule, instigating the assassination of the tyrant Aristodemus, and, helped by Aratus, ridding their city of his successor, his brother Nicocles (1.3–4). It was apparent that Philopoemen was weaned on this spirit of democratic ideals. Philopoemen's moral principles were extolled by Plutarch, who pointed out how much the young man attempted to emulate Epaminondas. Following in the Theban's footsteps, Philopoemen was a man of action, integrity and a strong moral character, a man both honest and prudent, unmoved by the lure of riches (Plut. Phil. 3.1). The fact that Philopoemen was so much admired, just as Aratus was before him, whose life and accomplishments had placed him high in the consciousness of friends and foes alike for his selfless and significant actions, this alone makes them worthy of praise. However, Plutarch also noted some less desirable qualities in his character, such as his tendency to become enraged, quick to argue and quarrel. When involved in political disputes, his behaviour was not always measured and charitable.

Philopoemen exhibited great zeal and aptitude in the art of warfare (3.2–3). His baptism by fire took place on the battlefield, participating with his fellow Megalopolitans in their marauding raids into Laconia. In these raids, he always took the lead during the attack and was the last to return (4.1–2). Plutarch's description illustrates the extent of the zeal the young man displayed for the adventure and excitement of

E. M. L. Economou, *The Achaean Federation in Ancient Greece*, Frontiers in Economic History, https://doi.org/10.1007/978-3-030-52697-9_5

actual battle and his aptitude for warfare; he deliberately chose to take on the most dangerous missions—the more daring, the better—both on the attack as well as the return. He took great care in maintaining himself in perfect physical condition, strong and robust, without excess body weight—always battle-ready; to that end, his spare time was devoted to either hunting or farming. He owned farmland not far away from Megalopolis that he visited every day, after either his morning or afternoon meal, where he would rest on a bed he had built made of branches. He rose early every morning and helped in the fields alongside the farmworkers or lent a hand herding cattle. He would later return to the city to involve himself with public affairs (4.3).

Any income derived from his military campaigns was spent on the purchase of horses and arms or for ransoming prisoners of war. Only his farm's income was allocated to his own well-being (4.4–5). To further his military education, he followed relevant discussions and read the works of philosophers. His favourite book was the *Taktika* of Euangelus, a military author who wrote about Alexander the Great. The first signs of Philopoemen's authentic military prowess were made evident by what transpired at the Battle of Sellasia (222), where the Megalopolitans with Philopoemen in the lead engaged with the Cleomenes' army. During the battle, he took the initiative, and in a very bold and dangerous action, launched an attack on the lightly armed soldiers of the Lacedaemonians, inspiring his fellow citizens to follow him. Philopoemen's action had not been approved by the commander of the combined Achaean–Macedonian forces, King Antigonus III Doson, who considered the young man's plan reckless. It was not so much Philopoemen's youth that caused the king to reject the proposal but the fact that it came from someone who had not yet proved himself; thus, it lacked the validity of seasoned experience. Of course, the action might not have had the success it achieved had Philopoemen been unable to bolster his men's morale and inspire them.

To encourage his men forward to engage the enemy, he dismounted and ran ahead. As a cavalryman, he was equipped with heavier armour and weapons than the *hoplites* he faced and, with total disregard for his safety, defying all odds, he forged ahead, fighting the enemy over difficult terrain, full of gullies and canyons until he was wounded. A light lance passed through both his thighs, pinning them together (6.6–9). The pain must have been excruciating; nevertheless, he insisted on removing the lance by shaking his legs until it broke in two and then having his men pull out the two pieces. Instead of withdrawing from the battlefield, given the severity of his wounds, according to Plutarch (6.8–9), he gathered his physical and mental strength and returned to the battle in full force. Philopoemen's action was instrumental in the successful outcome of the battle. Antigonus' men declared they had been swept into the fray by the young Megalopolitan horseman's enthusiasm. It was only natural that Philopoemen acquired a glorious reputation and widespread fame as a result. Antigonus asked him to remain in his army, offering a high command and wealth (7.1). Plutarch (7.1–3) notes that Philopoemen refused the offer, preferring to remain faithful to his choice of being a loyal soldier of Megalopolis and the Sympolity. So as not to stay inactive, he chose to leave for Crete. It is said that he probably fought there as a mercenary in the wars between the island's city-states.

While there, he certainly improved his military skills as he associated mainly with military combatants, men of sound mind, austere in their way of life. When he finally returned to Achaea, he assumed command of the Sympolity's cavalry.[1]

Upon his return to Achaea, and having added to his fame with his exploits in Crete, Philopoemen, newly appointed *ipparchos* of the Achaean Sympolity at the age of 31, threw himself with great zeal into the radical reorganisation of the cavalry. He had been handed an organisation in total disarray: the horses were unfit for battle while the men themselves were lazy, unmotivated and lacking any sense of duty. Plutarch gives us a socio-economic dimension to the cavalry's problem: just as what most likely prevailed throughout the Hellenistic states of the period, the cavalry was made up of members of the wealthy class. No commander was willing to clash with members of his own class (7.5) despite being aware of the cavalry's dismal state. Philopoemen, however, was no ordinary man! To him, mediocrity was anathema, and he was not about to put up with it. He never backed away from what he believed to be right, never yielding to any kind of pressure. With great determination, he toured the Sympolity's city-states to seek recruits, appealing to the sense of honour of every young man. In training, he instituted military exercises that included parades and games among the cavalrymen, turning the sessions into spectacles with bystanders present to encourage the men. Within a very short time, the state of the cavalry improved drastically, undergoing a complete reversal. The formerly spoilt, lackadaisical and unmotivated young well-to-do Achaean cavalrymen had been transformed into an exceptionally intrepid and willing fighting force. Their skills now finely honed, they had become a very quick and adaptable unit, capable of executing successful manoeuvres, moving rapidly in tight formation, so cohesive that it seemed to surge forward like a single giant fist (7.6–7). The Achaeans considered the metamorphosis of their cavalry from an underperforming military tool into a formidable fighting war machine no small feat.

The next reference to Philopoemen occurs during the war between the two neighbouring sympolities, the Aetolian and Achaean, during the so-called Social War (220–217). In this new, significant conflict, the Achaean Sympolity allied with the Macedonian king, Phillip V, to confront the Aetolian Sympolity. Following the Achaeans' victory, the defeated Aetolians turned for support to Rome which, meanwhile, had been searching for an excuse to intervene in Greek affairs. In the end, it were the Greeks themselves, worn out by internal strife, who were responsible for opening Greece's doors to the Roman invader, as discussed in Chap. 2, whose initial approach in her intervention into Greek affairs was to function in the role of referee.

On one occasion during the Social War, Philopoemen, commanding the Achaean cavalry, confronted a force of Aetolians and their allies, the Elians, near the Larissos River.[2] The clash was particularly brutal. Plutarch (7.7–8) does not clarify the makeup of the opposing forces but does tell us of an Elian cavalry commander,

[1] He assumed the rank of *ipparchos,* as will be discussed in Sects. 6.1 and 6.4.

[2] According to Strabo, the cities of Dyme and Achaean Larissa were near this river.

Demophantes, who took it upon himself to attack Philopoemen directly. Stepping out of his formation, he headed on his own straight for the Achaean who warded off the Elian's attack and killed him with his *sarisa.* Demophantos' compatriots, seeing this, chose immediately to withdraw from the fray. This was yet another victory for Philopoemen, further enhancing his reputation. As Plutarch (7.8–9) points out, despite his youth, the Megalopolitan did not lack either the courage or the wisdom of any of his older fellow officers. He was a tactical genius who had an instinct for making the right battlefield decisions. He had successfully reorganised the army and whipped his troops into a capable fighting machine, a match for any adversary. Strong leadership is crucial in securing victory, as a commander, personally leading his troops into battle, sets the example by his bravery, encouraging his men and instilling fear in the enemy (Plutarch Phil. 8.4–7).

It is clear that when troops feel their commander is a born-to-win master warrior such as the likes of Cleomenes or Philopoemen, they tend to be less fearful, more confident, shedding some of the anxiety associated with the fear of dying, transforming their uneasiness before going into battle into positive energy. In short, an army that identifies with its leader is willing to sacrifice for him since it fights for him. Without a doubt, Philopoemen, with his leadership qualities and his emblematic personality, had succeeded in transforming those indifferent rich young men into a force to be reckoned with—an exceptional battle-ready cavalry.

5.2 Philopoemen Becomes *Strategos* of the Achaean Sympolity, Increasing His Military Power Considerably

In recognition of Philopoemen's contribution to the Sympolity, the Achaeans honoured him by electing him *strategos* in 208 (Polyb. 11.9.1–10; Plut. Phil. 9; Paus. 8.50.1; Anderson 1967; Errington 1969, pp. 62–66). Upon his election, and with the blessing of the Achaean's military hierarchy, Philopoemen undertook to transform the Sympolity's whole army radically. Up to that point, the army's battle worthiness had been well below par, its arms dated and inadequate, its tactics old-fashioned and no longer equal to circumstances. He introduced new types of weaponry and armour, abolishing the small, light, thin shield which did little to protect the body, as well as the short spear that was no match for the Macedonian *sarissas* (Fig. 1.2).

The Achaean army was little more than a lightly armed force in contrast to Macedon's 'heavy infantry'. Philopoemen also realised that the Achaeans were not training their troops in carrying out specialised tactical manoeuvres, nor did their *phalanx* have a strong front line and the necessary cohesion like that of the Macedonians. In battle, it was easily penetrated and overwhelmed by an adversary. Aware of these failings, he undertook to persuade the Achaeans of the necessity of developing a 'heavy infantry' along the lines of the Macedonian *phalanx* which, together with the Roman *legion*, at the time, was the most potent battle formation, a formidable force. Successful in convincing those of military age to bear arms, Philopoemen then turned his efforts to deal with the psychology and low morale of the rank and file, helping to give them renewed courage, as if they had become invincible, and then change from their previous way of life that had been one of luxury and pleasures.

Philopoemen's significant reforms, with their various social aspects, related to the general behaviour and customs of the Achaeans and were described by both Pausanias and Polybius (Polyb. 11.9.1–10.9; Plut. Phil.7.6–7; Paus. 8.50.1).[3] His efforts bore fruit quickly when the combined Macedonian and Achaean cavalry defeated the Elians in the summer of 209 (Livy 27.31.9–11; Plut. Phil. 7.6–7). In 208, in a battle at Mantineia, Sparta and the Achaean Sympolity clashed again, evidence that Sparta still possessed a military force to be reckoned with, at least within the givens of the Peloponnesus. Sparta's head of state at the time was the tyrant Machanidas who had come into power the year before. Walbank (1967, p. 282) estimates that the forces of the two adversaries were equally matched in numbers, about 14,000 on each side. Philopoemen, with his courage and military expertise, led the Achaeans to victory. The Spartans lost more than 4000 men on the battlefield, including Machanidas who was killed in action by the hand of Philopoemen himself (Plut. Phil. 10; Polyb. 11.11–18).

The battle of Mantineia had significant repercussions for both the victors and the vanquished. For the Achaeans, this was the first time the Sympolity had managed to achieve a victory of such proportions against such a powerful adversary. According to Errington (1969, pp. 66–67), this victory served to mark the beginning of the end of the Macedonian Kingdom's manipulation of the Sympolity. What was more, the losers suffered heavy losses. Although the defeat may not have dimmed the Spartans' morale, those losses were too great for the city-state ever to recoup. From that time on, the Spartan army avoided engaging in pitched battles. It would not be an exaggeration to claim that Philopoemen, from 209 on, having assumed the highest office of the Sympolity, with his decisions, choices and policy measures, had created a new state of affairs in Achaea. Step by step, he had succeeded in transforming the prevailing attitudes of excess, faint-heartedness and intolerance of militarism into virtues. A propensity for taking on challenges now bonded the Achaean *hoplites*, inspired by lofty ideals such as patriotism, a newly developed sense of social responsibility and altruism, endowing them with a true spirit of camaraderie. The Achaeans, acknowledging the contribution of their great new leader who had given them such a significant victory, wished to honour him during the festival of Nemea. But, as Plutarch (Phil. 11.1–2) describes, Philopoemen was not a person to rest on his laurels; apparently, his soul and his mind were aflame with passion for new glory. So, as the lyrist Pylades began to sing the *Persians* by the poet Timotheus from Miletus:

> ...all the spectators turned their eyes upon Philopoemen and gave him glad applause; for in their hopes the Greeks were recovering their ancient dignity, and in their courage, they were

[3] See also, Anderson (1967) and Errington (1969, p. 63).

> making the nearest approach to the high spirit of their fathers. But when it came to perils and battles, just as young horses long for their accustomed riders, and if they have others on their backs, are shy and wild, so the Achaean army, when someone other than Philopoemen was commander-in-chief, would be out of heart, would keep looking eagerly for him, and if he but came in sight, would at once be alert and efficient because of the courage he inspired. For they perceived he was the one general whom their enemies were unable to face, and whose name and fame they feared, as was evident from what they did. (Plut. Phil. 11.3-12.1)

It was therefore understandable that all acclaimed Philopoemen at the Nemean festival; the Achaeans had begun to take courage, seeing in his person a leader equal to the legendary heroes of the past. The Macedonian king, Phillip V, observing the speed with which the strength and influence of the Achaean Sympolity were expanding because of Philopoemen's activities, sent men to Argos to assassinate him. When the king's plans came to light, he was reviled by all the other Greeks (Plut. Phil. 12.2). An excellent example of the extent of Philopoemen's impact was on the occasion when the Boeotians laid siege to Megara; a false rumour circulated that an army led by Philopoemen himself was headed their way to engage them in battle. The result was that the Boeotians immediately turned tail and fled, even abandoning their ladders resting against the city walls (12.3)!

On another occasion, when Nabis succeeded Mahanidas as tyrant of Sparta in 202, he mobilised his forces and occupied Messene. Lysippus, the *strategos* of the Achaeans at the time, decided not to move against him despite Philopoemen's insistence. His 1-year term as army commander over, acting as a private citizen, he called to arms his loyal fellow-citizens of Megalopolis and rushed to the Messenians' aid. As soon as Nabis heard that Philopoemen was advancing with a military unit and was closing in rapidly, he secretly abandoned the city in a panic together with his men, terrified at the mere thought of coming face to face with Philopoemen. He considered himself lucky that he managed to get away (12.4–6)! This event was indicative of the fear and awe the name Philopoemen instilled in his adversaries.[4]

Why did the Achaean *strategos* Lysippus not act and prevent Philopoemen from acting on his own? Was he afraid he might have faced defeat or was it that he did not think much of the idea of putting the Sympolity in harm's way because of something that, officially at least, was of no concern to the Sympolity at that time?[5] This is one more question which cannot be answered because of the lack of verifiable sources. The following year, 201/202, Philopoemen was again elected *strategos* and, indomitable as ever, continued the war against Nabis, carrying hostilities over into Laconia itself. Because of the Achaeans' superior organisation and discipline, his forces quickly advanced all the way to Sellasia, defeating a mercenary detachment near the town of Pellana (Polyb. 16.36–37). However, Philopoemen's success was rather short-lived as the next year, 200, Nabis resumed his raids into Megalopolis.

[4]Archaeological findings have not rescued any portrait or statue representing Philopoemen. A modern statue of Philopoemen depicting him in his old age is in the Louvre Museum. See: https://www.louvre.fr/en/oeuvre-notices/philopoemen

[5]Messene did not join the Sympolity until 191.

Heeding an appeal for assistance by the citizens of Gortyna on Crete, Philopoemen accepted the appointment of *strategos* of that city-state. That earned him the disapproval of his fellow citizens who accused him of abandoning his homeland. The situation in Megalopolis became extremely dire, even touch and go for the town and its citizens. The Megalopolitans were trapped behind the city walls, resorting to growing their own vegetables along the city's alleyways to survive, while the countryside was devastated (Plut. Phil. 13.2).

There are some discrepancies in these accounts, concealing what we believe are some crucial questions. It seems odd that while a Megalopolitan army, led by Philopoemen, had driven out the Spartans in 202, only 2 years later, Megalopolis found herself in such a desperate state. What had happened? How did Nabis manage in less than 2 years to raise an army, the might of which put the Megalopolitans in such a difficult position, forced behind their city walls to save themselves? Was it they were so terrified because Philopoemen was no longer there to lead them?

Moreover, as the Achaean Sympolity's armed forces had been completely restructured and proven their effectiveness, first, at the Battle of Mantinea in 208, and again, at the Battle of Pellana in 201, why did they not come to Megalopolis' defence in a situation which constituted a 'constitutional' obligation of the Sympolity towards a member city-state? Why did Cycliadas, the *strategos* at the time, most likely with the blessing of the Sympolity's governing body, refuse to come to Megalopolis' aid? Even if there were serious concerns regarding providing that aid, perhaps related to the balance of power in the region, why did he not deploy some units to harass the besiegers or at least attempt to set up a supply line into the city to provide food and weapons to her desperate citizens?

Could it have been that the Achaeans were seeking to take advantage of the opportunity to weaken Megalopolis to the point of collapse, then step in at the last minute, saviours to the rescue? Perhaps the Achaean federal government policymakers felt that a powerful Megalopolis in the future would be in a position to affect the balance of power within the Sympolity, shifting its centre of power from the north—the locus of cities that formed the nucleus around which the federation had emerged—to south. The geostrategic importance of this city-state as the first line of defence against Sparta was such that it offered her a position of strength within the Sympolity. Were the latter's leaders afraid that Megalopolis would evolve into a Peloponnesian 'Thebes'?[6] Was a shift in power from north to south a real possibility? Were that to happen, it would mean a redistribution of privileges between the various powerful groups within the Sympolity.

As it turned out, after 209 and until 146, most of the Sympolity's *strategoi,* such as Aristaenus, Lycortas, Diaeus and Critolaus, were from Megalopolis—and some of them were even elected to that office more than once. Even other *strategoi* of that

[6]As already mentioned, Thebes was the capital of the Boeotian *Koinon*. At least during the time of the peak of her powers, during the fourth and third centuries, as the most powerful of the member city-states, she had been able to manipulate the federal Boeotoian institutions (Larsen 1968; Buckler 1980).

time, like Archon, may have been Megalopolitans as well. In the past, during the period 370–234, Megalopolis had been the capital of the Arcadian Sympolity which was then absorbed by the Achaean. Kralli (2017, p. 149) notes that Megalopolis was undoubtedly a formidable city-state in terms of territory and population, consisting of several communities, and there are indications that it had always exercised an expansionist policy within Arcadia.

That the Sympolity's policymakers were either reluctant or incapable to handle the situation with Nabis with resolve was obvious. Perhaps Nabis' military might was too much for the Sympolity to handle. However, given the Sympolity's recent reorganisation of its armed forces, mentioned above, that is unlikely. When the Second Macedonian War[7] broke out that very same year, Philip V proposed the Achaeans join him to fight the Romans, in exchange for helping them get rid of Nabis, expecting them to jump at the opportunity. The Achaeans found themselves in a dilemma. The so-called Pan–Hellenic alliance established by Antigonus III was officially still in effect, and the Sympolity was a significant member. At the meeting that took place in Argos, after weighing all the facts, for and against, they concluded they feared the Romans more than the Spartans. Though their response to the Macedonian king was evasive, in effect, they rejected his offer.

Meanwhile, Philopoemen had returned to Megalopolis from Crete. The Achaeans, blaming him for their problem with Nabis, denounced him as a foreigner and tried to have him expelled. The Sympolity's government, however, did not allow that and instead despatched an envoy to Megalopolis, the serving *strategos,* Aristaenus, who made sure that the decree was not executed, even though Philopoemen was his political rival (Plut. Phil. 13.6–7).[8] Philopoemen had returned at a time when the Achaeans, together with their new allies, the Romans, were at war with Nabis. Plutarch (Phil. 14.2) writes that a little after the above events took place, he was again appointed *strategos*, indicating that the Achaeans did an incredible reversal in their opinion of him, once more showing him the appreciation and respect he was due.

Following this, Philopoemen gathered his forces in Tegea and invaded Laconia to put an end to the siege of Gytheion. Nabis, however, succeeded in occupying that city and then turned to march against Philopoemen's army. After numerous clashes over the next 2 days, the Achaean army prevailed, with the Spartans having lost three-fourth of their total forces. Nabis, together with the remnants of his army, was

[7] The Macedonian Wars were a series of conflicts between the Roman Republic and the Kingdom of Macedon. The Battle of Cynoscephalae took place in 197 during the Second War (200–196) where Philip's army was crushed, resulting in the Treaty of Tempe which forbade Macedon from interfering in any affairs beyond her borders, a term which Philip upheld until his death. In 194, Rome declared Greece's independence and withdrew her troops from the Balkans. On the surface, it appeared that Rome no longer had any interest in the region.

[8] Just one example of how 'short-sighted' a people can be. Another example of a radical reversal in the public consciousness for a personality initially admired is that of Themistocles who was lionised at first, but then despised and reviled, ending up an exile in Persia where he died years later, by some accounts, forced to drink hemlock.

in full retreat, heading back to Sparta. They barricaded themselves behind the city walls while the Sympolity's army plundered and pillaged Laconia at will for a month, without facing any resistance (Liv. Hist. 35.12, 35.27–30). Nabis finally signed a treaty with the Romans, only to be assassinated a short time later by the Aetolians, in 192 (Plut. Phil. 15.1–3).

It is clear that during that period, Sparta was at war with the Achaean Sympolity as well as battling Roman units in the Peloponnesus. During the unrest that followed the assassination of Nabis, Philopoemen took full advantage of the situation, seizing the opportunity to incorporate Sparta into the Achaean Sympolity. But he showed no interest in interfering in the city's local affairs, nor in making demands for territory. Perhaps Philopoemen, savvy politician that he was, wisely looking ahead to the future, realised that Sparta joining the Sympolity would only be sustainable if the Spartans did not consider their participation as subjugation, but instead saw it as an opportunity. It seems that this was how he dealt with the defeated Spartans, in a conciliatory, moderate manner, instead of imposing his will by use of military force.

After this, Philopoemen's reputation was enhanced even further. His success was no small matter, as not only did he succeed in solving one of the Sympolity's most significant age-old problems—security—he also succeeded in incorporating all the geographical territory constituting the Southeast Peloponnesus into the Sympolity (see Fig. 1.1). Even the *aristoi*, that is to say, Sparta's wealthiest citizens, praised this action, hoping to curry his favour (Plut. Phil. 15.5). It was evident they felt secure in the belief that Philopoemen, though an exceptionally competent polemarch, was not a social reformer-visionary like Agis IV, Cleomenes III or Nabis. In this context, for them, this exceptional foreigner was a lesser threat than their previous visionary leaders. Like Aratus before him, Philopoemen was not envisioning socio-economic change, but rather the Sympolity's consolidation through the unification of the whole of the Peloponnese under its umbrella, something which did not clash with the financial interests of the *aristoi*.

Nevertheless, in the spring of 191, the Spartans withdrew from the Achaean Sympolity, without having completed even 1 year as a member city-state. Diophanes, the Sympolity's *strategos* at the time, wanting to set an example, decided to punish the Spartans by collaborating with Rome's forces in Greece. Against Philopoemen's advice to exercise caution as a joint intervention by the Sympolity and Rome, although ensuring Achaean sovereignty over Sparta, would again allow the Romans to interfere in the Sympolity's internal affairs, Diophanes proceeded anyway and, entering Laconia together with the Roman legate, Titus Flamininus, prepared to attack Sparta (16.1–2). The Romans' involvement was ostensibly to provide support to their ally, the Achaean Sympolity. In effect, however, their intervention was just one more excuse to meddle in Peloponnesian affairs.

Philopoemen, however, did not just sit back and do nothing. Even though at the time he was only a private citizen, between terms as *strategos*, he took the initiative and headed for Sparta. He consequently not only succeeded in obstructing the Achaean and Roman joint effort against the city-state and put an end to the prevailing unrest, he even convinced the Spartans to rejoin the Sympolity (16.3–4). A short time later, however, before autumn of that same year, supporters of Nabis overthrew Sparta's pro-Archaean faction, driving them out of the city. The Spartans went even further: in the winter of 191–190, they sent a delegation to Rome demanding the return of some neighbouring territories as well as the five hostages Flamininus had come away with as part of the arrangement Philopoemen had achieved a few months earlier.

The fact that Sparta had addressed their demands to Rome provides evidence of two things. First, Sparta, in essence, did not recognise Achaean jurisdiction over their territory, and second, on another level, the Hellenistic world was now headed on a 'course of no return': the conscious acceptance of Rome as the primary regulator and arbitrator of Greek affairs. The Spartans saw only the tree and not the whole forest. By asking the Romans to mediate in their favour, they may have gained on a local level in the short term. Longer term, however, their insular, opportunistic policy, whether intentionally or not, contributed to the mortgaging and undermining of the independence of the Peloponnesus as a whole.

In the end, the Romans agreed only to Sparta's second demand. They returned the hostages, probably considering that satisfying the first demand would bring them in direct conflict with the Sympolity which, at the time, was not something they wanted to do. Meanwhile, the situation between the Sympolity and Sparta, its member-in-name-only, had degenerated into a smouldering dispute, reaching a peak in the autumn of 189 when remnants of the late Nabis' inner circle persuaded their compatriots to occupy all the neighbouring towns populated by pro-Achaean sympathisers. Initially, they attacked and occupied Las, a town southwest of Gytheion where their exiled fellow countrymen had settled. However, the pro-Achaean Spartan exiles, together with their neighbours, succeeded in driving them out.

Philopoemen demanded the Spartans hand over all those who were responsible for the affair. They refused and, exacerbating the situation, in an outburst of rage, killed 30 supporters of the pro-Achaean group in Sparta. According to Livy (38.30.6–7), lacking the military might of yore, and confronting the Achaean Sympolity militarily was out of the question, Sparta turned once again to the Romans to act as an intermediary. Philopoemen took immediate action, probably intending to forestall any meddling by Rome. He invaded Laconia, plundering and pillaging; the arrival of winter, however, postponed further action. Thus, the situation was not resolved by the use of arms, and the Romans were once again able to insert themselves into Peloponnesian affairs. The Spartans appealed to the Roman Senate while the Achaeans, under Philopoemen's friend, Lycortas, argued that Rome had no right to intervene in the Sympolity's internal affairs.

According to Livy (38.32.10), the Senate's verdict was ambiguous, presented in such a way that the Achaeans interpreted it as acceptance of their claims. At the same time, the Spartans were left believing they did not have to give the Achaeans everything they had demanded. We believe that Livy's view was accurate. As analysed in Chap. 1, the Romans had one overriding strategy they applied in Greece: divide and rule. From time to time supporting one side or the other, their long-term goal was to weaken all the players progressively. This resulted in the gradual loss of power along with any desire to resist, forcing those players to submit to Rome's will and her long-term plans for conquest—'ripe fruit ready for the picking'.

Philopoemen, as a skilful military commander and keen strategist, as well as an astute analyst of the geo-strategical situation, had more than likely perceived the above. Aware of the ancient saying, 'idleness is the root of all evil', he decided to take immediate action. Instead of accepting a political solution, where it would have been certain that any benefits or advantages would have had to be shared among the three parties involved—the Achaeans, Spartans and Romans—he opted for aggressive action. He believed taking the initiative with a bold move would greatly favour the Achaean Sympolity. So, as Philopoemen himself was physically active and tireless, in May of 188, he ordered the city walls torn down, appropriated a large section of Laconian territory from Spartan administration, restoring it to Megalopolis, and also abolished all the social reforms set in place by Nabis, dismissing all *helots* and mercenaries who had served in the Spartan army. These last unfortunately met with an even worse fate, as the Achaeans hunted them down, capturing about 3000 of them and selling them into slavery (Plut. Phil. 16.4–5).

Philopoemen did not stop there. Sparta's humiliation and exemplary punishment were not enough. He allowed the return to the city of all exiles. He abolished, too, many local customs, like the *agoge* for boys, established originally by the lawgiver Lycurgus in the seventh century, as well as the *syssitia,* replacing them with Achaean equivalents. According to Plutarch (16.9), Philopoemen intended that all characteristics which had formed the unique nature of Sparta and its people would be forever erased. However, the Romans later helped the Spartans reclaim their customs, not because they recognised the moral or political right of the Spartan people to have them—that was of no interest to them—but more to impede the Achaean Sympolity from becoming too powerful.

Philopoemen had grasped the new state of affairs created by Rome's behaviour when dealing with the Greek world. However, being a savvy realist, he knew when to back down and accept certain situations, fully aware of the Romans' military superiority. On the other hand, he tried hard to maintain outward appearances and defend the Achaean Sympolity's independence, offering resistance whenever possible. In our opinion, he was following Thucydides' unwritten 'golden rule of geopolitics': 'the powerful impose their will on others as far as their might will allow it, while the weak accept and back down as far as their weakness requires them to do'.[9]

Philopoemen, Lycortas and all the other policymakers who belonged to the group that favoured an independent foreign policy were continually working to motivate the Achaeans in favour of independence and against Roman intervention in their internal affairs. Because of this, Philopoemen very often clashed with the group of Achaean politicians who were pro-Rome. A characteristic example is an incident that occurred when Aristaenus from Megalopolis, one of the most powerful and influential Achaeans, was urging his compatriots not to go against the Romans, not

[9]See in Thucydides' *Histories* (5. 84–116), the so-called *Melian Dialogue.*

even to displease them. Philopoemen angrily responded: 'Man, why are you in such a hurry to see the day that seals the fate of Greece?' (Larsen 1968, p. 227). Another incident occurred when the Roman general Manius, who had defeated Antiochus III's Seleucid forces in 192 near Thermopylae, and Titus Flamininus, insisted on returning certain exiled Lacedaemonians to Sparta, and Philopoemen refused to allow it. The following year, when Philopoemen was *strategos* once more, he repatriated them himself, in an attempt to give the impression that this was being carried out solely by the Achaean Sympolity (Plut. Phil. 18.4–7), even though it indirectly satisfied the Roman demand. Philopoemen wished in every way to show and also force the Romans to respect the national sovereignty of the Achaean Sympolity and not interfere in its internal affairs.

5.3 The Inglorious End of a Glorious Old General

In 183, Philopoemen, now aged 70, was once again elected *strategos*. It was evident that, at that late age, having endured a lifetime of hardships, albeit of his own making, he no longer possessed his trademark physical strength of earlier times. His indomitable will and zeal, however, were undiminished. Where he had hoped that his service would be relatively uneventful, it instead was destined to be his last command, one that turned out to be accompanied by insufferable pain and anguish.

Deinocrates of Messene, an enemy of Philopoemen, renowned for his malice and debauchery, on the heels of a successful coup by oligarchic circles leading to the overthrow of the city-state's democratic regime, convinced his compatriots to break away from the Sympolity (Freeman [1893] 2013, p. 636). In an act of aggression, he attempted to occupy the town of Colonida. Philopoemen was in Argos at the time, on the other side of the Peloponnese. When he learned of the Messenian's actions, even though running a high fever, he decided to act immediately. He marched over 300 *stadia* (approximately 55 km) in 1 day to reach Megalopolis. Once there, he gathered a force of volunteer horsemen, eager to serve under the great *strategos*, and headed for Messene. Near Mount Euandrou, they clashed with Deinocrates' forces, defeating them and forcing them to turn tail and flee (Plut. Phil. 18.1–5).

Philopoemen's handling of Deinocrates' apostasy was problematic from the start. As commander of the Sympolity's armed forces, why did Philopoemen not mobilise, if not all his army, at least a few of its units, preferring instead to rely only on his Megalopolitan compatriots? One reason may have been that Philopoemen, based on his vast experience together with the available information, decided that Deinocrates' forces were not much of a threat—neither in quantity nor quality—and that he could defeat them quickly, by mobilising only the local federal forces from Megalopolis. Even if he had wanted to gather troops from other regions, in all probability, he would have risked losing valuable time, which Deinocrates would no doubt have exploited, and which might have reinforced his anti-Achaean insurgency.

However, 500 men who had been left behind to guard Messene suddenly appeared on the battlefield. Gathering heart, the scattered Messenian troops regrouped, coalescing around the 500, forming a renewed fighting force. Observing this, Philopoemen reassessed his position and most likely fearing being surrounded, ordered the retreat, unwilling to sacrifice his cavalry. He was the last to withdraw, attempting to draw the enemy's attention on him alone so that his men could pull back safely. The Messenians, not daring to attack him head-on, took to shouting at him from a safe distance while circling him on their horses (18.5). Plutarch continues (18.6–8):

> Withdrawing from the line frequently, then, to spare his young men, and sending them one by one into safety, before he was aware of it, he was left alone among numerous enemies. Even then no one ventured to come to close quarters with him, but he was pelted with missiles from a distance and forced upon rocky and precipitous places so that he had difficulty in managing his horse and kept tearing him with the spur. His age, owing to his generous exercise, was not burdensome, and in no way impeded his escape; but at that time his body was enfeebled with sickness and worn out with a long journey, so he was heavy and stiff, and at length, his horse stumbled and threw him to the ground. His fall was a heavy one, and his head was hurt, and he lay for a long time speechless so that his enemies thought him dead and tried to turn his body over and strip him of his armour. But when he raised his head and opened his eyes, they threw themselves in a throng upon him, tied his hands behind his back, and led him away, treating with great insolence and contumely a man who could never have even dreamed he would suffer such a fate at the hands of Deinocrates.

It is evident that Philopoemen had miscalculated the ultimate size of the enemy's force, But, proving what a great leader he was, magnanimously, he refused to abandon his men, an act of great valour. At that moment, it should have been of primary importance for him to have saved himself, given that not only was he the commander-in-chief of the federal armed forces, he was also the head of state. Thus, Plutarch shows us yet another side to Philopoemen: his altruistic character—personal sacrifice for the common good. Philopoemen's actions were somewhat like those of a 'father-protector' of his troops, willing to sacrifice his life for them. When the people of Messene heard what had transpired, they were overcome with joy and filled with pride. They rushed to gather at the city gates to witness the return of their troops.

> ... wonderfully elated at the news.... But when they saw Philopoemen dragged along in a manner unworthy of his fame and of his former exploits and trophies, most of them were struck with pity and felt sympathy for him, so that they actually shed tears and spoke with bitterness of the inconstancy and vanity of human greatness. (Plut. Phil. 19.1)

As usually is the case in such situations, some people with extremely low morals demanded that Deinocrates have Philopoemen tortured and then executed. They believed that if Philopoemen ever managed to escape, he would be unforgiving and ruthlessly vengeful, and Deinocrates would have to answer for that. The decision was eventually taken to move him to the *thesaurus,* an underground structure without light or fresh air, its entrance sealed shut by a huge boulder and surrounded by armed guards (19.3–4). Meanwhile, the surviving members of Philopoemen's cavalry had regrouped and realised their commander was not among them. Convinced he had been killed, they berated themselves: how shameful and unjust it was that they had survived while leaving behind their leader, who had no regard for his own safety, in the enemy's hands. When they discovered that Philopoemen had been captured and was being held prisoner, they spread the news throughout the Sympolity. The Achaeans saw this as a terrible calamity and sent an envoy demanding the release of Philopoemen. Meanwhile, they began to mobilise their forces, planning their military campaign against Messene (19.5).

As soon as night had fallen and the crowds had dispersed, Deinocrates, fearing time would be to Philopoemen's advantage, sent a public servant with a vial of poison to the *thesaurus* with orders to administer it to Philopoemen and remain with him until the end. Philopoemen was not asleep but was stretched out on his cape, depressed and agitated. As soon as the great commander noticed the boulder had been moved and perceived the figure of the servant approach, despite his weakness, he made an effort and sat up. He took the vial of poison. Aware of what it meant, he asked the man if he had heard any news of the Achaean cavalrymen, and mainly his friend Lycortas. Plutarch gives us the following description of what followed (20.2–3):

> . . .and on being told by him that the greater part of them had escaped, he nodded his head, and with a kindly look at the man said to him: 'That is good news, if we have not wholly lost.' Without another word and even without a sigh, he drained the cup and laid himself down again. He did not give the poison much to do, but breathed his last speedily, so weak was he.

Even in his last moments, he placed duty and the fate of his compatriots over and above his own survival! Never once did he ask to see a Messenian official, nor lose his dignity by stooping to ask his arch-enemy Deinocrates to meet with him, to plead for mercy or attempt to negotiate with him for his life, given his immense political weight. On the contrary, an honourable man, he acknowledged the cost of his actions and stoically faced his cruel and prescribed fate. Without doubt, an admirable leader, Philopoemen possessed the purest of souls and a steadfast character, a rare gift in those days, and today more relevant than ever for a modern democratic society in the global arena. He was a patriotic soldier, a true supporter of the Sympolity's democratic ideals to the very end. Even in that, his last act, he distinguished himself as a heroic, dignified and magnificent hero.

The news of Philopoemen's inglorious end shocked the Achaeans, and they were overcome with grief (21.1), a justifiable reaction to the loss of such an outstanding man. With Lycortas,[10] their new *strategos*, at the head, they marched against Messene, laying waste to the country until the Messenians capitulated (20.1). This point is unclear but most likely implies that they agreed to put an end to their revolt and rejoin the Sympolity, this time under precise terms and procedures. As discussed earlier, thanks to Philopoemen, the remaining regions of the Peloponnesus (Laconia,

[10]The procedure whereby the Sympolity replaced a *strategos* or other elected member of the government who died while serving is not described so clearly from the sources. We believe that an extraordinary federal Assembly known as *synkletos* was called for the election of a new leader by vote. We revert to this in Sect. 6.1.

Sparta, Messenia, Elis) had been incorporated into the Achaean Sympolity almost a decade earlier, in 191.

Deinocrates took the easy way out and took his own life, while those that had conspired with him in Philopoemen's death were all executed. Those who had called for him to be tortured were also put to death by Lycortas, condemned on the specific charge of torture (20.2). Such was the fate of Philopoemen's murderers, disgraced and made to suffer a horrible end, forever remembered as the executioners of a great man. Philopoemen was cremated, his ashes placed in an urn and returned to Megalopolis. It was a strange procession to behold, of men wearing wreaths commemorating the victories over the Messenians, sometimes joyful, other times tearful, captives, hands bound, dragged behind them. As the procession passed, people came out to greet it, to welcome the mean as if they were returning from some victorious campaign. When the procession finally reached Philopoemen's homeland, the women and children joined it:

> And so when they had been joined by the old men and by the women and children, a lamentation at once spread through the entire army and into the city, which longed for the presence of Philopoemen and was grievously cast down at his death, feeling that with him it had lost its supremacy among the Achaeans. (Plut. Phil. 21.4)

That last sentence implied that the Megalopolitans feared the loss of Philopoemen would undermine their city's influence within the Sympolity hierarchy. This fear proved to be unfounded, as Megalopolis continued to 'supply' *strategoi* to the Sympolity. In fact, the last *strategoi* of the Sympolity in 147 and 146, Diaeus and Critolaus, were Megalopolitans. One should take into account that Philopoemen, with his achievements and actions, had been accepted and well-liked not only by the Megalopolitans but by all Achaeans as well. To a large degree, this accounted for their spontaneous reaction to his death. Perhaps in some way, to varying degrees, they felt that Philopoemen was, above all, one of their own, and they needed to honour him and mourn him. It also should be mentioned that, as is common throughout history, the true scope and value of leaders is realised and appreciated by their fellow countrymen only after their death. Maybe it is not easy for people to evaluate the significance and contribution of a living person, for when he is with them, and the state prospers, although a great deal is clearly owed to that individual's innate abilities, the others around him feel that they deserve a good share of the credit as well. This way, their actual (and lesser) contribution is revealed only when the individual is no longer around, and when they are called upon to take on a much greater share of the responsibility.

Philopoemen was a rare leader, not only because of his military abilities but also for his ethos. He was 'an excellent captain who managed and courageously steered the Achaean Sympolity through rough, stormy seas, guiding her to a safe harbour'. His compatriots would understand what a truly great man he was by comparing him with the successors that followed him. We are not implying that after Philopoemen, all the Sympolity's *strategoi* were incompetent, but rather that they could not compare in stature with their predecessor. It follows then that Philopoemen, in terms of the value of his contributions, can be compared only with Aratus.

Glorified in death, he was buried with full honours. Around his tomb, the Messenian prisoners condemned to death were stoned. He was called *the last great Greek* as after his death there was no other remarkable leader in Greece. Many city-states issued resolutions in his honour and statues of him were erected in many parts of the Sympolity. After the Battle of Leucopetra near Corinth in 146 that marked Greece's subjugation by Rome, one Roman proposed that all the monuments dedicated to Philopoemen's memory be destroyed, accusing him of being an enemy of Rome—as if he was still alive (21.10)! The Romans were annoyed by this forceful personality from beyond the grave who was not at all like the crop of subservient administrators who, above the objective interests of their homeland, prioritised the interests of the powerful foreigner! They had not forgotten Philopoemen's stance against Manius and Titus Flamininus in the past when the former refused to grant any concession of the Sympolity's sovereignty to Rome, at least not to the extent it would irreparably harm his country's interests. The role of standing up to the conqueror and protecting the memorials erected in Philopoemen's memory fell to Polybius who succeeded in persuading Mummius (the Roman victor at Leucopetra) and the other Roman officials not to erase the monuments dedicated to a great man who had fought for his country.

> These judges distinguished, as it would appear, between virtue and necessity, between honour and advantage. They rightly and fitly considered that benefactors ought always to receive reward and gratitude from their beneficiaries, and good men honour from the good. (Plut. Phil. 21.6.)

Chapter 6
The Political Institutions of the Achaean Sympolity

In Chap. 2, we examined the historical context for the formation, operation and actions of the Achaean Sympolity. Then, in Chaps. 4 and 5, we briefly examined the lives and achievements of its two greatest figures during the second phase of the Sympolity's function (280–146), Aratus and Philopoemen. In this chapter, we will analyse the Sympolity's political institutions. We believe the analysis in this chapter and the next, which examines its economic organisation, is of paramount importance. Approaching the material from the viewpoint of an Economic Historian, we have gone to great lengths to gather and assemble the evidence from the sources, archaeological research and the modern bibliography in a way that is coherent and comprehensible for the reader.

We stress from the outset that it is that viewpoint that characterises our research since, as we mentioned in our Preface, surviving ancient texts (which comprise our primary material, and which we consider eminently worthy of close examination) frequently present disconnected and contradictory information regarding the historical context and how the state and economic institutions of the Achaean Sympolity and other federations functioned. Our ambition here is to present a coherent series of evidence that will highlight and clarify the way those institutions operated, examined through the prism of an economist. As in previous chapters, here too, we follow a multidisciplinary approach.

Concerning the Greek federations, Mackil (2013, p. 3) correctly argues that, generally, a host of issues such as the composition of federal assemblies, councils, and public offices, the determination of where these were located as well as their overall operation over time, are all very difficult to identify. Naturally, this has raised a good deal of disagreement among historians. In that light, the ultimate aim of our analysis is to generate questions as food for thought in our readers by examining whether the institutions and the lessons derived from the development and function of the Achaean administrative system provide policy proposals for societies today, especially at a time when democratic values and perceptions are increasingly being

E. M. L. Economou, *The Achaean Federation in Ancient Greece*, Frontiers in Economic History, https://doi.org/10.1007/978-3-030-52697-9_6

challenged as a result of failures in the formation of policy and its administration by the political elite of today's democratic societies.

6.1 The Organisation of Political Institutions

The Achaean Sympolity was based on democratic principles. It consisted of three key state political institutions: the federal *Ecclesia of the Demos*, the *Boule* and the federal government. As Rizakis observes (2015, p. 123), it is much safer to discuss these bodies as they were during the period of the reconstitution of the Sympolity in 280/279, as the information provided in the sources of that time is much greater than that of the prior period (389–281).

As Polybius (Hist. 29.24.6) notes, the *Ecclesia of the Demos* or the *Synodos*, was the popular federal Assembly with the right of participation by all male citizens. Polybius (2.43.3) emphasises that the principles of *isegoria* and *parrhesia* characterised these assemblies. *Isegoria* meant freedom of speech and the right of anyone who wished to propose legislation (Kralli 2017, p. 53).[1] *Parrhesia* was an extension of *isegoria* and meant the right (and obligation) of a citizen to speak the truth freely, for the common good, even at personal risk. Thus, the principle of *parrhesia* implied a high moral standard, requiring conscientious, active citizens acting in favour of the common good.[2] The principle of *parrhesia* was, in effect, the antidote to demagogy.

According to Livy (32.20), each Achaean citizen had the right to vote in the universal Achaean elections upon reaching 30 years of age. At the city-state level, however, a citizen acquired the right to vote as of age 20, after fulfilling his military service as a *hoplite*, but acquired the right to stand as a candidate only upon reaching 30. At the federal level, on the other hand, the right to vote and that of standing as a candidate for holding a public office (either in the city-state or the federal level) both occurred at age 30 (Walbank 1984, p. 245). We presume here that as far as a citizen's right to vote was concerned, the Achaeans were probably influenced by the Athenian model, although with some adjustment.[3] It goes without saying that the right to vote or stand for election was not a prerogative of *metics* who happened to be working in a member city-state, nor of slaves.

As we have already mentioned, there seems to be a considerable divergence between researchers as to the number of pan-Achaean federal assemblies that took place every year. Our principal resources on this subject, Polybius (2.43.1–2) and

[1]For the development of *isegoria* even earlier, during the Archaic Period in Greece (750–510), see Economou and Kyriazis (2019a, b). This principle was one of the cornerstones of the Athenian *Ecclesia* of citizens, during the Classical and Hellenistic Periods.

[2]Manville and Ober (2003) provide a quite important and convincing discussion on this issue.

[3]For the relevant provision of the Athenian political system as to the age limits for the right to vote (20 years of age) and to stand as a candidate (30 years of age), see Xenophon (*Memorabilia* 1.2.35) and Hornblower et al. (2012, p. 435).

Livy (38.30.2) offer differing data. Larsen (1972, 1975) argues that probably a federal 'pan-Achaean' Assembly was called once a year some time from late April to early May. The meeting place of the Assembly was initially the sanctuary of Zeus Homarios, outside Aegion, but at some point, it moved into the polis of Aegion itself (Paus. 7.7.2). However, in 188, upon a proposal by the *strategos* Philopoemen, it was decided that Assembly gatherings would be held at different city-states in rotation (Livy 38.30.2). This was a decision designed to guarantee that the capital Aegion would not manipulate the federation's decision-making process. Errington (1969, p. 138–139) believes that this decision must not have gone down well with the citizens of Aegion, obviously because they felt they would be losing some of their privileges to the other city-states of the Sympolity. Kralli (2017, p. 153), on the other hand, argues that this decision mirrored the expanded character of the Sympolity, and the need to give access to the Assembly to as many citizens as possible.

Schuckburgh ([1889], 2012, p. iviii), Freeman ([1893] 2013, p. 260–161), and Davis (1978, p. 31) believe that the Achaean Assembly took place twice every year. Mitsos (1947), Larsen (1968, p. 216), Walbank (1984, 1993), Mackil (2013, p. 342) and Kralli (2017, p. 52), however, argue in favour of four annual assemblies. The confusion seems to arise because Polybius uses the terms *synodos* and *synkletos* interchangeably (Larsen 1955, p. 75–76), both meaning 'Assembly'. However, according to Larsen (1968, p. 223), Walbank (1984, p. 245) and Rizakis (2015), the term *synodos* referred to the regular federal assemblies, while *synkletos* referred to extraordinary assemblies. This seems to resolve this issue that troubled earlier researchers.[4] Some historians, such as Aymard (1938, p. 63), held that the *synodos* was not a representational body, although this view has since been rejected (Larsen 1955, p. 157–159, 1972, p. 178–185).

On this issue, keeping in mind that the neighbouring Aetolian Sympolity held two national assemblies every year, one in the capital, Thermos, very likely in the spring, and a second one, probably in the autumn, on a rotational basis with other member cities,[5] we tend to believe the notion of two regular pan-Achaean assemblies to be correct, keeping in mind that it was very likely that the two neighbours exerted some influence on each other. The degree of such an influence, however, is unknown. In any event, the number of national assemblies is not the critical issue here, but rather that there did exist a hybrid procedure of direct and indirect democracy that allowed the Achaean citizens to have a voice in the critical issues of the Sympolity, even if only twice (at least) a year.

The federal *Ecclesia of the Demos*, or *Synodos*, which constituted a pan-Achaean national Assembly, was convened only for serious issues, such as deciding on alliances, declaring war, setting the federal budget, etc. An extraordinary federal Assembly, or *Synkletos*, was convened in urgent cases, or when circumstances were serious enough to require it. The logic behind regular and irregular Assembly

[4]See Larsen's (1972) informative analysis on this issue.

[5]See Larsen (1952), Mackil (2013, p. 112) and Economou et al. (2015).

meetings was a wider Panhellenic political-institutional practice in the Hellenistic period. It was implemented in Athens (and probably, in other city-states as well) during the Classical and the Hellenistic period (Lambert 2017) and it was practised by federal states during the latter period, too.

We believe that this problem regarding the exact number of federal Assembly gatherings is related to the territorial expansion of the Sympolity. Perhaps, during the period 280–252, when the Sympolity was restricted to the original Achaean territories (in geographical terms), four annual assemblies were feasible in practical terms, but later, as the Sympolity expanded, they were reduced in number to two because the cost of the journey of the average Achaean citizen to participate gradually became too great. Larsen (1972, p. 183) thus believes that due to the distance, participation by many citizens became prohibitive, especially given the high 'opportunity cost', the loss of wages because of not working during the time it took to travel to and from, plus the time spent at the Assembly. In earlier research, Caspari (1914) and Briscoe (1974) brought up this issue, and we, too, raised it in 2.3 and 3.3 where we noted the socio-economic aspects and social division (high number of mid- and low-income citizens, low number of wealthy citizens) related to the Sympolity's decision-making. Briscoe (1974) notes that it was a serious issue in the Aetolian Sympolity as well, while less so in the *Koina* of Boeotia and Acarnanians, where geographic distances were smaller. In effect, he notes, political decision-making at the national assemblies rested to a very large extent in the hands of the wealthier classes that could afford to attend.

This problem, in theory perhaps, must have been acute. Even today, the distance between Aegion and, say, Argos is 140 km by automobile, while that between Megalopolis and Aegion, essentially from one end of the Sympolity to the other, is 222 km. Given the state of the travel system in those days, the distance Aegion-Megalopolis must have taken around 4–5 days to traverse on foot or even some form of transport under normal conditions—one way. That meant the loss of daily wages just for travel to and from amounting to at least 1/5 or 1/6 of a citizen's monthly income. In this light then, the scope of democracy in political decision-making was restricted since there was no fair representation from each city-state and the whole range of social groups. This lent the assemblies, in practice, to some extent, an oligarchic, non-democratic character. On this issue, Walbank (1993) argues that, from a political point of view, the Sympolity may have been democratic to the extent that vital decisions were taken in an Assembly in which all males of age had the right to participate, its officials, however, came from a limited number of families from only a few member cities. Larsen (1968, p. 88) writes on this that on account of the distances involved, it is likely that only men of property with sufficient leisure normally attended the meetings of the federal Assembly. Thus, the real influence of the lower classes may have been exercised more effectively in the election of representatives to the federal Council. Thus, it is likely that, even under the democracy, the federal government normally was directed by the moneyed upper classes.

Nevertheless, our view is that promoting an argument that the Achaean Sympolity resembled a form of covert oligarchy does not appear to be confirmed by hard evidence beyond the scattered reference by Polybius and other ancient sources. For this reason, anyone claiming that in practice, the Sympolity was an oligarchy under a cloak of democracy must offer much more persuasive evidence. Larsen (1968, p. 232) argues that during the Hellenistic period, the meaning of *demokratia* had changed, so that states which once would have been considered oligarchic, could be called democratic. Robinson (2003, p. 26–27) disagrees with this view, arguing that despite the ascendance of oligarchic circles in the politics of the Sympolity's city-states for a time, that role and its influence gradually receded and, from the fourth century on, the Achaean city-states had all established democratic governments.

Although the persistence of oligarchic governments cannot be excluded with absolute certainty, we believe that Robinson's view is correct and is supported by two facts: first, as was explained in detail in 4.1 and 4.2, the Sicyonian *strategos* Aratus, who was elected as head of the state of the Achaean Sympolity, launched a huge initiative in 251 to restore democracy in every city of the federation, replacing all the pro-Macedonian tyrannical regime. Second, the city of Messene, which had joined the Sympolity in 191, was subject to an oligarchic coup in 183. Attempting to subdue the rebellion, Philopoemen was captured and put to death by poison. Nevertheless, according to Freeman ([1893], 2013, p. 636, 647), Messene's citizens rejected the oligarchs, and democracy was restored. This shows that, although oligarchic tendencies persisted in many city-states within the Achaean Sympolity, only rarely did they manage to prevail politically, and then, only briefly, until they were overthrown by democratic administrations.

It seems odd that in the Aetolian, as well as the Achaean Sympolities, there was no provision for reimbursement for participating representatives to the federal assemblies, as Larsen (1968, p. 231) believes, arguing that the Sympolities were actually in the hands of men of property (oligarchs). There is no evidence in the sources that either of the two Sympolities adopted the institution of *ecclesiastica* that prevailed in the Athenian Democracy. The *ecclesiastica* was a mechanism by which citizens who attended the Athenian Assembly (*Ecclesia of the Demos*) after travelling a great distance were granted a stipend of three *obols* as compensation for loss of wages. This was adopted at the end of the fifth century (ca. 403/2) by the politicians of the democratic faction as an incentive to encourage broader participation in political decision-making that concerned the future of the state (Tridimas 2017). It was abolished by Demetrius of Phaleron, a statesman appointed by the Macedonian king, Cassander, to govern Athens, where he ruled as sole ruler for 10 years. However, after he was deposed and exiled in 307, it is possible that it was implemented again. Lambert (2017, p. 260–261) provides epigraphic evidence of this and further bibliographic evidence that the *ecclesiastica* was also implemented on the island of Rhodes during Hellenistic times.

Based on this evidence, we believe that there is a strong possibility that other city-states or federations introduced *ecclesiastica* at least for some time during the Hellenistic Period. We believe that it is highly unlikely that the leadership of both Hellenistic Sympolities were not aware of that institution as a workable and effective vehicle that could have been adopted, giving, if not to the extraordinary *synkletoi*, at least to the regular *synods*, a more representative number of Achaean citizens, further validating decision-making through expanded participation. As we have mentioned, keeping that in mind, as well as for reasons of maintaining the balance of power between the Achaean city-states, in 189/8, Philopoemen abolished the practice of holding the federal assemblies only in Aegion, the Sympolity's capital. This gave the right to hold the pan-Achaean assemblies to other cities, e.g. Argos (Livy 38.30.1–6; Aymard 1938, p. 293–302; Rizakis 1995, p. 131, 2015, p. 124).

The second major political institution of the Sympolity was the Council, or *Boule*, which had a role and responsibilities similar to those of the Athenian *Boule* and that of the other democratic federations. This consisted of the preparations for the issues to be discussed during the federal *Ecclesia*. All Achaean citizens over the age of 30 had the right of participating (Walbank 1984, p. 245, 1993). Polybius (2.46.6) mentions that, in 229, the parallel functioning of both the *Ecclesia* and the *Boule*, where the latter functioned as a body to prepare the topics for discussion and decision by the former, equivalent to the Athenian *Boule* (Mackil 2013; Economou and Kyriazis 2016a).[6] This was similar to the federal Assembly of the Aetolian Sympolity (Economou et al. 2015). Accordingly, the importance of the federal Assembly was greater than that of the federal Council. There are plenty of references to the role of the Achaean Council in the ancient sources, such as in Polybius, verse 22.7.3 in Diodorus Sicilus, verse 29.17, and Livy, verse 38.30.2.

Ehrenberg (1964) offers another dimension to this issue arguing that the members of the Achaean *Boule*, although serving in a federal organ, in practice, functioned as representatives of their city-states. According to Larsen (1968, p. 88), the Achaean members and federal public magistrates were certainly chosen in the city-states of their origin by vote, and not by lot. They were selected based on population criteria in each municipality of each city-state. This differed from the Athenian practice where *Boule* members, again depending on the size of the population in each municipality, were selected by lottery[7] to undertake their years' service. That the number of *Boule* members was ultimately dependent on population size was common to a host of other federations such as the Aetolian, the Boeotian, the Arcadian, as well as the Lycian in Asia Minor (Larsen 1955, p. 68–75, 1968, p. 226; Economou and Kyriazis 2015b; Rizakis 2015, p. 127). The 28 city-states of the Lycian *Koinon* all had the right to vote on the federation's issues, with the larger ones sending three delegates, the middle-sized, two, and the smaller ones, one (Knoepfler 2013). Rizakis (2015, p. 127) argues that this might have been so in the Achaean *Boule* as well since there exist reasonable conjectures by some researchers that the Lycian *Koinon*, established sometime after 189, was essentially a copy of the Achaean

[6]Frank (1914) and Aymard (1938) argue that the *Boule* was a smaller *Ecclesia*, a view with which Larsen (1972, p. 178–180)—rightfully, we believe—disagrees, based on Polybius (2.46.6).

[7]In ancient Athens, 500 *Boule* members were selected by lottery from 1000 candidates from the city's 139 municipalities. The 500 who were not chosen served as a reserve, known as *epilachontes*. See Economou and Kyriazis (2019b).

Sympolity's state system. Mackil (2013, p. 10) argues that active cooperation and negotiation based on population criteria was required in coming to an understanding as to how many delegates/*Boule* members each city-state was entitled to send to the federal bodies.

Lastly, in reference to the eligibility of *Boule* membership at the city-state and the federal level, although lacking any relevant evidence, we believe that, at least for practical reasons, it was unlikely that the same individuals could serve at both levels. In other words, members selected for the local *Boule* of, say, Corinth or Megalopolis, could not also be selected to serve concurrently in the federal *Boule*. Considering the structure of the Sympolity, we argue that each city-state selected its local and federal delegates for each *Boule* separately. Of course, exceptions cannot be excluded conclusively, although the Achaeans, as well as the Aetolians and other democratic federations, must certainly have kept thorough registers and demographics to avoid double-entries, the same persons being selected too frequently and other anomalies.

As we have proposed elsewhere (Economou and Kyriazis 2016a), that to convene the Assembly of the Sympolity, the Council first had to assess and approve the topics for evaluation clearly indicates that it was in the Greek democratic federations that for the first time in history there appeared a 'bicameral' democratic system, harmonically combining elements of direct (Assembly) and indirect (Council) democracy. Behind the creation of a representational system lies the problem of inadequate representation of citizens and city-states in the elections of the federal Assembly. As discussed above, because of the great distances, especially for the more distant regions from the location of the two annual assemblies, the likelihood of underrepresentation was significant. Therefore, the system of representation that was developed can be seen as an indirect way of ensuring, if only partially, that citizens who, for practical reasons, were unable to participate in the functions of the federal Assembly could indirectly decide on issues of concern to them.

One must also consider the number of representatives in the Council of the Sympolity. This is important because, at least theoretically, the larger the number of participants in the process, the more democratic it is. Unfortunately, on this issue, too, ancient sources do not provide specific information. Again, we will attempt to draw out some relevant data employing an 'indirect strategy'. First, Rizakis (2015, p. 127) argues that it was likely the number of members sent by city-states to the federal Council changed from one period to another, with such changes accelerating in the second century as the Sympolity expanded markedly. One piece of information that relates to the possible numerical size of the Achaean federal Council is provided by Livy (45.28.7) indirectly where he recounts a sad event—the slaughter in Rome of 550 members of the Aetolian federal Council in 168/7 because they were against Roman aspirations.[8] Consequently, the Aetolian Council must have

[8]Obviously, just as in the Achaean Sympolity, in the Aetolian, and probably in many Greek city-states toward the end of the Hellenistic Period, there existed men like the Achaean Callicrates who toadied to the aggressively demanding Romans against the will of their compatriots who disagreed with their opportunistic, pro-Roman sentiments.

consisted of a far larger number of members; Funke (2015, p. 112) has estimated it to have been around 1500. It is worthwhile noting that Livy (34.51.6) and the inscription (*IG* IX.2.261) mention that the equivalent forum of the Thessalian *Koinon* numbered 354 members. To put this in context, according to Wade-Gery (1924) and Larsen (1960), the Thessalian *Koinon* was an oligarchy, was divided into administrative districts run by *tagoi*, later renamed *archontes* (leaders) and *polemarchs* (warlords).

Taking all the above into consideration, and given that the Achaean Sympolity, in terms of the number of member city-states and population, probably exhibited higher, or at least similar, levels to the Aetolian, by extension, even if arbitrary, we can argue that it was not unlikely that the Council of the Achaean Sympolity consisted of a similar number of delegates, around 1500, chosen in their city-states of origin, a view seconded by Rizakis (2015, p. 127). Even though it is based on an elaboration of information that we assemble into a reasonable induction, our estimate of the Achaean Council's size cannot be too far off the mark.

As for the government of the Achaean Sympolity, it was composed of specific individuals, elected by the federal Assembly. The highest office was that of the *strategos*—literally, 'general'. The *strategos* held the ultimate political and military power of the state in matters of executive and political power (Freeman [1893], 2013). Originally, there were two *strategoi,* serving concurrently as commander of the armed forces, and alternating between each other. In 253, however, the *strategia* was made the purview of a single individual (Frank 1914; Larsen 1972, p. 183). Aymard (1938), Larsen (1968, p. 86, 217), Walbank (1993), Mackil 2013, p. 342–343), Rizakis (2015, p. 123) and Kralli (2017, p. 154), however, relying on Polybius (2.43.1–2) and Strabo (Geo. 8.7.3), suggest it was in 255, not 253. In any event, in our view, what matters more was the restriction of the term of office to 1 year, without the right to re-election in the following year. The first *strategos* to be elected after this change was Margos, from Ceryneia (Larsen 1968, p. 217; Kralli 2017, p. 154).[9]

Within the highest ranks of the Sympolity's administration was the post of *grammateus*, or secretary (Mackil 2013, p. 342–343) but it is not quite clear what his duties were. As the democratic federations of Greek antiquity presented many similarities with each other in terms of their political institutions, it will not be far off the mark to argue that the *grammateus* had a variety of duties such as collating and archiving documents on the functioning of the state, notification to member states and third countries and was probably also responsible for collecting and maintaining the General Records of the State, while also handling other duties which one associates with those of today's minister of the interior.

As we have analysed extensively in the previous Chapters, based on available resources, the most significant *strategoi* of the Sympolity are considered to have

[9]The institution of *strategos* as both political and military leader is not unlike the role of the American President, i.e. George Washington during the War of Independence 1776–1783, or that of Napoleon 1798–1814, a view supported by Freeman ([1893], 2013).

been Aratus and Philopoemen. It is possible that the initial idea of having two *strategoi* instead of one was derived from the proximity of the Sympolity to Sparta. The Spartans' highest office was held by two kings, one from each of the two tribes, the Argiadai and the Eurypontidai, providing a 'system of checks and balances' between the two. The 'founding fathers' of the Achaean 'constitution' might have seen fit to adopt this system, believing two *strategoi* would provide a better balance of power and more transparency to the political system. It is not known why they later abandoned the system. It shows, however, that beyond the basic institutions (Assembly, Council, federal government), the Ancient Greek federations did present some institutional differences between them, a view verified by Mackil (2013) as well.

It is important to note that, while the *strategos* was the highest-ranking official of the Sympolity, his authority was not absolute; he was subject to the control and the satisfaction of the wishes of the federal Assembly. In other words, the *strategos*' duty was to execute the wishes of the Achaean citizens as expressed by the Assembly (Rizakis 2015, p. 128). That the authority of the *strategos* was not unconstrained is related to the fact that his term of office (as well as that of the rest of the members of his government) was limited to 1 year,[10] and he and his government were ineligible for a consecutive term. This practice was decided, according to Kralli (2017, p. 155) to curtail individual power. In the hierarchy of the Sympolity, after the *strategos*, the second-highest rank, (*deuteria*), was held by the *ipparchos* (cavalry commander), who was probably then followed by the *nauarchos* (admiral). There was also the office of the *hypostrategos*, equivalent to major general. According to Larsen (1968, p. 220), this was the commander of the troops of a district (*synteleia*). The specific institutional/governmental duties of the *hypostrategos* remain unspecified in the bibliography (Caspari 1914; Larsen 1971, 1972; Mackil 2013, p. 342).

A reasonably safe assessment of the hierarchy of the state's administration should include the *strategos*, the *grammateus* ('secretariat'), the *ipparchos*, the *hypostrategos* and *nauarchos* who, together with ten so-called *damiourgoi* (or *demiourgoi*)[11] or *probouloi* or *synarchontes* ('co-governers'), formed the highest echelon of the Sympolity, coming from its member city-states. They were supplemented by some other lower-ranked officers (Strabo 8; Livy 32.22.2, 38.30; Polyb. 4.4, 27.2.11, 23.5.16; Larsen 1968, p. 86; Mackil 2013, p. 343). Larsen (1968, p. 221–222), based on Livy (32.22.2), argues that it is uncertain whether the number of *damiourgoi* was always ten. Moreover, it may have been a provision of the Sympolity's 'constitution' that the *damiourgoi* be of a certain age because, in one passage (38.5), Polybius refers to them as the *gerousia*, ('senate'), as in the Senate of Sparta. Mackil (2013, p. 343) argues that although it is not clarified in the ancient

---

[10]Although in practice this was not always the case, as it is known that in some cases Aratus and Philopoemen retained their posts as *strategos* for consecutive years. See also Table 6.1 below.

[11]Possibly, the word *damiourgoi* derives from the Greek word *demiourgo* for 'create', here meaning those elected representatives who 'create' i.e. produce and enact policy.

sources or by archaeological evidence, some modern researchers tend to support the idea that this government body (which more or less could be seen as a federal cabinet) was comprised of members who came from all the city-states on a rotating basis.[12]

Further expanding on what has been discussed so far are some extra issues: the first refers to the possibility of the federal administration's officers being elected not by the Assembly but by the Council or, alternatively, by a combination of the two bodies. This, however, does not apply as it is not indicated in any of the primary sources, nor any modern research. The administration's officers were elected only by the federal Assembly. The second issue, related to the first, refers to which of the two annual convocations of the Assembly served as the occasion for the election of the administration for the next year; at the first in the spring, held in the capital, Aegion, or at the second, in the autumn, held in another city-state of the Sympolity. Polybius (2.43, 4.6.37) states that the members of the new government were elected in the spring, at the time when the constellation Pleiades made its appearance. Walbank (1984, p. 245) goes further, arguing that until 217 they were elected in the spring, but after that, it was done in autumn, with the new administration assuming power in time to plan the military campaigns of the following spring and summer. Walbank further notes that the institution of extraordinary federal assemblies, the *synkletoi*, was introduced right after 217.

One might also consider the possibility of a new federal government assuming power as the result of an extraordinary *synkletos* because of some unusual event such as, for example, the death of a serving *strategos*, as happened in the case of Philopoemen. Of course, in such a case, the complications involved in convening a *synkletos* may have precluded such a course of action, with one of the other members of the government, the *hypostrategos,* for example, assuming the position until the end of the term instead. That is not known. What is known is that in the event of the death of a sitting member of the administration, the post would be filled by his predecessor. Polybius does not specify if this included the posts of *strategos* or h*ypostrategos* and in at least two occasions we know of, there was an exception. Upon the death of Timoxenos, it was Aratus and not his predecessor who replaced him. Similarly, when Philopoemen was murdered by Deinocrates and his cohorts in Messene in 183, he was replaced not by his likely predecessor, Archon, but by Lycortas.

Another issue would have been the length of the term of office of a new, interim administration. If, for example, it had assumed power in May, would its term end at the next regular bi-annual convening of the federal Assembly in autumn or the following May? The former is more logical. However, the essential element in this analysis of the Achaean governmental hierarchy is that all the high officials were elected democratically. It is certain, too, that the Achaean and probably the rest of the

[12]However, O′ Neil (1984–1986) believes that the political leaders of the Achaean Sympolity came from a few major cities, notably Sicyon, Megalopolis, and the four western Achaean city-states that comprised the reconstituted federation in 280.

Greek democratic federations elected each official directly. This institutional arrangement is essential in terms of the transparency and orderly functioning of democracy. That might be clarified if that practice of those ancient federations were to be compared with the analogous practice in the European Union today, where the institutional administrative bodies such as, for example, the members of the European Commission, are appointed, and not elected. This has resulted in a bloated 'Brussels bureaucracy' that is based only on indirect democratic legitimacy. Only the members of the European Parliament are elected directly. Finally, it should be noted that on matters of policy and governance, in the Achaean Sympolity, the decision-making and the details of execution were shared between the federal and the regional institutional bodies.

Another significant issue regarding the composition of the Sympolity's government concerns the dual role with which government officials were tasked: they also held the responsibilities of a high military hierarchy. This dichotomy must not be construed to mean that the Achaean and the other Greek federations were covertly run by a military staff (or junta, in today's terms) and were thus not actually democratic. In fact, the opposite was the case: democratically elected officials were charged with the running of the federal armed forces. This was so because citizenship implied the obligation to serve as a *hoplite* in the military up to age 20, and after that be recalled for service should the need arise. Therefore, inherent to one's identity as a citizen was his status as a *hoplite*. This was no 'militocratic society', but one composed of citizens with a self-evident obligation to be called to arms when circumstances demanded. Just as a democratic city-state could be seen as a '*hoplite* democracy', where the citizen had an obligation to bear arms, by extension, one could adopt the term '*hoplite* federations' to describe the democratic (and, for that matter, the non-democratic) Ancient Greek federations. Of course, citizens elected to serve in the highest offices were those that were felt by the electorate to possess the necessary expertise to defend the state from outside aggression. This may have limited the pool of potential candidates, but that did not alter the fact that those who were elected were chosen by the general federal Assembly by a direct and democratic procedure (Economou and Kyriazis 2019b).

6.2 The Crucial Institutions of *Isopoliteia*, the Concession and the Sale of Political Rights, *Asylia* and *Proxeny*

Another dimension of our analysis concerns the relations between city-states and small cities (known as *polismata*) within the Sympolity. One major basis for the creation of a Sympolity was equal rights among its member city-states (Polyb. 2.37). Larsen (1971) states that the institutional basis of the Achaean Sympolity allowed a great degree of flexibility between its members, as well as specific schemes for cooperation with city-states beyond its borders.

In the Achaean Sympolity and the other Greek federations, there existed the right to *isopoliteia*, meaning the right of every citizen of a member city-state to have full political rights anywhere throughout the federation. That meant that a citizen could live anywhere within the Sympolity, retaining all his rights plus eligibility to participate in all sociopolitical functions there. Anyone who chose to move, say, from the city of Cleitor in Arcadia to Patras in Achaea, automatically could participate in the local political life, e.g. vote in the next election. Aside from being an Achaean citizen, the only prerequisite was that to participate in the electoral procedure in the new city-state of his residence, he had to be stricken first from the registry of his city-state of origin (Larsen 1968, p. xx).[13] This sounds logical; for example, a federal citizen who resided in Sicyon could not simultaneously be a voting citizen, say, of Megalopolis. Thus, each Achaean citizen had the right to retain only one city-state citizenship and corresponding rights at any given time. This institutional principle was undoubtedly a pioneering step for that time because it meant the voluntary consolidation of different state entities under a single framework of cooperation essentially.

Regarding citizenship rights, it is imperative to clarify some additional issues. First, theoretically, under *isopoliteia*, any Achaean citizen could change citizenship any time he chose to do so. Second, another theoretical possibility was that any Achaean citizen, say of Aegeira, could choose to stay in any other city-state, say, in Dyme, for a relatively short time, for example, for business purposes, while retaining his citizenship rights in Aegeira. That meant that, while ineligible to participate in any political electoral procedure in Dyme during his stay there, theoretically, he could travel back to Aegeira to take part in an electoral procedure there, and then travel back to Dyme to resume his business there. Larsen (1968, p. xx), however, believes that as far as military service was concerned, this citizen would fight alongside the citizens of the city-state in which he lived at that moment rather than of the city-state in which he was formally a citizen.

Third, *isopoliteia* was not limited to the status of citizens within a federation, as instances have been recorded of relationships between federal city-states and city-states beyond their borders as well. Based on inscriptions that have been found (*SEG* 2.258, *SEG* 18.245, *BE* 77.231, *Syll.*3472), it can be argued that around 240, the Aetolian Sympolity had signed a treaty of *isopoliteia* with Messene in southwest Peloponnesus (Mackil 2013, p. 102, 263). On another occasion, in 200, the city-state of Athens granted *isopoliteia* to all the inhabitants of the island of Rhodes out of gratitude for the naval assistance it had received (Polyb. 16.26.9). Polybius, however, does not say whether the Rhodians reciprocated, as was the general principle in such cases. It appears this was a case of a unilateral grant of *isopoliteia*, a voluntary act granting political rights to all the citizens of another city-state—without reciprocity. A similar case of the unilateral grant of *isopoliteia* occurred on the island of Crete: a city-state there, Ierapetra (or Ierapytna), granted *isopoliteia* to several other

[13]For the application of *isopoliteia* in the Aetolian, Arcadian and Achaean Sympolities, see, among others, Economou et al. (2015), Economou and Kyriazis (2015a, b, c, 2016a, c).

Cretan city-states without receiving the equivalent in return. Chaniotis (1999a, p. 230) believes this may have been because Ierapetra was hoping to attract settlers and investment or was attempting to 'alleviate' overpopulation in those city-states that burdened their economies. The incentive in such cases was clearly economic/commercial, a position with which Walbank (1993) agrees.

A grant of political rights through the institution of *isopoliteia* normally implied the catholic coverage of another city-state's citizenry, as evidenced in the cases mentioned above; however, it could also be applied to individual citizens. For instance, an inscription found in Dyme, a member of the Achaean Sympolity (*Syll.*^{3}, 529), dating from 219, contains a list of 52 individuals with the following statement:

> Those listed below are declared citizens of this city because they fought in the war, and because they contributed to the salvation of the city, each one was chosen specifically.

Walbank (1993) argues that this refers to events during the war between the Achaeans and Aetolians in 220–217, and referred to mercenaries and some others, possibly members of a Macedonian garrison, as one of them was named Drakas, a Macedonian name. In the case of the Achaean Sympolity, as Larsen (1971) confirms, the success of the practice of granting *isopoliteia* was such that it led to the easing of conditions for accepting citizens of other city-states into its fold. As for the practice of selling political rights to citizens of other city-states, Mackil (2013, p. 388) argues that this did exist, citing an inscription (T35) from the third century. It is obvious that the purchase of political rights implies the automatic acquisition of citizenship in the Sympolity as well, and, by extension, all the perquisites that entail e.g. free movement throughout the Sympolity, right to vote and to stand for election at the city-state as well as the Sympolity level, civil rights throughout the Sympolity, etc. In that light, this practice of the Sympolity is mirrored by that of the European Union today, where, say, if Greece grants an Albanian emigrant or Syrian refugee citizenship, he or she automatically acquires the rights laid out in the treaties in force and accepted by all EU member states.

Mackil notes that, along with rights, a new citizen of Dyme and the Achaean Sympolity also acquired all the relevant obligations deriving from the Achaean constitution. The sale of political rights to foreigners was a source of income for a city's coffers as well as a means of increasing population. In one case, during the third century, another Achaean city, Tritaia sold political rights, controlling every aspect of the integration of a new citizen from start to finish (*SEG* 40.400; Rizakis 1990, p. 129–134). The inscription (T35) from Dyme mentioned above refers to *epoikoi* and *synekoi* in Epidaurus, with Mackil (2013, p. 260–262) arguing that the difference between the two was not very clear, but it is certain that *epoikoi* were those who had purchased their citizenship in Dyme; the inscription describes the economic obligations the new citizens of Dyme and the Sympolity had to meet. Therefore, the practice of granting political rights to foreign citizens, the great majority of which were Greeks from other city-states, was not a rare phenomenon occurring in just a few cities but was widespread throughout the city-states of the Sympolity.

The other important state institutions were those of *asylia* and *proxeny* (Mackil 2015). In a constantly reordering Hellenistic world, city-states had become aware that cooperation between them was a serious affair that could forestall any misadventure—mainly, war. For this reason, they adopted two institutions which can be seen as coherent and interconnected with *isopoliteia* and the granting (or sale) of political rights at a time when the movement of people throughout the Hellenistic world had intensified a great deal and was even encouraged by the corresponding state institutions. *Asylia* was the waiver of retaliation that one city-state could impose on another of which a citizen somehow damaged the interests of the former. Under *asylia*, it was forbidden to exercise *sylis*, or one city-state initiating legal reprisal against another. In our view, this provision was crucial because it effectively separated any criminal or moral liability that could be attributed to a citizen of one city-state from his activities in another, that may have harmed the interests of the former. This was particularly important because it rendered invalid the notion of collective responsibility for acts committed by a specific individual weighing on all the inhabitants of the city from which that individual originated (Rigsby 1997). It is obvious that this institutional arrangement created better conditions for cooperation between city-states, within a broader context of mutual tolerance and understanding (Economou and Kyriazis 2019a).

Originally, this applied only to temples, which were considered sacred and thus inviolable because of *sylis*. It was then extended to city-states. An example is provided by a surviving inscription (*P. Herman, Anadolou 1967, 13, v. 17–20*) which highlighted the efforts of Teo, a city-state in Asia Minor, to draw up a treaty for *asylia* with city-states of the Aetolian Sympolity and Crete because both the Aetolians and Cretans were notorious for their involvement in piracy (Walbank 1993). Of course, it could have been the reverse: the Aetolian and Cretan city-states could have sought *asylia* from Teo, which apparently was suffering the effects of the predatory raids on some of their inhabitants. In fact, during the third century, as evidenced by several surviving inscriptions, the Aetolian Sympolity had signed treaties of *asylia* confirming that it was not her intention, nor of any of her citizens, to commit acts of piracy or predatory raids.[14]

As for *proxeny*, this was closely linked with the age-old institutions of *philoxenia* (hospitality) and *philia* (friendship). Historically, the competences of consuls of Greek cities was not only to represent their city-state in general but to represent it in the *Ecclesia of the Demos* or the *Boule* of the city-state where they were serving as well (Mack 2015; Woolmer 2016, p. 77–79). They were also obligated to receive and host in their home, ambassadors and representatives in general of the city-state of which they were consul. For example, the Spartan ambassadors that arrived in Athens in 378 were hosted by Kallias, Sparta's ambassador to Athens (Xen. Hell. 5.4.22).

[14]*IG* IX.12 1.179 l. 19, from around 260 BCE; *IG* IX.12 1.4c l. 18; *IG* IX.12 1.135 ll. 2–3, ca. 220; *IG* IX.12 1.192 ll. 9–10, from 204/3(?), *IG* IX.12 1.176 l. 5, shortly after 228; *IG* IX.12 1.169a ll. 2–3, b ll. 1–2, ca. 222; *IG* IX.12 1.189 ll. 3–4, around 214/3(?).

During the Hellenistic Period, this institution of *proxeny* referred to the granting of privileges to citizens of other city-states in recognition of their service to the city. As an example, according to (*Syll.*^{3} *137 II 116*), the Athenians granted *proxeny* to Phanocritus from Phaneion and his progeny because 'he warned the Athenian leaders that enemy ships were nearing the shores and, if they acted quickly, they could capture them', which, in the end, they did not do. Nevertheless, the Athenians acknowledged their moral debt to Phanocritus and chose to honour him. This institution was expanded in the third century, the granting of *proxeny* became more frequent and even came to be accompanied by many distinctions, including the concession of civil rights. Walbank (1993) argues that extending the institution of *proxeny* served to promote and expand commercial relations between city-states and had less to do with the traditional role of consuls. For instance, an inscription dating from 266, *Syll.*^{3}, *492*, states that in the city of Hestiaia in Euboea, the local authorities had granted rights of *proxeny* to 31 citizens from other Euboean cities. On another occasion, during the 270s, the Aetolian Sympolity granted those rights to Aristion, son of Androcles, from the city of Haleion in western Locris, while granting *isopoliteia* to several citizens of Amphissa (*IG* IX.12.1.5, *IG* IX.12.1.12a; Scholten 2000, p. 29).

6.3 Conflict Resolution Regime between City-States on Civil and Territorial Matters

In the event of differences between member city-states, as a rule, common to every federal government of the Hellenistic world was the right to intervention and mediation to resolve them. According to Ager (1997, 2015, p. 478), the normal procedure to do that which was normally adopted was to choose a third city-state to intervene by providing competent judges to arrive at a resolution. Walbank (1993) argues that this was a widespread practice during the Hellenistic Period, noting that the main differences between city-states were those involving disputes over land rights in border regions.

Such recorded instances related to differences between Achaean city-states include an intervention by Megara between Corinth and Epidaurus somewhere between 242/1 and 238/7, and by Patras between Thourioi and Megalopolis. More than one city-state could offer arbitration services as in the case of a conflict between Epidaurus and Arsinoe in 228 where, through their delegated representatives, 11 cities took part in a joint effort. Another case of more than one city-state providing such services was in the case of a land dispute between Epidaurus and Ermione, around 200, where Miletus and Rhodes jointly provided arbitration (Ager 2015, p. 480). Ager argues that in certain cases, the Achaean Sympolity invited several third city-states to offer arbitration services and, on other occasions to a large number of city-states, to ensure a more objective resolution between opposing member city-states through a collective arbitral body. One might ask, why do something that essentially constitutes an indirect intervention in the Sympolity's internal affairs? It can only mean that there were occasionally some cases that only adjudication by a third party, outside of the Sympolity, neutral to the state parties involved, could provide impartial counsel.

Larsen (1971) provides an additional dimension of the federal relationship between the members of the Achaean Sympolity. Referring to the example of two city-states, Stymphalos (in Arcadia) and Aegeira, that had drawn up a treaty between them in 219, based on which any legal issue would be resolved jointly under their legal system. Larsen believes that such a treaty gave them considerable autonomy and freedom of movement. Such an agreement might have presented a problem for the federalist organisation of the Sympolity, however, Larsen notes that there did exist certain legal circumstances (perhaps based on both criminal and civil law) that the federal courts took into consideration in cases of disputes between member city-states that had signed that type of agreement with each other.

Another instance, in 194, concerns special commercial arrangements that Stymphalos had established with city-states outside the Sympolity; these, however, must have been done with the knowledge and consent of the federal administration. Another case worth mentioning is that of an embargo by the Sympolity against the city-state of Elateia (which was not a member of the Sympolity) after it attempted to appropriate and cultivate land belonging to Stymphalos. The citizens of the latter appealed to the federal courts who declared the Elateians' action as illegal and prohibited it. The imposition of commercial sanctions by the whole of the Sympolity as a countermeasure against third parties that somehow harmed member(s) of the Sympolity highlights yet another significant dimension of the scope and cohesion between its members: their real solidarity—to the extent possible—not only in military terms but beyond that, in terms of safeguarding their interests. Any action that harmed the interests of one city-state automatically involved the others, in the same way, for example, that the destruction wreaked by Hurricane Katrina in 2005 in the South of the USA was not solely the concern of Florida and New Orleans in Louisiana but involved bringing to bear the full might of all of the United States' emergency forces. That is significant because it shows that the Achaean Sympolity was prepared to protect the interests of all its members, requiring all its members to impose sanctions on any third state that wronged any one member.

Before resorting to appealing to third states to act as arbitrators, the Sympolity could initially attempt to resolve conflicts internally. Several surviving inscriptions attest to this (*IG* VIII 189, 24ff, *SIG*^{3} 471; Aymard 1938, p. 166–169). The consent of the federal Assembly was required (Rizakis 2015, p. 129) to appeal to a third state to resolve intra-Sympolity conflicts. One such instance occurred between Messene and Megalopolis in 180 where, upon an appeal by the latter to the Achaean *Synodos*, the case was adjudicated ad hoc by a committee of 17 *hegemons*, likely members of the Sympolity's political elite (Livy 32.31.1; Aymard 1938, p. 328; Arnaoutoglou 2009–2010; Rizakis 2015, p. 130). This case did not end there: it was again adjudicated by a committee of judges specifically from Aegion, the Sympolity's capital. There followed a third phase to this case, probably following an appeal by the Messenians, because there exists a reference to a committee of judges from

Miletus issuing the final, definitive verdict. Throughout the three phases of this case, the Sympolity maintained a supervisory role in the judicial process (Rizakis 2015, p. 131).

In each of these cases, the decisions on borders, commercial and various other issues, were binding—in theory, at least—on the city-states involved, which were supposed to comply with them. However, it is not known what the limits were to intervention by the Sympolity regarding enforcement. There are four relevant scenarios. The first, the 'optimal', concerns a verdict of a third state's arbitration, with which the city-states involved comply. The second scenario concerns the case where one or both parties to the conflict reject the verdict.

What happened in such cases? Would the Sympolity then appeal to another city-state to act as arbitrator, or would it resort to the use of force to induce compliance? A definitive answer to this is unknown, but we believe that given that the desire to maintain the Sympolity's cohesion was paramount in the consciousness of its leaders, we speculate that if the federal policymakers felt new arbitration might yield a viable and acceptable solution, then this was the initial resort. The abovementioned instance involving Messene and Megalopolis is a case in point. The first adjudication by a committee of *hegemons* was not successful, leading to a second attempt, by Aegion, the Sympolity's capital, also unsuccessful, leading to yet another and ultimately successful effort, this time by a third state, Miletus. This case clearly illustrates how deeply ingrained—at least, among the Sympolity's leadership—the desire to cultivate and maintain a constructive and sincere spirit of cooperation by all parties was, with the ultimate aim achieving the common good, the well-being of all the city-states.

The third scenario concerns the case of one party to the conflict, a member city-state of the Sympolity, while the opposing city-state was a third party. In such cases, the Sympolity undertook to defend the interests of its member in the event the decision by the other state's arbitration proved unacceptable. How would this have been accomplished? By diplomacy? By military means, or a combination of the two? That is not known, but one can reasonably suppose that in any event, the Sympolity would not abandon its member and would defend its interests—to one extent or another. The instance mentioned above concerning the dispute between Stymphalos and the Elateians of Phthiotis, who attempted to appropriate cultivatable land belonging to the former, with the Sympolity intervening on behalf of Stymphalos, attests to this.

The fourth scenario concerns a case of a third city-state, acting as arbitrator, decides against a member of the Sympolity, and in favour of another, state. What was the reaction in such cases? Was there a specific protocol to be followed, or would the Sympolity demand its member comply with the verdict from a third city-state, or would it support its member by all means necessary, even if its leaders felt its member was at fault? All of the above are difficult issues and, as with much issues relating to our analysis up to this point, there is no verified evidence to support one over the other with certainty. Accordingly, what we have presented here is food for thought, issues for future research related to the Sympolity, and how it functioned.

What does appear to have been the Sympolity's practice regarding justice in general was that court cases, as well as the legal backdrop for a host of agreements (e.g. of a commercial nature), could be resolved directly between involved complainants or, if that failed, such litigants (persons, merchants, ordinary citizens or even city-states) could appeal to the federal legal services. The regional courts considered cases only at the city-state level (Larsen 1972, p. 81–83). Generally, in the Greek federations, both the regional as well as the federal courts were obligated to provide legal services and adjudicate civil and criminal cases. One case was that of a wealthy woman, Nicareta, who had loaned substantial sums (10,085 *drachmae* and two *obols*) to the city of Orchomenos, a member of the *Koinon* of Boeotia. The city's failure to repay her led to a legal battle between the two in which Nicareta eventually prevailed in the federal courts. It is obvious that secondary level (federal) courts would have also existed in the Achaean Sympolity. We will revert to this interesting case involving Nicareta in 7.1.

That there existed higher federal courts in at least some of the federal formations of the Hellenistic Period is attested to by an important piece of information provided by Chaniotis (1999b) and Ager (2015, p. 479) on the island of Crete where, at that time, a Hellenistic *Koinon* functioned. There existed what was called the *Koinodikion* that adjudicated disputes between its member city-states. Furthermore, common judicial practices between states throughout the Hellenistic world have been verified by various researchers.[15] The existence of federal courts in Achaea is also supported by historians such as Larsen (1971) and Cartledge and Spawforth (2002, p. 75). The Achaeans had functional federal courts similar to those in the neighbouring Aetolian and Boeotian federal states. For the Achaean and Boeotian federations, there is much epigraphical evidence and many sources which attest to the existence of courts at both the local city-state and the federal level (*SEG* 23.271; *IG* VII. 3172.77; Polyb. 24.8.4–5; Mackil 2013, p. 352, 354). It should also be noted that according to Polybius (2.37), at the time when he was recording the events, the Achaeans had succeeded in '. . .having. . .the same laws. . .and judges. . .', indicating that there was a specific framework of laws under which the judges of every city-state had to try all cases. Larsen (1968, p. 220) mentions the existence of federal laws and *dicasts* (judges), indicating that the federal administration of justice was more highly developed than in some other federal states.

Put differently, we argue that, yes, each judge in each city-state had the authority to dispense justice in accordance with his own free will; nevertheless, he had to follow a specific model of procedural principles, practices and laws put in place by the pan-Achaean federal Assembly. In support of this, Larsen (1968, p. 231) refers to

[15]On this, see Müller (2016), who provides further references. In fact, economic cooperation between the Greek city-states had already been achieved during the Classical Period. A characteristic example is the Delian League (also known as the Athenian Alliance) which consisted of a very large unified military and economic/commercial area of 316 city-states (Figueira 1998, p. 52). These states, with Athens the leader, shared common economic, commercial and judicial practices and rules of behaviour (Woolmer 2016; Bitros et al. 2020). Thus, the idea of cooperation on judicial issues was already familiar to the Greeks from the Classical Period.

an inscription discovered listing 24 *nomographoi*, public magistrates whose role was to record the legislation passed in the Achaean Sympolity, from 17 city-states, plus one secretary. Rizakis (2015, p. 126) refers to the existence of the institution of *nomographoi* as well, referring to an inscription (*IG* IV I^2.73) relating to the period 207–201. The city-states each had their own *nomographoi*, which means that the city-states had laws and law-making machinery of their own (Larsen 1968, p. 234). Each city-state, depending on its size, sent one, two or three citizens to this service of the Sympolity for this purpose. Most of the city-states were entitled to just one representative, but three had two each, and two others had three each. This separation of judicial jurisdiction between the city-state and regional/federal levels is a key intertemporal principle that applies to all true federal states.

Thus, the Achaean Sympolity had a formulated, organised system to dispense justice, under its aegis and supervision. The *nomographoi* were also empowered to review the laws periodically (Larsen 1968, p. 235). Specific examples that attest that justice at the federal level functioned in practice, dispensing either punishments or large fines on public officials found guilty. Pausanias (7.13.3) refers to one case where an especially large fine of 50 *talents* was imposed on the *strategos* Damocritus in 148, as already mentioned earlier. The judges also adjudicated cases of high treason, and occasionally, the federal Assembly itself acted as a court, punishing the guilty with heavy penalties, even exile or death (Aymard 1938, p. 182–183; Larsen 1968, p. 236–237; Rizakis 2015, p. 129). A sentence of exile mentioned here meant that the Achaean Sympolity had probably adopted the institution of *ostracism*, or some version thereof, along the lines of the Athenian model.[16]

Larsen (1968, p. xxiv) further argues that, in addition to the *nomographoi*, another key institutional body existed as well, not only in the Achaean but also in the Aetolian and Acarnanian Sympolities. This had to do with *nomophylakes*, meaning ‘guardians of the laws’. This special body was first introduced in the fourth century in Athens, and it was responsible for the safety and protection of written laws from forgery, loss or damage to the inscribed passages, etc. For this purpose, the *nomophylakes* had full access to the *metroon*, also known as *nomophylakion,* which was a special purpose building designed for the preservation of all these important archives (Sickinger 2004, p. 95–86, 102–104; Lanni 2006). With that in mind, an Achaean *metroon* or *nomophylakion* must have existed as well and was probably located in the capital, Aegion.

Finally, according to Mackil (2013, p. 385), the decisions of local magistracies, laws, and courts did not conflict with federal Aetolian Sympolity’s laws. This is a very important qualitative element that is vital and necessary for the success of a federal political structure. Mackil states that local and regional law and local/regional responsibilities did not overlap with the federal ones. Every judge or magistrate knew which were his responsibilities and to what degree he had the discretion to exercise them so that they did not overlap with those of the federal magistrates and

[16]For a detailed description of the policies of exile and *ostracism* in ancient Athens, see, among others, Forsdyke (2005).

judges. This Aetolian practise can be interpreted as an early application of the *principle of subsidiarity* as it exists in the European Union today. In all probability, it was practiced too in the Achaean Sympolity as a general principle of functioning of the public administration.

6.4 The Military Organisation of the Achaean Armed Forces

The federal structure of the Sympolity was reflected in its military organisation. As discussed above, both the political and military head of state was the *strategos* who had the authority to call to arms a part or all federal units, as Philopoemen had done in 200. All three bodies, the *strategos*, the *ipparchos* and the *nauarchos* headed the armed forces which consisted of units provided by the member city-states (Strabo 9; Polyb. 4.59, 5.95, 28.6), while, as Larsen (1968, p. 220) notes, the *hypostrategoi* were the regional commanders of the troops supplied by the administrative districts (*synteleiai*).

Table 6.1 below is based on Russell and Cohn (2012, p. 36) and presents a list of *strategoi* in their order of service, dependent on available and reliable records. Larsen (1971) and Walbank (1985, p. 28) both further note that there existed a measure for administrative autonomy in the use of the federal military forces. For example, in the western reaches of the Sympolity, four cities, Dyme, Pherae, Tritaia and Patras, in 219, fielded a separate federal military force known as the *synteleia of Patrikis,* under the command of a *hypostrategos.* There may even have been other such instances, though Larsen (1971, p. 84) does not believe it likely—mistakenly, we believe—claiming that instance of a semi-independent federal force was the result of particular geopolitical circumstances.

Polybius (Hist. 4.59) reports that during the time of the Social War (220–217), under the *hypostrategos* Mikkos, from the city of Dyme, federal forces unsuccessfully attempted to resist an Aetolian raid against several cities led by their *strategos*, Euripidas. Larsen (1971) reports that each city-state of the Sympolity could undertake individual military initiative at its discretion in defence of its territorial integrity, as in the case of Corinth in 197, until the full might of the Sympolity's armed forces could be brought to bear.

Anderson (1967) and Larsen (1971) all report that the military formations of the Sympolity were essentially based on those of the Greek *hoplite phalanx*. On the back, though, of innovations introduced by Aratus, among others, the Achaean forces were now backed by units of light infantry, more flexible, such as the *thureophoroi.* Later, in 208/7, with the reforms of Philopoemen, the Achaeans adopted the Macedonian-type *phalanx*. Meanwhile, characteristically, in 217, the Sympolity possessed a mixed mercenary force of 8500 troops (8000 infantry and 500 horsemen), whereas a citizen's militia from all the regions of the Sympolity contributed a further 3000 infantry and 300 horsemen. The Sympolity also had at its disposal six battle-ready *triremes* (warships) (Pol. 91.5–8; Mackil 2013, p. 119–120,

Table 6.1 The Achaean *strategoi*, from 256 to 146 BCE

Year of service	Strategos	City of origin	Year of service	Strategos	City of origin
256/5	Margus	Ceryneia	**208/7**	Philopoemen	Megalopolis
245/4	Aratus	Sicyon	**200/199**	Cycliadas	;
244/3	Dioedas	?	**199/8**	Aristaenus	Megalopolis
243/2	Aratus	Sicyon	**198/7**	Nicostratus	Megalopolis
242/1	Aegialeas	?	**195/4**	Aristaenus	Megalopolis
241/234	Aratus	Sicyon	**193/2**	Philopoemen	Megalopolis
234/3	Lydiades	Megalopolis	**192/1**	Diophanes	;
233/2	Aratus	Sicyon	**191/186**	Philopoemen	Megalopolis
232/1	Lydiades	Megalopolis	**186/5**	Aristaenus	Megalopolis
231/0	Aratus	Sicyon	**185/4**	Lycortas	Megalopolis
230/229	Lydiades	Megalopolis	**184/182**	Archon	;
228/7	Aristomachos	Argos	**183/2**	Philopoemen	Megalopolis
227/6	Aratus	Sicyon	**182/1**	Aristaenus	Megalopolis
226/5	Hyperbatos	?	**180/179**	Callicrates	Leontion
225/4	Timoxernos	?	**175/4**	Xenarchos	;
225/4	Aratus	Sicyon	**172/169**	Archon	;
224	Timoxenos	?	**151/0**	Menalkidas	Sparta
224/218	Aratus	Sicyon	**150/149**	Diaeus	Megalopolis
218/7	Epiratos	?	**149/148**	Damocritus	;
217–213	Aratus	Sicyon	**148/147**	Critolaus	Megalopolis
210/9	Cycliadas	?	**147/146**	Diaeus	Megalopolis

123). In total, this amounted to a force of 11,000 infantry and 800 horsemen, composed of conscripted and mercenary *hoplites* and officers—professional soldiers, in the modern sense. The deployment of mixed military formations, composed of both infantry and cavalry, was common in all the federations, most characteristically, in the Aetolian Sympolity (Diod. Sic. 20.20.3; Rzepka 2009, p. 19–31).

The existence of cavalry in the Achaean armed forces is significant in that it underscores directly a socio-economic dimension to the Sympolity's military organisation. There may have even been some cavalry units financed by citizens with the wherewithal to maintain horse and rider, such as the young horsemen that followed Philopoemen to suppress the insurrection of the Messenians, as mentioned in 5.3. Non-mercenary Achaean horsemen must certainly have been well-off citizens since the cost of maintaining a horse was extremely high (Kagan and Viggiano 2013, p. 11). However, it would be misleading to claim that they were part of private armies employed by the wealthy as was not uncommon in the kingdoms of that time, or much later, during the Middle Ages in Europe, where private armies were, in fact, quite common. Therefore, private armies, either paid and controlled by well-off nobles, or ad hoc military units composed of wealthy aristocrats did not exist as a general rule, although the possibility cannot be ruled out entirely.

Figure 6.1 that follows presents a version of military organisation in terms of its administrative structure. Based on what we have discussed to this point, it shows the

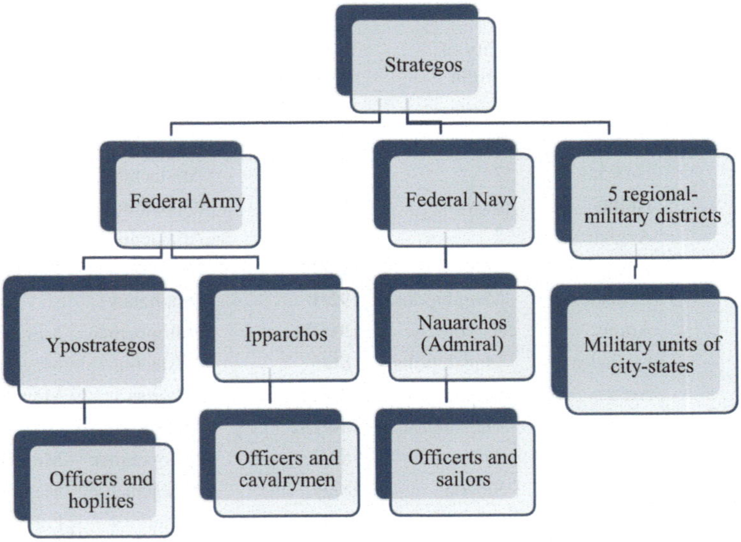

Fig. 6.1 The administrative structure of the military organisation of the Achaean Sympolity

organisation at the top level of the hierarchy (the *strategos*), the two main branches, the land army (the *hypostrategos* and *ipparchos*) and the naval force (*nauarchos*) and at the level of the regional military formations (the *synteleia of Patrikis,* the regions of Megalopolis, Sparta, Aetolia, Elis). We must also mention the term of service of these officers of the Achaean armed forces. Starting from the bottom up, the lower-ranked officers were either conscripted or hired by the state. They offered their services as public functionaries for military matters, similar to the logic of modern armed forces, where commissioned and non-commissioned officers staff the armed forces. As far as the mercenary *hoplites* were concerned, they were probably hired on a short-term basis—'time-restricted hires'—probably on an annual basis.

As far as the upper echelons were concerned—*strategos, hypostrategos, ipparchos, nauarchos*— the term of service was for a single year. One might consider that this must have affected the efficiency of the federal armed forces since frequent changes in military leadership can only adversely affect the training and maintenance of a cohesive fighting force. Each incoming administration inevitably wants to introduce its adjustments to existing policies and methodology, tending to disrupt the armed forces' effectiveness.[17] In all likelihood, this problem was resolved, or at least mitigated, by electing officials from a pool of limited—but tried and tested—personnel with considerable experience in administration in general, both civil and military. Moreover, there remains the question as to when a newly elected military hierarchy actually assumed their duties. We addressed this

[17]This problem affected civil administration as well.

issue in 5.1, where we argued that until 217, elections were held sometime in the spring, but from that year on, they were held in early autumn.

Finally, one additional issue was whether there was any form of a standing federal army or whether the Sympolity's fielded force was an amalgam of the contributions by each city-state. On this, Larsen (1968, p. xxvii) notes that the armies of the Greek federations were composed of contingents contributed by the various city-states under the direct command of their local officers. The central command rested with the federal officials. This strongly suggests that the units of the city-states were gathered together to form the unified Achaean armed forces.

6.5 The Administrative Organisation at the State/Regional Level

Based on the model of the military organisation, we can draw information on the organisation of the Sympolity at the regional level. We believe that the five (or three) military districts mentioned above could have been mirrored in the civil administration, as well. Although we have no relevant information from sources, extrapolating from the significant expansion of the Sympolity during Aratus' time and beyond, it is logical to infer that the new regions (Sparta/Laconia, Elis, Messenia, etc.) that were added to the Achaean Sympolity's territory in 191 would have led to the reconfiguration of its administrative division at the regional level.

The neighbouring Aetolian Sympolity was divided into seven regional units. Each one had a civil administrator, the *boularchos*, a military commander, the *epilectarchos*, the head of a troop of 1000 professional *hoplites*, or *epilectoi*, as well as an economic administrator called the *tamias*. This last, together with his counterparts in the other units, was responsible for the federal treasury. One of them must have functioned as the head ('chief') *tamias*, acting also as the Sympolity's 'Finance Minister', to use modern terminology (Economou et al. 2015). We assume a similar organisation at the regional level existed in the Achaean Sympolity. And just as in the Aetolian Sympolity, the post of the Achaean regional 'chief *tamias*' was obviously highly crucial to the implementation and success of the overall federal policy. Thus, the chief *tamias* should be included among the Sympolity's highest-ranking officials such as the *strategos*, the *ipparchos* and the *grammateus*. As regards how the chief *tamias* was elected, we believe we can reasonably assume that it was by a committee of his peers, the other regional *tamiai*.[18]

Regarding the interaction between administration at the federal level and the city-state level, Rizakis (2015, p. 128) condenses the basic elements of that interoperability, arguing that although the point where one side's impact on issues ended and the other's began was inconclusive, Greek federalism as a whole was characterised

[18]However, the possibility that the Achaean Finance Minister was elected instead, in one of the annual major pan-Achaean federal assemblies, cannot be excluded.

by some common features. Each member city-state retained its autonomy in terms of its right to maintain its own laws and 'constitution', while concurrently, those of the Sympolity were also applicable. Moreover, every city-state had its own administration as well as its own currency (Walbank 1993). On this, Larsen (1968, p. 220) notes that although there were federal laws and magistrates, city-states had their own magistrates and undoubtedly special local regulations as well in some city-states. Nevertheless, federal justice did not overlap with local city-state justice, and the duties of federal magistrates did not overlap with those of the city-state level magistrates.

Mackil (2013, p. 375) adds that each city-state retained its autonomy regarding control over its sanctuaries; control over its own finances; the preservation of local magistracies, laws, and courts, insofar as these did not conflict with federal laws; control over its citizenship rolls; and interaction by the city-states with other states in ways that had neither military nor political implications. Furthermore, in 6.3., we provided evidence regarding the institution of *nomographoi*, one of whose duties was to periodically develop and revise state laws (Larsen 1968, p. 235). According to Larsen (ibid., 231), there were *nomographoi* at both the city-state level as well as the federal. That means that the city-states had laws and law-making machinery of their own (ibid., 234). This separation of judicial jurisdiction between the city-state and regional/federal level is a key intertemporal principle that applies in true federal states. Thus, the Achaean Sympolity disposed of a coordinated, organised system of dispensing justice under its supervision and aegis.

According to Aymard (1938, p. 166) and Larsen (1968, p. xxviii), the Achaean Sympolity retained the right of binding decision over all member city-states in a number of issues such as international relations and foreign policy, defence and security in terms of military and economic organisation. The city-states, however, did retain a high level of autonomy not limited to religious, athletic and general cultural matters. Larsen (1968, p. xxviii) writes that when cities seem to take independent action in foreign affairs, this action usually turned out to be connected with some such innocuous matter as the recognition of a religious festival or the inviolability of a sanctuary. Although the city-states did not have the right of drawing up foreign policy agreements with the 'outside world'—unless approved by the central authority—nevertheless, proportional participation in the principal state institutions provided the conditions for effective integration with the framework of the Sympolity since the city-states could express their positions and be heard through the state machinery of the *synkletos*, the *synodos* and the *Boule*.

Finally, Table 6.2 refers to the 103 city-states listed as members during the period of the Sympolity's greatest extension, in 191, when, with the inclusion of Laconia, Messenia and most of Elis, it had unified almost the whole of the Peloponnesus under the Achaean umbrella. There may have been even more city-states included, but the 103 listed are verifiable. It is not at all certain that they disposed of a uniform population composition between them. According to Hansen and Nielsen (2004) and Ober (2008, p. 85–86; 2011, p. 7) during the Archaic Period (750–510), the approximately 1000 listed cities of the Greek world presented a uniformity in the

Table 6.2 The distribution of 103 cities of the Achaean Sympolity within the seven municipalities of the Peloponnesus today

Municipality	City-states
Achaea (14)	Aigeira, Aiges, Aegion, Boura, Dyme, Helice, Ceryneia, Leontion, Patra, Pellene, Rypai, Tritaia, Pherae, Ophelos
Arcadia (35)	Athenaion, Alipheira, Alea, Asea, Gortyna, Dipaia, Heraia, Thelpousa, Theisoa, Thyrea, Kallista, Caphyae, Cleitor, Kynaetha, Lousio, Lycosura, Lyrkeia, Mainalos, Manthyrea, Mantineia, Megalopolis, Methydrion, Nemea, Orgees, Arcadian Orchomenos, Palladion, Paos, Stymphalos, Pheneos, Phygaleia, Tegea, Teuthis, Phleious, Psophis
Argolis (10)	Aegina, Alea, Argos, Asine, Epidauros, Ermione, Cleonae, Nauplia, Tiryntha, Troezen
Elis (9)	Epitalio, Zakynthos, Elis, Helida, Kyllene, Lasion, Oenoe, Olympia, Pylos
Messenia (11)	Abia, Ampheia, Andania, Aepeia, Asine, Thouria, Kyparissia, Lepreo, Methoni, Samiko, Phares
Sparta/Laconia (24)	Akries, Alagonia, Asopos, Boies, Brasies, Bilemina, Geronthes, Gytheion, Epidauros, Limera, Therapyes, Zaras, Kainopolis, Kardamili, Karyes, Krokaies, Kythera, Las, Leuktro, Oitylo, Prasies, Sparta, Teuthrone, Pharis

distribution of the population, except for the 'super-poleis': Athens, Sparta and Syracuse. Between 750 and 190, this must have shifted quite a lot. New large cities had appeared, mostly in the Hellenistic East, such as Antioch and Alexandria. This, though, had little impact on the situation in mainland Greece.

On the other hand, significant researchers, such as Morris (2004), Ober (2010, 2011, 2015) and Harris (2016), have argued that at least for a while during the Classical Period, economic development had been achieved, at least in mainland Greece, although, in the absence of specific data, this is extremely difficult to quantify. However, this development was not sustained, and it is certain that some time in the middle of the Hellenistic Period—probably—or perhaps later, on the verge of the Roman conquest, it had come to an end (Tridimas 2018). The picture becomes rather obscure because of the constant warfare, mostly intramural conflicts in the Peloponnesus and the Greek world in general, the recruitment of mercenaries and the emigration of a large percentage of the Greek population eastward after Alexander the Great's conquests. This makes it exceedingly difficult to estimate the size of the cities' populations, especially of war-torn Peloponnesus, which concerns us here.

Of course, given the institutions of *isopoliteia, asylia* and *proxeny* (especially the first), it is certain that the mobility of the population within the Sympolity increased dramatically. Perhaps, too, there was migration from other parts of Greece to the Peloponnesus, or by Achaeans away from the Peloponnesus. We must assume that the union of the Peloponnesus through the Sympolity's expansion must have increased population mobility in all directions, although without altering the characteristics of its city-states to any significant extent.

6.6 The 'Common Foreign and Security Policy' of the Achaean Sympolity

As, among others, Larsen (1944), Mackil (2013), Ager (2015) and we have stated in many relevant publications on the Greek federations,[19] one, if not the most basic reasons for banding together in a Sympolity, was the need of smaller, weaker city-states to achieve more effective defence. On its own, if faced by a more powerful foe, such as the Kingdom of Macedon, such a city-state had but two choices: either resist and be defeated or submit to becoming a protectorate or satellite. The weaker state would then be obliged to accept the will and political and geopolitical aims (see Clausewitz [1832], 1989) of the more powerful state, which would enforce its policies through what J. Nye (1991, 2009, 2011) terms *hard power*.

As is clear from our analysis up to this point, to avoid this, smaller city-states resorted to banding together, first, in *amphictyonies* and alliances, and later, in more sophisticated formulations, sympolities or *Koina,* to address this issue of defence. As mentioned earlier, although the Macedonians had prevailed in southern Greece after the Battle of Chaeronea in 338, the death of Alexander created the opportunity for a significant number of Greek city-states in the south to declare their independence, a development that subsequent Macedonian monarchs tried to reverse (Finer 1997). As we have analysed, within this context, both the Achaean and Aetolian Sympolities grew progressively stronger. However, the *raison d'être* of the sympolities was not limited to the fear of smaller city-states of a more powerful neighbour, it was also related to the growing sophistication of the citizens of the Greek city-states who had become aware that participation in some form of alliance would reduce the cost of defence, freeing resources for other public and private needs.

A significant dimension to this issue is provided by Ager (2015, p. 478), who refers to the case of one city-state, Epidauros, which was hoping to join the Achaean Sympolity. Epidauros had serious issues with one of the Sympolity's members, Corinth, and could only join on condition they were resolved. This was an important prerequisite to ensure that no territorial disputes would be raised between member city-states, and crucial to ensuring harmony and peace within the Sympolity was maintained. Both the Achaean and the Aetolian federations defended their members militarily if necessary, against any third state. To express clearly the significance of the provision of defence by a federation (or of a military alliance) against a third state, below, we resort once again to game theory (as analysed in 3.3) in Table 6.3.

Initially, the table presents two cases—Argos and Corinth. Let us say that the Achaean Sympolity did not exist and that these were two independent city-states that had serious issues in their relations and, militarily, were of equal strength. This is not unlikely as both these city-states historically had always been powerful players in the Peloponnesus. Their dispute could easily escalate and lead to military confrontation.

[19] Economou et al. (2015), Economou and Kyriazis (2015a, b, c, 2016a, c, 2018) regarding the Aetolian, Arcadian and Achaean federal states.

Table 6.3 Game and payoffs regarding war and peace strategy of Argos as an independent city-state and as a member of the Achaean Sympolity

Argos	Scenario 1		
		Corinth	
		Peace strategy	War strategy
	Peace strategy	(8, 8)	(1, 10)
	War strategy	(10, 1)	(5, 5) Armed peace (0, 0) War
Argos and Achaean Sympolity	Scenario 2		
		Corinth	
		Peace strategy	War strategy
	Peace strategy	(8, 8)	(7, 1)
	War strategy	(10, 1)	(7, 3) Armed peace (5, 2) War

Table 6.3 presents the outcome for either state, based on two armament and disarmament scenarios. If the two city-states choose to resolve their differences amicably, this would be the ideal scenario, receiving the grade of (8, 8). If Argos resorts to war and Corinth disarmament, the score would be (10, 1), assuming that Argos would win and gain further in strength, acquiring new wealth through war booty as well as land and other resources from the enemy. The opposite scenario, where Argos chooses disarmament and Corinth war, would reverse the score: (1, 10).

The fourth case, that of 'armed peace', is the most interesting. In this, based on Scenario 1, Argos and Corinth indulge in an exhaustive arms race which does maintain peace, but at a high price, ruinous defence expenditures that limit resources that can otherwise be applied for the well-being of their citizens.[20] Thus, the score, in this case, is a standoff: (5, 5). In the event of war, however, given their approximately equal military capability, the result would be a long-term struggle, exhausting both city-states—a zero-sum game where both lose their power and their soundness: (0, 0).

On the other hand, in Scenario 2, Argos decides to join the Achaean Sympolity, while Corinth does not. The first two sub-scenarios have the same result as in Scenario 1. The third and fourth, however, differ. In the third case, even if Argos chooses not to arm itself, if Corinth does attack, Argos will prevail because the other members of the Sympolity will back her militarily. Corinth will be defeated (in all probability) and the victors, including Argos, will reap a portion of the vanquished's

[20] Modern cases of arms races include, for example, the USA and the USSR during the Cold war period.

wealth in the form of war booty or land or war compensation or infrastructure assets: labour (in the form of slavery) and capital (machinery).

The fourth sub-scenario is the case of an arms race which, for Corinth, would again be burdensome; for Argos, however, because the member city-states share the cost of defence, it would be considerably less. An 'armed peace' would cost Argos only a 3, leaving a rating of 7, while Corinth would have to undertake much more military expenditure to efficiently confront Argos and her allies. Thus, for Corinth, the cost for armed peace would be high and she rates only 3 for this sub-scenario, thus, the score would be (7, 3). In the event of extended war without a clear victor, this would be less burdensome on Argos since the damage would be shared with the other member city-states. For Corinth, on the other hand, the effect would still be almost ruinous—score: (5, 2) in favour of Argos.

In support of the above and to demonstrate that the matter of common defence and security was the paramount concern over all others, we refer again to an incident concerning the attitude and behaviour of three Achaean cities—Dyme, Tritaia and Pherae—during the so-called Social War of 220–217. The Aetolian forces advancing from the north into the Sympolity wreaked considerable damage to these cities. The Aetolians were notorious for their propensity to pillage areas they occupied. These three cities were the first to face the Aetolians' onslaught and, despite appeals to the Sympolity for help, it never came because, according to Polybius (4.60.4–5), the Achaeans were unable to pay their mercenaries that had fought against Cleomenes III of Sparta.

Polybius here implies that the Achaeans' coffers were empty, and they had no resources to hire new mercenaries to face the Aetolian threat. Polybius' observation reveals the Sympolity's serious problem at that time: exhausted by successive defeats by Cleomenes' forces, the Achaean federal army had not been able to regroup properly. This problem, however, obliged the three city-states to refuse to pay the annual tax to the Sympolity (*koinas eisphoras*) for the year 219, using those funds to hire mercenaries of their own (Polyb. 5.30., 5.91., 5.94; Larsen 1968, p. 233). From the moment the Sympolity was unable to meet its obligations to defend them, automatically, any obligation of the three city-states toward the federal government was null and void (*SEG* 40.393).

Polybius criticizes their stance, believing that it only served to weaken the Sympolity further. Mackil (2013, p. 497), however, observes that by acting as they did, the three city-states were only serving notice that they would not accept the failure of the Sympolity's defence obligations. In this light, as Mackil further notes, the three city-states' refusal to accept their tax obligation not only did not harm the Sympolity but, on the contrary, served to strengthen it; the three's refusal can be seen as a direct effort to exert pressure on the central authority of the Sympolity to live up to its commitments to its members. The Sympolity imposed any penalties on the three members, but simply accepted their act, recognising the fact that the basic principle of the forming the Sympolity was the provision to all its members of security and defence.

This incident indirectly underscores another dimension which had evolved as a basic principle binding together the federal government, the member city-states and their citizens: reciprocity of obligation between the Sympolity and its members. This enduring principle, the instance with the three city-states mentioned above notwithstanding, constitutes, we believe, one of the basic reasons for its success as a historical phenomenon.

Chapter 7
The Economic Institutions of the Achaean Federal State

Several institutions and political/management strategies have been identified so far, which relate to policy options and practices that, over time, one encounters in federal or confederal states. We have confirmed and analysed the existence of participatory and representative bodies such as the Achaean federal Assembly (*Ecclesia,* or *Synodos*) and the extraordinary federal Assemblies (the *Synkletoi*), as well as the federal Council (*Boule*). We have confirmed that there was a democratically elected government at the federal level, and respectively, in each member city-state as well.

Also, in Chap. 6, we noted how the Sympolity was organised at the regional level, both in terms of civil administration and military organisation, and examined the political institutions that facilitated the emergence of a unified space within which existed equality of political rights and the right to free movement for all citizens—*isopoliteia*—and for anyone else residing therein as well, either by concession or because of bilateral agreements (*asylia, pryoxeny*).

In this chapter, we examine the practices by which the Sympolity's economic activity was carried out. This chapter effectively complements the sixth chapter's analysis, homogenising the factors that ensured the success of the political experiment that was the Achaean Sympolity, by ensuring its coherence, efficiency and sustainability as a whole for the period 389–146, and especially for the period 280–146, the second phase of the Sympolity's existence. Essentially, Chaps. 6 and 7 contain detailed information on several important criteria of political institutions and economic policy related to states organised along federal lines.

In Sect. 7.1, our analysis is concerned with the concepts of *enktesis* and *epigamia,* both related to property rights, civil rights and the right to do business anywhere within the Sympolity; all these together constitute what in today's parlance is called basic principles of economic freedom. In Sect. 7.2, we refer to the question of whether there was a federal currency union, a key element in the success of a federation. Section 7.3 concerns public finances and expenditures, examining how the federal budget was prepared, what happened in cases of budgetary deficits and how public debt statements were prepared, both at the federal and at the city-state level. Section 7.4 focusses on the issue of the provision of public goods and that of

E. M. L. Economou, *The Achaean Federation in Ancient Greece*, Frontiers in Economic History, https://doi.org/10.1007/978-3-030-52697-9_7

positive externalities, on the issue of economic development, on welfare redistribution and taxation. This section also addresses the criteria of *economic/fiscal federalism*[1] as a factor in creating a viable federation. Section 7.5 analyses the status of the other social groups, focusing on women, children, *metics* (foreigners) and slaves. Finally, Sect. 7.6 summarises our analysis, focussing on the value added by the political and economic institutions of the Achaean state.

7.1 The Economic Freedom and Market-Type Institutions of the Unified Market of the Achaean Federal State

Historians who have studied Ancient Greek federalism have focused relatively less on the economic issues and the institutions of the sympolities, given that the key primary sources focussed on historical and political issues and information. However, from the perspective not of a historian, but an Economic Historian or an Institutional Economist, one can extrapolate a great deal from the historical information concealed within those ancient sources and from the archaeological research.

Beginning with the great economist-philosopher and Nobel laureate F.A. Hayek ([1948] 1996) who, in his book *Individualism and Economic Order,* referring to the issues of the federal organisation, finds three significant reasons why, in its political expression, federalism entails economic cooperation between members. First, because the federal authority must retain the right to control exports and imports as this is a serious issue that could lead to conflict. Second, if barriers are put in place on commerce between members of a federation, that undermines the basic commitments between members on common defence and security, leading to *regional protectionism*, limiting the movement of goods and services. Third, *economic federalism* promotes solidarity and thus, peace between members.

Hayek's second axiom refers to economic protectionism and relates to Mercantilist Theory which prevailed as an economic model of the international economy during the Early Modern period in Europe (1549–1789). This economic model was based on one state strengthening at the expense of another, a neighbour or a rival, inevitably leading to extended military confrontation, the main reason being that it was ethnocentric and not cooperative/transnational. In other words, national well-being was not guaranteed through the collective prosperity of the involved states, or at least, a group of states with which the homonymous national economy maintained economic, trade and civil-military and diplomatic relations. This mercantilistic system was strongly challenged by the proponents of *Physiocracy*, whose leading figures were François Quesnay (1694–1774) and Pierre Samuel Du Pont de Nemours (1739–1817). With his work, *An Inquiry into the Nature and Causes of the Wealth of Nations,* the great Scottish Classical philosopher of economic thought, Adam Smith,

[1]These terms have been employed by, among others, Pauly (1973) and Musgrave (1998).

disavowed economic protectionism with even more structured arguments, introducing the concepts of the *invisible hand* and the *free market economy.*

Hayek's ([1948] 1996) third axiom that economic cooperation within a federal state model creates the preconditions for solidarity and, in consequence, peace among its members is considered now a given concept of the international economic system. For instance, the correlation between improving financial position as an incentive to participate in federal state forms is well-certified in the modern bibliography (see, among others, Pauly 1973). Hayek's third axiom also relates to the *Liberal School* of International Relations which, as opposed to the *Realist School,* holds that economic and commercial activity creates a potent interaction between countries that benefit from the increase in their prosperity, making the cost of stopping it and war extremely unbeneficial. War over understanding and cooperation is discouraged.

For the *Liberal School,* nations characterised by liberal economic institutions such as the protection of property rights and competitive markets are generally less aggressive than those that are not, i.e. nations whose economies are state-run (McDonald 2007, 2009; Copeland 2014, p. 1, 7, 18–19). Accordingly, the interdependence between countries through commerce is strongly related to more peaceful behaviour by those nations.[2] Mackil (2015, p. 488) further argues that the acute fragmentation of the Greek world into small city-states, mini-states and towns had resulted in severe contractual restrictions on the movement of people and capital. This fragmentation was, to a large extent, due to the geomorphology of the Greek countryside, characterised by frequent changes in the landscape without large and extended agricultural expanses, with the exceptions of the regions of Thessaly, Laconia, Messenia and a few others. Foxhall (1995) and Fleck and Hansen (2006) hold this view as well.

Gradually, between the Archaic and Classical Periods (750–323), institutions were introduced that facilitated greater movement of people and capital between the city-states of the Greek world,[3] initially by granting privileges to a few, such as benefactors and consuls of the cities, as we analysed in 6.2. The next step was affording legal protection for this inter-city-state commerce. In this, the Athenian Democracy was the pioneer introducing during the fifth century a substantial institutional system for the protection of international commerce and of commercial contracts. Typical examples were the *nautodikeia* (maritime courts), and the *dikai emporikai* (trials related to economic/commercial issues) where experienced judges weighed on such issues—impartially, as far as we know—to ensure an active

[2]On this issue, see, among others, Polachek (1992, 1994, 1997), Oneal and Russett (1997, 1999), Caruso (2006, p. 53), Polachek and Seiglie (2007), Dumas (2011), Massoud and Magge (2012), Copeland (2014), Cortes and Montolio (2014), our work (Economou and Kyriazis 2016b), Kollias and Paleologou (2017) and the extensive further references therein.

[3]For these developments, see Lyttkens (2006, 2013), Ober (2010, 2011) and our own, Economou and Kyriazis (2017, 2019b).

economic/commercial environment for both local merchants as well as foreign and other Greek merchants doing business in Athens.[4]

Generally, the Athenian Democracy, to a very significant degree, had evolved a plethora of institutions related to a market-type economy such as the protection of individual property and commercial contracts, as well as the rapid dispensation of justice,[5] private and public banking, insurance against catastrophe and piracy for overseas commerce, consumer protection by the *agoranomoi* against profiteering, the adoption of standard weights and measures for the sale of products, supervised by the so-called *metronomoi,* as well as, of course, the introduction of reliable currency—the Athenian *drachma,* or *glauke*—for city-state and interstate transactions.[6] It is certain that during the Classical Period, these new economic institutions found their way beyond Athens, to the other city-states of the Athenian League in the Aegean.[7] Just as in the British Commonwealth or the USA in recent times, then, Athens, as the leading city-state of the League, on the back of its power, exported many socio-economic and cultural standards and rules of conduct which were adopted by the smaller members (Bitros et al. 2020). Therefore, Athens, as the driving force of political and economic freedoms in the Classical Period, just as the British Commonwealth did in the nineteenth century and the USA in the twentieth century and today, exported its civilisation to the rest of the world, as evidenced in ancient texts, for example, Pericles' *Funeral Oration*, rescued by Thucydides in his *Histories.*

That the Greek world during the Classical Period gradually became more and more familiar with these new tools of economic policy, both the sources and archaeological research, as well as the modern bibliography, confirm it. For instance, Roberts (2011) argues that the banking system was developed not only in Athens[8] but in other places as well, such as the island of Delos towards the end of the third

[4]On these developments, see, among others, the significant work of Cohen (1973, 1992), Woolmer (2016), Economou and Kyriazis (2017, 2019a, b) and Bitros et al. (2020).

[5]As supported by the French political philosopher of the Enlightenment, Montesquieu, among other things, the speedy dispensation of judgment and verdict forms the very foundation of effective justice.

[6]For the development of market-type institutions during the Classical Period in Athens and other city-states, there is a recent vast bibliography with persuasive arguments (the so-called Formalist's approach). See, for example, among others, Cohen (1992), Amemiya (2007), Bitros and Karayannis (2008, 2010, 2013), Kyriazis (2009), Burke (2010), Engen (2010), Halkos and Kyriazis (2010), Lyttkens (2010, 2013), Ober (2010, 2011, 2015), Mackil (2013, 2015), Economou et al. (2015), Economou and Kyriazis (2016a, 2017, 2019a), Harris (2016), Woolmer (2016) and Bitros et al. (2020). This approach revisits the older views of scholars such as Finley (1973, 1985) and Austin and Vidal Naquet (1977), who had argued that the Ancient Greek economy was 'embedded' and characterised by primitive and simple economic activities (the Substantivist's approach). In fact, this debate (*Formalists/Modernists* vs *Primitivists*) goes back to the end of the nineteenth century with the so-called Bücher-Meyer controversy.

[7]On this, see Harris (2016) and Woolmer (2016), in detail.

[8]According to Cohen (1992, p. 31), at least 30 citizens were active in providing banking services in ancient Athens during the Classical Period.

century, beginning of the second century, or in Olympia, because of the Games. He mentions 35 Hellenistic city-states where it has been confirmed that they had instituted advanced banking (banks were known as *trapezai*) during the second century. Banking and the institutions it entails were certainly a part of the wider Hellenistic world, both at the city-state level and up to that of federations and kingdoms.[9] This framework of values, based on a market economy and the free movement of goods, services and people, became a key cornerstone of the economic organisation of the sympolities as well. Mackil (2015, p. 489) notes that most federal states of the Hellenistic world seized the opportunity offered by the new trends of commercial extroversion that were now prevailing everywhere. They adopted a host of innovative forms of economic behaviours such as a common currency, common standards of weights and measures, the expansion of property rights to all citizens residing anywhere within their domain, while some even adopted common taxation policies.

Two new significant economic institutions were embraced as a universal practice between city-states: *enktesis* and *epigamia*, both significant factors in the evolution of property rights over time and their upgrading from the city-state level to that of a federation. The first concerned the right to own property in another city-state. By extension, this meant that in the event of trespass, the complainant could appeal to the federal courts to seek justice as in the case of Nicareta, described in 6.3 above. Related to this was the institution of *epigamia* that confirmed the right for a groom to legally acquire property from his bride's dowry, even if that property was located in another member city-state (Economou and Kyriazis 2017).

Inscriptions have been found confirming that *enktesis* prevailed in the Achaean Sympolity. Inscription (*IPArk* 16), for instance, bears witness that with the incorporation of Arcadian Orchomenos into the Sympolity, all Achaean citizens henceforth enjoyed the right to hold property in that city-state (Mackil 2015, 491–492). That *enktesis* was a general principle valid for all Achaean citizens has been confirmed definitively (Larsen 1968, p. xviii; 1971). Two characteristic cases: Aratus himself owned property in Corinth, and a citizen of Aegeira named Hieron, also owned a house in Argos (Plut. Arat. 41.4, 42.3; Cleo. 19). That was also the case in the other federal states: the Aetolian Sympolity,[10] the Chalcidian *Koinon* (Xen. Hell.5.2.19), as well as the Lycian *Koinon* in Asia Minor (Larsen 1957). For example, the alliance of the Acarnanian *Koinon* with that of the Aetolian Sympolity from the second quarter of the third century gave the citizens of both federal states the right to own property in either one.

Larsen (1968, p. xix) furthermore writes that with *enktesis* and *epigamia,* by extension, any Achaean citizen had the right to contract business anywhere within the Sympolity's territory. Mackil (2013, p. 257) argues that *enktesis* was a natural

[9]For banking in Ptolemaic Egypt, see Manning (2003, 2007), von Reden (2010) and Economou and Kyriazis (2019a).

[10](*IG. IX 1^2*; Xen. Hell. 5.2.19; Scholten 2000, p. 110; Mackil 2013, p. 255, 302–303; Economou et al. 2015; Funke 2015).

response to the need to promote economic mobility between the regional units controlled by the *polis* of each of the Sympolity's city-states, free from the restrictions created by the territorial boundaries that existed before. This strategy of abolishing border restrictions, thus encouraging commercial interaction, is intelligently characterised by Mackil (2013, p. 281) as *interpolis* (inter-city-state) *economic transactions* and as *microregional interdependence.*

In one sense, the Greek federations' member city-states, in practice, followed the basic principle of *comparative advantage*, as propounded by David Ricardo, one of the fathers of the Classical Economics school of thought, which can be condensed into the general idea that each country has a comparative advantage in a particular branch of production, with a corresponding lower opportunity cost. Accordingly, it can offer the products it produces with a lower opportunity cost while importing those that would be too costly to produce, i.e. would have a higher opportunity cost. The general principle of comparative advantage is regarded as a starting and axiomatic principle of modern international trade.

We believe that Ancient Greek politicians and entrepreneurs had a pretty good idea of that basic principle since, according to Xenophon (Ath. Const. 2.3), Plato (Rep. 2.370e – 2.371a) and other philosophers the concept of commercial exchange and interdependence had been instilled as an economic practice in the consciousness of the Greeks of that era. The Ancient Greek economy, during the Hellenistic Period, had, with a few obvious exceptions, gradually but surely moved away from economic nationalism and protectionist practices. A salient exception was Sparta, although sometime in the third century, no longer able to ignore the general economic trends in her neighbours, she abandoned her policy of national self-sufficiency and opened her borders to international trade.

At this point, we must admit that to support with absolute certainty that economic interaction between the Sympolity's members and with other city-states contributed to a rise in the general level of prosperity, we would have to provide tangible cliometric data—GDP, GDP per capita, rate of economic growth, the extent of 'foreign direct investment', the trade balance and the current account balance, in time series format—to prepare a reasonably accurate statistical analysis estimate of the economy's performance, as well as its impact on the population at large.

Unfortunately, because of the lack of pertinent evidence, our estimates are inferred from a synthesis of the historical data at hand, ancient sources and inscriptions, as well as the arguments put forth in the modern bibliography. This approach is not wrong, nor does it lessen the value of the assessment of such research. In any event, at least during a time in Greek antiquity, there was economic growth in Athens and a large part of the Greek world during the Classical Period (North 1990; Morris 1994, 2004; Ober 2010, 2011, 2015; Harris 2016; Tridimas 2018). Mackil (2013, p. 273, 281, 305) believes that the strong commercial interaction between the city-states of the Sympolity was beneficial in terms of economic prosperity. We agree with this, keeping in mind what Hayek ([1948], 1996, p. 255) held as an axiom, that the great advantage of the federal states was that they broke down the barriers to the free movement of people, goods and capital between states and that they were receptive to the creation of common rule of law and a single monetary policy. He writes that the material benefits that would spring from the creation of so large an economic area can hardly be overestimated, and it appears to be taken for granted that economic union and political union would be combined as a matter of course. On a practical level, this axiom relates to what Polybius reported (2.37):

> ...Achaeans, as I have stated before, have in our time made extraordinary progress in material prosperity and internal unity. For though many statesmen had tried in past times to induce the Peloponnesians to join in a league for the common interests of all, and had always failed, because everyone was working to secure his own power rather than the freedom of the whole; yet in our day this policy has made such progress, and been carried out with such completeness, that not only is there in the Peloponnesus a community of interests such as exists between allies or friends, but an absolute identity, of laws, weights, measures and currency. All the States have the same magistrates, senate and judges. Nor is there any difference between the entire Peloponnesus and a single city, except in the fact that its inhabitants are not included within the same wall; in other respects, both as a whole and in their individual cities, there is a nearly absolute assimilation of institutions.

We consider Polybius' description of the Achaean Sympolity as the distillation of what federalism must be. This reference to the harmonisation of laws, weights, measures and currency is significant evidence of a functioning internal market, customs union, similar to that of the German states in 1834, known as the *Zollverein* which eventually contributed to the establishment of the Second *Reich* under Bismarck in 1873. The existence of common weights and measures constitutes the first step towards such unions and a precondition for new countries to join any form of federation or alliance. For example, Great Britain adopted the European weights and measures before its entry into the European Union in 1973 (*kilometre* and *metre* instead of *mile* and *yard*, the *kilo* instead of the *pound*, etc.).

To complete the picture of the creation in the Greek federations of conditions for an environment favourable for commercial activity, one must include additional economic institutions that are related to securing such a state. Beginning with banking, above we have mentioned that at least 35 Hellenistic city-states have been recorded as having banks. It would be paradoxical to consider that this might not have been so within the Sympolity as well simply because, as far as we know to date, none have been recorded in the sources during the Hellenistic period. An indirect approach to trace elements of a banking organisation in the Achaean Sympolity is to try to find any evidence regarding each of the 103 city-states that were members of the Sympolity, as mentioned above. Perhaps one of the most representative cases is that of Corinth where the existence of banks dates back to the fifth century with the case of Philostephanos who was conducting banking transactions during the years that followed the Persian Wars and is said to have received the enormous sum of 70 *talents* as a deposit from the Athenian *strategos* Themistocles (Calhoun 2002, p. 94).[11] Thus, Corinth, a major commercial rival to Athens during the Classical Period and a member of the Achaean Sympolity during the Hellenistic period had already established banking activities as of the Early Classical period, and there is no evidence or reason to believe that this was not continued in

[11]Themistocles was the victor of the famous naval Battle of Salamis in 480.

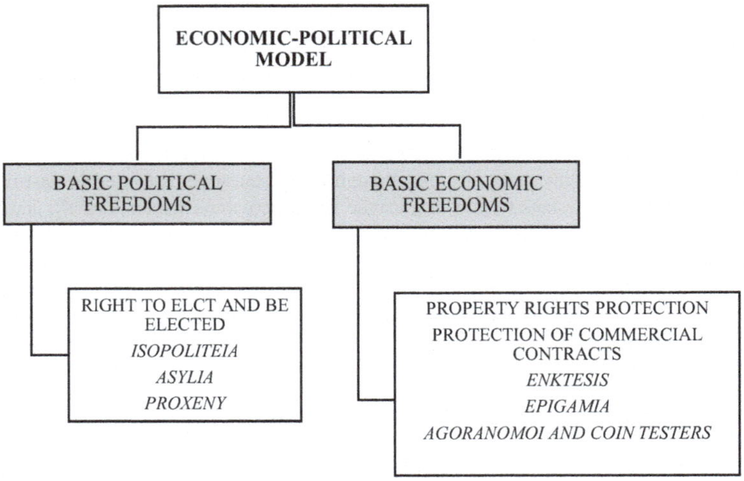

Fig. 7.1 The basic political and economic institutions of the economic success of the Achaean Sympolity

later times. Thus, it is verified that at least one-member city-state of the Achaean Sympolity did have banking activities.

Furthermore, as with the case of Athens mentioned above, Mackil (2013, p. 268–269) mentions that the Achaean state had also introduced *agoranomoi*, who were local magistrates (under the supervision of the federal authorities) whose duties were to punish those who were selling goods at exorbitant prices. Thus, the main objective of the *agoranomoi* was to prevent sellers from profiteering, thereby protecting the smooth functioning of the market and the interests of consumers. As in Athens, in the Achaean and Aetolian Sympolities, the *agoranomoi*, in concert with the federal courts, were charged with enforcing the application and the legal protection of commercial contracts and monetary transactions (Mackil 2013, p. 268–269, 272).

Polybius (2.37) informs us that the Achaean federal authorities also introduced another pivotal institution that had been first developed in the pioneering Athenian economy, which went hand in hand with the *agoranomoi*: the *metronomoi*. Their responsibility was to check and make sure that the weights and measures used by sellers of goods in the markets were correct. Their job was critical in preventing profiteering (Bitros et al. 2020). To the above, a supplementary and undoubtedly crucial role in the smooth functioning of the economy was that of federal currency. The Sympolity, like the other federal states, had adopted the use of a common federal currency, to facilitate commerce. We examine the role of the common currency further in 7.2. Figure 7.1 summarises the political and economic institutions that have been analysed up to this point that contributed to the success and sustainability of the Achaean Sympolity.

Two more institutions—the *argyramoiboi,* or *kolyvistai* (money changers), and the *dokimastai* (coin testers), further analysed in the next section. There is no doubt that all these institutional tools functioned as 'dynamic multipliers' by which the success of the Greek federal experiment was achieved. Had these tools not been developed, it is highly uncertain whether the grand visions of those that imagined and designed the federal institutions would have succeeded. A functional and viable array of economic institutions was vital for commercial transactions and market mechanisms to function properly and efficiently. As a final observation, it can be safely argued that the above institutions comprise what is in modern economic theory called *transactional cost reduction*, a basic principle in further assisting trade.

7.2 The Adoption of a Common Currency as a Means of Expanding Economic Activity

In antiquity, money as a means of exchange had *intrinsic value*, meaning that the value inscribed on the coin was equal to the value of its metal. In modern times, transactions are conducted in so-called *fiat money,* where the value inscribed on the bill or coin is not equal to the value of the paper or metal of which either is made. The ancient Greeks understood the basic functions of money as they are known today. *Nomisma* (currency) was considered to be something that can be shared and used as a means of exchange under the auspices of the state issuing it (Arist. Pol. 1. 1256b. 25–30).

The innovation of currency is related to the evolution of societies as a need was created for a commonly accepted means of payment as commerce expanded beyond the bounds of the city and began to internationalise. Beyond the case of the Achaean Sympolity being examined here, the general practice followed by either independent city-states or those part of a Hellenistic federal states was that each had the right to mint its own coins providing it had the technical know-how to undertake the task effectively. According to Polybius (2.37), these coins had to be of the same weight and standard to facilitate transactions either within the city-state or with others. According to Mackil and Van Alfen (2006) and Mackil (2013, p. 245–255), the Achaean city-states had established common monetary practices amongst themselves, a feature that can be found in monetary unions.

Coins have been found at archaeological sites from a host of city-states such as Dyme, Helice, Aegeira and Pellene, across a broad expanse of the northern Peloponnesus. Regarding this dispersion of coins throughout the territory of Achaea, Thompson (1939, p. 116) reports that 119 coins from 22 different city-states have been found, dating from the third to the second centuries. A typical format for a coin produced at a local member city-state mint was to bear on the one side the head of a local deity, while on the obverse side was inscribed the initial or first few letters of the name of the city, or a small relief relating to the worship of that deity, surrounded by a wreath (Davis 1978, p. 19–20; Mackil 2013, p. 251). Based on what has been revealed by the archaeologist's rake, the majority of coins found that were issued either by the Achaean or Aetolian city-states were *hemidrachms* (half *drachma*)

Fig. 7.2 *Hemidrachm* minted in Argos between 196 and 146 BCE. Source: http://www.wildwinds.com/coins/greece/argolis/argos/Clerk_139.jpg. With permission of wildwinds.com

known also as *triobols* (three *obols*) (Thompson 1968; Mørkholm 1991, p. 9; Warren 1999).

Figures 7.2–7.7 present some characteristic examples of the multitude of coins that have been found throughout the Peloponnesus. These images depict *hemidrachms*. Figure 7.2 is of a *hemidrachm* believed to have been minted in Argos between 196 and 146; on one side is a depiction of Zeus while on the reverse, the letters 'AX' indicate the coin was minted in the name of the Sympolity and was thus a federal issue. Also on the reverse, the lower part depicts the head of a dog, while on the upper part, barely discernable, are letters which indicate its provenance, Argos.

Figure 7.3 presents another *hemidrachm* believed to have been produced in the city-state of Messene between 191 and 183. Here, again, one side depicts the head of Zeus in profile, while the reverse, the letters 'AX', denoting the coin was minted in the name of the Sympolity. At the bottom of the reverse side is inscribed the letter 'M', indicating the coin was minted in Messene. It is worth noting that, as is apparent from the coin's chronology, from the moment Messene became a member of the Sympolity, it acquired the right to mint coins bearing the letters 'AX', denoting its status as federal currency.

Figure 7.4 depicts a coin confirmed to have been used in Sparta. On one side, again, a profile of Zeus is depicted. Again, the reverse bears the letters 'AX', the federal insignia, but includes the letters 'EY' and a depiction of the two *Dioscuri*—Castor and Pollux. Figure 7.5 depicts another similar type of coin, made and used in Elis circa 191. Like Messene, as soon as the city-states of the regions of Sparta/Laconia and Elis became members of the Sympolity, they were obliged to issue federal coins, replacing the local ones with federal ones of the same weight and standard so that they could be circulated within every city-state of the federation, or be used for commercial transactions with even third (non-federal) city-states, in the name of the Achaean Sympolity. These two *hemidrachms* offer evidence of this policy.

Figure 7.6 depicts yet another *hemidrachm,* this one found in the capital Aegion, issued between 160 and 150, which, on its face, depicts Zeus Omarios while the

Fig. 7.3 *Hemidrachm* issued by Messene between 191 and 183. Source: http://www.wildwinds.com/coins/greece/messenia/Messenia/Clerk_106v.jpg. With permission of wildwinds.com

Fig. 7.4 *Hemidrachm* minted in Sparta around 192. Source: http://www.wildwinds.com/coins/greece/laconia/lacedaemon/Clerk_321.jpg. With permission of wildwinds.com

Fig. 7.5 *Hemidrachm* minted and used in Elis circa 191. Source: http://www.wildwinds.com/coins/greece/elis/SNGCop_297.jpg. With permission of wildwinds.com

Fig. 7.6 *Hemidrachm* minted in Aegion between 160 and 150. Source: http://www.wildwinds.com/coins/greece/peloponnesos/achaia/aigion/Clerk_044.jpg. With permission of wildwinds.com

Fig. 7.7 *Tetrobol* issued in the city of Argos between 350 and 228. Source: http://www.wildwinds.com/coins/greece/argolis/argos/BMC_055v.jpg. With permission of wildwinds.com

reverse bears the letters 'AX' and the name Aristodamos. Warren (2007) and Benner (2008), who have extensively studied the coinage of the Achaean Sympolity from the third through the first century, and Mackil (2013, p. 251) argue that the wreath on these coins is a declaration they were minted during the Hellenistic Period.[12] As has already been mentioned, the greatest volume of commercial interstate transactions was taking place using *hemidrachms* (*triobols*, 3 *obols*).

There is, however, the case of Fig. 7.7 which depicts a federal *tetrobol* (four *obols*), issued in the city of Argos in the name of the Achaean Sympolity circa

[12]For proof of this, see in detail the following lists of Achaean coins found: http://www.wildwinds.com/coins/greece/peloponnesos/achaean_league/i.html, https://www.coinarchives.com/a/results.php?results=100&search=Achaean+league, https://coinweek.com/ancient-coins/ancient-spartan-coins/

350–228, and whose value is higher than that of a *hemidrachm*. One side depicts a forepart of a wolf while on the reverse side, there is a triskelion of crescents rotating left, enclosed in the lower part of the letter 'A'. Of course, various other city-states, such as Sicyon and Pallantion, were also issuing *tetrobols*.[13]

However, it seems strange that the Achaean federal authorities did not issue currency of a value higher than four *obols* as that would have been beneficial for high-value commercial 'interstate' transactions between the federal city-states, and especially with other non-federal city-states.[14] In ancient Athens and probably in most of the city-states that were monetised in metropolitan Greece, the currency was the *drachma*. Each Athenian *drachma* was equal to six *obols*, cast in bronze or silver. The *obol*, in turn, was denominated in bronze coins of still lower value known as *chalkoi*[15] and *kollyboi*, issued by private persons, and not by the state mint (Aristophanes, *Peace* 1199–1201). These were introduced because there was an insufficient amount of currency in circulation in small denominations to cope with daily retail transactions of recurrent but small value like, say, for purchasing bread. The *chalkous* was of an even smaller denomination than an *obol*. One *chalkous* was equal to one-eighth of an *obol*. These coins were used to perform even smaller value transactions than those of *obols*, as was the case in ancient Athens, where there is recorded and verified evidence of this. Probably issuing *chalkoi* in the Achaean Sympolity was undertaken by private persons, not by the state mint, as was the case in ancient Athens.[16] The member city-states of the Achaean Sympolity also held the right to issue coins of even smaller denominations that could also be circulated throughout the Achaean federal sovereignty.

Figure 7.8 depicts an Achaean *hemiobol* (half an *obol*) issued in the city-state of Patras circa 175–168. On the face, it depicts the head of Zeus while on the reverse, the monogram 'X' in a wreath (denoting its Achaean Sympolity origin), the letters 'ΛΥ', 'A', 'Π', and a dolphin below. According to Warren (1999, 2007), the Achaean *hemiobol* coinage was extensively used in the Sympolity as a means of efficiently performing retail commercial transactions. Using small denominations of federal currency sounds logical since this would have been an important prerequisite for an efficient unified market of exchange of goods and services consisting of more

[13]For proof of this, see, among others:

https://www.vcoins.com/en/stores/london_ancient_coins/89/product/argolis_argos_circa_343146_bc_ar_tetrobol_r_sol/819303/Default.aspx

https://www.vcoins.com/en/stores/calgary_coin/27/product/sikyon_in_sikyonia_prior_to_146_bc_silver_hemidrachm/1087987/Default.aspx

http://www.wildwinds.com/coins/greece/arkadia/pallantion/BCD_Peloponnesos_1593.2.jpg

[14]There is always the possibility that future archaeological evidence may reveal Achaean federal coins of a higher value, such as an Achaean *drachma*.

[15]*Chalkoi*, in plural, meaning 'bronze'.

[16]By doing this, as was the case in Athens, the private sector covered a need not covered by the official mint. One reason that the state did not issue bronze coins may have been that it did not have the capacity to do so (insufficient qualified personnel for the production of low-value coins) and that the cost incurred in relation to any seigniorage was deemed to be too high to make the production of bronze coins by the state mint worthwhile (Bitros et al. 2020).

Fig. 7.8 An *hemiobol* minted in Patras ca. 175–168. Source: http://www.wildwinds.com/coins/greece/peloponnesos/achaia/patrai/SNGCop_244.jpg. With permission of wildwinds.com

Fig. 7.9 A federal *tetrachalkon* found in the Achaean city-state of Cleonae. Source: http://www.wildwinds.com/coins/greece/argolis/kleonai/BMC_157.jpg. With permission of wildwinds.com

than 103 city-states. Smaller denominations of currency (made of copper) for small value retail would have been necessary for reducing transactional costs to use modern terminology, with R. Coase's theory in mind (Coase 1937).

For example, Fig. 7.9 presents an Achaean *tetrachalkon* (four *chalkoi*, half an *obol*, one-twelfth of a *drachma*) found in the city-state of Cleonae, used between 191 and 146. Similar coins have been found in other federal city-states such as Asine, Dyme, Kaphyai, Kleitor, Phenaios and Sicyon. On the face, it presents Zeus, nude, standing left, holding Nike and a scepter, while on the reverse is a female figure (Achaea, seated left, holding wreath and scepter).

A very important issue is related to the volume of currency issued by the member city-states. We believe that the intertemporal deduction of the modern *Fisher Equation* regarding the *Quantity Theory of Money* applies in our case as well: if every member produced coinage at will or arbitrarily, the logical consequence would be an inflation increase, and possibly a large one resulting in lower purchasing power as each monetary unit buys fewer and fewer goods and services. The truth is that already as of the fifth century, both the Athenian as well as the Greek economies, in general, faced inflationary pressures (Figueira 1998, p. 72, 493–495), but in the case of Classical Athens, these were not severe (Bitros et al. 2020). However, determining the impact of (possible) inflationary pressures in the Achaean Sympolity is not easy due to the lack of sufficient data.

On this issue, Mackil and van Alfen (2006) and Mackil (2013) argue that new currency issued by each city-state was determined not only by currency needs to perform market and commercial transactions effectively but was part of an overall federal monetary policy strategy. That meant that the total amount of currency (of the same weight and standard) issued in each of the city-states was part of the broader annual objectives of federal monetary policy. Mackil and van Alfen (2006) and Mackil (2013, 2015, p. 489) characterise this kind of money creation and supply under federal supervision, as 'cooperative coinages'. This was not only an Achaean practice. It was also introduced in other Greek states as well, such as several city-states of the Aegean Sea and Asia Minor, the Boeotian and the Aetolian federal states, as well as some Macedonian cities. Caspari (1917, p. 182), in earlier research, confirms that this system of issuing currency was an interim stage between local freedom to issue currency at will and the exclusive monopoly to do so by the central federal authority, preventing local mints from issuing indiscriminately, but rather, in line with the general policy laid out by the Sympolity.

To make the monetary regime of the Achaean Sympolity more understandable, we could argue that it resembles the basic modern practice of the current European Monetary Union (EMU). For example, contemporary Greece, as an EMU member, has the right to issue a 'Greek' *euro*, which, however, can be used as a means of exchange throughout the European Union, equal in value to all the other EMU member *euros*, e.g. the 'German', 'Italian', etc.

In fact, monetary networks for cooperation had already been established during the Classical Period (510–323). According to von Reden (2010, p. 67–68), the Greek city-states decided to introduce new series of coins of common weight standards to facilitate trade through monetary communication across political boundaries; thus, they made their currencies compatible with each other. She further argues that military coalitions and short-term alliances provided further reasons for adopting common weight standards. However, Thompson (1939), who dealt in detail with the issue of the circulation of money in the Peloponnesus, provides the crucial piece of information that there were some cases of strong states which were members of the Achaean Sympolity, such as Megalopolis, Argos, Sicyon and Corinth, that retained the right to issue currency with their local weight and standards to perform local city-state transactions. Thompson (p. 143) argues that:

Fig. 7.10 A *hemidrachm* issued in Megalopolis between 151 and 146. *Source*: http://www.wildwinds.com/coins/greece/arkadia/megalopolis/Dengate_72a.jpg. With permission of wildwinds.com

> ...Megalopolis continued to issue these coin types[17] after she joined the Achaean League, that she issued them in the tradition of the Arcadian Federation[18] to serve as her standard municipal currency....Then in 234 she joined the Achaean League[19] and found her identity submerged in that of a highly organized *politeia*[20] whose communal functions included the issuing of a standardized currency. There is every evidence, in the form of coin types to prove that Megalopolis, as well as Argos, Sicyon, Corinth and other cities, exercised the privilege of independent coinage even after she gave allegiance to the League. Not impossible is the conjecture that at that time she decided to keep the Pan type *for her local uses*, adopting the syrinx as her city symbol on the League denominations.

Megalopolis issued local coinage that bore the symbol and initials of the god Pan (Fig. 7.10), while the federal coins (Fig. 7.11) bore an image of a *syrinx*, a type of windpipe associated with the mythology surrounding Pan. It appears that Megalopolis and some other strong city-states, such as Argos, Sicyon and Corinth, retained this right until the dissolution of the Achaean Sympolity by the Romans in 146, as the coin in Fig. 7.11, issued between 151 and 146, denotes. The image depicts a *hemidrachm* (three *obols*, *triobol*) issued in Megalopolis with the head of Zeus on the face, the reverse bearing the letters 'ΜΕΓ' and 'ΑΝ' (possibly denoting Pan, the god who the Megalopolitans historically liked to use as an archetype on their coins).

We believe that Larsen (1968, p. 234) provides a concise and very well-written view regarding the system of money supply within the Achaean Sympolity that summarising what has already been described above. He writes that:

[17]She means, the coin types bearing the Megalopolitan (not federal) symbols.

[18]We remind our readers that from 370 to 234, Megalopolis was the capital of the Arcadian Sympolity It was then incorporated into the Achaean Sympolity. For information on the Arcadian Sympolity, see Larsen (1973), Economou and Kyriazis (2015) and Nielsen (2015).

[19]She means the Sympolity.

[20]She means *polity*, political entity.

Fig. 7.11 Achaean federal *hemidrachm*—or *triobol*—minted in Megalopolis between 160 and 146. Source: http://www.wildwinds.com/coins/greece/arkadia/megalopolis/Clerk_212.jpg. With permission of wildwinds.com

> The Achaean system of coinage went well with the system of taxation. Polybius has made famous the fact that the members of the Confederacy[21] used the 'same coins', that is, they had a uniform system of coinage. Yet there was no federal mint, but the constituent cities minted coins which bore on the obverse the Achaean monogram and the monogram or symbol of the cities issuing them. The standard silver coin was an Aeginetan triobol, which apparently was the chief coin in use in the entire Sympolities. Many cities also issued autonomous triobols, that is, coins without any federal insignia. Some of these may have been issued before the city joined the Confederacy,[22] but it is clear that several cities issued autonomous coins as well as federal coins after they had joined. Such a demonstration was considered neither treasonable nor objectionable. Most remarkable was the case of Megalopolis, which, in addition to federal and autonomous coins, also minted coins marked as Arcadian. This city, at the very time when its citizens played a prominent part in the leadership of the Achaean Confederacy,[23] liked to keep alive the impression that it was the chief city of Arcadia.

One issue that arises is whether local and federal coins could be circulated and exchanged freely within the borders of those strong city-states that were authorised to issue coins bearing local insignia in parallel to those with the federal insignia, such as Megalopolis, Argos, Sicyon and Corinth. Taking, for example, the case of Megalopolis, it meant that sellers and buyers there accepted both local and federal coins interchangeably to perform their transactions. We believe that this was indeed the case. But why did some states such as Megalopolis enjoy the privilege of issuing both local and federal currency? We believe there were three main reasons.

The first was for practical commercial purposes: Megalopolis, Argos, Sicyon and Corinth and possibly some other states had large populations and historically, a large

[21]He means the Sympolity.

[22]*Op. cit.* ftn. 21.

[23]*Op. cit.* ftn. 21 and 22.

volume of commercial traditions.[24] These city-states, because of that volume of commercial transactions they performed each year, required larger quantities of currency than the median Achaean city-state. If the Achaean federal policymakers did not provide such a privilege to these specific city-states, it might have given them cause to reconsider their membership in the Sympolity; their political leadership might have felt that such a 'restrictive monetary policy' (to use a modern term) would 'suffocate' their economies, that the money supply would not be adequate to cover the volume of commercial transactions; if alternatively, their city-states were independent, free to issue currency with no federal restrictions, they could determine their own monetary policy based on their true needs.

Second, in geopolitical terms, secession would be a very bad precedent, jeopardising not only the 'international prestige' of the Achaean Sympolity and its capability to attract new members city-states to join, but also lead to a crisis that could spread throughout all its member city-states. This, to some extent, resembles the case of Grexit in 2015; if that had happened, it might have led to a negative chain reaction within the whole of the EMU's structure, leading possibly to a lengthy crisis. It also resembles the Brexit decision of 23 June 2016 (finally accepted in January 2020) which eroded the prestige of both the EU and the EMU as a unified environment of stable and guaranteed economic and political benefits for their members. Brexit is a development that can possibly discourage prospective candidate states from joining the EU.

Finally, for 'prestige', Some powerful Achaean member city-states could not easily abandon some customs or practices that denoted their greatness and glory of the past. That is why, according to Thompson (1939, p. 144), the city-state of Megalopolis while deciding to retain the Pan image for her local coinage and adopting the *syrinx* as her symbol for her Sympolity coins, added an eagle on the knee of the seated Pan, possibly as a symbolical reminder of her former power and importance in Arcadian affairs. Thus, although according to Mackil and van Alfen (2006) and Mackil (2013), the quantity of money issued by the Achaean member city-states as a whole was determined by overall federal monetary policy, there were still some key and economically stronger member city-states which had (more or less) an autonomy to produce the quantity of money they wished. This autonomy could increase the total amount of money circulating among the Achaean city-states and be responsible for causing inflation.

However, we believe that each Achaean federal administration, to some degree, was able to grasp the debilitating nature of inflation and take some measures to control the amount of money in circulation. The federal authorities demanded that

[24]For example, it is very well-known from Thucydides' *History of the Peloponnesian War*, that one major reason for this devastating war was the harsh economic/commercial competition between the economically powerful states of Athens and Corinth, the former being the leader of the so-called Delian League (a military alliance), and the latter belonging to the Peloponnesian League, a military alliance created as a 'countermeasure' to the Delian League, with Sparta as its leader. In modern terms, this antithesis was mirrored in the NATO vs. Warsaw Pact status quo during the Cold War Era (1945–1991).

the quantity of currency issued in each city-state be defined by the broader objectives of federal monetary policy, a strategic decision that Mackil and van Alfen (2006) and Mackil (2013) have characterised as 'cooperative coinages', as mentioned above. As a final comment on this, based on the above information, it can be argued that the federal government's monetary policy was 'mixed', with certain privileged city-states accredited with issuing their own currency while the rest were under some measure of control, subject to some form of restrictions. Based on the above, we further believe that the federal monetary authority provided the appropriate guidance to all city-states as to the proper quantity of currency they should issue in order to satisfy their needs.

Another important issue is whether there was a central federal mint, perhaps in the capital, Aegion or not. Larsen (1968, p. 234) argues that there was no central federal mint in existence but rather, a 'system of mints' that implemented overall federal monetary policy in conjunction with each other. Larsen's view comes as a supplement to the above findings, that in reality there was cooperation between city-states and the federal government on how to implement the annual monetary policy in the federation. In Aegion, it must be said, there was a mint, as evidenced by the number of coins found there such as the federal *hemidrachm* pictured in Fig. 7.6.

Another question is whether each of the 103 city-states had its own mint or whether the smaller cities, perhaps lacking the know-how or the necessary infrastructure, relied on larger neighbours to produce their coins. There is no relevant information on this. It is possible, too, that some of the smaller city-states used coinage of other states for their transactions exclusively. Furthermore, it is unknown from where the silver and gold processed by the city-states that did have mints came. This question relates broadly to the overall monetary system of the Greek world and, accordingly, is worthy of extensive and thorough analysis, which is, however, beyond the scope of this work. One can, however, supply a general overview. Evidence dating from as early as the Late Mycenean Period, around 1250, indicates that gold, silver and copper was being extracted from mines within Greece. That is attested to in Homer's poems, *The Iliad* and *The Odyssey*, as well.

Records dating from even before the eighth century confirm that gold was mined in, for example, northern Greece (Macedonia, Thrace and the island of Thassos). Gold objects have been found in the Peloponnesus, but the possibility that those were not imported from elsewhere cannot be excluded. Verified evidence of gold and silver mines exists in Rodope, at Mount Paggaion near Kavala and on Thassos in Northern Greece. The famed silver mines of Laurion and Thoricos in Attica, on the islands of Kythnos, Serifos, Sifnos, as well as on Cyprus, etc., are all a matter of record as well. It is certain that three cities with a significant commercial orientation in the Greek world—Aegina, Athens and Corinth—as early as 560, used a substantial amount of coinage. While Athens had her source for silver from the mines of Laurion and Thoricos mentioned above, the other two centres had no such advantage.

The question then arises as to how those two city-states obtained the silver used to issue their coins. It can only have been with the import of unprocessed or partially processed ore, possibly from the areas mentioned above, or from other areas outside of Greece—perhaps Spain, for instance. This last possibility is not to be excluded since colonisation by Greeks of many locations throughout the Mediterranean basin had occurred centuries earlier. According to Herodotus (Hist. 3.115.1–2), even before 1000, Mycenean traders imported large quantities of tin from overseas, from the so-called *Cassyterides Nesoi* (tin islands), believed to have been the southwestern tip of the British Isles, in Cornwall, where the largest deposits of tin in Europe were located. Copper was produced in Chalkis and on Cyprus (both of whose names are derived from the word 'copper' or the Greek word for it, *chalkos*), Anatolia in Asia Minor and Etruria, Brutium and the island of Elba in Italy, as well as in Spain (von Reden 2010, p. 30, 32).

Another issue has to do with the fact that the Achaean Sympolity, according to Larsen (1968) chose to adopt the Aeginetan standard in their coinage, instead of, say, the Athenian standard, which, after all, was the main currency of the Eastern Mediterranean world during the Classical Period and beyond (Thompson et al. 1973; Kraay 1976; Kroll 2011).[25] Figueira (2016, p. 29) offers the significant information that the high purity Aeginetan *drachma* (also called *chelone* as, on the reverse, they bore an image of a turtle, the city-states' insignia) became the currency of choice among wealthy Peloponnesians as a reserve for their property against disaster, just as the US dollar, the British pound, the Swiss franc and the Euro function today. It is not known whether these Peloponnesians, in later years, as the Sympolity gained in power, were persuaded to abandon this practice, and replaced their precious *chelones* with Achaean coins.

But why did the Achaeans choose the Aeginetan standard instead of, say, the Athenian? Opting for the Athenian standard would have been a wise choice regarding the familiarity and acceptance of the Achaean *hemidrachm* in international commerce. But the Achaeans chose a standard which was actually 'competitive' to the Athenian, perhaps along the same logic by which the US dollar, currently the universal currency, faces 'competition' from the Euro (see, for example, Cohen 2011; Wang 2016). Adopting the Aeginetan standard probably was not an irrational choice since the 'Aeginetan turtles' were probably still familiar and recognisable during the Hellenistic Period. However, Larsen (1968, p. 234) argues that the use of the Aeginetan standard and the *triobol* as the chief denomination minted made the Sympolities somewhat 'a land apart within Greece'. This last phrase implies that the Aeginetan standard was used among the Greeks during the Hellenistic period as, more or less, an exception to the rule. Then, why did the Achaeans make such a choice?

[25]The Athenian *drachma* was a currency of excellent craftsmanship, of high silver content, and of stable value for about two centuries during the Classical Period. During the Hellenistic Period that followed, the gold Macedonian *tetradrachm* (four *drachmas*) became the universal coin in the Balkans, the Mediterranean, the Middle East and India because of the conquests of Alexander the Great (see Manning 2003, 2007; von Reden 2010). However, during the Hellenistic Period, the Athenian *drachma* was still considered an important means of performing international transactions and a reliable currency to be used as a depository by city-states.

Fig. 7.12 Macedonian *tetradrachm* minted in Sicyon between 225 and 215. Source: http://www.wildwinds.com/coins/greece/macedonia/kings/alexander_III/Price_0721.jpg. With permission of wildwinds.com

Perhaps they did not want to suffer any (even indirect) kind of dependence on Athenian or any other strong state monetary practices (e.g. the Kingdom of Macedon or the Ptolemaic Kingdom) and chose a more 'neutral' system of weights and standards, such as that of Aegina. Furthermore, as has already been mentioned, from 237 to 229, the Achaean Sympolity was actually in dispute with Athens, intending to make the latter its latest member city-state, something that never materialised. However, Aegina became a part of the Achaean Sympolity in 229, remaining a member until 211.[26] Thus, taking all the above into account, we tend to believe that the decision of the Achaean policymakers to adopt the Aeginetan standard was also related to the geopolitical environment of their times.

That the geopolitical developments in the Peloponnesus were related to the Sympolity's choice of coinage can also be verified by Fig. 7.12, which depicts a Macedonian *tetradrachm,* issued is Sicyon between 225 and 215. On the face, it shows the head of Heracles wearing a lionskin headdress, and on the reverse, it shows Zeus, seated facing left, and a boy. This complicates even further the whole picture of the Sympolity's currency regime. How was it that Sicyon was able to issue Macedonian currency? Had the city entered into some form of relationship with the Kingdom of Macedon? Did the Sympolity authorise this? Could such a *tetradrachm* or any other coin with Macedonian symbols issued by Sicyon circulate freely there and elsewhere in the Sympolity? If so, under what authority? As a transaction with a 'supranational' currency? These are all questions that cannot be answered easily and demand a thorough study of the monetary circulation of Greek antiquity, not only by historians who specialise in Political History and archaeologists but by Economic Historians as well.

[26]In 211, Aegina become a part of the Aetolian Sympolity and in the following year, in 210, part of the Hellenistic King Attalus of Pergamum's domain. Finally, in 133, it came under Roman rule.

We speculate that such coins were issued by some of the Sympolity's members for a limited period when the Macedonians, under Antigonus III Doson and Philip V, returned dynamically onto the Peloponnesian stage just before the Battle of Sellasia in 222. As detailed in Chap. 4, this was the time that the Achaeans under Aratus were under threat by Sparta. Possibly, this Macedonian influence, as expressed by these coins, must have gradually receded as the Sympolity 'regained' its national integrity, limiting the Macedonian impact. We believe that after the Macedonians' defeat by the Romans at Cynoscephalae in 197, it came to an end.

In closing, it must be emphasised that, as in Classical Athens and other city-states, the laws of the Achaean Sympolity on counterfeiting were very strict. Mackil (2013, p. 387) mentions one case in Dyme, where six counterfeiters were arrested and sentenced to death. The fact that they were dealt with so severely is indicative of how seriously the Achaeans took the smooth and unhindered functioning of the market as an essential parameter of the overall well-being of the citizenry. Thus, according to the Achaean legal system, anyone attempting to undermine the basic foundations of the market, by tampering directly with the reliability and purity of the Achaean federal currency, jeopardising the very state, deserved the ultimate penance.

7.3 Public Revenues and Expenses of the Sympolity and the Issues of State Budget, Taxation and Public Debt Management

Public Revenues (PR) are the cumulative financial flows by which the state can carry out a number of its obligations vis-à-vis its citizens such as public works (roads, hospitals), defence spending and transfer payments—compensation for war veterans, support for the disabled, the poor, the aged, those injured by accident, orphans, etc. Conversely, Public Expenditures (PE) are the expense incurred by the state to serve its ultimate obligations. It is a fact that when (PR) > (PE), the annual state budget is in surplus, and when (PR) < (PE), it is in deficit, while when (PR) = (PE), it is balanced.

First of all, we are interested in whether it is possible to provide an estimate of the size of public revenues produced in the Sympolity. The higher the number, the more robust the economy would appear. In 6.4 we attempted to estimate the cost of a specific defence expenditure of the Sympolity, and in 7.4.1 we calculate roughly that in 217, the amount came to approximately 880 talents, leading us to estimate that total defence expenditures probably were in excess of 1000 talents. That number seems quite high for the times in metropolitan Greece, indicating that the Sympolity was, in fact, a credible focus of growth and economic prosperity, probably the brightest star in the south of Greece during the Hellenistic Period. It is worth mentioning that in 323, Classical Athens reached the apex of its economic performance for that century since public revenues reached 1200 *talents* due to the expansionary fiscal policy of public works instituted by two influential policymakers, Eubulus and Lycurgus (Economou and Kyriazis 2016b, 2019b). Athens at that time was considered a very strong and prosperous economy. Thus, the 1000 *talents* for the defence budget of the Achaean Sympolity in 217, which constituted a large part of the overall federal budget, meant that the overall budget was certainly higher than 1000, and may have been even higher than 1200 talents. This is another indirect indication regarding the economic might of the Achaean economy as a whole.[27]

Below, we attempt to approach how the Sympolity's Public Revenues and Public Expenditures were determined. We know little of the income side of the federal budget. However, gathering data from a number of sources (Xen. Hell. 5.2.16), including archaeological evidence, an inscription found in Dyme (T35) that provides some relevant information, the findings of Scholten (2000, p. 103, 115) in the neighbouring Aetolian Sympolity, as well as Mackil and van Alfen (2006, p. 224), Mackil (2013, p. 290, 387) and the methodology we developed for determining the public revenues of the Achaean Sympolity in Economou and Kyriazis (2016a), we conclude that the Sympolity's sources of revenue originated:

- First, from tax contributions from each city-state according to the size of the population and economic strength, as drawn from its local public revenue and the overall picture of its annual total trading volume.
- Second, probably, each city-state paid a direct tax called the *telos* to subsidise federal war campaigns.
- Third, there may have been a 2% tax imposed on the value of overseas imports as existed in ancient Athens and the port of Piraeus. It is quite possible, especially if we assume the existence of an internal market, as, in 7.1, we have shown, did exist.
- Fourth, possibly, from tariffs imposed on all products from third countries entering the Sympolity, as is the policy today between the EU and non-EU countries.
- Fifth, from donations by wealthy citizens to the federal public fund, hoping to increase their chances of gaining political clout. This, too, may have been a source, as it had been even in Classical Athens.
- Sixth, inspired by the Athenian example, the Achaeans may have introduced the so-called *liturgies*, a special type of taxation applied to the wealthy, responsible for undertaking certain state activities such as *trierarchy*—the maintenance of a warship.[28]
- Seventh, loans to the public treasury by private citizens.

[27]It must also be acknowledged that the Hellenistic kingdoms of the East were much larger in territorial extent—with some of it especially fertile, such as the Ptolemaic Kingdom's Nile Valley—and had much larger public revenues, something that has been confirmed by historians such as Walbank (1993), Manning (2003, 2007) and van Reden (2010).

[28]For *liturgies*, see, among others, Davies (1967, 1981) and for *trierarchy*, see Kaiser (2007), Tridimas (2013), Ober (2017) and Economou and Kyriazis (2017).

- Eighth, it is possible that loans were made to the federal government or individual city-states throughout Achaea by temples, which also functioned as state/public treasuries and state banks. This function of temples was a customary practise in Athens during the Classical Period. There is no reason to believe that such a practise was not introduced by the Achaeans, as well—at least under extreme circumstances, such as the need to finance military campaigns.[29]
- Ninth, from income from *seignorage* on the minting of federal currency, the difference in value between that of a coin's metal (gold, silver) and its market value, less the cost of minting it.
- Tenth, from war booty captured during successful military action against the state's enemies, part of which was retained by the federal government. It is well-known that plundering during military campaigns was a common practice, wide-spread in ancient times. For example, De Laix (1973, p. 60), based on Thucydides (1.5.3.) and Polybius (4.3.1–5), argues that the troops of the Aetolian Sympolity were especially notorious in that respect.
- Eleventh, from ransom for the release of prisoners of war.

As far as public expenditures were concerned, it consisted of state obligations, the principal one being defence, which accounted for the largest amount, although there are no particular data regarding the Achaean federal government's related expenditures. In the sources, there is no indication of the other particular public expenses, but we assume that they more or less followed the Athenian model[30] and, at least, included public works such as building roads, temples, athletic installations, paying the salaries of public officials and, of course, the erection and maintenance of city walls and other federal infrastructure. We further analyse this issue in 7.4.

The above analysis concerning the sources and the approximation of the level of the federal budget is also related to the issue of taxation. Taxation was imposed on both citizens and each member city-state separately. Regarding personal taxation, this was imposed on citizens in the city-state of their origin, but similar to the Athenian practise, Achaean low and medium-income citizens were not taxed;

---

[29]In Athens, these temples were known as the *Treasuries of* (goddess) *Athena and of the Other Gods*. At first, the *Treasury of Athena* and the *Treasury of the Other Gods* were separate funds. The former managed the treasures of the Parthenon, which had been established before democracy, whereas the latter, established in 434, handled the treasures of all the other temples in the city. The treasuries were merged into one in 406/5, separated in 384, and finally merged again in 346. They functioned as bankers to the state during peacetime and as lenders of last resort in periods of war. These treasuries were administered by magistrates called *Tamiai*. They were funded from the tributes of either devout Athenians or foreign residents who had lived in Athens for an extended period (either as *metics* or as foreign merchants). In addition, they raised funds from the payment of fines, from renting out public property allocated by the state, even from private donations and tributes paid by allies to the city of Athens, known as *aparchai* (Aristotle, Ath. Const. 47.1; Samons 2000, p. 35–38; Marcaccini 2015, p. 517). According to Blamire (2001, p. 108) and Rhodes (2005, p. 93), until 427, the Athenian state paid an interest rate of 6% on her borrowings by those temple-funds but from 426 on, only 1.2%. On these issues, see in detail our own recent detailed analysis, in Bitros et al. (2020).

[30]See, among others, Kyriazis (2009), Halkos and Kyriazis (2010).

taxation only applied to the rich, and only in urgent situations such as war, who were taxed according to their total personal wealth. This tax was called the *eisphora*, and it was a pan-Hellenic practice as a means of raising public revenues under urgent circumstances. Aside from Athens, it was applied, among other places, in the Boeotian *Koinon* and the Kingdom of Macedon, and only on the wealthy elite, at least for some time during Philip II reign, etc. (Pritchard 2015, p. 58–59; Müller 2016, p. 13). Larsen (1968, p. 232) argues that the Achaean Sympolity never imposed personal taxation at the federal level, meaning that this happened only at the city-state level.

Regarding taxation imposed on each member city-state by the federal government (called *eisphorai*), Larsen (1968, p. 233) and Mackil and van Alfen (2006, p. 224) argue that a common practice of the Ancient Greek federal states was that their member city-states were obligated to pay a tax to the federal government in proportion to the size of their population, a practice that applies to modern federations, too. Furthermore, the existence of the regional magistrates, the *tamiai*, mentioned above, whose duties, among others, included the collection of federal revenues, meant that at first, city-states contributed taxes as a whole (based on population criteria).[31] The taxes were collected by the *tamiai*, gathered as an aggregate sum and then paid to the federal authority. According to Larsen (1968, p. 226), this sum was then stored at the federal treasury, possibly in the capital, Aegion. Mackil (2013, p. 312) argues that the Achaeans paid the *eisphora* in silver coinage to subsidise their war efforts.

Further examination of the issue of taxation, seeking evidence concerning the existence (or not) of an egalitarian system of federal taxation, probably raises more questions than answers.

In Chap. 4, we mentioned the social uprising throughout Achaea during the period of Aratus and of Cleomenes III. This was related to a general demand by the people for the abolition of debts. This demand was also related to *anadasmos* (land reclamation). The social uprisings in the Aetolian and Achaean sympolities and other federations were based on the following social demands: the cancellation of debts and/or the redivision of property, through the confiscation of property and its redistribution (known as *ges anadasmos* and *anaplerosis*) among the masses (Mendels 1982, p. 87–88, 91). These uprisings took place during the Late Hellenistic Period, when the economic decline of the Hellenic world had already begun, according to Tridimas (2018). Perhaps they were related, among others, to unfair taxation. Social uprisings due to unfair taxation is an intertemporal phenomenon throughout history. For example, in Economou and Kyriazis (2019b), we provide instances regarding the Medieval Ages, such as Wat Tyler's movement in 1381 in England, also known as the *Peasant's Revolt*.[32]

---

[31]This means that a part of each city-states' public revenues was applied to payments to the federal budget.

[32]For further intertemporal historical evidence on social rebellions due to (unfair) tax measures, see Burg (2004).

However, in our case, the Achaean Sympolity, determining the degree to which social uprising should be attributed to unfair taxation is not an easy task since there is no evidence in the ancient sources or modern bibliography that any social uprising took place against the federal authorities specifically concerning taxation. Furthermore, if there was indeed a situation of unfair taxation in the city-states of the Achaean Sympolity (as a wider symptom of the Greek world at the time), there is a strong possibility that this was not related to predatory taxation federal policies but due to implementation of unjust taxation at the local city-state level that the Sympolity's government may not have been able to control or discourage for reasons that we do not know. On the other hand, we acknowledge that such an argument may be regarded only as partially convincing since there is always the possibility that federal taxation was not fair, but the citizens themselves may not have managed or failed to effectively coordinate themselves, for a variety of reasons, to force both the local and federal authorities to establish a fairer taxation system.[33] On the other hand, one should not disregard the fact that no ancient source refers to the issue of unfairness in implementing federal taxation policies.

Finally, another important fiscal policy issue has to do with the management of the federal public debt. Contrary to the popular view of previous decades, that ancient societies did not recognise public debt due to their primitive institutional framework, based on available evidence, we believe that this was not the case. In Footnote 6 in 7.1, we referred to Finley (1973, 1985), Austin and Vidal Naquet (1977) and some other authors who argued that the Ancient Greek economy was characterised by primitive institutions that were not related to what we call today a 'market economy'. We then provided just a small portion of recent literature that recalls such views. The issue of acknowledging public debt by a state is an important axiom which is a basic prerequisite regarding the smooth functioning of the modern international system. We believe that it has origins in Ancient Greece, but this is an issue that exceeds the scope of the current essay. However, we promise future research on this.

A characteristic example is the Athenian Democracy. According to Aristotle (Oec. 2.1.15), the principle on which the Athenian state managed its finances called for keeping the annual budget balanced by holding public expenditures in line with public revenues. In this passage, Aristotle argues that the Athenians had adopted this practice as an established citizen's mentality on their private and public affairs. Moreover, on this very crucial issue, he informs us that the *Council of the Five Hundred* supervised how the state budget was applied in any given year, striving to avoid systematic deficits.

As stated above, in the Athenian state, when there were extreme cases such as wartime that forced a deficit due to increased defence expenditures, this shortfall was balanced by borrowing from the *Treasuries of the Gods*. In the event of a surplus,

[33]We think that, among others, the seminal work of Mancur Olson (1965) provides some intertemporal explanations as to why coordination and collective action sometimes fails among a group of people or a society as a whole.

however, that was transferred to the *Treasuries*, partly for safekeeping purposes and partly as donations. Thus, the *Treasuries* played a key role in the budgetary process. Apart from serving as safekeeping depositories, in normal times they kept their assets at arm's length from the fiscal authorities, considering them as dedicated to the gods and hence untouchable in all but compelling circumstances. Davies (2001) conveys this view by arguing that these sacred funds functioned as monetary reserves.[34]

Far from the case of Athens, it appears that this practice of acknowledging public debt was a widespread phenomenon during the Hellenistic Period. A characteristic example is the case of the woman Nicareta, referred to above, a citizen of the Boeotian *Koinon* who sued the city-state of Boeotian Orchomenos, a member state that had failed to repay debts owed her. Nicareta had supplied Orchomenos with four loans (10,085 *drachmae* and two *obols,* 2500 *drachmae*, 4000 *drachmae* and 1000 *drachmae* respectively). Nicareta appealed to a federal court seeking justice and was vindicated. Unfortunately, we know nothing of the court's level nor its synthesis. The case was very likely adjudicated in Orchomenos. We speculate that such disputes regarding serious cases were resolved in high-level federal courts.

The city-state of Orchomenos and Nicareta eventually reached a new agreement with each other. According to Schaps (1979, p. 13, 63–65), a particularly significant element, in this case, was that a woman, by law and as a matter of principle, had the power to demand justice and, consequently, compensation. Other cases of women winning similar trials throughout the Greek world include Kleuedra and Olympichia (Mackil 2013, p. 415–448). In another case, sometime between 230 and 210 BCE, Orchomenos signed a settlement with Eubolos, a citizen of the city of Elatia in Phocis (which was not a member of the Boeotian state). In the settlement, it is stated that the city of Orchomenos had fully repaid the loan to Eubolos and had no further obligation to him (Migeotte 1984, p. 48–53).

These cases of Nicareta, Kleuedra, Olympichia and Eubolos indicate that city-states did take loans from private persons, assuming the obligation to repay them within a specific time frame in the future. If they did not, lenders could apply to federal courts (considered superior to local city-state courts in terms of providing justice) for vindication. In general, according to Larsen (1968, p. 235), federal judges were competent not only to impose fines but even to inflict the death penalty. From an Institutional Economist's point of view, this also relates to property rights protection of both the lender and the borrower and is an important prerequisite for a prosperous economy (Hodgson 2015a, b, c).

Another proof of this was the institution of *nomographoi*, introduced in both the Achaean and Aetolian Sympolities (Larsen 1968, p. 231). During the First Macedonian War (214–205), because of social frustration caused by the general increase in public debt in the city-states of Aetolia, the authorities appointed two magistrates, Dorimachos and Scopas, known as *nomographoi* (see 6.3), to resolve debt problems. This information is important for two reasons: First, it verifies that in the Aetolian

[34]We extensively analyse this issue in Bitros et al. (2020).

state, there existed a regime of formal state laws. Second, the two magistrates were appointed to achieve a 'social compromise'[35] between, on the one hand, the majority of citizens favouring debt relief, and on the other, the wealthy oligarchic groups, the lenders. Had there been a powerful social uprising, the latter might perhaps have lost their property—a violation of their property rights.

Social uprisings with the basic request of wealth redistribution were very common during the third century in Ancient Greece. Cases include the Achaean federal state's social turmoil during the reigns of the Spartan Kings, Agis IV and Cleomenes III (235–222) (Plut. Arat. 39.5; Cleo. 17.3; Mendels 1982), as we have already analysed in 4.3. The fact that the Achaean Sympolity was against any socio-economic change that was related to the redistribution of wealth and debt cancellation, which indirectly implies protecting the property rights of the wealthy or oligarchic elites, although of others as well, can be proved by the ferocious struggle of the Sympolity's policymakers to suppress any such uprisings during and after the period of the socio-economic reformists of Sparta, Agis IV, Cleomenes III and the tyrant Nabis. By defending the socio-economic status quo against any reform that was related to wealth redistribution, the Achaean federal policymakers were protecting the property rights of their constituents.

7.4 The Provision of Federal Public Goods and the Issue of Positive Externalities

In his 1954 paper entitled *The Pure Theory of Public Expenditure*, the eminent scholar, Paul A. Samuelson, defined a public good, or a 'collective consumption good', as follows:

> [...goods] which all enjoy in common in the sense that each individual's consumption of such a good leads to no subtractions from any other individual's consumption of that good... (p. 387)

A good is defined as public good if it has one or both of the characteristics of jointness in consumption and non-excludability. A good is nonexcludable if, once produced, the producer cannot prevent people from consuming the good.[36] Of course, public good theory is not only applicable regarding unitary states but also includes the federal ones. The theory of *Fiscal Federalism* regarding the modern federal experience proves that the more a federal budget is sufficient and satisfies at least a series of critical socio-economic cohesion policies regarding the provision of public goods, the more the federal bonds of trust between the citizens themselves and

[35]As Solon did in Archaic Athens in 594 (van Wees 2013).

[36]For this basic economic principle regarding public goods see the seminal works of Musgrave (1939, 1959), Samuelson (1954, 1955) and Olson (1965).

the federation itself strengthens (Pauly 1973, Rubinfeld 1997, p. 1587).[37] The reverse also applies: an inadequate federal budget weakens the bonds of trust among the state and its constituents. In this section, we attempt to assemble all the available evidence that is related to the provision of public goods and services by the Achaean Sympolity, as a part of their overall federal strategy.

We will analyse the issue of the provision of federal public goods by the Achaean state. It appears that this practice was a phenomenon that characterised Ancient Greek federal states in general. Ober (2015, p. 113) writes on this that some Greek states encouraged investment by citizens in learning skills relevant to the provision of valuable public goods, notably security and public services (e.g. clean water, drainage, reliable coinage, honest market officials) that conduce to the general welfare. Thus, public goods benefited all citizens, and in, some cases, all members of the community. As will be further explained below, this view was indeed the case since the citizens of the Ancient Greek federal states were very much aware of at least the basic privileges of cooperation and coordination under a federal structure. They understood that by creating a unified area of economic cooperation through their federations, they could increase their prosperity by achieving higher economic welfare standards in the long term. Such 'zones of economic cooperation' appeared in later times as well, for the same reasons, such as the fifteenth century CE Hanseatic League, the German Zollverein during the nineteenth century and the current EU and the EMU.

7.4.1 Provision of the Public Good of Defence and the Operational Cost of the Achaean Federal Armed Forces

So far, it has been argued that the primary reason for the establishment of the Ancient Greek federal states was the provision of the public good of defence if we interpret the issue of military spending from an economist's point of view. Because of its *Common Foreign and Security Policy* (CFSP),[38] the Achaean Sympolity was able not only to confront successfully the expansionary adventures of Macedon in

[37] *Fiscal Federalism* is a subfield of public finance, which deals with the division of governmental functions and financial relations among different levels of government. This theory assumes that a federal system of government can be efficient and effective at solving problems governments face, such as macroeconomic stabilisation, fair distribution of income in the society as a whole, efficient and effective allocation of resources, and economic stability etc. According to Oates (1999), *fiscal federalism* is concerned with understanding which functions and instruments are best centralised and which are best placed in the sphere of decentralised levels of government. For an extensive analysis regarding the theoretical foundations on *fiscal federalism*, see the seminal works of Musgrave (1959) and Oates (1972). See also Pauly (1973), Rosen (1988), Inman and Rubinfield (1997), Rubinfield (1997), Oates (1998), and Musgrave (1998).

[38] We borrow this term from the European Union's glossary.

Southern Greece, powerful Sparta under Cleomenes III and, later, the Aetolian Sympolity for a time, along with secessionist tendencies from within, it even managed to unite the whole of the Peloponnesus at one point. If the Sympolity had been able to achieve the latter accomplishment before 191 and succeeded in maintaining its independence longer, it may have been able to avoid its violent dissolution by the Romans in 146. Effective CFSP is a precondition of a successful federation.

In 6.4, we argued that, in 217, the Sympolity possessed a mixed mercenary force of 8500 troops (8000 *hoplites* and 500 horsemen), whereas the citizen militias from all member city-states could contribute a further 3000 *hoplites* and 300 horsemen; the Sympolity maintained a fleet of six battle-ready *triremes*. Based on this, a reasonable estimate can be made of the annual federal defence budget. We assume in Table 7.1 that in time of war, professional and enlisted *hoplites* received a daily compensation of 1.5 *drachmae,* which, according to Loomis (1998), was the average daily wage of a labourer during the third century, while horsemen received five *drachmae.* We also assume an 8-month length of service since, during the winter, there was no military activity. Accordingly, we have an average daily cost of $11{,}000 \times 1.5 = 16{,}500$ *drachmae* for *hoplites* and $800 \times 5 = 4000$ *drachmae* for horsemen, for a total of 20,500 *drachmae* per diem for the Sympolity's fighting force.

Multiplying that amount by 365 days $\times$ 8/12 (8 out of 12 months per annum): $21{,}700 \times 365 \times 8/12 = 5{,}280{,}333.30$ *drachmae* or $5{,}280{,}333.30/6000 = 880$ talents (since one talent was equal to 6000 *drachmae*). Table 7.1 presents the mathematical equations in detail, taking into consideration that the Sympolity also maintained a fleet of six *triremes* patrolling the seas off the coastal areas of the Peloponnesus, especially in the north, in the Gulf of Corinth, vigilant against the ever-threatening Aetolian Sympolity. That is affirmed by Polybius (5.91.1–5) who notes that the Sympolity maintained three *triremes* in the Gulf, patrolling between Patras and Dyme, while the other three were at sea off Argolis. Each *trireme*, based on the Athenian model, was manned by a crew of 200 sailors and officers,[39] requiring the Sympolity to pay wages for the 1200 seamen on its six warships. If one estimates that each man received a daily wage of 1 *drachma*, for their 8 months of duty, that amounted to a total annual charge to the budget of 292,000 *drachmae.* Accordingly, including the operational cost for the six warships (around 49 *talents*), the total cost of the Achaean military forces (infantry, cavalry and navy) amounted to 880 talents.

In 231, a joint Achaean–Aetolian fleet of possibly ten *triremes* was defeated by an Illyrian fleet somewhere among the Ionian Islands (Walbank 1970; Scholten 2000, p. 107, 141). We estimate that in this particular naval engagement, the two sympolities each disposed of a fleet of five *triremes.* Also, in Table 7.1, we assume a fleet of at least six warships was maintained, a probably very conservative number given that the Sympolity included among its members several city-states with a

[39]With this Athenian model of a fifth-century *trireme* in mind, where each warship was manned by a crew of 200 (Morrison et al. 2000), it follows that the six ships required 1200 men. That number must be added to the total manpower of the Sympolity's military forces for the year 217.

Table 7.1 Total cost of the Achaean Sympolity's armed forces in 217 BCE

	Infantry (*hoplites*)	Cavalry	Navy	Total cost (in *drachmae*)[a]
Daily cost in *drachmae*	11 × 1000 × 1.5 = 16,500	800 × 5 = 4000	200 × 6 × 1 = 1200	21,700
Total cost in *drachmae* for 8-month service	16,500 × 365 × 8/12 = 4,015,000	4000 × 365 × 8/12 = 973,333, 33 ~ 973,333	1200 × 365 × 8/12 = 243,333.3 ~ 292,000	5,280,333
Converted into *talents*	4,015,000/ 6000 = 669.166 ~ 669	973,333/6000 = 162.2221 ~ 162	292,000/6000 = 48.66 ~ 49	**880 *talents***

[a]Infantry, cavalry and navy

centuries-old maritime tradition, especially Corinth. Those cities may have maintained their own fleets, to provide security to their commercial activities; in the event the Sympolity was at war, such capacity would have been put at the disposal of the Achaean admiral.

Table 7.1 presents an indicative estimate of the cost of maintaining a combat-ready military force. To that, one must add the additional operational cost of military bases and installations, training of recruits, other possible costs related to the logistics of maintaining such a force, as well as any related extraordinary costs. Larsen (1968, p. xxvii) writes that in some periods, the Achaean armed forces relied heavily on mercenaries rather than citizen-soldiers. That would have resulted in increased costs. It is obvious, based on available data, the total cost of the Achaean armed forces would have been even higher, perhaps reaching, or even surpassing, 1000 talents, as has already been mentioned.

It is also pertinent to mention whatever information is available regarding the deployment and geographical divisions of the Sympolity's forces in the Peloponnesus. Polybius (5.92.7–10) reports that, in 217, Aratus proceeded to reorganise the structure of the Achaean armed forces, resulting in establishing three new geographical/regional units relative to the bordering states: Elis to the west, the Aetolian Sympolity to the north and Sparta to the south. However, this analysis is somewhat complicated by the existence of an additional, independently organised military region called the *Synteleia of Patriki*, a region of an unknown size around the city of Patras (Rizakis 2015, p. 125–126). There are even some who claim that there was a fifth military region, Megalopolis, and that it was Philopoemen who established the three main regions mentioned above in 207. Unfortunately, no further clarification is available regarding this issue; however, it is almost certain that there did exist federal military departments in specific locations on the Achaean territory.

Finally, Larsen (1968, p. 232) argues that at the time when the Achaean Sympolity practically controlled the entire Peloponnesus, after 191, it could theoretically mobilise as many as 30,000 or even 40,000 *hoplites*, but this practically never materialised. Such army ceilings could only be practically achieved by the Hellenistic kingdoms (e.g. the Kingdom of Macedon or the Ptolemaic Kingdom of Egypt) or the Roman Republic due to their vast financial resources and ample human capital.

7.4.2 Other Federal Public Goods: Federal Courts and the Road Network

Considering the overall structure of the Achaean state, as it has been described above, we think that, except for the provision of public good defence, at least a part of the federal budget expenses was intended for implementing, in practice, a series of other federal social policies too, through the provision additional public goods. Regarding the issue of the federal justice system, in 6.3, we have stated that the Sympolity had introduced the *koinodikia* (federal courts) to provide justice to its constituents. These courts' decisions were binding between parties and meant they had to be implemented in practice by the federal authorities. In 7.1, we reported that there were also certain institutions such as the *agoranomoi* (whose job was to protect the markets from profiteering) and the *metronomoi* (whose duty was to guarantee that products were sold in standard weights and measures).

Furthermore, we guess that under the same logic, the federal authorities must have taken some measures to subsidise the development of a road network connecting all the Sympolity's city-states. Possibly funding for this was co-financed by the federal budget and the local city-states' budgets. According to modern methodological approaches such as *Economic Geography* and *Spatial Economics* theory, the existence of an efficient road network is considered as a competitive advantage for an economy since the proper development of the transport road network not only reduces the cost of transportation, both in terms of money and time, but also helps in the integration of various regions within a country. The relationship between transportation infrastructure and economic development has been the focus of increasing analysis in the recent literature (see among others, Xie and Levinson 2011; Wood and Roberts 2012; Percoco 2016[40]). This means that as the economy grows, it becomes more dependent upon its transport sector.

Our guess regarding the existence of an efficient road network as a means of promoting interstate economic/commercial transactions and what Mackil (2013) characterises as *microregional interdependence* is strongly supported by the findings of Pikoulas (2000) who found that an extensive road network was in existence in Arcadia, a region in the central part of the Achaean Sympolity and the Peloponnesus in general, even as early as the Late Archaic Period. He found that even the smallest settlements were linked through this network. Moreover, Marchand (2009) verifies that interstate routes were common in the Peloponnesus, by focusing on the main road that was passing through the city of Cleonae, connecting the important and (economically strong) cities of Corinth and Argos. Finally, in their extensive study, Sanders and Whitbread (1990) prove that there was indeed an extensive and functional road network between the city-states of the Peloponnesus including, for example, Corinth, Patras, Argos and Epidauros.[41]

[40]On this issue, see also the recent and the older volumes of the academic Journal *Networks and Spatial Economics* published by Springer.

[41]Further evidence on these as well as further issues which we study in the next subsection such as the existence of an efficient system of water supply and management would be welcomed. However, due to space limitations, this lies beyond the scope of this work.

7.4.3 Provision of Public Goods Under the Discretionary Supervision of the Achaean Federal Authorities (Health, Education Etc.)

Regarding the issue of public health, in Athens and other Greek city-states, there was a parallel two-tier system for the provision of health services. The so-called *Asclepieia* formed the first tier and consisted of large medical care centres that also included temples of worship. According to Risse (1990, p. 56), an *Asclepieion* included carefully controlled spaces conducive to healing.

The *Asclepieia* were sacred places of worship of the hero, divine doctor and healer, the god Asclepius. They were, in fact, the first hospitals in Ancient Greece and offered their services for many centuries.[42] Each *Asclepieion* consisted of a large complex that also included a temple, a stadium, a gymnasium, a library and theatre; access to these amenities promoted self-therapy through rest, relaxation and exercise (Luce 2001). Additional activities, such as baths and *enkoimeses* (incubation) were central to the healing process. Athletic facilities such as the stadium, the *hippodrome*, the *gymnasium* and the *palaestra* (wrestling arena), all found near the temples, were used as training sites and areas where gymnastic games and entertainment took place. These facilities were considered necessary for the psychological component of the patient's recovery regime (Lyttkens 2011). *Asclepieia* like that of Epidaurus belonged to and were run either jointly, by several city-states, or by one city-state alone. Scattered throughout the ancient world, they numbered over 300, the largest and most famous being those of Trikke, Athens, Corinth, Epidaurus, the island of Kos and Pergamon in Asia Minor.

As for the Achaean Sympolity, in addition to the famous *Asclepieion* of Corinth, built next to the *gymnasium* and close to the theatre and the *odeon* of the Agora (the marketplace),[43] there was another *Asclepieion* in Sicyon, directly connected with the city's theatre. Another one was located in Troezen close to the *gymnasium* there, while an *odeon* was built there during the Roman period. In Messene and Megalopolis, the *Asclepieia* appear to form unified complexes together with the theatre and the stadium (Christopoulou-Aletra et al. 2009). Thus, there are at least five verified cases of *Asclepieia* within the Achaean Sympolity. There is no information on any federal contributions regarding the running expenses of the *Asclepieia* in the Sympolity, but we believe that the federal authorities could contribute in cases where city-states that hosted *Asclepieia* did not have the financial means to cover the operating cost for a particular period.

The federal authorities could intervene as a part of their strategy of providing health as a public good among their federal constituents. Although doctors provided

[42]Some primitive versions of such facilities are mentioned as early as the Trojan war period.

[43]*Gymnasiums* were large public athletic facilities which consisted of multiple spaces with extensive sports installations. In Athens, there were three, the Academy, the Lyceum and the Kynosarges (Fisher 1998). The *odeon* was a building devoted to music: singing exercises, musical shows, poetry competitions, and the like.

their services on a private basis and expected to be paid by their patients, in the second tier, they offered medical treatment to individual patients but were remunerated by the local communities on an annual basis. The availability of medical services along the second tier was considered as a fundamental obligation of state authorities, and the citizens viewed it as an acquired right. The communities outsourced the services of those doctors who worked for the public interest on condition the latter would be available on demand by potential patients. We know of this arrangement from Aristophanes (*Acharnians*, 1027–1032) reference to Dikaiopoles who prompts a poor and blind farmer to visit the famous surgeon Pittalos. The annual wage of public doctors in Classical Greece was around 500 *drachmae*, but in the following centuries, their pay increased considerably, a famous example being Asklepiades from the Perge who, in the second century, received 1000 *drachmae* from the city of Seleucia, a city-state in Asia Minor. To be selected, a candidate doctor had to convince the community's citizens of his talents and exceptional abilities. Also, public doctors had to be present at all public events, i.e. at feasts and, of course, at athletic contests so that they could immediately treat athletes in cases of accident. Public doctors had other duties as well, such as medical supervision during military training and service. Doctors, both public and private, were organised in associations centred around the cult of Asclepius, a sort of rudimentary union.

Regarding the provision of public or private athletic facilities, this can be extrapolated from the archaeological evidence. For example, the archaeological site of ancient Sicyon lies on a flat section of Vasilikos Hill; it includes the excavated area of the *Agora* of the Hellenistic and Roman city, the theatre, the stadium and the Roman Baths, which have been restored and modified in order to be used as a Museum.[44] On the southern side of the *Agora* of Argos, dating from the fifth century, on the crossroads from the Heraion of Argos, Corinth and Tegea, there is, among other structures, a large building, a *palaestra*, with porticoes of Doric columns. Another excavated area includes the starting line of the *dromos* (road, street) located in a *stadium*.[45] *Palaestras* and *stadiums* have also been identified in other Achaean city-states too such as Messene,[46] Nemea (Miller 1980), Sparta, Megalopolis etc.

Provision of public athletic facilities can also be verified indirectly regarding the Achaean Sympolity since the *Asclepieia* were public facilities that included public *gymnasiums*, run by the state. They were part of the overall pan-Hellenic mentality encapsulated in the motto 'a healthy mind in a healthy body'. During the Hellenistic Period, the *gymnasiums* were a well-developed and much-frequented institution. One famous in the Achaean Sympolity was Corinth's *gymnasium* (Wiseman 1969). Another famous one was in the city-state of Messene.[47] Another enormous *gymnasium* was located on the western side of the *Agora* in Sicyon, constructed with two

[44]http://odysseus.culture.gr/h/3/eh352.jsp?obj_id=2538

[45]https://www.gtp.gr/TDirectoryDetails.asp?ID=39174

[46]http://www.magicmessinia.gr/item/ancient-messini/

[47]See http://www.magicmessinia.gr/item/ancient-messini/

separate terraces. Argos's *gymnasium* was called Kylarabis and was located just outside the city, while Mantineia also had one (Dickenson 2017, p. 111–112).

Another public good partially provided by the state was education. Griffith (2001, p. 66–67), based on ancient sources, argues that by the late sixth century at least, some recognised schools which provided educational services existed all over Greece; and by the end of the fifth century, they were quite widespread, at least in urban communities, even if in smaller towns and villages, schools must have been (at best) quite rudimentary, and the *grammatists* and *kitharistai* may often have been the same individual. He further argues that by no means did every community boast a separate gymnasium or *palaestra* before the fourth or third centuries. Ober (2001, p. 185) adds that the concern with educating the youth through public institutions may well be a general feature of the Greek city-state: the Spartan *agoge* (upbringing) can be seen as one remarkable and extreme manifestation of this general concern in a non-democratic context. Thus educational procedures as a part of public institutions did exist in the ancient Greek world. In some cities like Athens, it was more sophisticated, while in others, the promotion of education was less organised.

In contrast to those who believe that education in Ancient Greece was based solely on private tutorship by *paidagogoi*, hired by well-off citizens to teach their children, the reality is that in Classical Athens and probably in a number of the rest of the Greek city-states, including those of the Achaean Sympolity, primary education came to be considered a public good, and thus, was partially undertaken by the state itself. Some scholars have found evidence corroborating that the Athenian state was significantly involved. For example, Beaumont (2012, p. 135) notes that while the state at first played no part in the provision of formal schooling with the result that all lessons were taught by teachers engaged and remunerated on a private basis, from the mid-fifth century on, the state intervened in the case of (i) boys whose fathers died in a battle, fighting for the city, (ii) sons of poor unpropertied families and (iii) sons of *thetes* (although there is not absolutely certain that this social group was indeed included in the provision of education as a public good).

Thus, public education was provided freely by the state to a large number of Athenian children: orphans (due to war losses etc.), sons of low-income families that owned no property, and the children of the lowest socio-economic class, the *thetes*, a large portion of the state's children were receiving public education at its expense, as a part of its social welfare policy. The Athenian public education system was a two-stage system, primary and secondary, and was exclusively dedicated to the education of boys. Primary education was undertaken by (i) *grammatists*, teachers that taught courses related to writing, reading and mathematics, basing courses on the works of the great poets, (such as Homer and Hesiod); (ii) *kitharistai*, guitarists that taught their students how to play the seven-string lyre and sing the works of lyric poets; and (iii) *paidotribai*, who were responsible for the physical development of the boys who were trained in wrestling, *pankration*, boxing, running, throwing the disc, jumping and various other sports in the *palaestra*.[48] Some other courses were

[48] *Pankration* was a mixed martial art, developed in Sparta.

occasionally included, such as literature, music and painting (Aristotle, *Pol.* 8.1336b-1337b). For the sons of the wealthier classes, primary education was financed privately. For those of the lower social strata, private teachers providing their services were paid by the state, under what it is today called a public–private partnership system, the so-called 'PPP' or '3P'. Primary education lasted for 8 years of study (6–14-year-olds). Formal education of poorer boys probably ended by age 14 and was followed by an apprenticeship in a trade. Wealthier boys continued their education under the tutelage of philosopher-teachers.

Based on the above evidence (even indirect one), we believe that there was an organised system of public education in the Achaean Sympolity similar to that of Classical (and Hellenistic) Athens, under the discretionary supervision of the Achaean federal authorities. We also believe that the authorities of each city-state provided the provision of a number of extra public services, such as policing and maintaining order in the streets, street cleaning, water supply and fountains inside the cities; the federal authorities did not intervene at all. In fact, such services were already being provided by the Athenian state authorities from as early as the fifth century,[49] and there is no reason to believe that they were not part of the ordinary state policy agendas of the Achaean city-states as well.

7.4.4 Water Management and the Positive Externalities

Water resources management in Classical and Hellenistic Greece was heavily affected by geophysical characteristics and climate. In earlier times, Eastern civilisations blossomed in large river valleys, with water in abundance (Mesopotamia's Tigris and Euphrates Rivers, India's Indus, Egypt's Nile). In contrast, Greece does not have large rivers and is divided by mountains into small plains. The major part of land cultivation takes place on plains covering approximately 20% of the Greek peninsula and islands (Foxhall 1995; Fleck and Hansen 2006).

Because of the above, Greek societies developed a framework of laws and institutions for water management. Verified evidence for Archaic Athens is provided by Plutarch (*Solon* 23), while Aristotle (Pol. 7.1330b) argued that the city of Athens must possess a plentiful natural supply of pools and springs as a guarantee for the

[49]In the city-state of Athens, a group of 10 policemen known as *astynomoi* were responsible for maintaining the city's cleanliness and keeping order. They were assisted by 300 publicly owned Scythian slaves. They were responsible for maintaining the peace, crowd-control and assisting in dealing with criminals, making arrests and handling prisoners (Arist. Ath. Const. 50; Cox 2007). Regarding street cleanliness, there was a service, the *koprologoi*, financed by the state, whose duty was to collect garbage and animal faeces found in the streets throughout the twin cities of Athens–Piraeus and turn it into fertiliser for sale (Ault 2007). Aristotle (Ath. Const. 50) and the inscriptions *IG* XII 5, 107 and *IG* XII describe the provision of such a service even in smaller towns, as was the case on the islands of Paros and Thassos. Thus, there is no reason to believe that such a service did not exist (in general or at least, partially) in the city-states of the Achaean Sympolity.

future prosperity of the population whereas regulations to ensure the fair distribution of water should be enforced (Aristotle Ath. Const. 43.1). For that purpose, the Athenians introduced, among others, the post of *epimelites epi ton udaton* (also known as *epimelites epi ton krinon*), a state functionary responsible for supervising the proper functioning and cleanliness of public fountains (Bitros et al. 2020). The fact that water management practices were implemented in the Greek federal states is verified indirectly with the paradigm of Lake Copais in the Boeotian *Koinon*, where there exists reliable evidence. The lake was vital to the efficient drainage and water supply of the Boeotian *Koinon*. The Boeotians exploited not only the edible resources of the lake, its fertile soil when it became dry in summer, but its waters as a transportation resource during the wet season as well. Fishing rights were offered to individuals under lease contracts; in cases of disputes concerning fishing rights, such as in the case of two neighbouring city-states, Acraephnium and Copai, federal courts could intervene and arbitrate over property rights of member city-states' disputes (*IG*, VII, 2792, reproduced in Mackil 2013, p. 415–448).

Federal courts could ensure (i) the legal status of usage of property rights in the lake, (ii) a relatively fair system of economic exploitation of the lake between neighbouring city-states and (iii) that the lake would be used in a way that ensured that it would not be profitable for only one group of users at the expense of the others (*negative externality*). This is related to the famous *tragedy of the commons* problem raised by Hardin (1968). More recent studies argue that Hardin's problem can be effectively solved providing that the many local communities that are related to the exploitation of a strategic resource, such a river or a lake, can cooperate over it under a commonly accepted set of rules which they all protect and respect (Ostrom 1990) (iv) that the lake will not be destroyed due to excessive consumption and misuse (*negative externality*). This issue, welfare maximization with and without environmental externalities is an intertemporal problem which is the core of the analysis of the modern Environmental and Natural Resource Economics (see among others Halkos and Psarianos 2016).

This situation was taking place also in the case of the Achaean Sympolity. The Peloponnesus is characterised by a complex river system that runs throughout the regions of the peninsula. Since: (i) an efficient water supply is a very important resource that determines the overall quality of life in a society (and this is an intertemporal axiom), and (ii) river and lake paths crossed territorial boundaries of more than one city-state, it is logical to believe that city-states were obliged to implement interstate cooperation with each other (such as in the case of the Sympolity and its neighbour, the Boeotian Koinon) to achieve efficient and mutually beneficial management of water sources, in a way that did not cause what is considered as a negative externality, to employ a modern economic interpretation. In other words, there must have been some kind of water management policy existed that included all rivers and lakes throughout the Peloponnesus. This is verified by the extensive analysis of Crouch (1994) who, by using a combination of literary sources (the ancient authors), geological and hydrological analysis, and archaeological evidence, proves the interaction between water management and the process of urbanisation in the ancient Greek world. Similarly, in an earlier study, Oleson

Table 7.2 The provision of federal public goods through the Achaean federal authorities

At the federal level		
Provision of a public good	Defence	□
	Justice	□
	Road network between city-states	?
Provision of a public good under the discretionary supervision of the Achaean federal authorities	Monetary policy	□
	Health	□
	Education	□
	Water management policy	□
	Lake management policy	□
At the city-state (local) level		
Provision of a public good	Cleanliness of the streets	?
	City water supply and fountains	□
	Road network within the city-state	?
	Police services	?
	Health	□
	Athletic facilities	□

"□" A policy that was in existence; "?" A policy that was probably in existence

(1984) provides evidence on the use of mechanical water-lifting devices to deliver water during the Hellenistic and the Roman periods, such as the water-screw, the force pump, the compartmented wheel, and the bucket-chain. Table 7.2 summarises the findings of 7.4.1–7.4.4.

7.5 The Other Social Groups: Women, *Metics* and Slaves in the Achaean Sympolity

Some scholars tend to downplay the political and economic achievements of Ancient Greek society expressing dismay over the fact that there existed discrimination at the expense of women, *metics* and slaves. The key distinction was the refusal to grant the right to vote to those three groups. Lyttkens and Henrik (2018), for example, characterise the Athenian Democracy was actually a 'direct male democracy'. However, this discussion is not very meaningful, nor does it make much sense, given that it does not take into account the different historical and social context, then and now. The universal right to vote for a woman in modern societies was first granted in 1893 in New Zealand and was only fully achieved in the twentieth century.

Can one honestly claim that until then, no western societies were democratic, not even, for example, the USA, whose constitution was ratified in 1787, but women's suffrage not achieved until 1918? The same holds for slavery as well, which was not abolished until the Civil War of 1861–1865. Was the USA not a democracy because slavery existed, and women could not participate in the public domain? If not, what was it?

In reference to women in Ancient Greece, we focus on their right to holding property. Women, under certain circumstances, did possess that right. By marriage, newlywed women received a dowry which consisted of precious objects, coins as well as land which the woman's father entrusted to the groom. Furthermore, a wife became *epicleros,* controlling the estate of her husband upon his death and until his male heirs became of age. Sources tell us of many instances of women that held inalienable and enshrined property rights. Among them, Epicteta, from the island of Thira, in around 200, owned a great deal of land. Another, Arete, in Megara, bought a garden from another woman in Aigosthena for 1000 *drachmae* in the third century while yet another, Timacreta, owned land in the domain of Ptolemy III Euergetes, the Hellenistic king of Egypt. Many such examples are recorded in Ancient Greece and throughout the Hellenistic world (Schaps 1979; Sealey 1990). In contrast to the entrenched view that the position of women was limited to the management of her household aside, many recorded cases refer to the active and significant participation of women in the business events of their city (Schaps 1979, p. 20, 50; Pomeroy 1995; Cohen 2002, p. 105; Kyriazis 2012, p. 74–76; Economou and Kyriazis 2019c).

As for the *metics*, who, for the most part, were citizens that had emigrated to another city to seek work, either temporarily or indefinitely, a tax of 12 *drachmae* was paid by men and 6 by women known as the *metoikion* or *xenicon.* Children were not subject to the tax as long as their mother paid her six *drachmae* (Gabrielsen 2013, p. 337, 341). If *metics* did not pay the tax, penalties were severe: not only were they punished for defiance of the law, the city even had the right to imprison them temporarily, or even sell them into slavery or expel them. A married couple's tax was 18 *drachmae*, equivalent to 18 days' wages, given that the daily wage was 1 *drachma* (Loomis 1998). Not a negligible amount but neither extremely burdensome. From an economic standpoint, it was the price paid to the city-state by non-citizens who enjoyed the use of the city's services and benefitted from them. Cohen (1973), who studied naval law as applied in ancient Athens, argues that under commercial law, *metics*, visitors to the city and even slaves had full legal rights as far as financial transactions were concerned. However, they could not own property, run for office or participate in the Athenian Assembly of citizens. *Metics* were not permitted to marry Athenian women, nor could they become citizens. However, a male Athenian could marry a female *metic*.

As far as slaves were concerned, despite the views of some very specific researchers such as Finley (1973, 1985), Austin-Vidal Naquet (1977) and de Ste. Croix (1989) that the Athenian, as well as the whole of ancient Greek society, did not present any economic progress because, in their view, they were based on rudimentary economic institutions and relied on slavery, the modern bibliography has almost completely discredited these arguments of Finley's *primitivism* mode. The treatment of slaves varied according to circumstances. Those that served in a wealthy household enjoyed a far easier life than the state/public slave who toiled under harsh conditions in the silver mines of Laurion. In Athens, some slaves served in households or private businesses while others belonged to the city, serving as scribes, messengers, officers of the law (300 archers served as policemen, for instance) etc. Slaves, for the most part, came from foreign lands (Illyria, Colchis, Scythia, Syria, Caria, Lydia) but there were cases of Greeks captured in war and consequently enslaved (Kyrtatas 2011, p. 93). However, what is important to note is that, in terms of civil and political freedoms, a slave in the ancient Athenian Democracy did enjoy at least a minimal level of civil rights. Of course, ownership of any property he might somehow acquire would revert to his owner (ibid., 106).

We believe, however, this was more of a formal rather than a substantive situation. There exist inscriptions found in Delphi dating from before 150 that attest to 368 such instances of ownership by male slaves and 123 by female slaves (Schaps 1979, p. 7). Therefore, it is not at all certain that a master did suppress his slave's 'property rights'. Slaves often received excellent clothing and sustenance from their owners so that they could perform their duties more efficiently. Slaves were also permitted to be involved in economic activities and to acquire property legally (Cohen 2000, p. 132–145). Such activities allowed them the opportunity to buy their way out of slavery and become free citizens (*apeleutheroi*), a significant incentive for them to remain honest and perform their duties for their master efficiently. The most characteristic case was that of Pasion who, from being a slave, eventually rose to become one of the wealthiest citizens of Athens, a shining example of social evolution and mobility. Additionally, torture of a slave was not allowed, and any sentence of death of a slave was punishable by law if the sentence had not been passed by court decision (Plato *Laws* 6.777; Demosthenes *Against Medias* 46). If their master or any other citizen killed a slave, the penalty imposed was exile, not death.

There did exist specific city-states and elsewhere in antiquity where the circumstances of a slave were particularly dire such as that of the *helots* in Sparta, the *penestai* of Thessaly or the *latifundia* of Rome, and who, for that reason, frequently rose in rebellion But, in general in the Greek world, the life of a slave was not as grim as some believe and a significant number worked in the markets of the Greek city-states carrying out trade activities alongside their masters, under decent working conditions that did not differ much from those of free citizens (see among others, Schaps 1979; Cohen 2000; Economou and Kyriazis 2019b, p. 96–97).

In 2.4, we provided a very characteristic case of tangible evidence regarding the existence of slaves in the Achaean Sympolity. Just before the Battle of Leucopetras, the *strategos* Diaeus released 12,000 slaves from bondage and enlisted them into the army. We believe that the general trend in the position of women, *metics* and economic migrants and slaves that transpired throughout the Greek world during the Classical and Hellenistic Periods existed in Achaean society (comprising at least 103 city-states) as well since it was part of the Greek world.

7.6 The Value-Added of the Political and Economic Institutions of the Achaean Sympolity. Was it a Successful Historical Federal Paradigm?

Figure 7.13 summarises some of the basic aspects of the economic organisation of the Achaean Sympolity. Figure 7.14, which is based on the above overall analysis, summarises the basic elements of the Achaean 'Constitution' concerning its political and economic institutions while Table 7.3 presents the most important institutions of the Achaean state that are related to its success as a federal entity. These institutions were responsible for the remarkable expansion of the Achaean Sympolity in the fourth and third centuries. In other words, through the establishment of such institutions, the federal structure was seen as a beneficial option for the majority of its citizens.

It was not only the issue of common defence and cultural, historical and social bonds that were vital for the advancement of the regional collaboration ethically

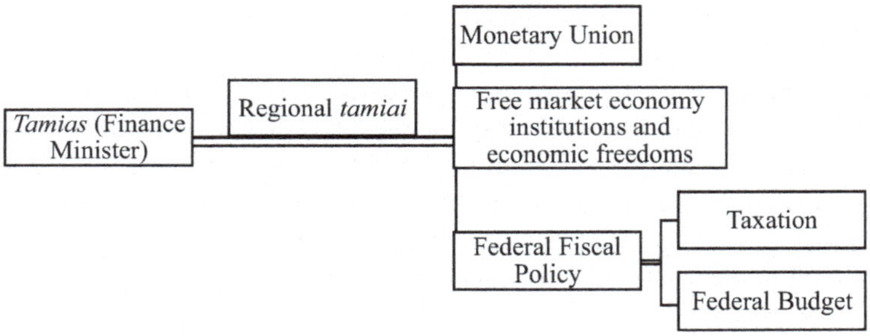

Fig. 7.13 The economic organisation of the Achaean Sympolity

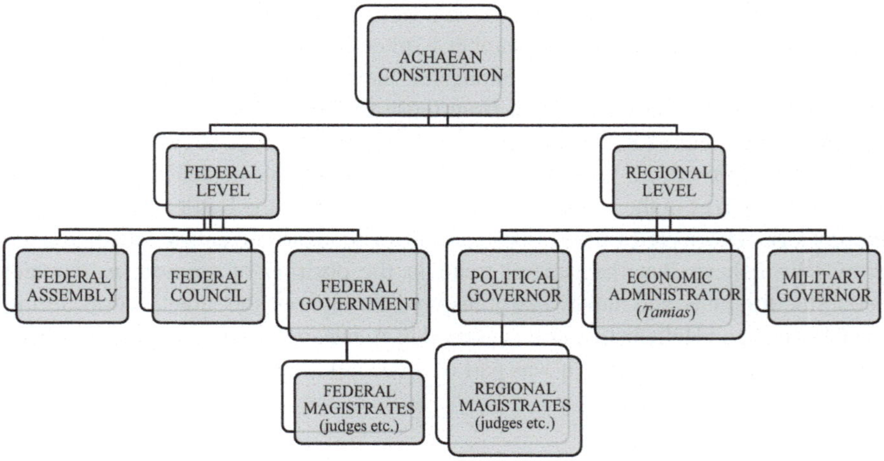

Fig. 7.14 The 'Achaean Constitution'

Table 7.3 The main political and economic institutions of the Achaean federal state

Federal political institutions	
Federal political posts and magistrates	Federal Assembly, (*Ecclesia*) Federal Council, (*Synedrion* or *Boule*) Federal Government (*Strategos, ipparchos, grammateus, hypostrategos, nauarchos*) Federal Magistrates
Equality of political rights	Eligibility of every federal male citizen to vote and to be elected
Regional level of organisation	The political head of the region The military head of the region
Single citizenship regime	*Isopoliteia:* A process of mutual concession of political rights between city-states
Federal judicial services on civic issues	For cases between individuals and for disputes between city-states (mainly territorial disputes)
Common external and defence policy	Regional military commanders under the *general*, and the rest of the high-ranking military officials.
Coexistence of complementary regional and federal institutional mechanisms	The responsibilities of local/regional magistrates and judges on civic and political issues did not overlap with those of the federal magistrates
Federal economic institutions	
Free market economy institutions	Organised markets and market mechanisms functioned in practice. *Agoranomoi* were introduced for preventing profiteering in the marketplaces
Federal judicial services on economic issues	Property rights protection through *enktesis* and *epigamia*
Protection of contracts	Through city-state and federal courts. A basic prerequisite for securing commercial transactions
Economic rights and freedoms	Free movement of goods and services, capital and citizens (labour)
Monetary union and common coinage	The seven federal *tamiai* (regional treasurers) and the 'chief *tamias*', responsible for introducing the federal monetary policy in cooperation with the mints throughout Achaea, which issued currency for the member city-states
Federal budget	The federal *tamiai* and the 'chief *tamias*' were responsible for managing public revenues and costs, for the upkeep of the federal treasury and for introducing the federal fiscal policy
Regional economic administration	*Tamias* (economic administrator in each of the seven regions)
Coexistence of complementary regional and federal institutional mechanisms	The responsibilities of local/regional magistrates and judges on economic issues did not overlap with those of the federal magistrates

legitimised by the Achaean citizens themselves, as emphasised by historians but also the obvious economic motives and opportunities that benefitted citizens through commercial transactions. Such an environment of rules of behaviour proved crucial for the step-by-step creation of a 'cognitive glue' between the federal state and its constituents.

If we exclude some Arcadian cases such as Mantineia, Tegea, Caphyae and Arcadian Orchomenos,[50] and if we exclude, too, the regions of Sparta/Laconia which joined *force majeure* due to Achaean military activities, and Messene and Elis which joined in 191 for specific geopolitical reasons, there is no evidence that any other city-state (or states) were forced into participating in the federal structure. In Table 6.2, we argued that of the 103 recorded cases of city-states that belonged to the Achaean Sympolity at its height in 191, 23 were from the region of Laconia/Sparta, 12 from the region of Messenia and 9 from the region of Elis.

If we add the four Arcadian cases mentioned above, we reach a number of 48 city-states or 46% of the 103. But the fact that the city-states of Messene, Elis and some from Arcadia, at an earlier time, joined the Achaean Sympolity due to current geopolitical realities does not necessarily mean that, say, the Laconian city-states were all against the process of federalisation. Of course, there were cases such as Sparta which, during the third and second centuries, was a sworn enemy of federalism, but this does not necessarily mean that all Laconian cities were against the progress of the Sympolity's federalisation of the entire Peloponnesus.

For example, it is almost certain that during the period of Spartan dominance in Greek affairs, from 750 to 372, there were cases of city-states in the wider regions of Laconia and Messenia that were against Spartan oppression but were unable to react effectively. These city-states were finally able to expose their true will after the Spartans' defeats at Leuctra in 371 and Mantineia in 362 and the intervention of the Boeotian *Koinon* under its *strategos* Epaminondas into Laconian and Messenian affairs that lead to the liberation of the *helots,* transforming the socio-economic status quo in the southern Peloponnesus.[51] Thus, it should not be taken for granted that during the late second century, the city-states of the region of Laconia and Messenia were all pro-Spartan or against the process of federalisation.

What the historians do not tell us on this point is what would have been the attitude of those city-states of Laconia, Elis and Messenia that were against federalisation, say, 100 years later, when the economic benefits from having participated in the federal structure would have been apparent and, likely, superior to those that these poleis could have managed to achieve, had they been autonomous, or fully—at least, theoretically—independent. In other words, Sparta/Laconia, Elis and Messene joined the Sympolity too late (in 191), possibly not in the 'best momentum' of time. When the Sympolity was dissolved, these regions had only had 55 years of membership, not enough time to take full advantage of the federal institutions that would eventually make them prosperous, not enough time to change their overall

[50]There is a controversy here among the ancient authors and modern historians regarding whether their joining in 241 or sometime from 239 to 228, was voluntary or due to geopolitical reasons.

[51]Regarding the political and socio-economic structure of Sparta see in detail Cartledge (1979, 1987, 2003) and Cartledge and Spawforth (2002).

attitudes and preferences towards developing a federal conscience regarding participation in the Sympolity.

In his very important passage 2.37., Polybius writes that the Achaean Sympolity was a successful political phenomenon because it succeeded in making Peloponnesians share a common interest; in the past, other states such as Sparta had tried but failed because their aim had been only to expand their power, and not to achieve a deliberate consensus. Polybius argues that before the Achaean federal experiment was implemented in practice successfully: every city-state was working to secure only his own power rather than the power of the whole but in his times the federal policy has made such progress that the Achaeans as a whole achieved: (i) a community of interests; (ii) uniformity of laws, weights, measures and currency; (iii) uniformity in federal procedures and federal institutions and practices; and (iv) equality among the city-states.[52]

These are key intertemporal federal axioms (Riker 1964; Oates 1972). What Polybius is saying here is that for a federal structure to flourish and become viable in the long run, the member states need to share a mutual package of benefits such as reliable security against foreign threats, political stability, economic development, prestige and equality among the city-states and the regions etc. The later was already observed by the eighteenth-century French philosopher, historian and writer, Abbé de Mably, who in his essay *Observations* written in 1764 regarding Greek antiquity wrote on the Achaean Federation specifically, that democracy, unlike other Greek cities caused no disorder in Achaea because:

> democracy was tempered by general laws agreed on by all its republics....Each republic renounced its right to forge alliances and agreed that the confederation should be based on the principle of equality. (Mably [1784] 2018, p. 226–227)

The majority of the Peloponnesian city-states had joined the federal Achaean experiment voluntarily. This is consistent with the argumentation of Kralli (2017, p. 148) who argues that partial loss of autonomy was not a sacrifice, provided that three conditions were being met: (i) that no or little coercion was exercised, (ii) that the Sympolity offered efficient protection from external enemies, and (iii) that there was no alternative. This view is almost identical to the groundwork argumentation of de Figuereido and Weingast (2005) who argued that the participation of a state in a federal structure could take place when: (i) there are gains from participation and (ii) these gains cannot be found elsewhere.

The basic gains were: (i) achieving a higher level of security against a foreign threat, (ii) establishing an environment of peace among the member city-states, reinforced by the fact that extensive commercial activity between the city-states

---

[52]This is implied by Polybius when he writes:

'Nor is there any difference between the entire Peloponnesus and a single city, except in the fact that its inhabitants are not included within the same wall.'

Here Polybius does not specify the nature of 'equality' he refers on; either economic or equality in power-sharing among member states or both of them. He probably wanted to refer on both of them.

functioned as a mechanism for neutralising conflict and disputes among them. The more 'international' and interstate commercial transactions taking place, the lower the threat of conflict and warfare. There is no evidence that during the entire period from 389 to 146, any of the Sympolity's members ever engaged in warfare against each other, which is consistent with the modern *Liberal* approach of *International Relations Theory* and even with the Kantian *perpetual peace* perspective that democracies (like the Achaean city-states or the current EU member-states) are not engaged in warfare with each other (Oneal and Russett 1997; Starr 1997). This was generally the case with the Greek federations. When commercial activity turned out to be mutually profitable for the member states, then the cost of abandoning that cooperation was much greater than any benefit that might have been derived from 'going it alone'. However, even under such an environment, there was always a trend in some city-states to revert to violence. Champion and O′ Sullivan (2017, p. 6) argue that individual poleis continued to pursue aggressive policies of territorial expansion against their neighbours and to define their civic prestige in terms of warfare.

However, such behaviours were exceptions to the rule. In fact, except for a few scattered cases such as Messene in 183/182 and Sparta, even after her inclusion in the Sympolity in 191, there is no mention in the sources, as far as we know, of any other instances of outbreaks of armed conflict between members of any of the Greek federations or of one or more members against the central authority of those federations. If any other such cases had occurred, we speculate they would have been isolated and short-lived incidents. Accordingly, it is possible to assert that the Ancient Greek federations, generally, fit the characterisation of 'zones of democratic peace', to borrow from Copeland (2014, p. 57).

In 6.3, we analysed the mechanisms and the protocols of behaviour through which the Achaean federal authorities could solve disputes between the member poleis, whether territorial or economic. A corollary to this is that by enjoying the privilege of actively participating in political decision-making procedures and thus having a sense of belonging to an environment of common values, ethics and principles, Achaean citizens found it extremely beneficial to cooperate and coordinate with each other, creating together what can be termed a 'federal conscience'. That is strongly related to the issue of direct democracy and the active participation of people in the political, social and economic life in every one of the Achaean city-states. When the average citizen saw that his actions had a real impact on the formulation of policy, he became more responsible, a better person, more effective as a member of his community. As Manville and Ober (2003, p. 65–66) argue in their seminal work, *The Company of Citizens*, referring to the seminal case of the Athenian state and the pioneering Athenian democracy:

> Cleisthenes and his colleagues transformed the existing status of 'being an Athenian'. They gave it deeper meaning, with language and passionate rhetoric celebrating the values of freedom and equality. They also made citizenship more reliable by formalizing the procedure of membership enrollment and certification… Now it was not some elite ruler but your fellow citizens as a community who guaranteed for you your status of citizenship. You became a citizen through a vote by the citizens, and no one but your fellow-citizens could

> ever take citizenship away from you. The formalisation of that status created a new and stronger sense of individual security. That in turn allowed for the growth of the deep mutual trust on which a true company of citizens must be built.

These values were also shared by the federal citizens of the Achaean Sympolity. Moreover, the Achaeans, whether fighting on the front lines or providing support to the federal armed forces, hammered out a common consciousness; they were fighting not only for their own city-state but for the Sympolity itself. The emergence of a federal conscience made the Achaeans willing to 'defend the system' according to B. Weingast's (1997) logic—an attitude vital to ensuring a federation's longevity and prosperity. As soon as this was achieved, the possibility of reverting to war was drastically diminished. Finally, this federal conscience was further reinforced by the rising levels of economic prosperity, as compared to the old environment of local, limited tribal/city-state economic cooperation.

The above views as a whole are related to the issue of measuring economic development through welfare distribution among the Achaean federal constituents. According to modern *fiscal federalism* theory, welfare distribution, both between citizens and cities/regions, is a key element in forging federalism. Aristotle (Polit. 1264a, 36–37) argues that fairer economic management and wealth distribution increase a state's coherence, a higher ideal in democratic states in general.[53] Obviously, economic development is related to political stability and based on the analytical evidence we provided above so far, we are confident to argue that, if we exclude some specific periods of social unrest (Cleomenes' III period) with mainly economic causes for the greatest part of the period of the reorganised Achaean federal state (280–146 BCE) member city-states achieved both political and economic stability and fruitful economic and political cooperation between them under the auspices of the federal government.[54]

Unfortunately, there are no recorded statistical data on macroeconomic issues such as GDP, growth rates, unemployment, the volume and the value of commercial transactions, etc. Thus, since no such data are available, we cannot provide a cliometric approach to measure the level of economic prosperity diffusion among the entire Achaean regions. Therefore, we do not know how and to what extent welfare was spread throughout Achaean society. However, based on the findings till this point, it can be assumed that there must have been a satisfactory level of distribution of wealth among the Achaean people.

---

[53]This is a timeless axiom that, as we have argued in Economou and Kyriazis (2019b), has been traced in a series of case studies such as Ancient Greece (Athens and the Aetolian Sympolity), the Old Swiss Confederacy, England, the United Provinces (the Dutch Republic), Great Britain, France, the USA, and the modern cases of Switzerland, Germany, the USA and the EU.

[54]The relation of political stability and economic development/growth in a democratic regime is an intertemporal one and has been analysed by numerous and prominent scholars such as Lipset (1959, p. 56), Friedman (1961), Hayek (1973), von Mises (1981), Ozler and Rodrik (1992), Riker and Weimer (1993) and Alesina and Perroti (1996). For a recent review on this bibliography, see Georgiou, Kyriazis and Economou (2015) and Economou and Kyriazis (2019b, annex no. 2) and the references provided therein.

As has been amply demonstrated, the establishment of the Sympolity, as well as all the other Greek federations, was initially based on the primary issue of forging a common defence and security policy. And as those alliances proved substantive and successful, new institutions were introduced to improve cooperation on a broader range of issues for mutual benefit. That trend served as an incentive to make this cooperation permanent, evolving into a true federation. And as this progressed, resembling what could be seen as a repetitive positive-sum game since, generally, it seemed that everyone—or at least almost everyone—was 'winning', the probability of this cooperation coming apart became less and less likely for three main reasons.

First, the investment in time and money, or, *sunk cost*, as modern economists would term it, incurred in the creation of the Sympolity would have been wasted since in the event it was decided sometime in the future to revive the alliance, it would require additional *transactional cost* to recreate the abandoned institutions. Second, because of *path dependence*. As cooperation between the city-states evolved and was perceived as mutually beneficial, *path dependence* developed gradually. In other words, the new morals and values that have proven successful have slowly been consolidated into a new permanent sociopolitical *status quo* making a return to the past less and less likely as citizens adopted them, became accustomed to them and made them a part of their everyday lives. Citizens would be loath to return to the past or introduce yet another new political experiment.[55]

Third, it appears that the Achaean Sympolity displayed a significant degree of flexibility in matters related to the social and political dimensions of the economic measures it decided to impose. If there were demonstrably valid explanations for a city-state's inability to meet its tax obligations towards the federal government, it was not punished, but instead, for the good of the Sympolity's cohesion, it was granted the privilege of *ateleia* (tax relief) for that fiscal year.

That was the case in Messene in 183/182. Deinocrates, the strongman in control of political events in the region, responsible for installing tyranny in Messene, requested support from the Roman general Quintius Flamininus to help ensure the city of Messene seceded from the Sympolity. At the time, Flamininus happened to be traversing the Peloponnesus heading a large force on its way to Asia Minor. There followed the Roman legate Quintius Marcius Philippus' intervention in favour of Messene's secession, the great *strategos* Philopoemen's death and the counterattack by the Achaean forces under the *strategos* Lycortas who arrested the rebels and plundered Messene. Deinocrates committed suicide. In the end, Messene was restored as a member of the Sympolity in 182/181. When Messene consented to rejoin the Sympolity, the terms stipulated tax relief for 3 years. Because of the destruction wreaked by Achaean troops during the campaign, the Sympolity effectively agreed to compensate the Messenians. As Polybius (Hist. 24.2.6–14;

[55]As mentioned in Footnote 64, for the meaning of *path dependence*, see the seminal work of David (1985) and Arthur (1989), but also Kyriazis (2006) and Kyriazis and Metaxas (2010), specifically in reference to the Athenian Democracy.

23.15.4–8) commented, this was 'so that the Achaeans would bear a burden no lesser than the Messenians'. Mackil (2013, p. 300–301) characteristically notes that when the cohesion of the federation was at risk, the Achaeans behaved with leniency towards its members, not arrogance.

Philopoemen's death at the hands of the Messenians had been no small matter. The Achaean leadership must certainly have been aware of the gravity of the loss. Nevertheless, rather than acting vengefully, it remained cool and mature, essentially applying a strategy of *stick and carrot*. Having already punished the Messenians for having attempted to secede by looting and pillaging their lands, it then pulled back and absolved them from paying federal taxes for 3 years to allow their economy to recover once they rejoined the Sympolity. The federalisation of the whole of the Peloponnesus had always been the ultimate aim of the Sympolity's visionaries. In furtherance of that goal, they were prepared to make objective sacrifices (*ateleia*) for the common good, as any true and functionally mature federation must be prepared to do. As a final comment, below we provide a concise quote by Ober (2015, p. 242–243) which conveys all the analytical framework developed above regarding the economic background of the historical success of the Achaean Sympolity (and the rest of the Greek federations of that time):

> Federalism allowed small states to retain the advantages arising from subsidiarity: That is, many decisions could be addressed at a local level by those most directly affected. But at the same time, the members of a federal state gained the security and welfare advantages of 'getting big'. In each case, the intensification of political relations among states in a region built upon, and subsequently fostered, productive intraregional economic relations, for example, between upland and coastal towns. Some degree of economic cooperation had long existed in each region, arising from shared interests and a sense of regional identity encouraged by attending religious ceremonies at regional sanctuaries. In the fourth century and continuing through the third and into the second centuries, the federal leagues became increasingly capable of acting as political entities, diplomatically and militarily. By credibly committing the member states to cooperative trade relations and by increasing security, the leagues were incubators of productive economic specialization. Pastoralists in upland poleis could, for example, plan to raise more sheep whose wool could be exported through coastal ports, without worrying about restrictions on movement across polis borders, or extortionate taxes. The leagues also helped to provide for better regional security, as potential counterweights to the hegemonic ambitions of their larger neighbors. The Achaean and Aetolian leagues[56] seem to have been especially well managed and are relatively well documented, but the idea of Federalism spread across much of the polis ecology in the course of the fourth and subsequent centuries. By the later fourth century, half of mainland Greek poleis were organized in federal leagues.

[56]Federal states.

Chapter 8
Further Key Issues Regarding the Achaean Sympolity

8.1 A Spatial Decision Model Analysis Between Aratus and Antigonus III Doson

In Chaps. 1 through 5, we have observed that many of the decisions of the main political figures who shaped the Achaean Sympolity's policies and grand strategies, such as alliances, war and peace, were based on a trade-off between an array of possible outcomes. In practical terms, this means that the Achaean policymakers tried to weigh the pros and cons and consequences of each policy before taking their decisions. In many cases, the decisions to be taken by either the federal policymakers or the pan-Achaean Assembly or both were not easy. The more complex the case was, the less predictable the outcome.

Thus, in some cases, the Achaean policymakers took prudent decisions, such as, (i) not to punish the city-states of Dyme, Tritaia and Pherae severely when, during the Social War of 220–217, they decided to retaliate against the Achaean government and not contribute to the federal budget after the federal government failed to protect them from the Aetolians, and (ii) to accept new poleis into the Sympolity by proposing voluntary membership to their political leaders, e.g. the tyrants Lydiades of Megalopolis and Aristomachus of Argos. In retrospect, these choices proved to be astute since, had the Achaeans chosen to incorporate these strong city-states by force, this may have been a very costly procedure, leading to severe losses in financial means, human resources and military equipment. However, in other cases, the Achaean policymakers took unwise (even catastrophic) decisions such as Diaeus and Critolaus declaring war against Rome in 147/146.

In Fig. 8.1, we provide another characteristic case. Under a *spatial decision model* analysis, it presents the strategic choices open to Aratus and Antigonus III Doson regarding a radical turn in their foreign policy by forming an alliance between the Achaean Sympolity and the Kingdom of Macedon, which had been, until then, a traditional foil to the Sympolity's grand strategy. Antigonus had understood Aratus' fear that a strong Sparta, allied with the Aetolian Sympolity, might turn against the

E. M. L. Economou, *The Achaean Federation in Ancient Greece*, Frontiers in Economic History, https://doi.org/10.1007/978-3-030-52697-9_8

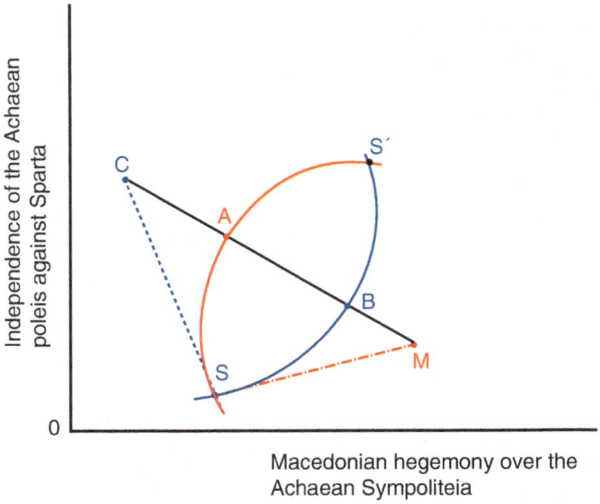

Fig. 8.1 A spatial decision model of diplomatic exchanges between the *Strategos* Aratus and King Antigonus III Doson

Kingdom of Macedon in the future. Thus, he considered accepting the 'deal' that Aratus proposed. This deal can be described in the stylised spatial decision model in Fig. 8.1. We assume a two-dimensional policy space. On the horizontal axis, we measure the degree of Macedonian hegemony over the Achaean Sympolity. On the vertical axis, we draw the degree of independence of the Achaean city-states from Sparta's hegemonic ambitions. Aratus and Antigonus are assumed to entertain Euclidian preferences over the two dimensions, so that utility increases the closer the actual settlement is to a player's ideal point. Points C and M, respectively, show those ideal points. Aratus prefers independence for the Sympolity with a low degree of Macedonian domination in compensation for military aid against Sparta. Antigonus, on the other hand, prefers a high degree of Macedonian hegemony over the Achaean Sympolity as compensation for providing that military aid against Sparta.

S = Status quo
C = Ideal point of Aratus
M = Ideal point of Antigonus III ⇒
Range of acceptable new international settlements = [AB]

The status quo before the Battle of Sellasia of 222 is shown by point S in the graph. It represents a low degree of security for the Achaean Sympolity because of Sparta's military success and dominance, and a low degree of Macedonian hegemony. We draw the indifference curves of C and M that pass through S and form the lens SABS' defined by the intersection of the indifference curves. Both players are better off with settlements represented by points inside the lens for they yield higher utility than the status quo. The points on segment AB on the straight-line CM represent Pareto improvements for both players. Any point on AB beats the status quo and is acceptable to both players, Aratus is thought as offering Antigonus Doson a deal represented by a point P∈[AB], although at this level of generality we cannot say which point on the AB will prevail.

As a final comment, based on the findings of 2.3 and 4.3, it can be argued that this deal between Aratus and Antigonus Doson, as analysed above, led to a short-term period of benefit in the Sympolity's favour (with Sparta's defeat in 222) but a longer period of benefit for Macedon (her partial dominance over the Sympolity from 222 to 197).

8.2 Was the Achaean Sympolity a Federation or a Confederacy? A Constitutional Economics Approach

In our Preface and at various points throughout the text, either directly or indirectly, the issue was addressed as to whether the Achaean Sympolity and the other states with similar institutions of Ancient Greek political history were federations or confederations. For us, and perhaps a large number of our readers who may not be involved in issues of Ancient Greek political history, that issue may not be particularly essential. More interesting is discovering what the Achaean Sympolity can offer us today as possible ideas and policy proposals to improve the democratic state institutions of modern societies. On the other hand, some might demand at least an attempt at assigning a particular integration of the Sympolity into a specific state/constitutional scheme to clarify the criteria whereby the functions of its institutions are described.

However, as we explained in detail in our Preface, this is not at all easy for two main reasons: first, because the information that has survived from ancient sources is not completely clear regarding the institutional framework of the Achaean 'constitution' while on some occasions, those sources even contradict one another. Even ancient inscriptions that have been discovered referring to this issue are insufficient. Up to this point, we believe that we have made a substantial effort to synthesise existing information in a coherent and scientifically and academically acceptable manner. Second, as Mackil (2013) has observed, although each of the city-states was very much like the others in terms of political and economic organisation, in certain cases, there did exist significant differences between them. A comparison between the Achaean and Aetolian Sympolities on the one hand and the Boeotian *Koinon* on the other, for instance, reveals a host of significant differences in the state organisation. Throughout our work, to avoid labelling the case we are dealing with here incorrectly concerning how it functioned, we used the safe ancient term, *sympolity*. We could have used the similar term *Koinon* and did so with regard to Boeotia. Only in cases where a practice of the Sympolity was clearly typologically correlated to the term *federation* did we use that term.

This issue of proper typological interpretation regarding a federalist structure is timeless: even today, the difference between a confederation and a federation is not always clear. For instance, Switzerland, Germany and Austria today are federations,

Table 8.1 The basic differences between the federation and confederation models

Type of government	Confederacy	Federation
Sovereignty	The central government is accountable to the member states who continue to hold significant power	The central government has the strongest power with which the member states must comply
Central government	Not a particularly strong body, appointed by the member states	A powerful body which takes decisions that the member states must follow
Sovereignty and federal government	A loose alliance of states. The member states strongly affect the decisions of the federal government	Decision-making competence shared between central government and regions and/or member states
Responsibilities and powers of the central government	Focus mainly on foreign policy, defence and security, but on other issues, the power of the confederacy's government to enforce its will is restricted	Has the power to demand member states adopt not only foreign policy, defence and security, but economic and judicial policy as well etc.
Basic responsibilities–functions (M): Mandatory (O): Optional	National defence (M) International cooperation (M)[a] International commerce (M) Common currency (O) Harmonised legislation (O) Taxation at the federal level (O, M)	National Defence (M) International cooperation (M)[a] International commerce (M) Common currency (M) Harmonised legislation (O) Taxation at the federal level (M)

[a]With the rest of the states at the federal level

just as are Russia and India. However, they each differ considerably from one another not only in geographical size but in a host of other issues of political and economic organisation. The USA and Canada are also federations, as is Mexico, Argentina and Brazil on the American continents, Belgium and Bosnia-Herzegovina in Europe, South Africa, Australia, Pakistan and Nigeria etc. Historical confederations include that of the Iroquois in North America, founded around 1142, the Old Swiss Confederation of 1291, the New England Confederation of 1643–1684, the 16 German states of the Confederation of the Rhine formed by Napoleon I in 1806 and lasting until 1813 and the states of the American South whose secession from the USA led to the Civil War of 1861–1865 etc. Some such alliances began as confederations and then evolved into federations, e.g. the Old Swiss Confederation and the USA, which latter, in 1776 was originally a confederation and only became a federation in 1787 with the ratification of the US Constitution.

Table 8.1, based on the views of theorists of federalism among whom are Davis (1978), Elazar (1982, 1987), King (1982) and Burgess (2000), presents the basic differences between a federal and confederate state. The main difference is that in a confederate state, the central authority is not as powerful and the final word in taking decisions rests with the member states; in a federal state, the central authority has the right to enforce decisions on all its members. So, of the two, which was the Achaean Sympolity?

To be precise, it must be assumed from the outset that, in the absence of prioritising one argument over another, although it is legitimate, requires very cautious handling. Based on the in-depth analysis of the material concerning the Sympolity in the previous chapters, one can argue that its institutions gave a very satisfactory degree of freedom of action to its member states: each maintained its own army and currency, its federal Assembly, Council, government board and courts. Moreover, each city-state was free to follow its own customs, cults and athletic events. One might assume then that the Sympolity was a confederacy.

Freeman ([1893], 2013, p. 260–261) presents the institutions of the Achaean Sympolity in comparison with those of the USA and, although each city-state was obliged to conform to certain rules (not to undertake unilateral action such as initiating military action or sending embassies to third countries without the approval of the central authority), his view is that the freedom of the city-states to act on their own was not as restricted as it is in the USA. The Sympolity offered its member states a fair amount of leeway. On the other hand, the Achaean Sympolity disposed of federal armed forces, which was the main reason for its establishment in the first place. On certain occasions, some city-states such as Dyme, Pherae and Tritaia or Megalopolis mobilised on their own to defend their territory from an imminent threat but, in principle, the defence of a city-state or a region was undertaken by the federal armed forces.

Major decisions were taken either in the two pan-Achaean assemblies or by the federal government policymakers themselves. These governed matters of foreign policy, defence and security, the adoption of common legislative constitutional initiatives and common weights and measures, the key issue of a common monetary policy, common taxation practices, ensuring a politico-economic/institutional set-up favourable to interstate commercial transactions as well as other common practices, binding on all member city-states. Similarly, the decisions of the federal courts were binding on all member city-states. Moreover, the fact that the Sympolity was divided into three or five regional units which each had its own political, economic and military administrators is suggestive of institutional elements one encounters mostly in an organised federation. Furthermore, Mackil (2013) states that local and regional law did not overlap with federal law. Every judge or magistrate was aware of his responsibilities and to what degree he had the jurisdiction to exercise them so that they did not overlap or conflict with the federal level. The bottom line that emerges from our analysis is that the central government of the Sympolity took decisions vis-à-vis all the member city-states. If, for instance, a region, say, the *Syntelia* of Patras, disagreed with a decision of the Sympolity, the latter was not obliged to recall its decision.

Before deciding on the correct typological classification of the Achaean Sympolity, we turn to two important historical facts. The first again relates to Aratus' decision to appeal to the Kingdom of Macedon for military aid. In order not to appear as the mastermind of this radical turn in foreign affairs policy he was proposing, and aware that certain city-states such as Argos and Megalopolis had strong pro-Macedonian elements, behind the scenes, he arranged to make it appear as if the local government policymakers of Megalopolis initiated the appeal for

Macedonian military aid against Sparta (Pol. 2.55.2–4). The apparent inability of the Sympolity to defend Megalopolis allowed the city-state's leaders to turn to Antigonus, who eventually agreed to support the city militarily. Several questions arise regarding this matter.

Since Megalopolis was a member of the Sympolity, did the city-state's leaders inform the relevant bodies of the federal government of their intention as they were obligated to do? As mentioned above, Larsen (1968, p. xviii) writes on this point that the Megalopolitans did not act without first obtaining permission from the Sympolity's leadership. In fact, it was only then that the Megalopolitans sent their embassy to King Antigonus. Larsen believes that their request was thus legitimate. That is because even under federal authority, each city-state did maintain a minimum critical level of autonomy in decision-making. On this issue, Polybius (2.50) writes:

> These arguments seemed to Antigonus to have been put by Aratus with equal sincerity and ability: and after listening to them, he eagerly took the first necessary step by writing a letter to the people of Megalopolis with an offer of assistance, on condition that such a measure should receive the consent of the Achaeans... He regarded it also as eminently favourable to his policy, that the people of Megalopolis were so eager to use the Achaean league as the channel of communication with Antigonus... Accordingly when Megalopolitan envoys appeared in the national council, and showed the royal despatch, and further declared the general friendly disposition of the king, and added an appeal to the congress to secure the king's alliance without delay; and when also the sense of the meeting was clearly shown to be in favour of taking this course, Aratus rose, and, after setting forth the king's zeal, and complimenting the meeting upon their readiness to act in the matter...

Kralli (2017, p. 225) provides the above passage of Polybius (2.50.6) on this, but she interprets it wrong when she writes that the Megalopolitans had decided to approach Antigonus anyway, without first asking Achaean permission, i.e. effectively breaking away from the Sympolity. By one measure, they would have had a fair excuse for this, given that the Achaeans had not offered them much protection against Cleomenes III. This point is crucial since it puts the degree of federalism of the Achaean state to the test: if the Megalopolitans believed that there would have been no serious consequences in not requesting permission from the Achaeans to conduct diplomacy with the Kingdom of Macedon directly, it could mean that here we are talking about a confederate state. But the fact that the Megalopolitans considered it a prerequisite to apply for the federal authorities' consent is proof that we are talking here about a practice that is associated only with true federal states.

The second historical incident that provides a further 'test' of the nature of federalism of the Achaean Sympolity occurred in 197 after Philopoemen had returned from Crete and King Philip V of Macedon had already been defeated at the Battle of Cynoscephalae. The Sympolity had cut off diplomatic relations with Macedon and had established an alliance with Rome. Argos and some other city-states refused to accept this decision and retained a pro-Macedonian stance, without, however, suffering any censure or penalties by the Sympolity. Some might argue that this demonstrates that the Sympolity was not really a federation but, rather, a confederacy. Had it been the former, they claim why did not the Achaeans censure

Argos? One response to that argument, perhaps a simplistic one, is elemental: the Achaean Sympolity was a democracy! That there should be differences of opinion among the dozens of city-states of which it was comprised, and especially on such a critical issue where one wrong move could have had serious consequences in the future, must be considered as completely normal. The only issue here is the lack of clarity on the part of the central government in dealing with a member city-state when there was a divergence in views.

From our standpoint, as we have elaborated it, in general, up to this point, the problem was not so much the reshuffling of relations between the city-states within the context of the diplomatic relations of the time as the latter adapted according to shifts in the balance of power. It was rather whether or not the means of enforcing the Sympolity's wishes existed in the first place in cases where a member city-state's position ran counter to the government's decisions on critical issues such as foreign policy, or a city-state wished to pursue a semi-independent policy or even to withdraw from the Sympolity outright.

Our view here is the Sympolity's leaders had foreseen such situations and put in place protocols for dealing with them. Simply put, we argue that the Achaeans were prepared to impose sanctions on Argos. That they did not, in our view, is not an indication that the Sympolity was not a true federation. Given the particularly confusing circumstances in the Peloponnesus at the time, perhaps the Sympolity did not have the means (military or otherwise) to impose its 'rules of the game' on a member city-state. Texier (1975, p. 66) provides support to this view, arguing that Argos had acted as she did because she had assumed the role of the undeniable leader of all radical socio-economic tendencies in the Peloponnesus (as elucidated in Chap. 5), as an alternative to the conservatism of the Achaean Sympolity.

Accordingly, Argos' revolt against the Sympolity and her ability to negotiate alliances with Sparta and Macedon was not an act that the Achaeans would normally have accepted, constituting an act of 'rebellion' by the city, an 'unconstitutional' derogation that at the time, for unspecified reasons, the Achaeans were not in a position to deal with effectively. Texier's view indicates that even in 197, 25 years after Sellasia, at a time when many radical socio-economic ideas had been emphatically invalidated, a trace of such sentiments lingered in the citizens of certain city-states. The environment of constant warfare, the looting and pillaging of cities, atrocities against their inhabitants, the constant parade of foreign troops, confusion as to how to manage the situation we speculate would have created an ideological mosaic, an explosive mixture whose manifestation was impossible to predict. All this could not have failed to have been considered by the Sympolity's leaders before they made any decision to punish a member for apostasy. Table 8.2 provides further support to the 'federalist' nature of the Achaean state's institutions.

By taking into account all the above analyses, we argue that the Achaean Sympolity was a unique state phenomenon that we would characterise as a 'mixture' of federation and confederacy. However, it appears to us that the term 'federation' is more accurate in interpreting the actions of the Sympolity and the way its political and economic institutions functioned.

Table 8.2 A principal set of federal institutional conditions practised in the Achaean state

Basic federal principles
• Central executive government implementing federal policies
• Joint activities regarding the implementation of federal public policy between city-states due to regional organisation
• Common foreign and security policy and common armed forces
• Double citizenship at both the city-state and the federation level (*Isopoliteia*)
• Full economic rights throughout all the member city-states
• A common legal system (local laws and courts did not conflict with federal laws)
• Federal budget
• Common currency. The overall federal monetary policy was the outcome of cooperation between the Achaean member states through monetary union

As far as we know, this is the first time this view appears in the bibliography. This typological determination of the Achaean and other sympolities of Greek antiquity is, we believe, significant in that it allows researchers examining political and economic institutions to compare politico-economic phenomena of the past with those of today.

8.3 The Achaean Sympolity and the US Constitution

From 1776 when the War of Independence began that led to the creation of the American federal state with the Constitution of 1787, the USA exhibited remarkable growth and rise in power and was responsible for a series of events whose outcome defined global developments in the course of history: her Civil War of 1861–1865, her participation in the two World Wars of the twentieth century, her role as defender of the 'free world' and her system of a free market economy and political liberalism arrayed against the Soviet threat during the Cold War, exemplified by the Truman Doctrine and the Marshall Plan, the creation of a mono-polar world as the sole superpower after the Soviet Union's collapse, a role currently being challenged by forces now emerging in the twenty-first century.

The USA, however, did not evolve into a superpower only because of a series of historical events and coincidences that created the conditions for her rise. It was as much a consequence of her political and economic system, which, to many political philosophers and institutional economists, remains the object of admiration and study.[1] However, it is not very well-known that the Founding Fathers of the American Nation, John Adams, John Madison, Thomas Jefferson, etc., were deeply influenced by the political texts of the Ancient Greek writers (Plato, Aristotle, Plutarch, Polybius and others) in fashioning the final version of the US Constitution

[1]For the USA's political system and its tools for transparency in the form of *checks and balances*, see, among others, the pioneering study by Buchanan and Tullock (1962).

in 1787. On a general level, the Greek political systems of antiquity had preoccupied the Founding Fathers at length. In their *Letters From a Pennsylvanian Farmer*, John Adams and John Dickinson discussed the political organisation of Sparta. They had studied the Persian Wars, read Plutarch's biography of Pericles and examined the Delian League and the other Greek alliances. Adams, Hamilton, Dickinson and others had delved into the history and nature of the Athenian Democracy (Richard 2009, p. 31–32, 47, 79–84).

The Founding Fathers such as Hamilton and Madison expressed a particular interest in the federalism of Ancient Greece, focussing on the Achaean Sympolity (Freeman [1893], 2013; Chinard 1940; Gummere 1962; Davis 1978; Millican 1990; Bederman 2008; Richard 2009; Lehmann 2015).[2] Champion (2013, p. 120) argues that the evolution of political theory in the USA, crystallised in the *Federalist Papers* (Nos. 16, 18, 19, 34, 38, 40, 44, 51, 63, 70), led the authors of the constitution to exhaustive discussions on the writings of Polybius. One of those documents of 1787, No. 30, *A Defense of the Constitutions of Government of the United States of America*, records that the future president, John Adams, discussing the extent of Polybius' influence on the Founding Fathers, stated that he should be declared an 'honorary' Father of the American Constitution (Momigliano 1987, p. 77). Thomas Jefferson, fearing that the under-development constitution was granting too much power to the central authority, suggested to Adams and the other committee members that they read about and be inspired by the ancient federations, offering each a copy of Polybius' *Histories.* In another letter, Dickinson wrote regarding the success of the Achaean Sympolity as an 'antidote' to monarchical and aristocratical arrangements:

> . . .The reason is plain. [Since] the energy of the government pervaded all the parts in things relating to the whole, it counteracted for the common welfare and designs hatched by selfishness in separate councils. (Richard 2009, p. 95)

Dickinson continues (*Letter of Fabius*, 58):

> How degrading would be the thought to a citizen of United America that the people of these states, with institutions beyond comparison preferable to those of the Achaean League,[3] and so vast a superiority in other respects, should not have wisdom and virtue enough to manage their affairs with as much as prudence and affection for one another as these ancients did. (Richard 2009, p. 95)

On the contrary, Madison in his *Federalist Papers* No. 18, No. 19 and No. 20 examined certain celebrated confederations of the past and present and asserted that everyone had failed through a lack of central power. Maddison wrote:

[2]The authors we cite here provide altogether an extensive analysis of the discussions of the Founding Fathers regarding the federal organisation in Ancient Greece. The purpose of our analysis to this point is not to retrieve all this evidence. This goes beyond the scope of our analysis. Thus, here we chose to retrieve some characteristic aspects of the research that are related to this discussion.

[3]The Achaean Sympolity.

> It appears that the cities had all the same laws and customs, the same weights and measures, and the same money. But how far this effect proceeded from the authority of the Federal Council, is left in uncertainty. It is said only, that the cities were in a manner compelled to receive the same laws and usages. When Lacedaemon was brought into the league by Philopoemen, it was attended with an abolition of the institutions and laws of Lycurgus, and an adoption of those of the Achaeans. The Amphictyonic confederacies of which she had been a member, left her in the full exercise of her government and her legislation. This circumstance alone proves a very material difference in the genius of the two systems... [T] here was infinitely more of moderation and justice in the administration of its government, and less of violence and sedition in the people, than were to be found in any of the cities exercising singly all the prerogatives of sovereignty. The Abbe Mably, in his observations on Greece, says that the popular government, which was so tempestuous elsewhere, caused no disorders in the members of the Achaean republic, because it was there tempered by the general authority and laws of the confederacy.[4]

James Monroe, another Founding Father on the floor of the *Virginia Ratifying Convention* observed that:

> The Achaean League had more analogy to ours... They [the city-states] were all democratic and firmly united. What was the effect? The most perfect harmony and friendship subsisted between them and they were very active in guarding their liberties...this league was founded on democratical principles, and, from the wisdom of its structure, continued a far greater length of time than any other. Its members, like our states, by their confederation, retained their individual sovereignty, and enjoyed a perfect equality. (Bederman 2008: p. 126)

In the end, the Founding Fathers rejected direct democracy, believing it would lead to the supremacy of the more populous lower social classes or chaotic disarray. Similar arguments were later used by conservative supporters of authoritarianism against even representative democracy. Preferring to follow the Roman model, the Founding Fathers chose to call their new state a 'republic' rather than 'democracy' with reference to the Roman state of the Hellenistic period. Moreover, Richard (2009, p. 96) argues that this is also related to the fact that in the end, the small decentralised cluster of democracies of mainland Greece failed to repel the centralised powers of the Kingdoms of Macedon and Rome. It was for this reason that the Fathers finally decided that their new state should be characterised by a certain degree of centralised power. The fact that later democracies after the USA also did not adopt institutions such as direct democracy or national congresses is why Freeman ([1893], 2013, p. 253), comparing the USA with the Achaean Sympolity, argued that the latter was the most perfected development of the federal principle which the world has ever seen.

With the above analysis in mind, we believe that the political systems and economic organisation of Greek antiquity continue to be of interest, as much from a historical perspective and the knowledge one may distil from delving into the relevant original sources, as is the possibility that by studying them, we may glean new ideas and policy proposals for the societies of today.

---

[4]He compared the Achaean Sympolity with the *amphictyonies* organisation.

8.4 The Achaean Sympolity and the European Union: An Interactive Comparison

The analysis that follows is a comparison of the political and economic institutions of the Achaean Sympolity and those of the European Union through a series of very specific and rigorous intertemporal criteria that have characterised federal states over time. We believe that if the EU finally proceeds in the future with more steps towards political integration, it is likely to take the form of a federation. As stated in our Preface, this, after all, was the intention of the Fathers of Europe, Jean Monnet, Robert Schuman, Konrad Adenauer, Alcide de Gasperi, Walter Hallstein, Paul-Henri Spaak, Altiero Spinelli and others. Such a comparison, aside from the element of originality, rests on the notion that conclusions drawn from past successful state models might offer solutions and proposals on critical issues related to policy management for modern governments, in general, but, more specifically, mainly for the EU's integration policy on which we focus here.

We consider it essential for a comparison of the Achaean Sympolity with the EU to cover several very specific federal criteria relating to the institutional organisation: (a) the number of members participating in each of the two entities, (b) the existence of institutional bodies for political decision-making (e.g. a federal legislative body), (c) the Sympolity's administrative bodies (e.g. *strategoi*, etc.), (d) the nature of common foreign and security policies, (e) the existence or not of a common currency, (f) the financing of the federal budget, e.g. for extraordinary expenses in wartime, or related to the contributions and financial burdens undertaken by the member city-states etc., (g) with the existence or not of a federal judiciary, and (h) with the level of *isopoliteia*, or the possibility of a citizen from elsewhere within a federation retaining his political rights throughout it. These criteria, proposed by McInerney (2013) and in some of our own academic publications,[5] characterise the federal states over time. Accordingly, we believe we avoid the trap of *historical anachronism* if we compare an ancient study with a modern one, within the context of a very rigorous framework of specific intertemporal criteria. Table 8.3 examines the two cases.

Beginning with the first criterion regarding the number of members, on a purely 'technical level', comparing the two is rather pointless as the Sympolity at one time had somewhere of 103 members, each with a relatively small population numbering in the thousands,[6] or, at most, tens of thousands, while the post-Brexit EU comprises 27 members. The first column assumes Brussels as the EU's 'capital'. In a future, federalist structure, the EU would have to have a true capital, and we suggest that Brussels holds the most promise, given that most of the EU's institutional bodies and related services are currently clustered there. Coupled with that, Brussels is

[5](Kyriazis and Economou 2015; Economou and Kyriazis 2015a, b, c, 2016a, b, c, 2018, 2019a, b; Economou et al. 2015).

[6]If we exclude the big city-states such as Argos, Corinth, Megalopolis, Sicyon etc. These possibly were habitated by several tens of thousands of people.

Table 8.3 Comparative analysis of the Achaean Sympolity's institutional structure relative to that of the EU

State	Main political institutions	*Isopoliteia* regime	Common foreign and security policy	Federal coinage usage	Federal budget	Federal courts
Achaean feder-ation (Sympolity) Capital Aegion 107 member city-states	Local city-state citizen assemblies Federal citizen assemblies (*Ecclesia*/*Synodos* and *Synkletos*) *Strategos* (Head of the state) *Grammateus* and *10 Damiourgoi/Synarchontes* *Hypostrategos, nauarchos and ipparchos*	▼	▼	▼	▼	▼ (Federal courts)
European Union 'Capital': Brussels 27 member states	European Parliament Council of the European Union European Commission European Court of Auditors	–	Not effective	▼ (EMU member states)	▼ (very low, only 1% of the EU GDP as a total)	▼ Court of Justice of the European Union (CJEU) (in Luxembourg) European Court of Human Rights (in Strasbourg)

Explanation: ▼: Institution in force
Source: Our own processing, based on the data in the above analysis

considered a 'neutral' centre, without associations that Belgium herself might be inclined to manipulate. The Greek sympolities had first addressed this issue. The Aetolians, for instance, had their capital in Thermion, in the very centre of the sympolity and thus considered neutral by all members (Economou et al. 2015). Consequently, decisions taken there were trusted to be fair and even-handed (as much as possible) vis-à-vis all the member city-states. We addressed this issue in 1.1 and at other points of the book. Modern cases of establishing a more 'neutral' federal capital include Washington in the USA and Brazilia in Brazil which replaced São Paolo and became the capital of the country in 1960.

The issue of the dynamic integration of new members has been addressed at various points in our analysis. In our view, the number of members is a significant indicator of the accessibility and success of a federation, but it cannot be considered the only factor. Large size is not necessarily proof of the possible success of a federal state. For example, both in antiquity and in modern times, there did exist successful small democratic federations in terms of political and economic organisation such as the states of Magnetes in eastern Thessaly, Arcadia, the Acarnanians, the Aegean Islands, the Chalcideans, the Locrians etc., alongside the large sympolities of Achaea, Aetolia and the *Koinon* of Boeotia, just as today there are several small successful federations such as Switzerland, Austria, Belgium and Uruguay which are considered more prosperous than other much larger federations such as Russia, India and Pakistan.

However, the main issue is to determine the 'optimal size' for a federation at which the addition of a new member will not reduce the overall prosperity and the smooth functioning of the state. The reasoning we develop here resembles somewhat the concept of *Marginal Product* in Microeconomic Theory where, from a certain point on, the addition of new workers does not increase but, rather, reduces the marginal product of a factory, resulting in diminishing returns. In this light, is there, let us say, an 'optimal point' whereby incorporating new members is no longer a viable proposition for a federal state?[7] In the case of the Achaean Sympolity, from the time the inclusion of new members was no longer consensual but an imposition, it became a detriment. Although on the surface the incorporation of the large territories of Elis, Messenia and Laconia/Sparta strengthened the Sympolity, based on the criteria of the power of a state, as was analysed in the Eqs. 1–11 in 4.2, that expansion ironically sped the demise of the Sympolity as it led to the dynamic, violent intervention of Rome in the Peloponnesus, resulting in the Sympolity's dissolution.

What can the historical progression of the Sympolity teach today's EU? One initial response is that the more the EU expands by enlisting new members, the more it risks its cohesion unravelling. During the first decade of the twenty-first century, after the dramatic expansion of the EU to the east in 2004 with the integration of ten new members, an impressive, bold and, we imagine, an unlikely to be repeated

[7]This is an interesting issue which we are determined to explore further, analysing a broad spectrum of federations from antiquity to the present.

number of simultaneous new memberships, there seemed to be an urge to keep adding to the roster. In 2007, Romania and Bulgaria joined, and in 2013, Croatia. Despite the British 'Brexit' from 2016 on, the plan even foresees that by 2025, the western Balkan nations of Albania, Northern Macedonia, Montenegro and possibly Serbia will have joined as well.[8] What characterises membership in European Union (former European Economic Community) is that it is voluntary, just as membership in the Achaean Sympolity was until 191. For instance, in 1973, Ireland's membership was supported by an overwhelming majority of 83.1%, Denmark's, by a still very respectable 63.3%, while the Norwegians rejected membership by a majority of 53.3%. Moreover, referenda to approve membership were held in all ten candidate countries during the 2004 enlargement.[9]

In earlier years, pent-up enthusiasm for enlargement spoke of Turkey joining, even Ukraine and perhaps Georgia. Are these last even thinkable now as we enter a new decade? The neo-Ottomanist aggression towards her neighbours backed by the distorted way in which they are handling the recent refugee problem and the issue of human rights (among others) of T. Erdogan's Turkey has dimmed that prospect drastically. In continuing to remain a candidate for membership in the EU, Turkey's candidacy undermines its design, especially given that Turkish values seem to be diverging dangerously from those of Europe. As far as Ukraine is concerned, this is a very complicated case, especially after the Crimean crisis and the annexation of Crimea by the Russian Federation in 2014 and the dynamic re-emergence of Russia in the region. As far as the other European countries that could become members are concerned, aside from Norway, mentioned above, Switzerland, Iceland and Lichtenstein have all elected not to join. The United Kingdom voted to exit the Union on 23 June 2016, a long process that took almost 4 years to complete (21 January 2020).

What would happen if the EU attempted to 'force' the situation and somehow integrate, say, Turkey and Ukraine, into its fold? Very likely, doing so would put its cohesion at risk given Turkey's current disdain for much of Europe's value system or norms of behaviour; moreover, Turkey's population of 83.2 million (in 2019) would result in a dramatic shift in the balance of power within the institutional organs of the EU, at all levels. Even further, because of the Treaty of Schengen, Turkey could 'flood' Europe with illegal immigrants or Turks where today more than 3 million live as German citizens, obviously influencing the politics of their adopted country. A sudden influx of new immigrants could alter the German and the rest of the EU member states' social landscape considerably. As far as Ukraine is concerned, membership in either NATO or the EU would put relations between Russia and the western alliances, already on edge, at grave risk. The EU's cohesion is already being tested further by other factors besides Brexit, such as immigration, with the Visegrád Group countries (the Czech Republic, Hungary, Poland and Slovakia) and the rest of the EU member states refusing to accept any more immigrants. There are

[8]On this, see Grieveson et al. (2018) among others.

[9]Regarding the referenda related to the EU and its direct democracy context, see: http://en.wikipedia.org/wiki/Referendums_related_to_the_European_Union, which is highly informative.

no set rules for establishing the optimum level of membership in a federation. The EU's could study the example of the Achaean Sympolity as we have explored it here to avoid actions of expansion policies that may at first glance seem promising, however, along the way, turn out to be dangerously deceptive.

As for the second column, referring to the political institutions of the Sympolity, based on our analysis so far, one can claim that the Sympolity had managed to achieve an effective combination of direct and indirect democracy, both in terms of federal organisation, as well as in terms of regional administration. Concerning the frequency of the citizens' direct and democratic expression of their will, in the Greek federations, the federal Assembly was obligatory and institutionalised—at least twice annually in the Achaean and Aetolian Sympolities—something which is not so for the EU, where, in the sense presented here, there are no established 'union-wide' referenda on an annual basis. In the USA, such annual referenda exist at the state/regional-level only and refer to issues exclusive to that state (e.g. the *Propositions* of California, South Dakota, Texas etc.). One such famous case was California's *Proposition 13* on taxation.[10]

Despite the influence exercised by wealthy oligarchic circles on decision-making, what was even more significant was that in the consciousness of the Sympolity's citizens, by one way or the other, and to one extent or the other, a conviction had been imbedded that they were masters of themselves and their fate. When average citizens see that their actions have an impact on forming political developments, they become more responsible, better as people and more effective as members of society, as argued by Manville and Ober (2003, p. 65–66) in their *A Company of Citizens*. The development of a federal consciousness made the Achaeans want what B. Weingast (1997) characterised as a desire to 'defend the system', contributing vastly to ensuring long life and prosperity in a federation.

In today's EU, the European Commission tables legislation for approval by the European Council and the European Parliament. Before the Commission proposes any citizens' initiatives, it first evaluates the economic, social and environmental impacts that they might have. It advises interested parties such as non-governmental organisations (NGOs), local authorities and representatives of industry and the citizenry, etc. In the event the European Council and the European Parliament cannot agree on amendments, the European Commission's decision can be blocked. That the Parliament acts as a *checks and balances* mechanism corroborates transparency and a democratic decision-making philosophy.[11] However, the principal initiator of legislation, as well as the administrating governing machine, is the Commission,

[10]In June 1978, California's citizens voted for the first time on a taxation issue, *Proposition 13* (*People's Initiative to Limit Property Taxation*). The proposition concerned a reduction (or non-increase) of taxation matched by a corresponding reduction of the provision of public goods. On 6 June 1978, the proposition was approved by California voters with an almost two-thirds' majority. This led to a reduction in property wealth (housing, businesses and farms etc.) of about 57%. For a more detailed analysis of *Proposition 13,* see Economou, Kyriazis and Metaxas (2017) and the references we provide therein.

[11]http://europa.eu/eu-law/decision-making/procedures/index_en.htm

whose members, including its president, are appointed and not elected, as is the president of the European Council as well. That suggests, to some extent, democratic deficit because the European Parliament has only limited powers. More and more, the citizens of Europe are beginning to believe that decisions affecting their lives are taken not by themselves but by an elite and 'distant bureaucracy in Brussels'.

Concerning the third column, the issue of *isopoliteia*, it was devised in the Greek federations and features in modern ones as well, such as the USA and India. However, it does not feature in the EU. For example, if a Swedish citizen of the EU were to move to Italy and choose to remain there indefinitely, he does not automatically acquire the right to vote in the next Italian national elections. As we have already stated, a citizen of ancient Sicyon that moved to Corinth, both city-states being members of the Achaean Sympolity, could vote in his newly adopted city-state. Of course, European citizens who remain in another member country for an extended period do have the right to participate in local elections, but voting in national elections is of substantially more significant political importance.

Regarding the EU's *Common Foreign and Security Policy* (CFSP), in our preceding analysis, we argued that the main reason for the Ancient Greeks to form federations was for common defence against external enemies. That is something they shared with all the federations that followed, including the old Swiss (1300–1798), the United Provinces (1581–1795) and the USA.[12] The members of Greek federal states had grasped that the best insurance for an effective level of security was provided by banding together in some form of federation. The Achaean Sympolity, because of its effective CFSP, succeeded not only in warding off the expansionary ambitions of Macedon in southern Greece, the powerful Sparta of Cleomenes III, the Aetolian Sympolity for a time, as well as secessionist tendencies from within, but also managed to unite all of the Peloponnesus under its leadership. Perhaps if the Achaeans had succeeded in doing that before 191, it might have been able to maintain its independence better and avoid its dissolution by Rome in 146.

There is no doubt then that effective CFSP is a prerequisite for a successful federation; until today, however, and despite the efforts of important intergovernmental conferences such as Maastricht in 1992, Amsterdam in 1997 and Lisbon in 2007, where steps were taken in furthering political integration, several more significant steps are needed for the EU to achieve an effective CFSP. There are different national interests, especially among the EU's more powerful members, that create distortions along that path. The divergence between member states regarding a series of occasions such as the two Gulf Wars (1991, 2003), the war in Bosnia in 1995 and Serbia in 1999, as well as, more recently, events in Ukraine (2013–2014), in Syria (2011–) and in Libya (2014–) reveals wide rifts on many issues, objectively unavoidable, given it is not always easy for so many nations to agree on such critical issues as CFSP.

In any event, when the European Economic Community was first formed in 1957, the North Atlantic Treaty Organisation (NATO) already existed as a defence alliance

[12]See Economou and Kyriazis (2019a, b).

against the looming threat of the Soviet Union. This means that the defence of post-WWII Europe was very much based on the US forces in Europe backed by their hegemonic role in world politics (Keohane 1984). According to Ikenberry (1989) and Lundestad (2003), the US hegemony in Europe was largely 'an empire by invitation' whose main purpose was to use its dominant position to guarantee an orderly and peaceful international system, based on economic cooperation and international trade exchanges, a situation similar to what Great Britain did in the nineteenth century. Thus, Europeans' efforts to create an efficient pan-European defence organisation, such as the so-called *European Defense Community* (EDC) in 1952 or the *Western European Union* (WEU) in 1954 scaled down due to the US key presence in Europe through NATO.

The road to a 'United States of Europe' of the twenty-first century, if it is ever achieved, is one of history's grandest experiments as the EU is composed of nations made up of peoples with a wide variety of historical peculiarities, differences and cultural norms. As a former Minister of Defence of Belgium, Mark Eyskens, in 1991, famously said, 'Europe is an economic giant, a political dwarf and a military worm'. However, since then, and mainly since the Treaty of Maastricht that created the EU in 1992, significant steps have been taken in the direction of the EU's politico-military integration such as the establishment of the so-called *Eurocorps*, the *EU Battlegroups*, *Organisation Conjointe de Coopération en matière d'Armement* (OCCAR) and the *European Defence Agency* (EDA), with the last two organisations related to energising the EU's defence industry.[13] A recent 'upgrade' agreement, the so-called *Permanent Structured Cooperation* (PESCO), signed in December 2017, expanded cooperation among member states on issues of the defence industry and European security.[14]

The fifth column presents the data on the circulation of money in the Sympolity. In 7.2, we listed some parameters such as the existence of a mechanism for protection from counterfeiting, restricting the number of mints, both at the local and the federal level, homogeneity in federal currency and policy mechanisms aimed at forestalling inflationary pressures. The Achaeans applied a parallel system for issuing currency whereby all coins of all city-states could circulate throughout the Sympolity; however, some of the stronger city-states (in terms of economics, military strength and demographics) could also use local coins, although only in performing local commercial and financial transactions. This meant that locally made coins with local (and not federal) insignia could only be used locally (such as the coin of Fig. 7.10) while the locally made coins with federal insignia (such as that of Fig. 7.11) could be used anywhere within the borders of the Sympolity and exchanged freely or used as payment in any city-state.

---

[13]For issues related to the CFSP and the European defence industry see, among others, Hartley (2003, 2008), Metaxas and Economou (2012), Kollias (2008) and Kollias and Paleaologou (2016) and references therein.

[14]https://www.eda.europa.eu/what-we-do/our-current-priorities/permanent-structured-cooperation, https://www.iiss.org/blogs/research-paper/2019/05/pesco

As far as the EU is concerned, as of 1999, the European Monetary Union (EMU) came into existence. Therefore, in parallel to EMU, the monetary system of the Achaean Sympolity resembles what we can call in today's terms, a monetary union since the Achaean federal currency had to be of the same weights and standards in every city-state. Furthermore, the quantity of money issued in each city-state was not decided arbitrarily but was part of the wider federal monetary policy. However, it must be said that how some particular issues, such as inflation, were addressed is not known as there are no relevant sources. For this reason, we have only offered a few cases.

The next criterion refers to the issue of the budget. In 7.3, we examined how the public revenue and expenses of the Sympolity were formed. We hypothesised that, given the nature of *power politics* in the ancient federations, defence expenditures at that time probably reached the highest portion of the annual budget. The balance served the rest of the Sympolity's needs. In the EU today, the 'federal' budget comes to about 1% of the Gross Domestic Product of the member nations, which seems very small, and of which only half is destined for an integrated policy in support of member states in terms of a broad redistributive umbrella of social cohesion policies according to its members' needs.[15] It is obvious that the weaker a federation's economic cohesion policies are, the weaker its legitimacy in the eyes of its citizens.

In the view of Weingast (1997) and de Figuereido and Weingast (2005), a federation must dispose of the means to improve the individual and collective well-being of its citizens in economic and social terms. Only then will its citizens be prepared to 'defend' it. If it cannot serve those two very basic criteria, it will come apart, frequently with onerous consequences for its citizens—a drastic plunge in living standards, erosion of political and economic freedoms, bloody internecine conflict (e.g. the fall of the Soviet Union, dissolution of Yugoslavia). When those criteria are met, their prestige is enhanced and endures (USA, Canada, Switzerland, Germany, India, etc.). When a federation fails to heed society's concerns, however, legitimacy in the eyes of its citizens begins to recede as has been happening recently in the European Union with the rise of *Euroscepticism*.

Therefore, fairer economic management and distribution of the wealth generated within a federation increase its coherence which constitutes a higher ideal in a democratic state (Arist. *Pol.* 1264a, 36–37). Our analysis has shown that until 191, the integration of new members into the Sympolity was voluntary. The exceptions of the city-states of Laconia, Messene and Elis, however, were (probably) integrated violently, for geopolitical reasons. It is almost certain that if geopolitical concerns had not been such a priority for the Sympolity's leadership at that time, those territories that were absorbed in 191, probably without their full consent, might have progressively decided to join freely and voluntarily, aware of the more effective level of security and prosperity doing so would provide. Borrowing the concept of *marginal utility* from Microeconomic Theory, we can say that in the case, for example, of three cities, A, B and C, the usefulness of participating in a federal

[15]http://ec.europa.eu/budget/annual/index_en.cfm?year=2017

structure is higher than not participating. This can be expressed mathematically with the following simple preference relationships:

$$U_{\mathrm{A}} > U_{\mathrm{F}} \tag{8.1}$$

$$U_{\mathrm{B}} > U_{\mathrm{F}} \tag{8.2}$$

$$U_{\mathrm{C}} > U_{\mathrm{F}}, \tag{8.3}$$

where U_{F} expresses non-participation in a federal structure. Moreover,

$$U_{\mathrm{A}} + U_{\mathrm{B}} + U_{\mathrm{C}} > 3U_{\mathrm{F}} \tag{8.4}$$

constituting the total *marginal utility* derived from participation in the federation for the three cities, respectively, which is higher than from non-participation.

In closing on this issue, we offer another brief interpretation of our own, based on the above argument, focussing on the Achaean Sympolity: as we have said, its establishment, as well as that of the other Greek federations, was based on the primary issue of a common defence and security policy. As the union proved itself substantive and successful, new institutions were developed that further secured and improved cooperation on a broader range of issues (e.g. economics) to the benefit of all. That provided further incentive to make cooperation permanent, evolving into a true federation. This process could be simulated with a repetitive positive-sum game since, in general, it appears that all parties involved (or at least most) 'win' making the prospect of dissolving the cooperation increasingly distant, for three main reasons.

First, the investment in time and money, or *sunk cost*, the sum of all the necessary expenditures made to create the Sympolity would be lost because if it were ever decided to reconstitute it, that would require additional expenditures to restore all the institutional bodies. Second, because of *path dependency*. As cooperation evolved between city-states, proving mutually beneficial, gradually, a state of what is called *path dependency* developed where the ethos and values that grew out of the new status quo, as time passed, evolved into a permanent socio-economic environment. Returning to the previous state, of being an individual city-state, became increasingly unlikely as the citizens adopted, became used to and accepted that new environment, making it a part of their permanent daily lives. They were hardly likely any longer to replace it with what, practically speaking, would be a new political experiment. Based on this argument, avoiding the loss of *sunk cost*, the new set of social values with the passage of time, if accepted by the society, tend to become permanent (*path dependency*).

Third, it appears that the Achaean Sympolity exhibited a fair amount of leeway in matters related to the social and political aspects of the economic measures that it chose to apply. In the event a city-state, during special or extraordinary situations (such as catastrophes due to war), was unable to meet its tax obligations to the federal government, it would be punished but, for the good of the Sympolity, the city-state could receive the privilege of *ateleia*, i.e. absolved from paying taxes for that year or for even more than one year. This was the case in Dyme, Tritaia and Pherae in 219, and in Messene in 183/182, as referred to in 7.6.

This resembles the current situation of global and extremely deadly Coronavirus pandemic. To face the crisis in the EU, on 13 March 2020, the President of the European Commission Ursula von der Leyen declared that 'We will do whatever is necessary to support the Europeans and the European economy'. On 10 March 2020, between European Council Members, as well as the ECB President Christine Lagarde, the Eurogroup President and the High Representative, agreed to take immediate measures to respond to the extraordinary human and economic crisis caused by the Coronavirus. For that purpose, at the time of writing ECB President Christine Lagarde announced a 'Pandemic' *Asset Purchase Program*, an extraordinary bond purchase programme worth €750 billion in order to help insulate the region's economy from the likely coronavirus-led recession. This has to do with the so-called *quantitative easing* (QE) policies. She further declared that 'Extraordinary times require extraordinary action'.[16] This declaration is a true federal supranational policy and falls under the general rationale with which the Achaean policymakers were taking decisions under extraordinary times, as the historical examples we mentioned above prove.

However, it remains to be seen in the near future if and how these measures will be put into practice with tangible results in favour of the deadly Coronavirus tested Europe.[17] For example, the pandemic is very severe in Italy and Spain. Until 30 April 2020, 10,779 people died in Italy and 7340 in Spain. At the time of writing, Italy is grateful for the disinfection plants and military health personnel sent by Russia in recent days, in contrast to the meagre response from other EU Member States. In a wider sense, such a situation belongs again to a 'federal' obligation; the less help Italians receive from other EU countries, the greater the feeling of lack of practical solidarity on the part of the EU to them, and vice versa.

The last column in Table 8.3 refers to the issue of the existence of a federal court system responsible for adjudicating civil and criminal cases for each of the member city-states. Although there are no extensive references regarding the administration of justice; however, in 6.3, we offered evidence that attested to its existence, confirmed by Larsen (1971) and Mackil (2013), who have dealt exclusively with the issue of ancient Greek federalism. There was no special court of human rights as there is in the European Union today. On a more general level, the reasoning of

[16]https://www.nytimes.com/2020/03/13/business/europe-germany-coronavirus.html

https://euobserver.com/coronavirus/147731

https://www.consilium.europa.eu/el/press/press-releases/2020/03/16/statement-on-covid-19-economic-policy-response/

https://www.cnbc.com/2020/03/19/ecb-launches-new-820-billion-coronavirus-package.html

About how QE is implemented in practice, see, among others, the recent works of our own Kyriazis and Economou (2017) and Papadamou et al. (2018) whereas, more generally, for the unconventional measures by the ECB, see Kyriazis and Economou (2019) and Papadamou et al. (2020).

[17]See in detail: https://www.worldometers.info/coronavirus/

ancient Greek thought focussed on the well-being of society as a whole rather than on the personal rights of individual citizens. However, we have referred to a few cases of the protection of property rights, which, after all, in a wider sense, are related to and should be considered a human right. In any event, the *Court of Justice of the European Union* (CJEU) does not serve to defend property rights per se except insofar as European law has been violated, as, e.g. in matters of taxation. Human (and property) rights violations are adjudicated by the *European Court of Human Rights* (ECHR) in Strasbourg, an institution of the Council of Europe, not of the EU.

In conclusion, we believe that the lessons learned from how the Achaean Sympolity also functioned of relevance to the current situation in the European Union. In our opinion, the EU needs something more than a President of the European Council. It demands a 'leader' with institutionally enshrined competences, as well as credible federal military forces and a unified (as far as possible) foreign policy to be seen as a would-be pan-European federation in the future and something more than 'an economic giant, a political dwarf and a military worm'.

If the European experiment forges ahead towards political integration, what form would it take? How feasible is the creation of a unified political entity through the EU members' integration policy into a single federal scheme? What messages can the Ancient Greek federations convey in this respect through their political and historical institutions? In closing, the main ideas and institutional proposals for the further integration of EU, stemming from the examination of the Achaean Sympolity can be summarised as follows:

- A harmonious relationship between direct and indirect democracy with institutionalised use of *referenda* of a binding nature, both at the member state and federal level, initiated by the citizens.
- The introduction of the institution of *isopoliteia.* This is directly related to the further political integration of the EU into a federal structure.
- A combination of a strong central authority under democratic governance in the form of a *strategos* (or President of the EU, for our purposes) flanked by a democratically elected supreme council of executive power as a European Government.
- A more equitable distribution of income between the member states aiming at 'pervasive prosperity' in economic terms throughout the European Union.
- The creation of a joint pan-European defence force under a mixed command staff.
- The implementation of more coherent and efficient management of the immigration crisis.

Regarding the first issue, first of all, as is apparent from our analysis, the Achaean Sympolity and, by extension, the other ancient Greek federations as well, had succeeded in cultivating a harmonious relationship between direct and indirect democracy. Balancing this relationship is, in our view, a primary issue for modern democracies. Into today's terms, this relationship can be translated through the institutions of *citizen initiatives, referenda, recall* procedures and *e-democracy* techniques. The first has a collective orientation and addresses the ability of citizens, through collective action, to demand the adoption of a new measure or commitment by the state. This entails that citizens, whether at the federal, state/regional or local level, can go out and gather signatures on a petition regarding an issue that concerns the community as a whole directly, and when a sufficient number have been amassed to meet the minimum required, they can demand a referendum to be conducted on that issue. Some federations today such as Switzerland, or states of federations, e.g. Swiss cantons, American states and German Lander, incorporate this feature.

In Europe, such *initiatives*, as mentioned above, are not binding. With the Treaty of Lisbon of 2007, the EU decided to carry out such *initiatives* which, however, do not possess the crucial element of being binding on the member states in which they are carried out. Still, *Regulation (EU) No 1095/2010[2] No 211/2011* of the European Parliament and of the European Council of 16 February 2011 concerning *citizen initiatives*,[18] foresees that the European Commission will accept them if the proposal carries at least 1 million signatures from at least seven member states. However, we believe that more active participatory, direct democracy through the EU's institutions, such as the election of its president by the Union-wide electorate rather than his appointment, is a key solution to the democratic deficit which has become particularly pressing in recent years. The institution of the *recall* of an elected state official, for example, in cases of corruption, etc., is also relevant. This is applied in more and more American states, in the Swiss cantons, in Bavaria in Germany and in Canada's British Columbia.[19]

Recall means that citizens can petition for the resignation of elected officials, whether they are members of a local council or school board, even if they are mayors, governors, parliament or congress members if they are deemed to be beneath their expectations (for incompetence, corruption etc.). The process begins with a *citizen initiative*, as described above. If enough signatures are gathered, usually 8–10% of the electorate that voted in the previous election, then a vote is called, and if the official loses, he or she forfeits the seat. This process works as a deterrent as well, since elected representatives, in principle, will take their constituents' preferences more seriously and will behave more cautiously. Many studies, most of them econometric,[20] reveal that countries that apply elements of direct democracy in decision-making display higher results in terms of economic development than democracies that do not. Elsewhere (Economou and Kyriazis 2019b), we have argued that for a democratic regime to flourish it demands a sound economy, offering its citizens prosperity and reason to support the 'system'.

Regarding the issue of *e-democracy*, the idea of using technology to bring back direct democracy is simply not 'something too good to be true'. That is, it is not impossible. After all, the use of the Internet for electronic voting on policy issues is already a reality in an extensive number of countries, such as Switzerland in many

[18] http://ec.europa.eu/citizens-initiative/public/legislative-frameworkec.europa.eu/citizens-initiative/files/guide-eci-el.pdf

[19] http://www.ncsl.org/research/elections-and-campaigns/recall-of-stateofficials.aspx#History

[20] See, among others, Feld and Savioz (1997), Blume et al. (2009), Feld et al. (2010), Blume and Voigt (2012) and Matsusaka (2005a, b, 2010).

iterations. *E-democracy* is technically feasible through using high tech. Many studies attest to this, including those of Moreno-Jimenez and Polasek (2003), Traunmüller (2004), Hilbert (2009), Spirakis et al. (2010), Achieng and Ruhode (2013) and Kerikmae (2014) among others, who claim that the electronic voting process will improve the quality of democracy.[21]

Regarding the introduction of *isopoliteia*, we consider this of paramount importance for the political integration of Europe. Achieving it in the form of the right of any EU citizen to vote in the elections of the member state in which they live, even if temporarily, is an essential step towards political unification. Regarding the key issue for the further legitimacy of the EU in the eyes of its citizens, this concerns its institutional leadership (President, European Commission) which, based on the Ancient Greek model, we suggest should not be appointed as they are today, but should be elected directly by the citizens of the EU at large. That would serve to lend the EU the high degree of legitimacy it lacks. By the findings of our essay, it can be assured with a high degree of certainty that the more the political institutions of a democracy enable citizens to participate actively in decision-making, the more citizens become more conscientious, the better they are informed about the issues they need to decide and vote on, believe 'more in the system', and in the end, generally take better and more mature decisions when they vote.[22] The issue of a gradual development of a federal consciousness by Europeans themselves was analysed by Monnet (1951, p. 523) during the first steps of the process towards the unification of Europe:

> One essential issue is to retain a few constant principles that have guided us from the outset: to create gradually in the Europeans the consciousness a greater common interest served by common democratic institutions to which necessary competence is delegated, this is the dynamic which has never ceased to function.

Of course, in representative democracies, it is difficult to motivate citizens effectively in mass democracy to become informed, because according to Achen and Bartels (2017, p. 187, 198, 199) the cost of becoming informed (in terms of time and effort devoted to this) outweighs the benefit of better information in decision-making. We believe that this very important issue raised by Achen and Bartels (2017) can be ameliorated with the implementation of direct democracy techniques in decision-making in practice, such as *citizen initiatives*, referenda, the *recall* procedure and *e-democracy* techniques.[23] Citizens tended to be informatively myopic. On the other hand, becoming informed on the issues permits a change in the

---

[21]However, further analysis at this point on direct democracy techniques for today is beyond the scope of our present work.

[22]For such an argumentation regarding direct democracy at the city-state level in Classical Athens, see again Manvile and Ober (2003) and Bitros et al. (2020).

[23]For the feasibility of implementing in practise direct democracy procedures in our modern societies, see in detail the proposals in the seminal works of Barber (2003), the importand contribution of Ober (2017) regarding the conceptual definitions of democracy and our own in Bitros et al. (2020).

policy outcome and leads to better decisions by citizens (including economic issues). Linked to this is the issue of deciding on the 'common good'. As Tirole (2017, p. 12) writes:

> The problem of limited (or 'asymmetric') information is everywhere at the heart of our institutional structures and our political choices and at the heart of the economies of the common good.

Regarding the issue of a more equitable distribution of income between the members of a federation, which we include as our third condition, this relates to the many economic and internationalised parameters affecting the system of cooperation of the EU's members. Many scholars have proven that inequality regarding income distribution may critically affect political stability and growth and may destabilise democratic governance (see among others, Alesina and Rodrik 1994; Alesina and Perotti 1996; Perroti 1996). Alesina and Perroti (1996, p. 1214) characteristically write:

> A large group of impoverished citizens, facing a small and very rich group of well-off individuals is likely to become dissatisfied with the existing socio-economic status quo and demand radical changes, so that mass violence and illegal seizure of power are more likely than, when income distribution is more equitable.

This is confirmed by the ancient Greek example of the Achaean and the other federations and is something that EU leaders should take great care in addressing as a critical asymmetry has been developing in recent years in terms of the diffusion of prosperity, especially between the north (Germany, Denmark, Finland etc.) and the south (Greece, Spain, Portugal etc.). This issue is beyond the scope of our analysis here, but by including it, we imply that if a 'fair' distribution of wealth and prosperity among the members is not achievable in some way, then the Union's future is uncertain. Of course, such a view could spark a great deal of debate about what is meant by 'fair distribution of wealth' and this is not the purpose of this research. But this idea, which, to a lesser or greater extent, could also be described as 'equitable distribution of income'[24] is also related to the so-called *Gini coefficient*, which measures the income or wealth distribution of a nation's residents, and is the most commonly used measurement of inequality and has long studied by scholars in economics.

The Gini coefficient is a leading indicator that is used to measure income inequality. The Gini coefficient may range from 0, corresponding to perfect equality (in other words, income is equally distributed among every individual in a given society) to 100, corresponding to perfect inequality (in other words, when all of the income is received by a single person); thus, a lower Gini coefficient reflects a more egalitarian distribution of income. According to data retrieved from Eurostat, in 2017 (see Fig. 8.2), the Gini coefficient for the (pre-Brexit) EU-28 was 30.7%. The highest income disparities among the EU Member States (with a Gini coefficient of at least 35.0%—as shown by the darkest grey shade in Fig. 8.2) were recorded in

[24]Equitable does not mean equal distribution of income.

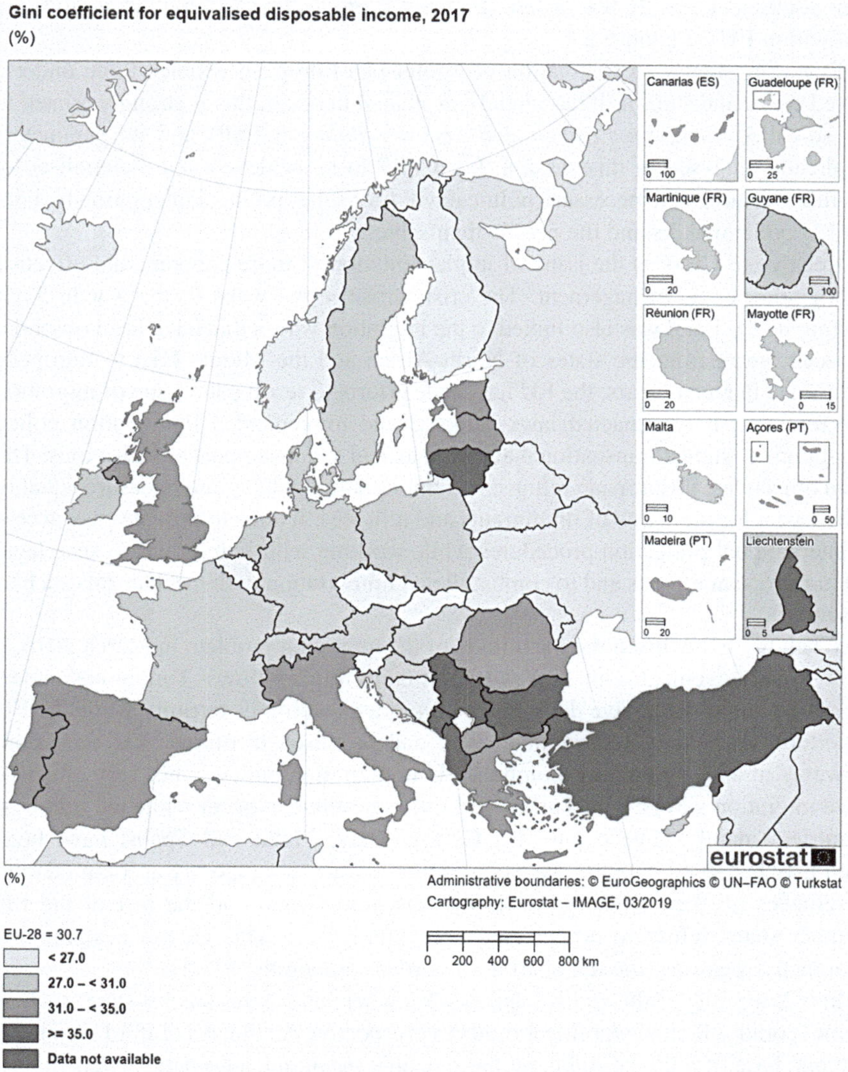

Fig. 8.2 Gini coefficient results for the EU-27 countries for 2017. Source: https://ec.europa.eu/eurostat/statistics-explained/index.php?title=File:Map_19_1_1.png

Bulgaria and Lithuania. A second group of countries, with a Gini coefficient above the (pre-Brexit) EU-28 average (in the range of 31.0–34.5%) comprised Estonia, Italy, Romania, the United Kingdom, Greece, Portugal, Spain and Latvia. At the other end of the range, income was more evenly distributed in Slovakia, Slovenia, Czech Republic, Finland and Belgium, as well as Iceland and Norway, where the

Gini coefficient was 26.0% or less. Figure 8.2 proves that income inequalities are real within EU-27 countries.[25]

Regarding the issue of creation of a joint pan-European defence force under a mixed command staff, as it has already explained in detail, this is strongly related to the so-called *Common Foreign and Security Policy* (CFSP) and its parameters as already analysed in this session. For CFSP to be achieved and materialised in the future requires the necessary political will for further political integration by both the EU policymakers and the people themselves.

Relative to CFSP is the issue of implementation of more coherent and effective immigration crisis management. The crisis arose in the wake of the war in Syria starting in 2011 and was also linked to the migration waves that have been observed in recent years from the states of North Africa and the Middle East to European territories. In recent years, the EU has made efforts to resolve the issue of migration and refugees. It has enacted laws, adopted and implemented immigration policy programmes, signed transnational agreements and set up support organisations. The main objectives of European refugee and immigration policies are to ensure equality and respect for the rights of immigrants and refugees. It aims to provide easy access to international protection procedures while working with immigrants to seek legal aid in European regions and to combat illegal immigration with mechanisms such as Frontex.

When the EU realised the magnitude of the migration problem in March 2016, it came to an agreement with Turkey to halt daily refugee flows. Turkey has undertaken to contain successive daily flows of migrants within its territory while the EU undertook to support Turkey financially and promised to discuss EU accession. However, it appears that this common EU immigration policy is not very effective since migration waves from Turkey and Libya continue to occur while the first-host countries (mainly Greece but also Cyprus, Italy, Malta and Spain) have been onerously burdened with the issue of granting asylum or temporary accommodation to refugees on their territory, while the Visegrád Group and the rest of the EU member states refuse to accept any more immigrants. This creates a significant asymmetry regarding the fair sharing of burdens among the EU-27.

In 6.2, we refer to the *epoikoi* and *synekoi* where any Achaean city-state (such as Dyme) could sell citizen/political rights to prospective candidates of third countries. The purchase of political rights by these people meant the automatic acquisition of citizenship in the Sympolity as well, and, by extension, all the perquisites that entailed (e.g. free movement, right to vote and to stand for election, civil rights etc.). What is important here is that the Sympolity (like today's EU) did not impose on any member city-state to accept as residents new citizens from third countries. On the other hand, if a member city-state opened its gates, e.g. seeking to enlarge its workforce, it had the right to do so freely.

Thus, based on the above, we believe that perhaps the best way to improve the immigration management policies in the EU-27 is to develop a more coherent

[25]Data for Iceland, Switzerland and Turkey are for 2016.

system of sharing the burdens of immigration between member states more 'symmetrically'. This means that (i) the external borders of the EU should be more properly secured through further enhancing mechanisms such as Frontex; (ii) existing immigrants should be distributed more equally in each EU member state, which means that they are distributed according to each member state's income and population power. We believe that such a proposal will be fairer and better both for the member states that are currently facing the problem of migration more severely (such as Greece, Cyprus, Italy, Spain and Malta) and for the living conditions and quality of life of the migrants themselves. Failure to manage migration flows from the Middle East, Asia and Africa more fairly may create shocks and disrupt cohesion among EU member states.

Epilogue

The preceding lengthy analysis concerning the case of the Achaean Sympolity leads us to present several conclusions as highlighted in our study. The sympolities of Greek antiquity have not enjoyed quite as much interest by historians as have, for example the Athenian Democracy or the Kingdoms of Sparta and Macedon. As we have said, the sympolities best-known to the general public are the Achaean, the Aetolian, and the Boeotoian, perhaps because of their historical importance, but more so because there are a fair number of primary sources from that era, invaluable to modern research. However, the occasional lack of information, in several instances, has obliged us to reach some, as we believe, well-reasoned conclusions. As we have said, there were over 103 city-states at the height of the Achaean Sympolity' unification of the Peloponnesian peninsula after 191. Those city-states were democracies, all following a common set of rules of action (a single code of standards and measures, regulated minting of coinage both at the local and at the federal level, common military organisation etc.) and federal policies (*isopoliteia, asylia* etc.).

Our second conclusion was that, in the course of our study, it became clear that during the Classical Period, and even more so, the Hellenistic, a federal state scheme was not limited to just a few individual cases but rather, was a widespread state structure prevalent throughout the wider Greek world. As we have noted, aside from the Achaean and Aetolian Sympolities, there are still more recorded instances of federations flourishing at that time.

In Chap. 2, we examined the historical framework through which the Achaean Sympolity ascended, in its first phase (ca. 389–281), and then its second phase (280–146), for which there exists a good deal more recorded evidence to explore. As we have analysed, in the wider Greek world, between the 4th and 2nd centuries, the environment that prevailed was characterised by what is known in *International Relations* theory as *power politics,* waged between the economically powerful politico–military agglomerations of Greece proper; the Aetolian and Achaean Sympolities, Macedon, Athens, Sparta, the Boeotian *Koinon*, and its peripheries, the Kingdom of Epirus, the rest of the Hellenistic kingdoms (Ptolemaic, Pergamon,

E. M. L. Economou, *The Achaean Federation in Ancient Greece*, Frontiers in Economic History, https://doi.org/10.1007/978-3-030-52697-9

Seleucid), and further east, Rome etc. This was a situation that could not fail to affect the leaders on Hellenistic Greece's federal schemes into enhancing central authority so that the head of state, the *strategos,* had expanded powers for greater flexibility in the use of state assets and policy measures.

The *strategos*, backed by his 'cabinet' of ministers had broad powers. He presided over the assemblies of the Sympolity, received foreign diplomatic representations, and introduced them to the federal Assembly. He was also empowered to draw up foreign policy agreements with other states. Essentially, he functioned in many parallel roles. His duties in today's terms included: head of state, president of the government, foreign minister, minister of defence, and head of the armed forces! In this sense, his role was expanded, with a wider range of politico–military responsibilities than the ten *strategoi* of the Athenian Democracy possessed. We assume that this plethora of responsibilities could not all be handled by one man and they were shared to an extent with the members of his administration, such as the *ipparchos*. Certainly, during the time the Sympolity was being governed by capable, worthy *strategoi* such as Aratus, Philopoemen, and Lycortas, it gained in power and the prosperity of its member city-states and their citizens improved. It expanded its territory significantly, achieving most of the geopolitical objectives of its overriding strategy, culminating in the integration of the whole of the Peloponnesus in 191 under a single political administration.

Furthermore, in Chaps. 6 and 7, we noted the reasons why the model of the Achaean Sympolity can be judged as successful, the main one being that its basic political and economic institutions were accepted by the average Achaean citizen, who deemed that his city-state's participation in it was more beneficial to him from a political and economic standpoint than non-participation. In support of this, an important factor is that, like the Athenian Democracy after 323, both the Achaean and the Aetolian Sympolities did not collapse internally since their citizens in their majority and as an overview, did not reject them in principle as state models,[1] but were defeated by the superior military power of an external foe. Athens became a satellite of Macedon and eventually of Rome, while the two sympolities, while succeeding in warding off the Macedonian threat, because of the prevailing anarchic environment and frequent warfare between the Greek state entities of the Hellenistic Period, gradually weakened, ultimately ending up provinces of the Roman Empire. The federalist phenomenon flourished at a time when none of the political entities in metropolitan Greece was strong enough to prevail politico–militarily and establish hegemonic influence over the others. The demise of the Achaean Sympolity was not the result of internal collapse but rather, of succumbing to the superior military power of an external force that finally prevailed.

The success of the Achaean state model was due to its institutions. For the critical decisions that determined the Sympolity's continuing survival, the pan-Achaean federal Assembly convened, either at set times as the *Ecclesia* or *synod*, most likely

[1]Even if there were occasional disruptive tendencies, such as in the era of Aratus and Cleomenes III, which was marked by social uprisings with mainly economic demands.

twice every year or, on extraordinary occasions, as the *synkletos*. It was at these convocations that the overriding strategy and other issues of the Sympolity's state policies were discussed and voted on by a direct and democratic procedure. In addition to taking decisions on national affairs, then, the elected administration was responsible for managing the various issues of implementing government policy as passed in the national assemblies by referendum.

That was how, in theory, at least, the critical decisions that guided the future of the Sympolity were taken by its citizens, who held the right of free participation in all democratic procedures of voting and standing for election, once they reached age 30. The items to be discussed and voted on in the federal Assembly were determined by the federal Council or *Boule*, which functioned as a pre-parliamentary body. Thus the federal Council could be seen, more or less, as and an indirect assembly of representatives elected directly by the member city-states. This provided one more form of indirect representation of citizens since those who were unable to participate in the national assemblies (e.g. because of the cost of travel, loss of work, personal reasons, and health) could do so through their federal Council representatives. These last were (probably) chosen by lot in their home city-state and sent to Aegion, to participate at the federal level.

In terms of the federal government, its success was due to what we believe was a crucial factor—combining a strong executive power, entrusted with taking and implementing decisions, with the character of its leader, the *strategos* of the Sympolity, but always through the prism and philosophy of democratic and collective governance of a participatory form. The *strategoi* of the Ancient Greek sympolities had extended responsibilities, much like, for example the American or French president today. There were three or five regional administrative units, each one with its own political and military commander as well as a financial administrator. A corresponding regime existed in the Aetolian Sympolity, which was divided into seven regional units (Economou et al. 2015).

In terms of the interaction between member city-states of the Sympolity, a regime was in place for allowing every individual citizen to operate seamlessly, both in the political and in the economic realms, anywhere within the Sympolity with full safeguards of their political and civil and rights. Through its institutional bodies, it appears that the Sympolity secured several essential benefits for its members (e.g. compensation for citizens who believed they had been wronged, *isopoliteia*, protection of property through either local or federal courts, a guaranty of integrity and fair pricing in the marketplace, a common currency of steady value, common defence, and security) quite advanced for the time.

The institution of *isopoliteia* permitted free movement and activity of the Achaean citizens throughout the territory of the Sympolity, while those of *ateleia* and *proxeny*, analysed in 6.2, offered non-Achaeans the possibility of transacting business in member city-states and acquiring civil rights as well as property. These institutions provided incentives to intensify commercial activity, to the benefit of the Sympolity and its citizens' level of prosperity.

The next critical factor was the guaranty of civil and property rights for every citizen of every member city-state or another state if he had been granted the rights of *enktesis* and *epigamia*. These two institutions guaranteed full political and economic freedoms between all Achaeans as well as any foreigners that may have acquired such rights or were active in commerce within the Sympolity's borders. There exist recorded cases of agreements between states of the Hellenistic world for the unilateral grant of the right of *isopoliteia* to citizens of only one of the two states involved. We cannot fail to note that the institution of *isopoliteia* has not yet been adopted in today's European Union.

Further element of the Sympolity's success concerned some additional institutions it offered such as market freedom, evidenced by the existence of laws regarding the proper function of the marketplace such as measures to forestall profiteering. Also, as Polybius (2.37) notes, the Sympolity had 'the same laws, standard weights, measures and coins, as well as common leaders, representatives and judges'. In short, the Sympolity possessed both common legislation and judicial system—both timeless and basic federal values—with the view of facilitating trade between the city-states. Although there is no clear evidence of the existence of banks, from all the available descriptions of the Sympolity's economic institutions, it is very likely that they did exist, most probably along the lines of the Athenian model. That can be confirmed, (1) directly, by the fact that the existence of banks in some city-states such as Corinth has been verified, (2) indirectly, by the existence of a common system of monetary circulation that was in force; to carry out wide-ranging trade between the more than 103 city-states would have necessitated the existence of investment and savings facilities related to banking, and (3) by the institution of the city-states' temples which in Athens and other city-states throughout the Greek world such as the island of Delos functioned also as treasuries, providing loans to the state. It is not very reasonable to believe that borrowing was only a state privilege. There is no reason to believe that private citizens were not able to borrow sums of money through banking services in the city-states of the Sympolity as they could in Athens.

Moreover, economic integration in a federation goes hand in hand with monetary integration or at least, with the parallel circulation of coinage of a standard form and type of and by all the city-states, as existed (at least[2]) in the major Ancient Greek federations. We also assume that the philosophy behind the formation of the Achaean Sympolity envisioned 'balanced' development of all its regions, as far as feasible. In this respect, we recalled Polybius' (2.37) important description. Mackil (2013) refers to this, as well. Certainly, any form and degree of economic development achieved were not limited to the capital, Aegion, but extended to other regions, giving rein to local initiative, aiming at sharing prosperity across the Sympolity as widely as possible, to all its city-states, villages, and settlements.

We suspect that, to a degree, it had become apparent to the Ancient Greek designers of the federal structures that the success of their ground-breaking institutions over the previous model of an individual city-state depended on fashioning a collective conviction that we name here as 'a state of mutual environment of welfare'

[2]We promise further research regarding this point in the future.

among the citizens participating in the Sympolity. In other words, participation in a lifestyle provided by a federal scheme was not just the political aim of each city-states' overriding strategy (e.g. that of Ermione and Epidauros concerning the prospect of a favourable resolution to their border dispute) nor that of some interest groups or power centre within such city-states, but constituted the instrument whereby it would be possible for a state of prosperity to pervade the whole of society collectively (*spillover effect*), improving prosperity and the standard of living of all subjects of the Sympolity's city-states. How else can one interpret Polybius' observation in the above verse that during that era 'those cities reached such great progress and perfection?'

It is no exaggeration to argue that Polybius' description is echoed in the basic tenets of modern *fiscal federalism* theory where important parameters in terms of the distribution of wealth in the state or the federal level are the improvement in the lives of its citizens as a whole, securing macroeconomic stability, redistribution of wealth to low-income households as well as providing basic public goods accessible to all (Oates 1972, 1999; Pauly 1973). Moreover, Inman and Rubinfeld (1997) argue that the basic conditions for a federal state model are (a) to encourage the effective pooling of national resources, (b) to encourage the participation of all members in decision-making, and (c) to protect the basic concepts of freedom. Musgrave (1998, 187), studying how a federal system functions, links its composition with several economic parameters, arguing that when independent states join a federation, it may be to secure common defence or to establish a customs union or to secure specific aims requiring the active participation of a central government in the economic life of its members. He adds that a set of targets (in participating in a federation) may involve a group or an individual aiming to eliminate/bridge economically the differences that exist with some or all the other members of the federation.'

We believe that all these principles and values, the basic criteria and tenets of federalism were implemented in the case of the Achaean Sympolity, one of the first, if not the first, democratically organised federations in history. Its main state and economic institutions are now reflected as the timeless basic principles of federalism.

In conclusion, one can argue that the Achaean Sympolity brought together all the basic characteristic institutional conditions set out in 8.1, qualifying as a functional and effective federal state structure. For over two centuries, the Sympolity succeeded in achieving the basic purposes for which it had been created: an effective defence policy and economic cooperation beneficial to all participants despite any weaknesses that may have occurred at times. The issue of improving the performance of federal state schemes becomes particularly topical when one considers that there are 28 registered federations on the planet right now, with the more representative, in terms of geopolitical gravity, the USA, Russia, Canada, Germany, Switzerland, and India. Finally, we close with the promise in the future to examine the issue of the Ancient Greek federations as a whole, given that more than 18 of them are attested (Beck and Funke 2015a). Here, from an interdisciplinary perspective, not limited to Historical Political Economy, we examined the Achaean Sympolity.

We hope the journey through the multi-level and interactive analysis that emerged with this book has succeeded in stimulating interest on related topics in both readers and researchers. After all, that is the essence that governs any work as, according to the great astronomer and astrophysicist, Carl Sagan:

> What an astonishing thing a book is... But one glance at it and you 're inside the mind of another person, maybe somebody dead for thousands of years. Across the millennia, an author is speaking clearly and silently inside your head, directly to you...Books break the shackles of time... (*Cosmos*, Part 11. *The Persistence of Memory* (1980)

In this instance, of the Achaean Sympolity examined here, we hope we have, to some degree, 'brought to life' time, space, and the personalities and events of 2300 years ago!

Glossary of Ancient Greek Terms

Agoge The upbringing of children combined with the educational procedure.

Agora The main marketplace of Athens where commercial transactions took place.

Agoranomoi A body of 10 magistrates that supervised the smooth functioning of the market; the prices to be fair based on the forces of demand and supply; the quality of the products to meet accepted specifications; and the currencies to be pure and unadulterated.

Amphictyonies (singular: Amphictyony) Autonomous societies with common ethnic characteristics uniting around a worship centre containing a temple, for the purpose of more effective political and military cooperation.

Anadasmos Land reclamation.

Aparchai The tributes paid by the allies of the Delian League to the city-state of Athens.

Apeleutheroi Freed men, such as the case of the wealthy banker and industrialist Passion.

Apokletoi High-ranking officials in the Achaean Federation.

Argyramoiboi (known also as kollybistai) Individual professional money changers in Classical Athens operating in the marketplaces of Athens and the port of Piraeus.

Aristoi The Spartan aristocracy; the well-off citizens of Sparta during the Hellenistic period.

Asclepieia (singular: Asclepieion) Large medical centres surrounded by an assortment of facilities, such as temples, baths, stadiums, gymnasiums, libraries, theatres etc.

Astynomoi A group of 10 policemen of the city whose main responsibilities were to watch over the cleanliness of the city and to maintain order.

Asylia Exemption from reprisals that, for example city A could take against city B, if the actions of a citizen of B damaged the interests of city A. In other words, with *asylia*, the practice of *sylis*, meaning that implementation of reprisals against another city, was not ethically (or legally) justified.

Ateleia Exemption from taxation for a year or years.

E. M. L. Economou, *The Achaean Federation in Ancient Greece*, Frontiers in Economic History, https://doi.org/10.1007/978-3-030-52697-9

Beltistoi Literally meaning 'the best of the citizens', it denotes the aristocratic group in many city-states in the Peloponnesus during the Hellenistic period.

Boularchos Each of the seven Aetolian regions (parts of the federal state) had a political administrator called the *boularchos*.

Boule Having its origin in the democracies of the Classical period, it was a preparatory body whose main competence was to set the agenda of discussions by the Achaean popular Assembly.

Chalkoi (in singular: chalkos or chalkous) A smaller coin denomination of the *drachma* made from copper. It was used for small value retail transactions.

Chelone The currency of the island of Aegina which bore on the reverse an image of a turtle (*chelone*), the city-states' insignia.

Damiourgoi (or demiourgoi) The annually elected members of the Achaean federal government. They were citizens from the Achaean city-states. Together with the head of the state, the *strategos,* they constituted the federal government. They were also called *probouloi* or *synarchontes*.

Demagogy The action or fact of winning support by exciting the emotions of ordinary people rather than by having good or morally correct ideas.

Democratia (also, democracy) The word derives from *demos* (meaning, the people) and *kratos* (meaning, holding power). Thus, democracy is the system where people actively participate in decision-making procedures, without exceptions.

Deutereia Meaning second in ranking. For example, a major general who is second in command in the army.

Dikai emporikai Commercial court cases judged by qualified and experienced judges (as was happening in Classical Athens).

Dogma A decree in the Achaean Assembly.

Dokimastai Two public slaves, one located in the *agora* of the city of Athens and the other in the port of Piraeus, responsible for certifying that the coins that were being circulated in the marketplace either had been struck by the Athenian mint, or that the quantity of their silver content was the same as that of an Athenian *drachma* (known also as *glauke*), thus allowing the coins to circulate freely in the Athenian economy.

Drachma (in plural, drachmae or drachmas) The currency that the Athenian state issued for undertaking all kinds of economic/commercial transactions. *Drachma* became also a universal coin throughout the Eastern Mediterranean.

Dromos Road, street.

Ecclesia of Demos (also known as Demos, or Assembly) A key political institution in Athens and the rest of the democratic city-states and federations, composed of all adult male citizens, and which had legislative, judicial and auditing powers.

Ecclesiastica A reimbursement of 3 obols (half a *drachma*) provided to each Athenian citizen when attending Assembly meetings.

Eisphora (plural eisphorai) A tax reckoned on the assessed value of one's property. In the beginning, Athenians introduced it as an extraordinary measure to apply only in times of extreme need, such as a war. However, during the fourth century, Athenians by vote rendered the *eisphora* permanent and imposed it on wealthier citizens and *metics*.

Enkoimeses Incubation.

Enktesis The right to hold property (of land and houses) in any member city-state within the territory of a federal state.

Epicleros When a man passed away, his wife became *epicleros*, that is she had property rights on his property (such as land property), in favour of her sons until they became adults.

Epigamia The right of transferring property in the form of women's dowries within the territory of a federal state.

Epilachontes In the case where an elected member of the Council of the Five Hundred could not undertake his position, he would be replaced in his duties by an *epilachontos,* one of 500 citizens forming a pool of substitute council members.

Epilectarchos The military commander in each of the seven regions of the Aetolian federal state. He commanded the 1000 *epilectoi* (meaning 'the chosen ones') who were professional and highly trained *hoplites* (much like modern special forces).

Epimelites epi ton udaton (Also known as epimelites epi ton krinon) A state functionary responsible for supervising the proper functioning and cleanliness of public fountains.

Epoikoi Citizens from non-Achaean member city-states who could buy citizenship when an Achaean city-state offered such an opportunity. An almost similar term was *synekoi*.

Gerousia A senate (e.g., in Sparta).

Ges anadasmos (also known as anaplerosis) Redistribution of land (among the masses).

Grammateus A post introduced in federal states such as the Achaean Sympolity, literally meaning the 'secretary' who had responsibilities similar to those of a modern head of state archives. His further responsibilities are not yet known.

Grammatists Teachers who taught courses in grammar (writing, reading) and maths, teaching their students through the works of the great poets, such as Homer and Hesiod.

Gymnasia (singular: gymnasium) Large public athletic facilities that consisted of multiple spaces with extensive sports installations. In Athens, there were three, i.e. the Academy, the Lyceum and the Kynosarges.

Harmosts Interim rulers in the Peloponnesus during the last decades of the Classical Period tasked with the smooth transition to a new democratic type of government after the oligarchs were dismissed.

Hegemon Literally meaning, a leader, it denotes a person or a country or group that is very strong and powerful and therefore able to control others. A *hegemon* is someone who enjoys *hegemony*, a predominating influence over others. A selected number of the Achaean Sympolity's political elite were called *hegemons*.

Helotes Slaves in Sparta.

Hemidrachm Half a drachma.

Hemiobol Half of an *obol*.

Hipparchos Cavalry's highest commander.

Hippodrome An ancient Greek stadium for horse racing and chariot racing.

Homoioi Literally meaning 'those who are alike', referring to Spartan citizens and hoplites sharing equal (political and social) rights.

Hoplites (singular: hoplite) Medium-income citizens who could bear arms by personally financing their military equipment. By participating in the so-called *phalanx* (heavy infantry) formation, they provided a potent fighting force whenever they were called upon to defend their homeland.

Hypomeiones A group of Spartans with limited rights.

Hypostrategos Literally meaning 'major general'.

Isegoria Freedom of speech. The right of anyone who wished to propose a decree.

Isopoliteia The possession of civil rights by every citizen of a member city-state throughout a federal state.

Kitharistai Guitarists who taught their students how to play the lyre and sing the works of lyric poets.

Koinas eisphoras The annual tax liabilities that the member city-states of the Achaean Sympolity had to contribute to the treasury of the federal government.

Koinodikia Federal courts.

Koinon (Koina, in the plural) Literally meaning common polity or joint polity, it denotes the federal state. In ancient times, *koina* meant also small cities.

Koinon politeuma The commonly established *polity* (political system).

Koinopoliteia A word similar to common polity or joint polity, which denotes the federal state.

Kollyboi (singular: kollybos) A smaller coin denomination of the Athenian *drachma* made of copper. One *chalkos* was equal to two *kollyboi*.

Komai (singular: kome) Small cities.

Latifundia Great landed estates specialising in agriculture destined for export: grain, olive oil or wine. A large portion of their workforce consisted of slaves.

Legati High-ranking Roman army officers. The title was also linked to the diplomatic representatives of the Roman state, with whom the *Senate* entrusted a mission to a foreign country.

Liturgies (singular: liturgy) A special tax imposed on wealthy citizens who undertook to finance the provision of a public service, such as the costly maintenance of a *trireme* warship for a year.

Merides (singular: merida) Regions or regional units.

Metics Citizens of other city-states who were residing in Athens for work.

Metoikion A personal tax on *metics*, both men and women. It was also known as the *xenikon*.

Metronomoi A body of 10 magistrates in Athens during the Classical Period whose responsibility was to check and make sure that the weights and measures used by sellers of goods in the markets were correct. Their post was very important because it prevented profiteering.

Metroon A special purpose building intended for the upkeep of all important archives regarding written laws or decrees.

Nauarchos The admiral.

Nautodikeia Maritime courts where special and experienced judges passed judgment on *nautodikai* (maritime/commercial cases) and *dikai emporikai* (as in Classical Athens).

Nomisma Currency.

Nomographoi Those who recorded the laws that were voted on in the Achaean Sympolity.

Nomophylakes Meaning 'guardians of the laws'. This special body was first introduced in the fourth century in Athens and was responsible for the safety and protection of written laws from forgery, loss or damage etc.

Obol A subdivision of the *drachma*; one *drachma* was equal to six *obols*.

Odeon An ancient Greek or Roman building built for music: singing exercises, musical shows, poetry competitions and the like.

Oligarchy A government in which a small group exercises control over the entire body of citizens.

Ostracism Was a procedure of the Athenian Democracy in which any citizen could be expelled from the city-state of Athens for ten years. *Ostracism* was often used pre-emptively. It was used as a way of neutralising someone thought to be a threat to the state or an aspiring tyrant.

Paidotribai Teachers being responsible for the physical development of boys.

Palaestra An athletic installation where athletes trained in various sports, mainly wrestling.

Pankration A mixed martial art practiced throughout Ancient Greece, developed in Sparta.

Parrhesia It is an extension of *isegoria* and means the right (and obligation) of a citizen to speak freely the truth for the common good, even at personal risk. Thus, the principle of *parrhesia* was related to a high moral standard and required conscious and active citizens acting for the common good.

Penestai Slaves in the Thessalian federal state.

Perioikoi A population group of non-citizen inhabitants of Laconia and Messenia, territory controlled by Sparta, concentrated in the coastal and highland areas.

Phalanx The most well-known and practiced military formation in Ancient Greece from the Archaic to Hellenistic times, composed entirely of heavy infantry armed with spears, pikes, *sarissas* (very long spears), or similar weapons. The *hoplites* in the *phalanx* were also known as *phalangites.*

Philia Friendship.

Philoxenia Hospitality.

Polis (in plural, poleis) Literally means a city (denoting a city-state).

Polismata Towns.

Polity (known also as politeia) Literally meaning political entity, it denotes any group of people who are organised into some form of institutionalised social relations. A *polity* can be any group of people organised for governance (such as a corporate board), the government of a country, or country subdivision.

Proxeny (also known as proxenia) An arrangement whereby a citizen (chosen by the city) hosted foreign ambassadors at his own expense, in return for being bestowed with honorary titles by that state. *Proxeny* was strongly related to interstate trade.

Sarissa A long spear or pike about 4–6 metres (13–20 ft) in length. It was introduced by King Philip II of Macedon and was used in his Macedonian *phalanxes* and later, by other armies, too (Sparta, Achaean Sympolity etc.).

Seisachtheia Literally meaning debt abolishment as happened in Archaic Athens in 594 through the so-called reforms of the lawgiver Solon.

Stadion (plural: stadia) Was an ancient Greek unit of length, based on the circumference of a typical sports stadium of the time. According to Herodotus, one *stadion* was equal to 600 Greek feet (today's 157 metres).

Stasis Revolt, mainly due to socio-economic reasons.

Strategos (plural: strategoi) Literally meaning 'general', and was the highest post in a federation, both military and civil. The *strategos* was an elected official and was limited to a term of just one year, termed the *strategia*.

Symmachia (plural: Symmachiai) An alliance of states with the purpose of assisting each other in case of a war. One of the most well-known in antiquity was the Athenian League.

Sympolity (also known as sympoliteia and as sympoliteiai in the plural) Literally meaning common polity or joint polity, it denotes the federal state (see also *Koinon, Koinopoliteia*). By the time of the Hellenistic Period, the term was often used for a federal state consisting of individual poleis (city-states) with shared political institutions and citizenship. Examples of this are the Achaean and the Aetolian federal states. The term was also used for the political merger of two or more neighbouring poleis. This could eventually, but not necessarily, lead to the disappearance of one of the participating poleis. This second form was especially common in Hellenistic Asia Minor.

Synkletos (plural: synkletoi) An extraordinary (unplanned) convening of the federal Achaean Assembly, depending on the circumstances.

Synodos (or Synod) The federal assembly of citizens with the right of participation to all male citizens.

Synteleiai (singular: synteleia) Federal Achaean districts (regions) with their own political and economic administrator and military commander and the regional level. A famous region in the Achaean Sympolity was the *synteleia of Patrikis* (the regional district of Patras).

Syrinx A symbol in the federal currency issued by the powerful city-state of Megalopolis.

Tagoi The political leaders of the Thessalian *Koinon*. This was an oligarchic state, divided into administrative districts and ruled by the *tagoi*, who were later renamed *archontes* ('leaders') and *polemarchs* ('warlords').

Talent A large amount of money. A talent was equal to 6000 *drachmae*.

Tamiai (singular: tamias) Each of the seven Aetolian regional states had a regional *tamias*, responsible for the economic administration in his region. At the same time, the seven *tamiai* as a whole were responsible for the collection and security of the revenues of the federal treasury. Probably one of them was the principal treasurer, who also acted (more or less) as Minister of Finance of the Aetolian federal state, in a modern sense. We assume that the Achaean federal state also had a similar organisation at the regional level.

Tamias tis koines prosodou (also known as Tamias ton koinon prosodon or epimeletes tis koines prosodou, or tamias epi tis dioikiseos) He was responsible for the overall supervision of the system of collecting and dispensing public revenues, reporting to the Athenian Assembly. In Classical Athens, tamiai were in charge of the so-called Treasuries of the Gods responsible for receiving and spending funds, reporting to a higher authority for reasons of accountability and transparency.

Tetradrachm Four *drachmae.*

Tetrobol 4 *obols.*

Thetes The lowest-income social group of Athens according to the reforms of Solon. *Thetes* were mostly farmers. Themistocles provided them the opportunity for social movement since under him and later on they became oarsmen in the navy.

Thureophoroi Lighter and more flexible Achaean military troops introduced by the *strategos* Aratus.

Trapezai (singular: trapeza) Private enterprises that provided banking services in the Classical and the Hellenistic Periods.

Trierarchy The most expensive *liturgy* in Classical Athens. It consisted of the maintenance of a state warship for a year by a group of wealthy Athenians.

Triobol 3 *obols.*

Trireme The main type of warship in the navies of the Greek world during the Classical and Hellenistic Periods. In Athens, each ship was manned by 200 personnel; 170 of them belonged to the low-income social group of *thetes*, who served as oarsmen.

Tyranny The government or rule of a tyrant or absolute ruler.

Bibliography

Ancient Authors (Perseus Digital Library)

Aristophanes. (1907). In F. W. Hall & W. M. Geldart (Eds.), *Acharnians, Aristophanes comoediae* (Vol. 2). Oxford: Clarendon Press.

Aristophanes. (1938). In E. O'Neill Jr. (Ed.), *Peace. The complete Greek drama* (Vol. 2). New York: Random House.

Aristotle. (1920). In E. S. Forster (Ed.), *The works of Aristotle (Oeconomica, Atheniensium Respublica)*. Oxford: Clarendon Press.

Aristotle. (1944). In H. Rackham (Ed.), *Politics*. Cambridge, MA: Harvard University Press.

Aristotle. (1952). In H. Rackham (Ed.), *Athenian Constitution*. Cambridge, MA: Harvard University Press.

Demosthenes. (1939). In A. T. Murray (Ed.), *Demosthenes Against Midias*. Cambridge, MA: Harvard University Press.

Diodorus Siculus. (1989). In C. H. Oldfather (Ed.), *Historical Library. Diodorus of Sicily in twelve volumes* (Vol. 4–8). Cambridge, MA: Harvard University Press.

Herodotus. (1920). In A. D. Godley (Ed.), *The Histories*. Cambridge, MA: Harvard University Press.

Homer. (1919). In A. T. Murray (Ed.), *The Odyssey*. Cambridge, MA: Harvard University Press.

Homer. (1920). *The Iliad. Homeri Opera in five volumes*. Oxford: Oxford University Press.

Isocrates. (1980). In G. Norlin (Ed.), *Panathenaicus*. Cambridge, MA: Harvard University Press.

Livy. (1912). In C. Roberts (Ed.), *History of Rome*. New York: E. P. Dutton.

Pausanias. (1918). In W. H. S. Jones, D. Litt, & H. A. Ormerod (Eds.), *Description of Greece*. Cambridge, MA: Harvard University Press.

Plato. (1968). In R. G. Bury (Ed.), *Laws. Plato in twelve volumes* (Vol. 10 & 11). Cambridge, MA: Harvard University Press.

Plato. (1969). In P. Shorey (Ed.), *Plato in twelve volumes* (Vol. 5 & 6). Cambridge, MA: Harvard University Press

Plutarch. (1920). In B. Perrin (Ed.), *Demetrius. Plutarch's Lives*. Cambridge, MA: Harvard University Press.

Plutarch. (1921a). In B. Perrin (Ed.), *Agis. Plutarch's Lives*. Cambridge, MA: Harvard University Press.

Plutarch. (1921b). In B. Perrin (Ed.), *Philopoemen. Plutarch's Lives*. Cambridge, MA: Harvard University Press.

Plutarch. (1926). In B. Perrin (Ed.), *Aratus. Plutarch's Lives*. Cambridge, MA: Harvard University Press.

E. M. L. Economou, *The Achaean Federation in Ancient Greece*, Frontiers in Economic History, https://doi.org/10.1007/978-3-030-52697-9

Polybius. ([1889], 1962). In S. Evelyn (Ed.), *Histories*. London: Shuckburgh.
Strabo. (1924). In H. L. Jones (Ed.), *Geography*. Cambridge, MA: Harvard University Press.
Thucydides. (1910). In J. M. Dent (Ed.), *The Peloponnesian War*. London: EP Dutton.
Xenophon. (1918, 1921). In C. L. Brownson (Ed.), *Hellenika*. Cambridge, MA: Harvard University Press.
Xenophon. (1923). *Memorabilia*. Cambridge, MA: Harvard University Press.
Xenophon. (1984). In E. C. Marchant (Ed.), *Constitution of the Athenians* (Vol. 7). Cambridge, MA: Harvard University Press.

Modern Authors

Achen, C. H., & Bartels, L. M. (2017). *Democracy for realists why elections do not produce responsive government*. Princeton: Princeton University Press.
Achieng, M., & Ruhode, E. (2013). The adoption and challenges of electronic voting technologies within the South African context. *International Journal of Managing Information Technology, 5*(4), 1–12.
Ager, S. (1997). *Interstate relations in the Greek world 337–90 BC*. Berkeley: University of California Press.
Ager S (2015) Peaceful conflict resolution in the world of the federal states. In: Beck H & P. Funke (eds), Federalism in Greek antiquity. Cambridge University Press, Cambridge, p. 471-486.
Alesina, A., & Rodrik, D. (1994). Distributive politics and economic growth. *Quarterly Journal of Economics, 109*, 465–490.
Alesina, A., & Perotti, R. (1996). Income distribution, political instability and investment. *European Economic Review, 40*(6), 1203–1228.
Amemiya, T. (2007). *Economy and economics in Ancient Greece*. London: Routledge.
Anderson, J. K. (1967). Philopoemen's reform of the Achaean army. *Classical Philology, 62*(2), 104–106.
Arnaoutoglou, I. (2009). Dispute settlement between poleis-members of the Achaean league: A new source. *Dike, 12–13*, 181–201.
Arthur, B. W. (1989). Competing technologies, increasing returns, and lock-in by historical events. *Economic Journal, 99*, 116–131.
Arvanitidis, P., & Kollias, C. (2016). Zipf's law and world military expenditures. *Peace Economics, Peace Science, and Public Policy, 22*(1), 41–71.
Ault, B. A. (2007). Oikos and Oikonomia: Greek houses, households and the domestic economy. *British School at Athens Studies, 15*, 259–265.
Austin, M. M., & Vidal-Naquet, P. (1977). *Economic and social history of Ancient Greece*. London: Batsford Academic and Educational Ltd.
Aymard, A. (1938). *Les assemblées de la Confédération Achaienne: étude critique d'institutions et d' histoire*. Bordeaux: Féret & fils.
Badian, E. (1952). The treaty between Rome and the Achaean league. *The Journal of Roman Studies, 42*(1/2), 76–80.
Baldwin, D. A. (1985). *Economic statecraft*. Princeton, NJ: Princeton University Press.
Barber, B. R. (2003). *Strong democracy: Participatory politics for a new age*. New York: Macmillan Press.
Bartholomees, B. (2012). *Theory of war and strategy. U. S. Army War College Guide*. Ashburn: Strategic Studies Institute.
Beaumont, L. (2012). *Childhood in ancient Athens: Iconography and social history*. Abingdon, NY: Routledge.
Beck, H., & Funke, P. (Eds.). (2015a). *Federalism in Greek Antiquity*. Cambridge: Cambridge University Press.

Beck, H., & Funke, P. (2015b). An introduction to federalism in Greek antiquity. In H. Beck & P. Funke (Eds.), *Federalism in Greek antiquity* (pp. 1–29). Cambridge: Cambridge University Press.

Beck, H., & Ganter, A. (2015). Boiotia and the Boiotian leagues. In H. Beck & P. Funke (Eds.), *Federalism in Greek antiquity* (pp. 132–157). Cambridge: Cambridge University Press.

Bederman, D. J. (2008). *The classical foundations of the American constitution*. Cambridge: Cambrdge University Press.

Benner, S. (2008). *Achaian league coinage of the 3rd through 1st centuries BCE [Classical numismatic studies no. 7]*. Lancaster, PA.

Bitros, G. C., & Karayannis, A. D. (2008). Values and institutions as determinants of entrepreneurship in ancient Athens. *Journal of Institutional Economics, 4*(2), 205–230.

Bitros, G. C., & Karayiannis, A. D. (2010). Morality, institutions and the wealth of nations: Some lessons from Ancient Greece. *European Journal of Political Economy, 26*, 68–81.

Bitros, G. C., & Karayiannis, A. D. (2013). *Creative crisis in democracy and economy*. Berlin: Springer.

Bitros, G. C., Economou, E. M. L., & Kyriazis, N. (2020). *Democracy and money: Lessons for today from Athens in classical times*. London and New York: Routledge.

Blamire, A. (2001). Athenian finance, 454-404 B.C. *Hesperia: The Journal of the American School of Classical Studies at Athens, 70*, 99–126.

Blume, L., Muller, J., & Voigt, S. (2009). The economic effects of direct democrat – A first global assessment. *Public Choice, 140*, 431–461.

Blume, L., & Voigt, S. (2012). Institutional details matter - more economic effects of direct democracy. *Economics of Governance, 13*(4), 287–310.

Bonner, R. J. (1910). The boeotian federal constitution. *Classical Philology, 5*(4), 405–417.

Bresson, A. (2016). *The making of the ancient Greek economy. Institutions, markets and growth in the city–states*. Princeton: Princeton University Press.

Briscoe, J. (1974). The Greek resistance to Rome. Der politische widerstand gegen Rom in Griechenland 217-86 v. *The Classical Review, New Series, 24*(2), 258–261.

Briscoe, J. (1981). The Achaean League. Wachstum und krise des Achäischen bundes. quellenstudien zur entwicklung des bundes von 280 bis 222 v. *The Classical Review, New Series, 31*(1), 89–90.

Brock, R., & Hodkinson, S. (2000). Introduction: Alternatives to the democratic polis. In R. Brock & S. Hodkinson (Eds.), *Alternatives to Athens: Varieties of political organization and community in Ancient Greece* (pp. 1–34). Oxford: Oxford University Press.

Buchanan, J., & Tullock, G. (1962). *The calculus of consent: Logical foundations of constitutional democracy*. Ann Arbor: University of Michigan Press.

Buckler, J. (1980). *The Theban hegemony, 371-362 B.C.* Harvard: Harvard University Press.

Burg, D. F. (2004). *A world history of tax rebellions: An encyclopedia of tax rebels, revolts, and riots from antiquity to the present*. London and New York: Taylor & Francis.

Burgess, M. (2000). *Federalism and European Union: The building of Europe, 1950–2000*. London: Routledge.

Burke, E. M. (2010). Finances and the operation of the Athenian democracy in Lycurgan era. *American Journal of Philology, 131*, 393–423.

Calhoun, G. M. (2002). *The business life of ancient Athens*. Washington, DC: Beard Books.

Cartledge, P. (1979). *Sparta and Laconia. A regional history c. 1300-362 BC*. London: Routledge and Kegan Paul Ltd.

Cartledge, P. (1987). *Agesilaos and the crisis of Sparta*. London: Gerald Duckworth and Company.

Cartledge, P., & Spawforth, A. (2002). *Hellenistic and Roman Sparta: A tale of two cities*. London: Routledge.

Cartledge, P. (2003). *Spartan reflections*. Berkeley: University of California Press.

Caruso, R. (2006). A trade institution as a peaceful institution? A contribution to integrative theory. *Conflict Management and Peace Science, 23*, 53–72.

Caspari, M. O. B. (1914). The parliament of the Achaean league. *The English Historical Review, 29* (114), 209–220.
Caspari, M. O. B. (1917). A survey of Greek federal coinage. *The Journal of Hellenic Studies, 37*, 168–183.
Champion, C. B. (2013). Polybios on government, interstate relations and imperial expansion. In H. Beck (Ed.), *A companion to ancient Greek government Malden* (pp. 119–130). Oxford.
Champion, C. B., & O'Sullivan, L. (2017). *Cultural perceptions of violence in the Hellenistic world*. London: Routledge.
Chaniotis, A. (1999a). Milking the mountains: Economic activities on the Cretan uplands in the classical and Hellenistic period. In A. Chaniotis (Ed.), *From Minoan farmers to Roman traders: Sidelights on the economy of ancient Crete* (pp. 181–220). Stuttgart: Franz Steiner Verlag.
Chaniotis, A. (1999b). The epigraphy of Hellenistic Crete. The Creatan Koinon: New and old evidence. In *Atti del XI congresso internazionale di epigrafia Greca a latina I* (pp. 278–300). Rome: Edizioni Quasar.
Chinard, G. (1940). Polybius and the American constitution. *Journal of the History of Ideas, 1*(1), 38–58.
Christopoulou-Aletra, H., Togia, A., & Varlam, C. (2009). History of medicine. *Archives of Hellenic Medicine, 27*(2), 259–263.
Clausewitz, C. ([1832], 1989). In M. Howard (Ed.), *On war*. Princeton: Princeton University Press.
Cline, R. S. (1977). *World power assessment: A calculus of strategic drift*. Colorado: Westview Press.
Cline, R. S. (1980). *World power trends and US foreign policy for the 1980's*. Colorado: Westview Press.
Coase, R. (1937). The nature of the firm. *Economica, 4*, 386–405.
Cohen, B. J. (2011). *The future of global currency. The euro versus the dollar*. London: Routledge.
Cohen, E. E. (1973). *Ancient Athenian maritime courts*. Princeton, NJ: Princeton University Press.
Cohen, E. E. (1992). *Athenian economy and society: A banking perspective*. Princeton: Princeton University Press.
Cohen, E. E. (2000). *The Athenian nation*. Princeton: Princeton University Press.
Cohen, E. E. (2002). An unprofitable masculinity. In P. Cartledge, E. E. Cohen, & L. Foxhall (Eds.), *Money, labour and land* (pp. 100–113). Abingdon: Routledge.
Copeland, D. C. (2014). *Economic interdependence and war*. Princeton: Princeton University Press.
Cortes, D., & Montolio, D. (2014). Provision of public goods and violent conflict: Evidence from Colombia. *Peace Economics, Peace Science and Public Policy, 20*(1), 143–167.
Cox, C. A. (2007). The "Astynomoi", private wills and street activity. *The Classical Quarterly, New Series, 57*(2), 769–775.
Cross, G. N. (2015). *Epirus. A study of Greek constitutional development*. Cambridge: Cambridge University Press.
Crouch, D. P. (1994). *Water management in Ancient Greek cities*. Oxford: Oxford University Press.
D'Amato, R., & Salimbetti, A. (2011). *Bronze age Greek warrior 1600-1100 BC. Osprey, Warrior, 153*. Midland: Osprey Publishing.
Daubies, M. (1973). Un chassé-croisé diplomatique dans le Péloponnèse au IIIe siècle avant. *J.-C. AC, 42*, 123–154. Retrieved from https://www.persee.fr/doc/antiq_0770-2817_1973_num_42_1_1696.
David, P. A. (1985). Clio and the economics of qwerty. *American Economic Review, 75*(2), 332–337.
Davies, J. K. (1967). Demosthenes on liturgies: A note. *Journal of Hellenic Studies, 87*, 33–40.
Davies, J. K. (1981). *Wealth and the power of wealth in classical Athens*. New York: Amo Press.
Davies, J. K. (2001). Temples credit and the circulation of money. In A. Meadows & K. Shipton (Eds.), *Money and its uses in the ancient Greek world* (pp. 117–128). Oxford: Oxford University Press.

Davis, R. S. (1978). *The federal principle: A journey through time in quest of meaning*. Berkeley Los Angeles: University of California Press.

De Figueiredo, R. J. P., & Weingast, B. R. (2005). Self-enforcing federalism. *Journal of Law Economics and Organisation, 21*, 103–135.

De Laix, R. A. (1973). The silver coinage of the Aetolian league. *Californian Studies in Classical Antiquity, 6*, 47–75.

De Ste. Croix G. E. M. (1989). *The class struggle in the ancient Greek world*. Ithaca: Cornell University Press.

Dickenson, C. P. (2017). *On the Agora: The evolution of a public space in Hellenistic and Roman Greece*. C. 323 BC-267 AD. Leiden: Brill.

Dumas, L. J. (2011). *The peacekeeping economy using economic relationships to build a more peaceful, prosperous, and secure world*. New Haven: Yale University Press.

Eckstein, A. M. (2007). Inttgcqra-Greek balancing, the Mediterranean crisis of c. 201–200 BCE, and the rise of Rome. In S. J. Kaufman, R. Little, & W. C. Wohlforth (Eds.), *The balance of power in world history*. New York: Palgrave Macmillan.

Eckstein, A. M. (2018). Rome, empire, and the Hellenistic state-system. In T. Ñ. del Hoyo & F. L. Sánchez (Eds.), *War, warlords, and interstate relations in the ancient Mediterranean* (pp. 231–253). Leiden: Brill.

Economou, E. M. L., & Kyriazis, N. (2015a). The Aetolian federation, the EU and Pakistan: An interactive analysis of federations. *Asian Journal of Humanities and Social Studies, 3*(2), 124–131.

Economou, E. M. L., & Kyriazis, N. (2015b). The Arcadian federation: A benchmark for the further EU integration. *Journal of Social Science Studies, 2*(2), 294–308.

Economou, E. M. L., & Kyriazis, N. (2015c). Ancient Greek democratic federations: A comparative study with the European Union. In H. Peukert (Ed.), *Taking up the challenge! Festschrift für Jürgen Backhaus* (pp. 289–306). Marburg: Metropolis.

Economou, E. M. L., Kyriazis, N., & Metaxas, T. (2015). The institutional and economic foundations of regional proto-federations. *Economics of Governance, 16*(3), 251–271.

Economou, E. M. L., & Kyriazis, N. (2016a). The emergence and the development of the Achaean Federation. Lessons and institutional proposals for modern societies. *Evolutionary and Institutional Economics Review, 13*, 93–112.

Economou, E. M. L., & Kyriazis, N. (2016b). Choosing peace against war strategy. A history from the ancient Athenian democracy. *Peace Economics, Peace Science and Public Policy, 22*(2), 191–212.

Economou, E. M. L., & Kyriazis, N. (2016c). The Achaeans and the Europeans: An interdisciplinary comparison of federations. *International Journal of Social Science Research, 4*(2), 8–23.

Economou, E. M. L., & Kyriazis, N. (2017). The emergence and the evolution of property rights in Ancient Greece. *Journal of Institutional Economics, 13*(1), 53–77.

Economou, E. M. L., Kyriazis, N., & Metaxas, T. (2017). Ancient Athenians, Californians and modern Greeks: A comparative analysis of choice set under direct democracy procedures. *Homo Oeconomicus, 34*, 47–65.

Economou, E. M. L., & Kyriazis, N. (2018). Ancient Greek Achaeans, modern Germans and EU integration: An interdisciplinary analysis of federations. In M. J. Holler & G. Tridimas (Eds.), *German-Greek yearbook of political economy* (pp. 137–160). Munchen: Verlag-Holler.

Economou, E. M. L., & Kyriazis, N. (2019a). The emergence of property rights in Hellenistic Greece and the Ptolemaic Kingdom of Egypt. *Journal of Institutional Economics, 15*(5), 827–843.

Economou, E. M., & Kyriazis. (2019b). *Democracy and economy: An inseparable relationship since ancient times to today*. Newcastle upon Tyne: Cambridge Scholars Publishing.

Economou, E. M. L., & Kyriazis, N. (2019c). The social position and the rights of women in ancient Greece: A Response to Barbara Klose-Ullmann's "Medea on Stage". In M. Holler & G. Tridimas (Eds.), *German-Greek yearbook of political economy* (Vol. 2, pp. 143–156). München: Holler-Verlag.

Ehrenberg, V. (1964). *The Greek state*. New York: W. W. Norton and Company.

Elazar, D. J. (1982). The principles and traditions underlying state constitutions. *Publius, 12*(1), 11–25.

Elazar, D. J. (1987). *Exploring federalism*. Tuscaloosa, AL: University of Alabama Press.

Engen, D. T. (2010). *Honor and profit: Athenian trade policy and the economy and society of Greece: 415-3-7 BCE*. Ann Arbor: University of Michigan Press.

Errington, R. M. (1969). *Philopoemen*. New York: Oxford University Press.

Feld, P. L., & Savioz, M. R. (1997). Direct democracy matters for economic performance: An empirical investigation. *Kyklos, 50*, 507–538.

Feld, L. P., Fischer, J. A. V., & Kirchgässner, G. (2010). The effect of direct democracy on income redistribution: Evidence for Switzerland. *Economic Inquiry, 48*(4), 817–840.

Figueira, T. J. (1998). *The power of money: Coinage and politics in the Athenian empire*. Philadelphia: University of Pensylvania Press.

Figueira, T. J. (2016). Aigina: Island as a paradigm and counter-paradigm. In A. Powell & K. Meidani (Eds.), *The eyesore of Aigina: Anti-Athenian attitudes across the Greek, Hellenistric and Roman worlds* (pp. 19–50). London: The Classical Press of Wales.

Fine, J. V. A. (1940). The background of the social war. *The American Journal of Philology, 61*(2), 129–165.

Finer, S. E. (1997). *The history of government* (Vol. 1). Oxford: Oxford University Press.

Finley, M. I. (1973). *The ancient economy*. Berkeley: University of California Press.

Finley, M. I. (1985). *Ancient history: Evidence and models*. London: Chatto & Windus.

Fisher, N. (1998). Gymnasia and the democratic values of leisure. In P. Cartledge, P. Millett, & S. von Reden (Eds.), *Kosmos: Essays in order, conflict and community in classical Athens* (pp. 84–104). Cambridge: Cambridge University Press.

Fleck, R. K., & Hanssen, F. A. (2006). The origins of democracy: A model with application to ancient Greece. *Journal of Law and Economics XLIX*, 115–146.

Flensted-Jensen, P. (1996). The Bottiaians and the poleis. In M. H. Hansen & K. Raauflaub (Eds.), *More studies in ancient Greek polis* (pp. 103–132). Stutgard: Franz Steiner Verlag.

Forrest, W. G. (1966). *The emergence of Greek democracy. The character of Greek politics, 800-400 BC*. London: Weidenfeld and Nicolson.

Forrest, W. G. (1968). *A history of Sparta 950-192 BC*. New York: W.W. Norton.

Forrest, W. G. (2000). The pre-polis polis. In R. Brock & S. Hodkinson (Eds.), *Alternatives to Athens: Varieties of political organization and community in ancient Greece* (pp. 280–292). Oxford: Oxford University Press.

Forsdyke, S. (2005). *Exile, ostracism and democracy. The politics of expulsion in Ancient Greece*. Princeton: Princeton University Press.

Foxhall, L. (1995). Bronze to iron: Agricultural systems and political structures in late bronze age and early iron age Greece. *The Annual of the British School at Athens, 90*, 239–250.

Frank, T. (1914). Representative government in the Macedonian Republics. *Classical Philology, 9* (1), 49–59.

Freeman, E. A. ([1893], 2013). *History of federal government in Greece and Italy*. London: Macmillan and Co.

Friedman, M. (1961). Capitalism and freedom. *New Individualist Review, 1*, 3–10.

Frier, B. W. (2000). Demography. In K. A. Bowman, P. Garnsey, & D. Rathbone (Eds.), *The Cambridge ancient history XI: The high empire, AD 70–192* (pp. 827–854). Cambridge: Cambridge University Press.

Funke, P. (2015). The Aetolian league. In H. Beck & P. Funke (Eds.), *Federalism in Greek antiquity* (pp. 86–117). Cambridge: Cambridge University Press.

Gabrielsen, V. (2013). Finance and taxes. In H. Beck (Ed.), *A companion to ancient Greek government* (pp. 332–348). Malden MA: Willey-Blackwell.

Gagarin, M. (2010). *Oxford encyclopedia of Ancient Greece and Rome*. Oxford: Oxford University Press.

Georgiou, M., Kyriazis, N., & Economou, E. M. L. (2015). Democracy, political stability and economic performance. A panel data analysis. *Journal of Risk and Control, 2*(1), 1–18.

Grainger, J. D. (1999). *The league of the Aitolians*. Leiden: Brill Academic.

Grieveson, R., Grübler, J., & Holzner, M. (2018). *Western Balkans EU accession: Is the 2025 target date realistic? wiiw Policy Notes 22*. The Vienna Institute for International Economic Studies. Retrieved from https://wiiw.ac.at/western-balkans-eu-accession-is-the-2025-target-date-realistic%2D%2Ddlp-4526.pdf

Griffith, M. (2001). 'Public'and 'private' in early Greek institutions of education. In T. Y. Lee (Ed.), *Education in Greek and Roman antiquity* (pp. 23–84). Leiden: Brill.

Gummere, R. M. (1962). The classical ancestry of the United States constitution. *American Quarterly, 14*(1), 3–18.

Habicht, C. (1999). *Athens from Alexander to anthony*. Cambridge, MA: Harvard University Press.

Halkos, G., & Kyriazis, N. (2010). The Athenian economy in the age of demosthenes. *European Journal of Law and Economics, 29*, 255–277.

Halkos, G., & Psarianos, I. (2016). Exploring the effect of including the environment in the neoclassical growth model. *Environmental Economics and Policy Studies*, 18(3): 339–358.

Hansen, M. H., & Nielsen, T. H. (2004). *An inventory of archaic and classical poleis*. Oxford: Oxford University Press.

Hanson, V. D. (1998). *Warfare and agriculture in classical Greece*. Berkeley: University of California Press.

Hardin, G. (1968). The tragedy of the commons. *Science, 162*, 1243–1248.

Harris, E. M. (2016). The legal foundations of economic growth in ancient Greece: The role of property records. In E. M. Harris, D. M. Lewis, & M. Woolmer (Eds.), *The ancient Greek economy: Markets, households and city states* (pp. 116–147). New York: Cambridge University Press.

Hartley, K. (2003). The future of European defence policy: An economic perspective. *Defence and Peace Economics, 14*(2), 107–115.

Hartley, K. (2008). Collaboration and European defence industrial policy. *Defence and Peace Economics, 19*, 303–315.

Hayek, F. A. ([1948], 1996). The economic conditions of interstate federalism. In F. Hayek (Ed.), *Individualism and the economic order* (pp. 255–272). Chicago: University of Chicago Press.

Hayek, F. A. (1973). *Law legislation and liberty. Rules and order* (Vol. 1). Chicago: University of Chicago Press.

Heiggs, R. (2012). *Delusions of power: New explorations of the state, war, and economy*. Oakland: Independent Institute.

Hilbert, M. (2009). The maturing concept of e-democracy: From e-voting and online consultations to democratic value out of a jumbled chatter. *Journal of Information Technology and Politics, 6*, 87–110.

Hodgson, G. M. (2015a). *Conceptualizing capitalism: institutions, evolution, future*. Chicago: University of Chicago Press.

Hodgson, G. M. (2015b). Much of the "economics of property rights" devalues property and legal rights. *Journal of Institutional Economics, 11*(4), 683–709.

Hodgson, G. M. (2015c). What humpty dumpty might have said about property rights – And the need to put them back together again: A response to critics. *Journal of Institutional Economics, 11*(4), 731–747.

Hornblower, S., Spawforth, A., & Eidinow, E. (2012). *The Oxford classical dictionary*. Oxford: Oxford University Press.

Ikenberry, G. I. (1989). Rethinking the origins of American hegemony. *Political Science Quarterly, 104*(3), 375–391.

Inman, R. P., & Rubinfeld, D. L. (1997). Rethinking federalism. *Journal of Economic Perspectives, 11*(4), 43–64.

Kagan, D., & Viggiano, G. F. (2013). *Men of bronze: Hoplite warfare in Ancient Greece*. Princeton, NJ: Princeton University Press.

Kaiser, B. A. (2007). The Athenian trierarchy: Mechanism design for the private provision of public goods. *The Journal of Economic History, 67*(2), 445–475.

Keohane, R. O. (1984). *After hegemony: Cooperation and discord in the world political economy.* Princeton: Princeton University Press.

King, P. (1982). *Federalism and federation.* Baltimore: Johns Hopkins University Press.

Kirk, G. S. (1965). *Homer and the epic.* Cambridge: Cambridge University Press.

Kerikmäe, T. (2014). *Regulating etechnologies in the European Union.* Heidelberg: Springer-Verlag.

Knoepfler, N. (2013). Un modèle *d'une* belle république fédérative? Montesquieu et le système politique des Lyciens, de la genèse de l'Esprit des lois aux découvertes épigraphiques les plus récentes en Asie Mineure méridionale. *Journal des Savants*, 115–154.

Knorr, K. (1956). *The war potential of nations.* Princeton, NJ: Princeton University Press.

Kollias, C. (2008). A preliminary investigation of the burden sharing aspects of a European Union common defence policy. *Defence and Peace Economics, 19*(4), 253–263.

Kollias, C., & Paleologou, S. M. (2016). Investment, growth, and defense expenditure in the EU 15: Revisiting the nexus using SIPRI's new consistent dataset. *Economics of Peace and Security, 11* (20), 27–36.

Kollias, C. (2017). *Defence economics.* Athens: Tourikis Publications. (in Greek).

Kollias, C., & Paleologou, S. M. (2017). The globalization and peace nexus: Findings using two composite indices. *Social Indicators Research volume, 131*, 871–885.

Kralli, I. (2017). *The Hellenistic Peloponnese: Interstate relations. A narrative and analytic history, from the fourth century to 146 BC.* Swansea: The Classical Press of Wales.

Kraay, C. M. (1976). *Archaic and classical Greek coins.* London: Methuen.

Kroll, J. H. (2011). The reminting of Athenian silver coinage 353 BC. *Hesperia, 80*, 229–259.

Kyriazis, N. (2006). Seapower and socioeconomic change. *Theory and Society, 35*, 71–108.

Kyriazis, N. (2009). Financing the Athenian state: Public choice in the age of Demosthenes. *European Journal of Law and Economics, 27*(2), 109–127.

Kyriazis, N., & Metaxas, T. (2010). Bounded rationality and institutional change. *Evolutionary and Institutional Economic Review, 7*(1), 1–19.

Kyriazis, N. (2012). *Why ancient Greece?* Athens: Psychogios Publications.

Kyriazis, N., & Economou, E. M. L. (2015). Macroculture, sports and democracy in classical Greece. *European Journal of Law and Economics, 40*, 431–455.

Kyriazis, N. A., & Economou, E. M. L. (2017). The relation of Brexit with UK's QE decisions and its impact on the Eurozone. *Journal of Central Banking Theory and Practice, 6*(1), 5–14.

Kyriazis, N. A., & Economou, E. M. L. (2019). Brexit and new perspectives of an unconventional way of Eurozone revival. *Journal of Central Banking Theory and Practice, 8*(3), 5–20.

Kyrtatas, D. (2011). Slavery and economy in the Greek world. In K. Bradley & P. Cartledge (Eds.), *The Cambridge world history of slavery* (The ancient Mediterranean world) (Vol. 1, pp. 91–111). Cambridge: Cambridge University Press.

Lambert, S. L. (2017). *Inscribed Athenian laws and decrees in the age of demosthenes: Historical essays.* Leiden: Brill.

Lanni, A. M. (2006). *Law and justice in the courts of classical Athens.* Cambridge: Cambridge University Press.

Larsen, J. A. O. (1925). Representative government in panhellenic leagues. *Classical Philology, 20* (4), 313–329.

Larsen, J. A. O. (1935). Was Greece free between 194 and 146 BC? *Classical Philology, 30*, 193–214.

Larsen, J. A. O. (1944). Federation for peace in Ancient Greece. *Classical Philology, 39*(3), 145–162.

Larsen, J. A. O. (1952). The assembly of the Aetolian league. *Transactions and Proceedings of the American Philological Association, 83*, 1–33.

Larsen, J. A. O. (1955). *Representative government in Greek and Roman history.* Berkeley and Los Angeles: California University Press.

Larsen, J. A. O. (1956). The Araxa inscription and the Lycian confederacy. *Classical Philology, 51* (3), 151–169.

Larsen, J. A. O. (1957). Lycia and Greek federal citizenship. *Symbolae Osloenses, 33*(1), 5–26.

Larsen, J. A. O. (1960). A new interpretation of the Thessalian confederacy. *Classical Philology, 55* (4), 229–248.

Larsen, J. A. O. (1968). *Greek federal states. Their institutions and history*. Oxford: Clarendon Press.

Larsen, J. A. O. (1971). The rights of cities within the Achaean confederacy. *Classical Philology, 66*(2), 81–86.

Larsen, J. A. O. (1972). A recent interpretation of the Achaean assemblies. *Classical Philology, 67* (3), 178–185.

Larsen, J. A. O. (1973). The Arcadian league in the fourth century. *Classical Philology, 68*(3), 224–225. Review on Dusanic, S. *Arkadski Savez IV Veka.*

Larsen, J. A. O. (1975). The Aetolian-Achaean alliance of CA. 238-220 B.C. *Classical Philology, 70*(3), 159–172.

LeDuc, L. (2011). Electoral reform and direct democracy in Canada: When citizens become involved. *West European Politics, 34*(3), 551–567.

Lehmann, G. A. (2015). Greek federalism, the rediscovery of Polybius, and the framing of the American constitution. In H. Beck & P. Funke (Eds.), *Federalism in Greek antiquity* (pp. 512–523). Cambridge: Cambridge University Press.

Lipset, S. M. (1959). Some social requisites of democracy. *American Political Science Review, 53*, 69–105.

Loomis, W. T. (1998). *Wages, welfare costs and inflation in classical Athens*. Michigan: Michigan University Press.

Luce, J. V. (2001). Greek medicine from Asclepius to Hippocrates. *Irish Journal of Medical Science, 170*(3), 200–202.

Lundestad, G. (2003). *The United States and Western Europe since 1945. From 'empire' by invitation to transatlantic drift*. Oxford: Oxford University Press.

Lyttkens, C. H. (2006). Reflections on the origins of the polis an economic perspective on institutional change in Ancient Greece. *Constitutional Political Economy, 17*, 31–48.

Lyttkens, C. H. (2010). Institutions, taxation, and market relationships in ancient Athens. *Journal of Institutional Economics, 6*(4), 505–527.

Lyttkens, C. H. (2011). Health, economics and ancient Greek medicine. *The Journal of Economic Asymmetries, 8*(1), 165–192.

Lyttkens, C. H. (2013). *Economic analysis of institutional change in Ancient Greece. Politics, taxation and rational behaviour*. Abingdon: Routledge.

Lyttkens, C. H., & Henrik, G. (2018). Understanding the politics of Perikles around 450 BC. The benefits of an economic perspective. In M. Canevaro, A. Erskine, B. Grey, & J. Ober (Eds.), *Ancient history and contemporary social science* (pp. 269–292). Edinburgh: Edinburgh University Press.

Mably de, A. ([1784], 2018). *Observations on the manners, government, and policy of the Greeks*. Engl. Trnsl Mr. Chamberland. Gale ECCO, Print Editions.

Mack, W. (2015). *Proxeny and polis: Institutional networks in the ancient Greek world*. Oxford: Oxford University Press.

Mackil, E., & van Alfen, P. G. (2006). Cooperative coinage. In P. G. van Alfen (Ed.), *Agoranomia: Studies in money and exchange presented to John H. Kroll* (pp. 201–246). New York: The American Numismatic Society.

Mackil, E. (2013). *Creating a common polity: Religion, economy, and politics in the making of the Greek Koinon*. Berkeley: University of California Press.

Mackil, E. (2015). The economics of federation in the ancient Greek world. In H. Beck & P. Funke (Eds.), *Federalism in Greek antiquity* (pp. 487–502). Cambridge: Cambridge University Press.

Manning, J. G. (2003). *Land and power in Ptolemaic Egypt: The structure of land tenure*. Cambridge: Cambridge University Press.

Manning, J. G. (2004). Property rights and contracting in Ptolemaic Egypt. *Journal of Institutional and Theoretical Economics, 160*(4), 758–764.

Manning, J. G. (2007). Hellenistic Egypt. In W. Scheidel, I. Morris, & R. Seller (Eds.), *The Cambridge history of the Greco–Roman world* (pp. 434–459). Cambridge: Cambridge University Press.

Manville, B., & Ober, J. A. (2003). *The company of citizens. What the world's first democracy teaches leaders about creating great organizations*. Brighton, MA: Harvard Business Review Press.

Marcaccini, C. (2015). The treasurers of Athena in the late 5th century B.C.: When did they take office? *Hesperia: The Journal of the American School of Classical Studies at Athens, 84*(3), 515–532.

Marchand, J. C. (2009). Kleonai, the Corinth–Argos road, and the 'axis of history'. *Hesperia, 78*(1), 107–163.

Massoud, T. G., & Magge, G. S. (2012). Trade and political, military and economic relations. *Peace Economics, Peace Science and Public Policy, 18*(1), 1–37.

Matsusaka, G. J. (2005a). Direct democracy works. *The Journal of Economic Perspectives, 19*(2), 185–206.

Matsusaka, G. J. (2005b). The eclipse of legislatures: Direct democracy in the 21st century. *Public Choice, 124*, 157–177.

Matsusaka, G. J. (2010). *A case study on direct democracy: Have voter initiatives paralyzed the California budget?* Ballot Propositions: The Council of State Governments. http://www.iandrinstitute.org/7-Matsusaka.pdf.

McDonald, P. J. (2007). The purse strings of peace. *American Journal of Political Science, 51*(3), 569–582.

McDonald, P. J. (2009). *The invisible hand of peace: Capitalism, the war machine, and international relations theory*. Cambridge: Cambridge University Press.

McInerney, M. (2013). Polis and Koinon. In H. Beck (Ed.), *A companion to ancient Greek government* (pp. 466–479). Malden MA: Willey-Blackwell.

Mele, A. (2002). Gli Achei da Omero all' Eta Arcaica. *Greco*, 67–93.

Mendels, D. (1982). Polybius and the socio-economic revolution in Greece (227-146 BC). *AC, 51*, 86–110.

Metaxas, T., & Economou, E. M. L. (2012). Security policy in the European Union and the United States through the issue of their defence expenditures. *Global Analysis, 3*(1), 52–79.

Michalopoulos, M. (2016). *In the name of Lykourgos: The rise and fall of the Spartan revolutionary movement (243–146BC)*. Barnsley: Pen and Sword Military.

Migeotte, L. (1984). *L'emprunt public dans les cités grecques: recueil des documents et analyse critique*. Paris: Les Belles Lettres.

Millican, E. (1990). *One united people. The federalist papers and the national idea*. Lexington: The University Press of Kentucky.

Miller, S. G. (1980). Excavations at Nemea, 1980. *Hesperia: The Journal of the American School of Classical Studies at Athens, 50*(1), 45–67.

Milner, H. (1991). The assumption of anarchy in international relations theory: A critique. *Review of International Studies, 17*(1), 67–85.

Mitsos, M. T. (1947). Thermika and Panaitolika. *Hesperia: The Journal of the American School of Classical Studies at Athens, 16*(4), 256–261.

Momigliano, A. (1987). *Essays in ancient and modern historiography*. Middletown: Wesleyan University Press.

Monnet, J. (1951). *Memoirs*. New York: Doubleday.

Morgan, C., & Hall, J. (1996). Achaian poleis and Achaian colonization. In M. H. Hansen (Ed.), *Introduction to an inventory of poleis: Symposium, August 23–26, 1995* (pp. 164–231). Copenhagen: Munskgaard.

Morgenthau, H. J. (1946). *Scientific man versus power politics*. Chicago: The University of Chicago Press.

Morgenthau, H. J. (1948). *Politics among nations: The struggle for power and peace*. New York: Alfred Knopf Publisher.
Mørkholm, O. (1991). *Early Hellenistic coinage from the accession of Alexander to the peace of Apamea (336–186 BC)*. Cambridge: Cambridge University Press.
Moreno-Jimenez, J. M., & Polasek, W. (2003). E-democracy and knowledge. A multicriteria framework for the new democratic era. *Journal of Multi-Criteria Decision Analysis, 12*, 163–176.
Morris, I. (1994). The Athenian economy twenty years after "the ancient economy". *CP, 89*, 351–366.
Morris, I. (2004). Economic growth in ancient Greece. *Journal of Institutional and Theoretical Economics, 160*(4), 709–742.
Morrison, J. S., Coates, J. F., & Rankov, N. B. (2000). *The Athenian trireme*. Cambridge: Cambridge University Press.
Mosse, C. (1967). *Les institutions Grecques à l'époque Classique*. Paris: Colin.
Müller, C. (2016). Globalization, transnationalism, and the local in Ancient Greece. *Classical studies, social and economic history*. Retrieved from http://www.oxfordhandbooks.com/view/10.1093/oxfordhb/9780199935390.001.0001/oxfordhb-9780199935390-e-42
Musgrave, R. A. (1939). The voluntary exchange theory of public economy. *The Quarterly Journal of Economics, 53*(2), 213–237.
Musgrave, R. A. (1959). *The theory of public finance*. New York: McGraw-Hill.
Musgrave, R. A. (1998). Approaches to a fiscal theory of political federalism. In W. E. Oates (Ed.), *The economics of fiscal federalism and local finance* (pp. 187–212). Chelterham: Edward Elgar Publishing Limited.
Nielsen, T. H. (1996). A survey of dependent poleis in classical Arkadia. In M. H. Hansen & K. Raaflaub (Eds.), *More studies in the ancient Greek polis, CPCPapers 3, Historia Einzelschriften 108* (pp. 63–105). Stuttgart: CPC Papers.
Nielsen, T. H. (2015). The Arkadian confederacy. In H. Beck & P. Funke (Eds.), *Federalism in Greek antiquity* (pp. 250–269). Cambridge: Cambridge University Press.
North, D. (1990). *Institutions, institutional change and economic performance*. Cambridge: Cambridge University Press.
Nye, J. S. (1991). *Bound to lead: The changing nature of American power*. New York: Basic Books.
Nye, J. S. (2009). *Soft power: The means to success in world politics*. New York: PublicAffairs.
Nye, J. S. (2011). *The future of power*. New York: PublicAffairs.
Oates, W. E. (1972). *Fiscal federalism*. Cheltenham: Edward Elgar Pub.
Oates, W. E. (1998). Introduction. In W. E. Oates (Ed.), *The economics of fiscal federalism and local finance*. Chelterham: Edward Elgar Publishing Limited.
Oates, W. E. (1999). An essay on fiscal federalism. *Journal of Economic Literature, 37*(3), 1120–1149.
Ober, J. (2001). The debate over civic education in classical Athens. In T. Y. Lee (Ed.), *Education in Greek and Roman antiquity* (pp. 175–208). Leiden: Brill.
Ober, J. (2008). *Democracy and knowledge. Innovation and learning in classical Athens*. Princeton: Princeton University Press.
Ober, J. (2010). Wealthy Hellas. *Transactions of the American Philological Association, 140*, 241–286.
Ober, J. (2011). Wealthy Hellas. *Journal of Economic Asymmetries, 8*(1), 1–39.
Ober, J. (2015). *The rise and the fall of classical Greece*. Princeton: Princeton University Press.
Ober, J. (2017). *Demopolis: Democracy before liberalism in theory and practice*. Cambridge: Cambridge University Press.
Oleson, J. P. (1984). *Greek and Roman mechanical water-lifting devices: The history of a technology*. Toronto: University of Toronto Press.
Oliver, J. H. (1978). Panachaeans and Panhellenes. *Hesperia, The Journal of the American School of Classical Studies at Athens, 47*(2), 185–191.

Olson, M. (1965). *The logic of collective action: Public goods and the theory of groups*. Harvard: Harvard University Press.

Oneal, J. R., & Russett, B. M. (1997). The classical liberals were right: Democracy, interdependence, and conflict, 1950–1985. *International Studies Quarterly, 41*(2), 267–294.

Oneal, J. R., & Russett, B. M. (1999). The Kantian peace: The pacific benefits of democracy, interdependence, and international organization, 1885–1992. *World Politics, 52*(1), 1–37.

O'Neil, J. L. (1984). The political elites of the Achaian and Aitolian leagues. *AncSoc, 15–17*, 33–61.

Ostrom, E. (1990). *Governing the commons: The evolution of institutions for collective action. Political economy of institutions and decisions*. Cambridge: Cambridge University Press.

Ostwald, M. (2000). Oligarchy and oligarchs in Ancient Greece. In P. Flensted-Jensen, T. H. Nielsen, & L. Rubinstein (Eds.), *Polis and politics: Studies in ancient Greek history presented to H.M. Hansen* (pp. 385–396). Copenhagen: Museum Tusculanum Press.

Ozler, S., & Rodrik, D. (1992). External shocks, politics and private investment: Some theory and empirical evidence. *Journal of Development Economics, 39*(1), 141–162.

Papadamou, S. T., Spyromitros, E., & Kyriazis, N. A. (2018). Quantitative easing effects on commercial bank liability and government yields in UK: A threshold cointegration approach. *International Economics and Economic Policy, 15*, 353–371.

Papadamou, S., Siriopoulos, C., & Kyriazis, N. A. (2020). A survey of empirical findings on unconventional central bank policies. *Journal of Economic Studies*. https://doi.org/10.1108/JES-04-2019-0186

Pauly, M. V. (1973). Income reduction as a local public good. *Journal of Public Economics, 2*(1), 35–58.

Percoco, M. (2016). Highways, local economic structure and urban development. *Journal of Economic Geography, 16*(5), 1035–1054.

Perotti, R. (1996). Growth, income distribution, and democracy: What the data say. *Journal of Economic Growth, 1*(2), 149–187.

Pikoulas, Y. A. (2000). The road-network of Arkadia. In T. H. Nielsen & J. Roy (Eds.), *Defining Ancient Arkadia*. Munksgaard: The Royal Danish Academy of Sciences and Letters.

Piper, L. J. (1986). *The Spartan twilight*. New York: New Rochelle.

Polachek, S. W. (1992). Conflict and trade: An economics approach to political interactions. In W. Isard & C. H. Anderton (Eds.), *Economics of arms reduction and the peace process*. New York: Elsevier.

Polachek, S. W. (1994). Peace economics: A trade theory perspective. *Peace Economics, Peace Science and Public Policy, 1*(2), 12–15.

Polachek, S. W. (1997). Why do democracies cooperate more and fight less: The relationship between trade and international cooperation. *Review of International Economics, 5*, 295–309.

Polachek, S. W., & Seiglie, C. (2007). Trade, peace and democracy: An analysis of dyadic dispute. In K. Hartley & T. Sandler (Eds.), *Handbook of defense economics* (pp. 1017–1073). Amsterdam: Elsevier.

Pomeroy, S. B. (1995). *Goddesses, whores, wives and slaves. Women in classical antiquity*. New York: Schocken.

Pritchard, D. M. (2015). Public finance and war in Ancient Greece. *Greece and Rome, 62*(1), 48–59.

Rahtjen, B. D. (1965). Philistine and hebrew amphictyonies. *Journal of Near Eastern Studies, 24* (1/2), 100–104.

Rhodes, P. J. (2005). *A history of classical Greek world: 478–323 BC*. Oxford: Black-well Publishing.

Rhodes, P. J. (2007). *The Greek city states: A source book*. Cambridge: Cambridge University Press.

Richard, C. J. (2009). *Greeks and Romans bearing gifts. How the ancients inspired the founding fathers*. Lanham: Rowman and Littlefiled Publishers.

Rigsby, K. J. (1997). *Asylia: Territorial inviolability in the Hellenistic world*. Berkeley: University of California Press.

Riker, W. H. (1964). *Federalism: origin, operation, significance.* Boston: Little, Brown and Company.
Riker, W. H., & Weimer, D. L. (1993). The economic and political liberalization of socialism: The fundamental problem of property rights. *Social Philosophy and Policy, 10*, 79–102.
Rizakis, A. (1990). La politeia dans les cites de la confederation acheenne. *Tyche, 5*, 109–134.
Rizakis, A. (1995). *Achaie I. Sources textuelles et histoire regionale*. Athens: Centre de Recherches de l'antiquite Grecque et Romaine.
Rizakis, A. (2015). The Achaian league. In H. Beck & P. Funke (Eds.), *Federalism in Greek antiquity* (pp. 117–131). Cambridge: Cambridge University Press.
Risse, G. B. (1990). *Mending bodies, saving souls: A history of hospitals.* Oxford: Oxford University Press.
Roberts, K. (2011). *The origins of business, money and market.* New York: Columbia University Press.
Robinson, E. W. (2003). *Ancient Greek democracy: Readings and sources.* New Jersey: Wiley-Blackwell.
Robinson, E. W. (2011). *Democracy beyond Athens: Popular government in the Greek classical age*. Cambridge: Cambridge University Press.
Roebuck, C. (1955). The early Ionian league. *Classical Philology, 50*(1), 26–40.
Rosen, H. S. (1988). *Fiscal federalism. Quantitative studies*. Chicago and London: The University of Chicago Press.
Rostovtzeff, M. I. (1941). *The social and economic history of the Hellenistic world.* Oxford: Oxford University Press.
Rubinfield, D. N. (1997). On federalism and economic development. *Virginia Law Review, 83*(7), 1581–1592.
Rummel, R. J. (1983). Libertarianism and international violence. *Journal of Conflict Resolution, 27*, 27–71.
Russell, J., & Cohn, R. (2012). *Aetolian league*. Edinburgh: LENNEX Corp.
Rzepka, J. (2009). The Aetolian elite warriors and fifth century roots of the Hellenistic confederacy. *AKME Studia Historica, 4*(2009), 5–34.
Samons, L. J. (2000). *Empire of the owl: Athenian imperial finance (Historia Einzelschriften).* Stuttgart: Franz Steiner Verlag.
Samuelson, P. A. (1954). The pure theory of public expenditure. *The Review of Economics and Statistics, 36*(4), 387–389.
Samuelson, P. A. (1955). Diagrammatic exposition of a theory of public expenditure. *The Review of Economics and Statistics, 37*(4), 350–356.
Sanders, G. D. R., & Whitbread, I. K. (1990). Central places and major roads in the Peloponnesus. *The Annual of the British School at Athens, 85*, 333–361.
Schaps, D. M. (1979). *Economic rights of women*. Edinburg: Edinburg University Press.
Scholten, J. B. (2000). *The politics of plunder: Aitolians and their Koinon in the early Hellenistic era, 279–217 BC*. Berkeley and Los Angeles: University of California Press.
Sealey, R. (1990). *Women and law in classical Greece.* North Carolina: University of North Carolina Press.
Shimron, B. (1972). *Late Sparta the Spartan revolution, 243-146 BC* (Arethousa monographs) (Vol. 3). Buffalo, NY.
Shuckburgh, E. S. ([1889], 2012). *The histories of Polybius* (Vol. 1). Cambridge library collection. Cambridge: Cambridge University Press.
Sickinger, J. P. (2004). The laws of Athens: Publication, presentation, consultation. In E. M. Harris & L. Rubinstein (Eds.), *The law and the courts in Ancient Greece* (pp. 93–109). London: Duckworth.
Spirakis, G., Spiraki, C., & Nikolopoulos, C. (2010). The impact of electronic government on democracy: E-democracy through e-participation. *Electronic Government International Journal, 7*(1), 75–88.

Starr, H. (1997). Democracy and integration: Why democracies don't fight each other. *Journal of Peace Research, 34*(2), 153–162.

Tarn, W. W. (1928). The Greek leagues and Macedonia. In *The Cambridge ancient history* (The Hellenistic monarchies and the rise of Rome) (Vol. 7, pp. 732–768). Cambridge: Cambridge University Press.

Tausend, K. (1992). *Amphiktyonie und symmachie: Formen zwischenstaatlicher bezienhungen in archaischen Griechenland*. Stuttgard: Fr. Steiner.

Texier, J. G. (1975). *Nabis*. Paris: Les Belles Lettres.

Thompson, M. (1939). A hoard of Greek federal silver. *Hesperia: The Journal of the American School of Classical Studies at Athens, 8*(2), 116–154.

Thompson, M. (1968). *The Agrinion hoard* (ANSNNM 159). New York: ANSNNSM.

Thompson, M., Mørkholm, O., & Kraay, C. M. (1973). *An inventory of Greek coin hoards*. New York: Numismatic Commission by the American Numismatic Society.

Tirole, J. (2017). *Economics for the common good*. Princeton: Princeton University Press.

Traunmüller, R. (2004). *Electronic government*. Heidelberg: Springer-Verlag.

Tridimas, G. (2013). Homo Oeconomicus in ancient Athens: Silver bonanza and the choice to build a navy. *Homo Oeconomicus, 30*(4), 435–458.

Tridimas, G. (2017). Constitutional choice in ancient Athens: The evolution of the frequency of decision making. *Constitutional Political Economy, 28*(3), 209–230.

Tridimas, G. (2018). The failure of ancient Greek growth: Institutions, culture and energy cost. *Journal of Institutional Economics, 15*(2), 327–350.

Urban, R. (1979). *Wachstum und krise des achaischen bundes. Quellenstudien zur entwicklung des bundes von 280 Bis 222 V. Chr. (Historia, Einzelschriften XXXV)*. Wiesbaden: Steiner.

Van Kreveld, M. (1977). *Supplying war: Logistics from Wallenstein to Patton*. Cambridge: Cambridge University Press.

Van Wees, H. (2013). *Ships and silver and taxes and tribute. A fiscal history of Archaic Athens*. London: I. B. Tauris.

von Mises, L. (1981). *Socialism: An economic and social analysis*. Indianapolis: Liberty Classics.

Von Reden, S. (2010). *Money in Ptolemaic Egypt: From the Macedonian conquest to the end of the third century BC*. Cambridge: Cambridge University Press.

Wade-Gery, H. T. (1924). Jason of Pherae and Aleuas the red. *The Journal of Hellenic Studies, 44* (1), 55–64.

Walbank, F. W. (1933). *Aratos of Sicyon*. Cambridge: Cambridge University Press.

Walbank, F. W. (1967). *Philip of Macedon*. Cambridge: Cambridge University Press.

Walbank, F. W. (1970). The Achaean assemblies again. *Museum Helveticum, 27*, 129–143.

Walbank, F. W. (1984a). Macedonia and Greece. In F. W. Walbank, A. Astin, M. W. Frederiksen, & R. M. Ogilvie (Eds.), *Cambridge Ancient history, Vol. VII part 1: The Hellenistic world* (Vol. 2, pp. 221–256). Cambridge: Cambridge University Press.

Walbank, F. W. (1984b). Macedonia and the Greek leagues. In F. W. Walbank, A. Astin, M. W. Frederiksen, & R. M. Ogilvie (Eds.), *Cambridge Ancient history, Vol. VII part 1: The Hellenistic world* (Vol. 2, pp. 446–481). Cambridge: Cambridge University Press.

Walbank, F. W. (1985). *Selected papers: Studies in Greek and Roman history and historiography*. Cambridge: Cambridge University Press.

Walbank, F. W. (1993). *The Hellenistic world*. Cambridge, MA: Harvard University Press.

Walbank, F. (2000). Hellenes and Achaians: Greek nationality' revisited. In P. Flensted-Jensen (Ed.), *Further studies in the ancient Greek polis* (pp. 19–34). Stuttgart: Franz Steiner.

Walt, S. M. (2009). Alliances in a unipolar world. *World Politics, 61*(1), 86–120.

Waltz, K. (1979). *Theory of international politics*. Reading, MA: Addison-Wesley Publishing Company.

Wang, J. (2016). *The past and future of international monetary system. With the performances of the US Dollar, the Euro and the CNY*. Singapore: Springer.

Warren, J. A. W. (1999). The Achaian league silver coinage controversy resolved: A summary. *The Numismatic Chronicle, 159*, 99–109.

Warren, J. A. W. (2007). *The Bronze coinage of the Achaian Koinon, the currency of a federal ideal*. London: Royal Numismatic Society in association with the British Institute of Persian Studies.

Weingast, B. R. (1997). The political foundations of democracy and the rule of law. *The American Political Science Review, 91*(2), 254–263.

Wight, M. ([1946], 1995). *Power politics*. New York: Royal Institute of International Affairs.

Wiseman, J. (1969). *Excavations in Corinth, the gymnasiu, area, 1967–1968*. Hesperia, American School of Classical Studies at Athens. Retrieved from https://www.ascsa.edu.gr/pdf/uploads/.../147640.pdf

Wood, A., & Roberts, S. (2012). *Economic geography: Places, networks and flows*. London: Routledge.

Woolmer, M. (2016). Forging links between regions: Trade policy in classical Athens. In E. M. Harris, D. M. Lewis, & M. Woolmer (Eds.), *The ancient Greek economy: Markets, households and city states* (pp. 66–89). New York: Cambridge University Press.

Xie, F., & Levinson, D. M. (2011). *Evolving transportation networks*. New York: Springer.

Index

E. M. L. Economou, *The Achaean Federation in Ancient Greece*, Frontiers in Economic History, https://doi.org/10.1007/978-3-030-52697-9

N

O

P

The manufacturer's authorised representative in the EU is Springer Nature Customer Service Centre GmbH, Europaplatz 3, 69115 Heidelberg, Germany. If you have any concerns regarding our products, please contact ProductSafety@springernature.com

Printed and bound by CPI Group (UK) Ltd, Croydon, CR0 4YY
30/09/2026
02225462-0008